SECOND LANGUAGE EDUCATIONAL EXPERIENCES FOR ADULT LEARNERS

Second Language Educational Experiences for Adult Learners provides an up-to-date review of the theory and practice of adult second language education. The primary objective is to introduce core ideas that should inform the design, development, and delivery of language learning experiences that take the typical forms of materials, courses, teaching, and assessment. Divided into three sections, the book first addresses what we know about adult second language acquisition and how individuals may acquire languages differently from each other. In the second section, key educational design elements—from pedagogical methods to curriculum to assessment—are then introduced from the perspective of research-based understandings about effective practices. Rounding out the volume is an overview of critical issues for language educational innovation, including supporting teachers, localizing materials and instruction, evaluating and improving education, and working with technology. Each chapter concludes with a set of recommended "design principles" that should guide readers toward high-quality, valuable, and empirically supported language educational experiences. This volume will be of interest to researchers and students investigating instructed language learning, designers creating useful language learning materials, and language teaching innovators seeking to improve outcomes in diverse instructional settings around the world.

John M. Norris is Principal Research Scientist in English language learning and assessment at the Educational Testing Service, USA.

John McE. Davis works at the School of Language Studies at the George P. Shultz National Foreign Affairs Training Center (formerly the Foreign Service Institute).

Veronika Timpe-Laughlin is Associate Research Scientist in English language learning and assessment at the Educational Testing Service, USA.

Innovations in Language Learning and Assessment at ETS

Series Editors: John M. Norris, James E. Purpura, Steven John Ross, and Xiaoming Xi

The goal of the *Innovations in Language Learning and Assessment at ETS* series is to publish books that document the development and validation of language assessments and that explore broader innovations related to language teaching and learning. Compiled by leading researchers, then reviewed by the series editorial board, volumes in the series provide cutting-edge research and development related to language learning and assessment in a format that is easily accessible to language teachers and applied linguists as well as testing professionals and measurement specialists.

Volume 1: *Second Language Educational Experiences for Adult Learners*
John M. Norris, John McE. Davis, and Veronika Timpe-Laughlin

Volume 2: *English Language Proficiency Assessments for Young Learners*
Mikyung Wolf and Yuko Butler

SECOND LANGUAGE EDUCATIONAL EXPERIENCES FOR ADULT LEARNERS

John M. Norris, John McE. Davis,
and Veronika Timpe-Laughlin

Routledge
Taylor & Francis Group

NEW YORK AND LONDON

First published 2017
by Routledge
711 Third Avenue, New York, NY 10017

and by Routledge
2 Park Square, Milton Park, Abingdon, Oxon, OX14 4RN

Routledge is an imprint of the Taylor & Francis Group, an informa business

Library of Congress Cataloging-in-Publication Data
A catalog record for this book has been requested

ISBN: 978-0-415-78406-1 (hbk)
ISBN: 978-0-415-78407-8 (pbk)
ISBN: 978-1-315-23080-1 (ebk)

Typeset in Bembo
by Apex CoVantage, LLC

CONTENTS

SERIES EDITORS' FOREWORD

The Educational Testing Service (ETS), the largest nonprofit educational research organization in the world, has a rich history of providing widely used and critically important educational assessments. It also supports ongoing research to instill innovation and rigor into its testing programs and to sustain forward-looking, wide-ranging foundational work that helps advance the field of education. ETS's offering of language assessments dates back to 1963 with the introduction of the Test of English as a Foreign Language (TOEFL®), currently used worldwide for higher education admissions decisions involving international students. The ETS portfolio of language assessments has grown substantially since then to include newer versions of the TOEFL (most recently the iBT), the TOEIC® tests, the TOEFL Junior Standard test, the TOEFL Primary test, and English language proficiency and language arts assessments for K–12 students in the U.S. Since the 1970s, ETS has supported an active validity research program for these assessments, as well as foundational research advancing English language learning and assessment around the world.

The goal of the new Routledge series, *Innovations in Language Learning and Assessment at ETS*, is to publish books documenting work undertaken at ETS and situated in relation to theories, research, and conceptual innovations by both ETS and external scholars. This work includes (a) the development and validation of ETS's language assessments, (b) contributions to assessment theory and practice, and (c) the exploration of innovations related to language learning and education. The purpose of the series is to disseminate cutting-edge research and development related to language learning and assessment organized around key issues and trends that appeal to a wide readership and to make this work readily available to the broader fields of applied linguistics and educational measurement. As assessments become increasingly diversified, including not only large-scale, standardized assessments but also learning-oriented assessments that are seamlessly embedded in instruction, this series includes work related to both language learning and assessment. The series thus encourages and facilitates the sharing of knowledge, ideas, and expertise across these two interconnected disciplines and provides opportunities for cross-pollination. Volumes on language assessment will focus on key issues, trends, and innovations in language assessment as reflected in research from a variety of fields such as first and second language assessment, cognitive and learning sciences, natural language processing, and speech technologies. Volumes related to language learning will include historical and conceptual explorations of critical topics to guide best practices in language learning and education, as well as empirical evaluations of language learning products and programs.

The debut of the volume *Second Language Educational Experiences for Adult Learners,* by Norris, Davis, and Timpe-Laughlin, marks the inaugural publication in this book series. This volume represents a unique contribution to the topic of language education program design, delivery, and innovation. It provides a comprehensive discussion of historical and recent developments in theories and practices related to second language education, ranging from the conceptual bases for designing language learning experiences to practical knowledge garnered from many decades of research on language teaching. Topics addressed in the first part of the book include second language learning theories and understandings about learner individual differences in relation to language acquisition. The focus then shifts to various facets of language program development, implementation, and evaluation. The focus here is on core design issues such as curriculum and materials development, teacher development and support, assessment as an integral part of teaching and learning, and the evaluation of language education programs. Additional, more challenging topics—which have attracted growing attention in recent years—are also addressed, such as language instructional sequencing and learning progressions, approaches to "localizing" language teaching and materials (i.e., adapting to the educational and social realities of local settings), and the role of technology in language learning and instruction. The book serves as a holistic, expansive reference on language education program design and innovation for researchers, curriculum and materials developers, and language program administrators and evaluators. It provides much needed macro-level guidance in designing second language education, as well as additional in-depth explorations of critical topics.

As we launch the book series with this first volume, we would like to thank Routledge Publishing for their interest in the series and for their commitment and behind-the-scenes hard work in bringing it to life. This inaugural volume on designing second language educational experiences will be followed soon by volumes addressing unique language assessment populations, roles for technology, and current issues in assessment theory and practice. We hope this book, and others in the series, will encourage and inspire cross-disciplinary dialogues revolving around key issues and ensuing innovations in language learning and assessment.

ACKNOWLEDGMENTS

The authors would like to acknowledge constructive feedback provided by five anonymous reviewers from the Educational Testing Service, as well as editors of this book series: James Purpura, Steven Ross, and Xiaoming Xi. The writing of this book was funded by the Educational Testing Service. Any opinions expressed are those of the authors and not necessarily those of the Educational Testing Service.

ILLUSTRATIONS

Tables

Figures

1

INTRODUCTION

Foundations for Designing Second Language Educational Experiences

Genesis and Purpose of This Volume

This volume is intended to provide an up-to-date review of relevant understandings about the theory and practice of primarily adult instructed language learning. The review was commissioned by the Educational Testing Service (ETS) in order to establish a foundation and primary reference for audiences interested in the nature of second language (L2) learning, including critical aspects of the learning context and learners themselves, as well as possibilities for thoughtful educational efforts that stand a good chance of encouraging successful and efficient second language acquisition (SLA). The focus on designing "educational experiences" is fundamental to the approach adopted here. Language learning currently occurs in a variety of possible settings and in response to a variety of factors. Although some learners have the opportunity and proclivity to acquire languages other than the first "naturalistically," immersed in target language settings and via daily exposure and interaction, many others attempt to learn languages in foreign language classrooms through planned courses of study, preselected materials, and the often-considerable efforts of language teachers. Increasingly, learners may also take advantage of self-access or tutored language learning in the form of burgeoning materials, courses, assessments, environments, and applications available via computers and the Internet. The range of possible language learning experiences, and the diversity of learning environments, is therefore considerable, as are the resulting outcomes in terms of learning achievements (i.e., ranging from quite dismal failure, to knowing a few words and phrases, to the development of functional degrees of proficiency). Given the plethora of routes into language learning, it is becoming decreasingly accurate to conceive of fixed-syllabus structures, textbook-driven courses, and prescriptive teaching methods as guidelines for the conduct of language instruction. Rather, language education (i.e., intentional efforts at fostering language acquisition) can be delivered in numerous ways—via numerous "experiences" from the perspective of the learner—and it is the accumulation of language learning experiences that determines, by and large, SLA achievements. At stake, then, is how those experiences (whatever they might be) can be designed, arranged, delivered, and supported in order to maximize learning.

The primary objective of this volume is to establish something of a baseline set of core ideas, along with attendant recommendations, underlying the design and development of language learning experiences that take the typical forms of materials, courses, teaching, tasks, assessment, and other activities.[1] The envisioned audience for this work is intentionally very broad: it includes *researchers* who are engaged in work that is informative of instructed language learning; *materials designers*, or those responsible for creating useful language learning curricula, syllabi, units, lessons, tasks, resources, and assessments; and *language teaching innovators and evaluators*, or those responsible for delivering and implementing new pedagogies in diverse instructional settings around the world, as well as those responsible for understanding and improving educational programs. Although some historical background is important for situating this work, the focus here is primarily on recent ideas that have emerged in the domains of instructed second language acquisition (ISLA), language education, and language assessment broadly conceived. Three basic questions are addressed in the volume:

1. How and to what extent does adult SLA occur, and in what ways does acquisition differ across learners in response to individual factors?
2. How can educational experiences be designed to bring about SLA, and what are the critical elements of education (i.e., from curriculum to assessment) in need of attention?
3. How are new educational designs to be delivered in diverse language learning contexts around the world, and what are the key concerns for supporting their ethical and effective use?

Although the scope of review required to answer these questions is quite broad, this work is not intended to serve as a systematic synthesis of research related to language teaching and learning—indeed, such a synthesis would comprise numerous volumes and thousands of pages given the range of topics covered. Rather, the approach adopted here is to provide high-level summaries of key issues, to make general recommendations, and to point to additional references and resources for more detailed information. Hence, each chapter offers a relatively brief overview of relevant content along with a deeper exploration of what seem to be the most critical contemporary issues for guiding future practice. The intent is to highlight major dimensions of theory, research, and practical knowledge that underlie current thinking about effective language education. Each chapter thus leads to a handful of concluding "design principles" that should guide future practice toward the delivery of high-quality, high-value, and well-supported language educational experiences—at least insofar as such goals are currently understood.

Overview of Chapters and Suggestions on Reading This Volume

The volume is divided into three sections. Although each section covers a distinct set of topics related to understanding, designing, and delivering L2 educational experiences, the sections are interrelated and cumulative. Thus, the largely *theoretical* ideas in part 1 provide a conceptual basis for the review of key *educational design components* covered in part 2, and these serve as a foundation for considering issues in *delivering and supporting language educational innovations* in part 3. Reading the entire volume, start to finish, should establish a substantial initial knowledge base for engaging in the development and implementation of language educational experiences. At the same time, we recognize that some readers may be particularly interested in only a selection of the topics covered here. Thus, each chapter, or each section, may also be read independently of the others and still provide relatively coherent advice. In addition, the inclusion of a summary and set of recommendations for educational design at the end of each chapter should enable readers to extrapolate the main ideas offered on each topic from the perspective of the upshot for language teaching and learning. Here, we provide a brief overview of each section to help guide readers.

Part 1 (chapters 2–4), "Second Language Acquisition and the Language Learner," reviews essential background information on language learning, including relevant theories and research addressing what we know about SLA, as well as the role that individual learner factors may play in impinging on or facilitating the language learning process. In chapter 2 we briefly introduce theories of foreign or L2 learning, acquisition, and development, and then summarize the relationship between theories of acquisition and instruction (i.e., planned language learning). In chapter 3 we review current thinking about a number of important learner variables that are relatively stable at any given moment of instruction or learning effort, such as age, L1, proficiency, aptitude, personality or identity, educational experience, and so on. By contrast, in chapter 4 we consider learner-related variables that are relatively unstable and therefore amenable to influence and change (e.g., in response to particular types of materials or particular efforts by teachers), such as motivation, strategies, and others. The basic thrust of these initial chapters is that adult SLA is a unique kind of learning that may benefit most from certain types of experience (and not from others) but that is also moderated considerably by the characteristics of individual learners. Understanding these ideas provides an important backdrop for current thinking in relation to the design of L2 educational experiences.

Part 2 of the volume (chapters 5–9), "Second Language Instruction, Assessment, and Educational Design," considers some of the main components that can be "engineered" to influence L2 learning. In chapter 5 we review contemporary approaches to language pedagogy, with an emphasis on educational practices that seek to foster the integration of knowledge and ability to use the target language for engaging successfully in "real-world" communication, whereas in chapter 6 we summarize current thinking related to the teaching of specific language skills (i.e., reading, writing, listening, and speaking). In chapter 7 we introduce the essential contributions of language learning assessment, including both formative assessments that are fully integrated into daily teaching and learning practices, as well as more summative assessments that offer important opportunities for reflection on learning outcomes. In chapter 8 we move on to an overview of considerations in designing curriculum and materials, and in chapter 9 we cover specific issues having to do with sequencing of language educational units for establishing systematic learning progressions. Note that the recommendations issuing from each chapter in part 2 are relatively agnostic to details of the teaching-learning context. Thus, although they are intended to suggest basic and up-to-date dimensions of good practice, it is also clear that many would require carefully considered adaptation in light of the particular, situated realities of language teachers, classes, programs, delivery approaches and platforms, and other dimensions of instructional settings (all considerations of part 3).

Finally, part 3 of the volume (chapters 10–13), "Second Language Educational Innovation and Support," explores important dimensions of the operationalization and delivery of effective language learning experiences that stand a chance of having positive impact. That is, what do we need to think about as we distribute new educational ideas and products to diverse possible users? In chapter 10 we address issues and practices in localizing instructional designs, and materials in particular, in response to the constraints and affordances of actual language learning contexts. Recommendations here focus on the distinct realities of language educational cultures in different parts of the world and the need to build processes of adaptation into delivery. In chapter 11 we turn to the specific challenges of innovation from the point of view of teachers, who are often the primary users of new materials and designs, and we suggest approaches to supporting teachers in the use of innovative language instruction. Key to the success of any educational innovation is the active monitoring and evaluation of overall design, as well as materials effectiveness, instructional implementation, and apparent effects on learning outcomes, all of which we cover in chapter 12. Finally, in chapter 13, we address the reality that constantly evolving technologies and their incorporation into education are having profound effects on language teaching and learning. Accordingly, we review implications of some of the main ideas presented in previous chapters in relation to the delivery of language education within technology-mediated environments.

Note

1 Whereas our intent is that the design of educational experiences for any target language should be amenable to the recommendations provided here, inevitably many of our examples and references to research will primarily have to do with English, given a primary interest in this language at ETS.

PART 1

Second Language Acquisition and the Language Learner

2

SECOND LANGUAGE LEARNING THEORIES

This chapter introduces theories of foreign and second language learning, acquisition, and development, and it summarizes current thinking regarding the relationship between acquisition and instruction (i.e., planned language learning). The chapter is thus intended to provide a basic *theoretical* foundation for considerations related to language instruction—that is, intentional efforts to bring about language learning. Although the theories covered here do not (and are not intended to) have specific implications for pedagogic design, they do sketch out the landscape of current thinking about second language acquisition (SLA) and some of the factors that foster or inhibit it (see also chapters 3 and 4 on additional factors related to learner variables). Accordingly, these theories offer something of a backdrop to design considerations that appear in later chapters, and the chapter concludes with a set of theory-generated recommendations that establish baseline assumptions antecedent to the development of language materials, instructional activities, assessments, and other components of educational design.

Second Language Acquisition

The term *second language* (L2) describes any language that is learned—regardless of the level of proficiency achieved—at any time after the acquisition of the first language (L1), be it in childhood, adolescence, or adulthood (Mitchell, Myles, & Marsden, 2013; Ortega, 2009c). Thus, the term encompasses literally a *second* language, as well as a third, fourth, fifth, or *n*th language, learned after earliest childhood, whether the learning context is local (e.g., in an English-dominant environment) or foreign (e.g., English in the classroom in a non-English-dominant environment) or other (e.g., English in a heritage or home-language environment). Subsuming local, foreign, heritage, and other language learning contexts under the term "second language" makes sense insofar as "the underlying learning processes are essentially the same for more local and for more remote target languages, despite differing learning purposes and circumstances" (Mitchell, Myles, & Marsden, 2013, p. 1). Moreover, the second-foreign distinction is becoming ever more blurred in the current era, as access to the target language via the Internet increasingly cuts across learning contexts.

SLA is a relatively new academic discipline devoted to studying the processes of, and factors related to, learning additional languages. It emerged in the 1960s as an interdisciplinary field of study that drew upon related disciplines such as linguistics, language teaching, L1 acquisition, and psychology. Ever since, SLA has grown into an established field of inquiry that has investigated aspects that influence and shape L2 acquisition processes and outcomes (e.g., Ellis & Shintani, 2014; Mitchell, Myles, & Marsden, 2013; Ortega, 2009c). Moreover, subdomains of SLA have emerged over the intervening years, such as instructed second language acquisition (ISLA), which focuses particularly on how systematic manipulation of learning mechanisms and environments can facilitate L2 acquisition in planned or taught contexts (Loewen, 2015). Although differing in scope, SLA and its subdomains jointly deal with the same immensely complex phenomenon of L2 learning. Thus, efforts to obtain a better understanding of L2 learning processes in an organized and comprehensive way are commonly guided by some form of SLA theory (Mitchell, Myles, & Marsden, 2013).

Theories of SLA

Two different types of SLA theory have traditionally been distinguished: property theories and transition theories. Although property theories tend to be concerned with modeling the language system that is to be acquired (i.e., the structure of the target language), sometimes in comparison with the system that is actually acquired (i.e., interlanguage or learner language), transition theories focus on describing the change and developmental processes involved in language acquisition (e.g., Gregg, 2003; Jordan, 2004; Mitchell, Myles, & Marsden, 2013). In SLA and its subdomains, a number of property and transition theories have been proposed over the years that represent different perspectives on language learning, including formal linguistic, psychological, cognitive, and social dimensions. Prominent theories pertaining to these perspectives will be discussed in the following sections (for detailed overviews see Lightbown & Spada, 2013; Mitchell, Myles, & Marsden, 2013; Ortega, 2007). Of these, only the first "innatist" perspective represents a true property theory, in the sense that it has focused primarily on how the L2 is represented (i.e., what it "looks like" or how it is structured) in the minds of language learners in comparison to the representation of L1s (i.e., what the language looks like in the minds of native speakers). Interestingly, though, in recent years, even the innatist perspective has been combined increasingly with cognitive and other accounts that are more transition (i.e., learning process) oriented, given the fundamental and overriding concern in SLA with questions regarding *how* language is acquired. As will be seen in the following sections, the original distinction between property and transition theories has therefore become somewhat moot, as researchers from all perspectives focus increasingly on trying to explain the process of L2 acquisition.

The Innatist Perspective

According to generative or formalist linguistic theory, human beings are endowed with an innate language faculty or, as Mitchell, Myles, and Marsden (2013) put it, a form of "language blueprint in the brain" (p. 83). This innate linguistic faculty, referred to originally by Noam Chomsky as universal grammar (UG), allows children to acquire their L1 in a relatively short period of time despite the disparity between the highly complex and often "messy" linguistic input they are exposed to (spoken language is full of slips of the tongue, false starts, incomplete sentences, etc.). Simply put, language acquisition occurs unconsciously in that the innate language faculty receives input and extracts rules and patterns that conform to universal linguistic constraints programmed into the learner's "genetic endowment" (Mitchell, Myles, & Marsden, 2013, p. 62). UG includes putative universal principles and parameters that allow for "constrained variation across languages" (White, 2012, p. 309). Hence, this formalist linguistic theory of first or second language acquisition is driven by two assumptions: (a) human beings are biologically endowed with universal grammatical knowledge prior to experiencing language use (so, they have a propensity to learn language, both the first and others), and (b) the human mind has a separate module dedicated to language processing and learning (Ortega, 2009c).

Originally developed as an account for first language acquisition, UG has been employed in SLA research since the early 1980s. Parallel to first language acquisition, SLA proponents of formalist theory maintain that innate UG also constrains L2 learning. Thus, the L2 should follow the basic assumptions about how languages are learned and how languages function, similar to the L1. Empirical studies have sought to investigate mental representations of grammar developed by L2 learners in order to shed light on whether these assumptions in fact hold true, and a particular emphasis has been on experimental studies of grammaticality judgments. In these studies, learners are asked to indicate whether various kinds of language input (typically individual sentences representing different grammar rules in the target language) are or are not "grammatical," or accurate or appropriate constructions in the language. This experimental approach has been used to investigate whether UG principles continue to operate in the L2 context, whether UG parameters associated with a learner's L1 can be "reset" to the L2 (i.e., adjusted so that new patterns, structures, grammar rules, and so on can be developed in the learner's mind), and to what degree evidence of learners' grammatical knowledge—which goes beyond the input they received (such as tacit intuition of language)—can be accounted for by putatively universal phenomena (for a detailed overview of research conducted within a UG framework, see White, 2007, 2012).

UG theory and research conducted in this tradition have been criticized for a number of reasons. First, there is considerable debate about the detailed functionality of the innate UG system; even among L1 learners, evidence does not always point to universal phenomena (i.e., there are always exceptions being found that counter what is supposedly a universal pattern). Second, UG-based approaches have focused primarily on morphosyntax (i.e., grammar rules), leaving phonology, pragmatics, discourse, and semantics largely unaccounted for (only more recent developments have begun to include these phenomena). Third, social and psychological variables, as well as learner individual differences are largely unaccounted for in the innatist framework, and findings tend to be generalized to all members of a given L1 population learning a given L2. Finally, and perhaps most importantly for our considerations here, UG theory and research have typically viewed language acquisition as an unconscious process that renders L2 instruction inconsequential or ineffective. That is, given that language acquisition, viewed from a UG perspective, occurs unconsciously and unfolds according to a preexisting, innate language structure, SLA processes fundamentally cannot be manipulated by L2 instruction (Loewen, 2015; Ortega, 2007). Nevertheless, despite this clear antipathy for instructed learning, in its focus on documenting and explaining the nature of the L2 linguistic system, SLA research adopting a UG framework has enhanced the understanding of particularly L2 morphosyntactic development, which in turn may inform teachers about which features to highlight in their L2 instruction at distinct points in the learning trajectory.

Though very general in nature, and despite the typical antipathy expressed toward L2 instruction, a handful of implications of UG accounts for L2 acquisition can be derived for pedagogic design that seeks to promote SLA. Already summarized several decades ago (e.g., Cook, 1994), the following still hold true today:

- Much of the target language can be learned on the basis of *large amounts of input* alone, and many things do not need to be taught explicitly, given that most languages share certain core similarities (e.g., word classes like nouns and verbs, syntactic structures like clauses and sentences); mostly, learners need to engage with the language as it is actually used so that they can cognitively discern the patterns that govern how it is used.
- Certain phenomena in the target language might best be taught through the intensive *provision of exemplars* that help focus on particularly problematic, distinct, new features. In English word order, for example, inversion of the subject and verb in question formation (e.g., Are you playing soccer today?) might best be taught through the use of concentrated, repeated exposure to such sentences.

- Similarly, procedures for *highlighting meaning* in the target language input such that new syntactic structures are understood (and thus available for acquisition) may be required. For example, bracketing of phrases might help learners acquire meaning implied by word order in English, as in the phrase "the boy the dog adores," which might be intonationally bracketed as "the boy [the dog adores]," thereby emphasizing that it is the dog who adores the boy, not vice versa.

- Finally, vocabulary learning, in addition to frequency of input, might also depend on the development of key syntactic knowledge about how certain words function within sentences; hence, vocabulary acquisition should be driven by the *provision of words in syntactic context*, not in the abstract (i.e., so that learners see how words are actually used, rather than merely what they mean conceptually). For example, understanding syntactic patterns—in this case, the rule that adjectives precede nouns in English—can help in identifying word classes and meanings, as in "the exorbitant price of gasoline," where learners can infer that *exorbitant* can only be an adjective modifying price.

Ultimately, the innatist approach to SLA serves as a reminder that language learning is, fundamentally, a mental endeavor, even though it is shaped by the social environment, a commonality shared with cognitive approaches to SLA reviewed in the next section.

The Cognitive Perspective

Since the 1990s, cognition broadly speaking has become increasingly central to SLA research, referring primarily to how information of all kinds is processed and learned by the human mind. A common theme underlying the cognitive perspective is that the computer constitutes a metaphor for the mind—that is, language acquisition is compared to a computer's capacity for processing, storing, and retrieving information. Among the many cognition theories of SLA are processability theory (Pienemann, 1998, 2007), input processing theory (VanPatten, 2002, 2007, 2012), efficiency-driven processor (O'Grady, 2005, 2008, 2010), associative-cognitive CREED (N. Ellis, 2007), and skill acquisition theory (DeKeyser, 2007).[1] Although united under the superordinate classification of cognition, these theories hold quite distinct perspectives and can be further subdivided into two broad categories: (a) traditional information processing theories (or implicit cognitive approaches), and (b) emergentist theories in which the role of memory systems and conscious learning feature more prominently (see Mitchell, Myles, & Marsden, 2013; Ortega, 2009b). Although these categorizations are very broad and theories often include elements of both traditions, two theories that have had a strong impact on contemporary thinking about SLA will be discussed to further illustrate the distinction: processability theory and skill acquisition theory.

As a transition theory, Pienemann's (1998, 2007) processability theory (PT) views L2 learning as the gradual acquisition of mental-procedural skills necessary for the processing of target language features. PT aims to reveal what Pienemann (1998) has called the "architecture of human language processing" (p. 4) and to clarify how learners acquire the computational mechanisms that operate on the linguistic knowledge they produce. Thus, L2 learners need to gradually develop the psycholinguistic capacity to process increasingly complex and linguistically "distant" or separated grammatical information; that is, they need to match "grammatical information contained within and across units in the linguistic material they encounter, and they are capable to do so gradually with more distant elements in linguistic units" (Ortega, 2009c, p. 132).

According to PT, this ability to match features across elements, in a clause or sentence, develops as L2 learners pass through certain cumulative stages of learning, gradually acquiring increasingly complex morphological and syntactic structures. The sequence of development for these morphosyntactic features is affected by how easy they are to process. Thus, processing at initial stages of L2 learning is constrained to small chunks, or lemmata, before it gradually develops to the processing of larger units such as noun phrases, clauses, and subclauses (see Pienemann, 2005, for a detailed outline of the acquisition sequence). A learner has to pass through all developmental stages successively, as they build upon one another. In short, higher level procedures depend on the mastery of lower level procedures. For one example in English, a commonly attested development sequence has to do with word order in question formation. Second language learners, it seems, acquire the ability to create English questions in the following order:

- subject-verb inversion in yes-no questions;
- movement of auxiliary verbs to the position following a *wh-* question word; and
- the reversal of subject-verb inversion in indirect questions.

According to PT and based on empirical observations, the ability to independently utilize higher level question formation rules (like reversal of inversion) is dependent on the prior acquisition of the ability to create "simpler" word orders (like subject-verb inversion) (see Norris, 2005).

A key qualification for PT is that, although morphosyntactic features are subject to this kind of acquisition sequence, other target language features are not affected by the same kinds of constraints (e.g., articles, prepositions, or pronouns) and are therefore referred to as "variational" features that are acquired in distinct ways depending on the learner and learning environment (and possibly in response to frequency or saliency of use in that environment). Hence, according to PT, there are two systematic and independent dimensions in SLA: development and variation (Lightbown & Spada, 2013).

Pienemann and colleagues have applied PT to the explanation of a number of developmental phenomena in L2 acquisition across a range of languages and in both syntax and morphology. The majority of empirical studies in PT have provided supportive evidence for Pienemann's theory (see Pienemann & Keßler, 2011, for details). Although proponents of ISLA have argued that PT implies that planned instruction has little impact on the advancement of L2 processing, studies conducted in the context of language teaching, such as Lightbown and Spada (1990), have shown that although instruction does not change the natural sequence of acquisition, it can promote and accelerate a learner's progress. Thus, PT has provided insights into development and acquisition processes that may make teachers more aware about L2 learners' developmental routes (see additional consideration of this view in chapter 9). For example, in teaching English question formation to L2 learners, it makes sense to first work with learners on developmentally simpler sentences, such as the following:

- "Do you play volleyball?"
- "Is she a good student?"

Once learners have demonstrated the ability to create such sentences independently, they would begin working with more advanced word order stages in question formation, such as the following:

- "When is the last flight to New York?"
- "Why are they so happy?"
- "Does he know where they went?"

As more representative of the emergentist tradition, skill acquisition theory (SAT) proposes that the learning of any complex skill proceeds from initial knowledge representation to changes in behavior, which—via repeated practice—eventually results in fluent, effortless, and highly skilled (proceduralized, automatized) performance. That is, declarative knowledge (i.e., explicit or conscious knowledge) is transformed into implicit or procedural knowledge (i.e., knowledge of how to do something). For example, an L2 English learner may have declarative, metalinguistic knowledge of the different uses of the adverbs "since" and "for" with the present perfect. Despite having this knowledge, though, the learner may not use the adverbs consistently in spontaneous communication. According to SAT, this inconsistent usage is an indicator that the learner may possess declarative knowledge about the form but that this knowledge has not been automatized in performance yet. The gradual process of proceduralization or automatization is achieved through continuous and relevant practice, which allows learners to deploy their explicit knowledge in increasingly fluent performance.

In general, three stages are distinguished in the automatization process (Mitchell, Myles, & Marsden, 2013). The first stage (cognitive, declarative, presentation) includes the establishment of new explicit knowledge, whether this knowledge is presented by a teacher, a book, or through conscious observation by the learner. Representations of this knowledge are temporarily activated in working memory (WM) and at the same time constrained by WM processing capability. In the second stage (associative, procedural, practice), declarative knowledge becomes procedural as the skill is performed and practiced. Learning tasks need to be constrained and skill specific to represent the original declarative knowledge, and the tasks need to be repeated regularly to activate the same processes (DeKeyser, 2007). However, the power law of learning maintains that at some point practice reaches saturation, yielding no further improvement, as optimal performance is reached (Ortega, 2009b). Although knowledge representations can still change in the second stage, the increasing proceduralization lowers the processing requirements for WM, providing for quicker access to the knowledge. The third stage (autonomous, automatic, production) includes the achievement of automaticity through extensive practice. Although still prone to error, the knowledge has become consolidated and stable, and the retrieval of implicit, procedural knowledge requires only limited cognitive resources. Furthermore, knowledge organization at this stage is free to further integrate other skills. Mitchell, Myles, and Marsden (2013) note that "[s]imple skills must become automatic before more complex ones can be tackled, thus explaining the step-by-step nature of learning" (p. 140). However, as discussed in Segalowitz (2003), automaticity should not be viewed as a mere increase in processing speed. Instead, it comprises an inherent quality change in the knowledge, once performance is automatized.

Although SAT does not claim to explain all phenomena of SLA, it provides accounts of several SLA phenomena such as fossilization, individual differences, incremental or step-by-step learning, and differences in the development of distinct skills (see Mitchell, Myles, & Marsden, 2013). Empirical studies have provided evidence that demonstrates associations in the proceduralization process (e.g., Roehr, 2007, 2008) or that documents the entire L2 acquisition process outlined in the SAT paradigm in experimental settings (e.g., de Jong, 2005; DeKeyser, 1997), as well as in the classroom (e.g., de Jong & Perfetti, 2011). Additionally, research has investigated the usefulness of an explicit focus on form in L2 teaching (e.g., Loewen, 2011; Norris & Ortega, 2000; Spada & Tomita, 2010), generally finding explicit instruction to be effective.

In sum, from a pedagogical design perspective, perhaps the key upshots of purely cognitive notions of SLA include the following:

• Learners tend to move through stages of acquisition for particular target language phenomena in relatively fixed ways; these stages may not always be from less accurate to more accurate (indeed, some times less accurate use of a target structure implies positive movement toward full knowledge); to the extent possible, "simpler" versions of target language forms should be introduced and acquired prior to work on more "complex" or higher level forms.

• Proceduralization and automatization of ability to use the target language takes time and effort; learners should not be expected to immediately acquire productive ability with the target language, and they should be provided with ample opportunities to practice particular forms repeatedly in communicative contexts.

• Language learning typically moves from knowledge of a form in a relatively isolated linguistic or communicative context, first, to the broader understanding of the form in multiple contexts of use; learners should be allowed to develop understanding of a target form in specific (perhaps most prototypical) contexts first, followed by exposure to (and acquisition of) the form in increasingly diversified linguistic and communicative contexts.

The Interactionist Perspective

Although it is widely accepted that interaction in the L2 is conducive to L2 learning, the essential issue—*how* L2 acquisition is facilitated by interaction—is addressed in the interactionist paradigm. With roots in the 1980s that saw the introduction of theories such as Long's (1981) first version of the interaction hypothesis (IH), Krashen's (1982) input theory, or Swain's (1985, 1995) output hypothesis, more recent interactionist research in SLA has drawn increasingly upon cognitive learning and language processing in combination with environmental conditions to explain L2 learning progressions (for a detailed historical discussion of interactionist theory, see Mackey, Abbuhl, & Gass, 2012; or Mitchell, Myles, & Marsden, 2013). In general, interaction (i.e., reciprocal communication with interlocutors in the target language) provides learners with input data that they need to process cognitively, it affords opportunities for producing output, and it creates key opportunities for the identification by learners of a mismatch between what they are able to produce and how that is received (and potential reactions to it in the form of feedback). Two highly influential, complementary theoretical approaches in this cognitive-interactionist paradigm are Long's (1996) revised version of the IH and Swain's (1985, 2005) comprehensible output hypothesis.

The IH posits that incidental learning is facilitated when a learner and interlocutor (i.e., a more proficient or L1 speaker of the target language) encounter some form of language breakdown in their communication. To address and solve the communication difficulty, meaning needs to be negotiated, which in turn requires discourse strategies and comprehension or clarification checks, as well as repetitions and recasts. Further, the breakdown often results in modified input—that is, input that is changed in some way to accommodate the learner's understanding. Although Long's first version of IH only proposed that negotiation of meaning results in L2 learning, his more recent version maintains two prerequisites for learning to occur: (a) in the negotiation process, the learner needs to notice the linguistic forms in the input (thus, Long incorporated Schmidt's, 1990, noticing hypothesis)[2] and (b) the linguistic forms attended to need to lie within the processing capacity of the L2 learner's WM. Additionally, drawing upon Pica

(1992), Long proposed specifically that corrective feedback needs to be provided, and that the learner needs to be pushed to produce more target-like output, in order for ongoing acquisition to occur.

A plethora of empirical research has been conducted within the interactionist paradigm testing the IH across a range of languages and L2 phenomena. Studies include investigations of individual grammatical structures such as articles (e.g., Sheen, 2007) or past-tense formations (e.g., R. Ellis, 2007), meta-analyses on corrective feedback (e.g., Lightbown & Spada, 1990; Lyster & Saito, 2010; Russell & Spada, 2006), and meta-analyses on multiple claims of the interactionist approach (e.g., Keck et al., 2006). In addition, contextual factors have been explored, for example, in recent studies on computer-mediated communication involving avatars as interlocutors (e.g., Petersen & Mackey, 2009). Overall, empirical findings have mostly substantiated IH to the extent that Gass and Mackey (2007) argued that "it is now commonly accepted within the SLA literature that there is a robust connection between interaction and learning" (p. 176).

As part of the input-output model of L2 acquisition, Swain (1985) proposed the comprehensible output hypothesis, which can be seen as complementary to the IH. Motivated by the observation that L2 learners, who were immersed in the target language and thus received plenty of input, did not necessarily develop high levels of grammatical competence, she proposed that L2 learners need to be pushed toward producing output. Output, Swain claims, is beneficial for three reasons. First, it has a consciousness-raising function insofar as productive communication requires bottom-up processing, which may assist learners in noticing gaps in their L2. Second, it helps learners test (new) hypotheses they have about L2 phenomena—whether these hypotheses stem from instruction or corrective feedback. Third, output allows learners to reflect consciously on L2 phenomena—indeed, it may force learners to move from a largely semantic orientation in how they process language (i.e., dealing with the content meaning of language input through comprehension) to a more syntactic orientation that requires attention to formal aspects of the language that have bearing on the meaning they are trying to construct (see Izumi, 2003). De Bot (1996) similarly proposed a fourth benefit reminiscent of SAT: producing comprehensible output assists SLA by helping learners "increase control over linguistic forms they had already partially acquired" (Ellis & Shintani, 2014, p. 207). More recently, Swain (2000) has repositioned her hypothesis to align it with sociocultural theory (SCT), arguing that output should be regarded as "participation" or "collaborative dialogue" or "languaging."

Empirical studies have investigated the effectiveness or contribution of L2 learner output for the acquisition of vocabulary (de la Fuente, 2002), question formation (e.g., McDonough & Mackey, 2006), and past-tense structures (McDonough, 2007), among other phenomena. Although some studies have found supporting evidence for the output hypothesis (de la Fuente, 2002; McDonough & Mackey, 2006), there are also inconsistent findings, for example, regarding how output should be systematically modified to facilitate L2 learning processes (see Mitchell, Myles, & Marsden, 2013, for a more detailed discussion).

Interactionist perspectives on SLA provide much food for thought in terms of pedagogic design, including the following broad ideas:

- Provision of *ample input* is key to enabling learners to experience how the target language works and to promoting comprehension development; however, it is not sufficient for developing advanced knowledge of target language structures or productive ability for using the language to communicate.
- Meaning-oriented *communicative interaction* between learners and other interlocutors in the target language should form a regular and considerable part of instruction, given the important dimensions of awareness, negotiation for meaning, feedback, and so on that interaction enables; critically, interaction creates both the opportunity and the need for learners to focus on form— that is, to pay attention to and work with the forms they are trying to use to convey ideas in the new language.
- Opportunities for *producing the language* are probably essential for SLA, not only in terms of developing productive abilities, but also in terms of focusing learners' attention on critical aspects of target language forms that lead to more or less accurate creation of what they intend to "mean" in their production; output may therefore be a necessary condition for full target language development.

The Sociocultural Perspective

Although interactionist theories view interactive communication as a source of data provided to the learner's mind to work toward acquisition, the sociocultural paradigm "rejects the separateness of environment and mind and sees interaction not as a source of data, but as a site where learning occurs" (Ellis & Shintani, 2014, p. 202). Thus, learning is not considered as something that happens because of interaction, but rather as something that happens within interaction. Hence, interaction is crucial because it mediates L2 learning, linking the social and interactional with the cognitive dimension. Learning is therefore a socially mediated process in which more expert individuals help move novice learners into higher levels of performance. As Ellis (2008) pointed out, it is important to note that "this paradigm, despite the label "sociocultural" does not seek to explain how learners acquire the cultural values of the L2 but rather how knowledge of an L2 is internalized through experiences of a sociocultural nature" (p. 517).

Within this sociocultural perspective, one approach has resonated strongly in SLA: Vygotskian SCT of mind (Lantolf & Thorne, 2006, 2007). Based on the work of Russian psychologist Lev Vygotsky, SCT proposes that learning takes place through a process of mediation that unites the social and psychological aspects of L2 learning. According to Lantolf and Thorne (2006), mediation constitutes "the process through which humans deploy culturally constructed artefacts, concepts, and activities to regulate (i.e., gain voluntary control over and transform) the material world or their own and each other's social and mental activity" (p. 79). In L2 learning, uniquely, the L2 is both subject and mediating tool at the same time. SCT holds that mediation and thus learning occurs in what has been labeled the "zone of proximal development" (ZPD). The ZPD is a sociocognitive construct or abstract space in which an expert (a more advanced speaker of the target language) interacts with a novice (a learner) to scaffold the learner to perform a task that they would not have been able to accomplish by themselves. This process of assisted performance accounts for how the more advanced person provides scaffolding for the less advanced, thus assisting in accomplishing a certain task that had been outside of the learner's scope of development. In sum, expert-novice sociocultural interaction in the ZPD leads to establishing new mental representations by the learner. Subsequently, these knowledge representations are internalized and thus available for self-regulated use—though it should be noted that this process is "the least theorized aspect of SCT" (Ellis & Shintani, 2014, p. 211). Overall, SCT conceives of L2 learning as a socially embedded, joint activity that may or may not involve planned and formal instruction.

Empirical research on key aspects within the SCT framework such as the ZPD has mostly been qualitative in nature. For example, teacher–student discourse was examined in a number of studies to outline the mediation and coconstruction of learning, as well as the impact of feedback (e.g., Aljaafreh & Lantolf, 1994; Nassaji & Swain, 2000; Ohta, 2000; Swain, Kinnear, & Steinman, 2011). Moreover, a controversy surrounds the idea of learning trajectories. Lantolf (2011), for instance, maintained that the core idea of SCT is to challenge "the existence of the natural syllabus" (p. 42). Song and Kellogg (2011) found empirical evidence for Lantolf's claim in that they identified no developmental trajectories for L2 vocabulary acquisition—a finding that clearly contradicts studies conducted in the cognitive paradigm. The still-very-limited body of empirical research on SCT notwithstanding, researchers have also developed the concept of "dynamic assessment" as an approach to overcome the traditional dichotomy between learning and assessment by applying the idea of the ZPD to the interpretation of learner abilities and the provision of feedback or guidance toward L2 development (Lantolf & Poehner, 2011a; Poehner, 2008; see also chapter 7 in this volume).

Perhaps the key upshot of SCT for pedagogic design is the idea that learners will benefit primarily from interaction with more knowledgeable others, be they teachers, natives speakers, or other learners. Pedagogy, then, should provide extensive opportunities for that kind of individualized interaction to occur, and where it does not, learning is likely to progress in less than ideal ways. Similarly, assessment plays a key role in promoting learning, principally when it is conceived as the regular, persistent provision of feedback to learners at those points when they are most in need of feedback and in focus on those phenomena that they need help with at a given point in time. Importantly, feedback should be instructive in allowing learners to adjust their knowledge structures, not simply indicative of right-wrong reactions to what they know.

Instructed Second Language Acquisition

Although different theories of SLA have provided selected implications for language instructional practice, as seen in the preceding review, there is also a particular branch of work related to ISLA per se. As a "burgeoning subdomain" (Ortega, 2013, p. 5), ISLA is primarily concerned with two questions: (a) is instruction beneficial for L2 learning and, (b) if so, how can the effectiveness of instruction be maximized (see also Loewen, 2015)? Thus, inquiry in the field of ISLA mainly deals with instruction in organized educational contexts such as the prototypical L2 classroom, and it addresses challenges or questions that tend to emerge in conjunction with these contexts. As such, ISLA is rooted in two prerequisites or underlying assumptions. First, it is essential that the learner wants to acquire the L2 and thus makes an effort to learn the target language. Second, in addition to the attempted acquisition, there must be some kind of systematic manipulation of learning conditions, or planned language instruction, that aims to promote learners' L2 development.

Research on ISLA for adult learners has tended to focus primarily on specific instructional techniques or principles applied to the teaching of distinct components of the target language system or in conjunction with improving specific skills. Thus, for example, there has been considerable research and debate over the past several decades on the role of error correction and other types of feedback in the improvement of L2 writing ability (e.g., Biber, Nekrasova, & Horn, 2011). Other areas that have received substantial attention include the design of tasks for eliciting different types of spoken interaction, the relationship between interaction and acquisition, the contribution of different types of feedback toward language development, the effectiveness of pronunciation or pragmatics instruction, the roles played by strategies instruction in promoting language learning, the use of input-enhancement techniques for developing vocabulary or morphosyntactic knowledge, the relative impact of implicit versus explicit approaches to instruction, and many others (see, e.g., Doughty, 2003; Housen & Pierrard, 2008; Loewen, 2015; Mackey & Goo, 2007; Norris & Ortega, 2006, 2010; Plonsky, 2011).

Two general observations are particularly relevant to this domain of research for our purposes here. First, the very large numbers of studies that have accumulated with respect to particular language instructional techniques or concerns has given rise to in excess of 150 meta-analytic syntheses of findings, providing a very substantial basis for making claims about the relationship between a given intervention and the likely magnitude of effect it may have on language learning. Indeed, it is by now very clear that planned language instruction can be quite effective at bringing about short-term L2 development, at least with respect to the specific language forms that have been targeted for instruction in these research domains (see Norris & Ortega, 2000, 2010; Plonsky & Oswald, 2014). Second, however, it is also clear that the vast majority of ISLA research has occurred at the level of what might be considered *microinstruction*—that is, what might be accomplished within a single lesson that strives to teach a particular rule, form, or structure. Although this type of research is useful in providing potentially good ideas for practice, it is not at all apparent to what extent these ideas translate into the much larger scale of educational design and implementation that is required for meaningful degrees of SLA to occur (e.g., developmental changes in overall proficiency levels). In the subsequent chapters of this book, we draw on findings of research syntheses and meta-analyses from ISLA in supporting particular claims about language educational design, where appropriate. At the same time, we would like to highlight the reality that there is much work remaining to be done in providing an evidentiary basis for the design and delivery of language instruction that seeks to promote profound, substantial, and lasting L2 acquisition among the diverse populations of language learners worldwide.

Summary and Recommendations

This brief overview of selected, if relatively influential, theories and research shows SLA as an "epistemologically diverse area of enquiry affording varying and sometimes conflicting accounts of the same phenomena" (Ellis & Shintani, 2014, p. 27). Thus, there is no unified framework or a type of SLA recipe that fully accounts for L2 learning. Nor is there evidence that would establish the superiority of a particular theoretical approach for informing best practice decisions about how to frame, design, or evaluate L2 educational experiences. Instead, the controversy and discussion of how L2 acquisition occurs is ongoing, driving the field forward and inspiring ever new inquiries and theorizing into the potential processes that constitute L2 learning. However, to the extent possible, we share Ellis and Shintani's (2014) proposition that teaching should proceed in accordance with how learners learn—that is to say, "[i]nstruction that is not compatible with the way L2 acquisition takes place cannot be successful" (p. 27).

Furthermore, the majority of the SLA theories discussed previously highlight the development of grammar and morphology as a core feature of L2 acquisition, yet it is important to note that language learning and the development of communicative language ability (CLA) in particular go far beyond mere grammatical knowledge. First, language ability is generally viewed as a complex communication system that needs to be acquired and analyzed on multiple levels,[3] including language skills (listening, reading, speaking, and writing) and components of the language system that cut across the four skills (phonology, lexicogrammar, semantics, pragmatics, and discourse).[4] Second, L2 language skills and components can be acquired for very different (communicative) purposes, such as "survival" in a foreign country, to develop literacy in a target language (McKay, 1993), for academic or esthetic (e.g., literary) language use (e.g., Johnson, 2012; Zwiers, 2008), or to communicate with other L2 learners using the target language as a lingua franca (e.g., Jenkins, 2000, 2012; Seidlhofer, 2011) or as an international language (e.g., McKay, 2002).

Given that language ability constitutes such a complex, protean phenomenon, L2 instruction needs to facilitate L2 acquisition for the learner by providing language learning experiences that aim to foster different language skills, language components, and their use in different language use contexts. SLA theories can function as a rough set of guidelines for educators to design these language learning experiences, as can findings from ISLA research. That is to say, although SLA theories cannot be translated directly into L2 pedagogy, certain principles can be derived from SLA theories that can then help operationalize and implement key ideas of SLA theories in L2 instruction, as suggested in the following recommendations.

2.1. *Determine a clear purpose and goal for L2 learning.*

Designing a language learning experience should always start with a particular objective, outlining which L2 skill(s), component(s), or type(s) of ability are to be developed.

2.2. *Take into account the order and sequence of L2 acquisition.*

A key idea and finding of different SLA theories is that many dimensions of the L2 system unfold according to a specific universal order or sequence and are bound to the cognitive development of the L2 learner. Ensuring that learners are developmentally ready, while accounting for individual learner differences, may prove challenging. Therefore, Ellis and Shintani (2014) recommend the following: "focus the instruction on explicit rather than implicit knowledge as explicit knowledge is not subject to the same developmental constraints" (p. 24). However, the development of more proceduralized L2 use requires instruction beyond declarative knowledge. A potential solution could be the use of tasks to provide for more individualized acquisition processes within a designed language learning experience (see chapter 5 section on recommendations and chapter 8).

2.3. *Create opportunities for learners to develop implicit knowledge.*

As implicit knowledge is a prerequisite to achieve automaticity and fluency in language use, the development of implicit knowledge needs to be at the core of successful language instruction. Although explicit knowledge is sometimes necessary and may also facilitate the process of noticing, learners should be given ample opportunity to practice L2 features in communicative tasks to develop their implicit knowledge and increase proceduralization.

2.4. *Implement a focus on meaning and form.*

SLA theories have highlighted the connection of meaning and form as necessary for successful L2 acquisition. Although meaning-focused instruction (e.g., immersive environments) can help develop some aspects of L2 learners' linguistic knowledge, a consensus of SLA theories seems to be that a focus on form is necessary to develop higher levels of linguistic accuracy and to increase efficiency or rate of acquisition. Such a focus on form can be achieved through awareness-raising activities or deductive, explicit grammar instruction that is otherwise embedded within a focus on meaning in purposeful communication.

2.5. *Offer extensive L2 input.*

Given that much of L2 learning is incidental and a result of exposure to the L2 (e.g., contextualized noticing), it is essential to provide learners with extensive, comprehensible L2 input. Moreover, given that the amount of exposure learners may have to the L2 may be limited to the formal instruction they receive (e.g., a few hours per week in many educational settings), maximizing the input is crucial. Two steps could be employed: (a) making the L2 the medium of instruction or (b) implementing opportunities for a broad variety of (authentic) input in L2 instruction, including via technology-mediated experiences.

2.6. *Encourage L2 output.*

Creating opportunities for output, including what Swain (1985, 2005) has referred to as "pushed output," is essential to allow students to deploy their L2 knowledge productively. Tasks that require oral and written production and do not limit output to constrained responses may be most beneficial in allowing students to practice language functions in legitimate communicative interaction.

2.7. *Foster opportunities for interaction.*

According to SLA theories, interaction helps increase not only automaticity but also the awareness of linguistic features and to assist in student development. Brown and Larson-Hall (2012) offer an account of activities that can be used in formal instruction, including the use of the L2 to manage the learning environment and the implementation of small-group work that revolves around contexts (e.g., problem-solving tasks) that require students to draw upon full performance abilities in the L2.

2.8. *Provide corrective feedback.*

Providing corrective feedback to L2 learners constitutes essential information communicated to the learner that is intended to modify their L2 knowledge in terms of either thinking or behavior for the purpose of improving L2 learning. Especially for lower level learners, implicit feedback may go unnoticed due to limited WM capacity in the L2 and will thus be ineffective unless carefully aligned with (i.e., focused on) their current levels of interlanguage development and consequent immediate learning needs.

Notes

1 CREED stands for construction based, rational, exemplar driven, emergent, and dialectic. For a detailed overview of cognition theories, see Mitchell, Myles, and Marsden (2013).
2 Though beyond the scope of the current summary, Schmidt's ideas provide important underlying concepts for much of how we theorize SLA. Fundamentally, he was the first to suggest that learners need to "notice" or become aware of a given form or function in their communicative use of the target language before they are able to acquire the associated rules or to understand "how things work" in the L2. Where learners are not aware of or paying attention to a given aspect of the language, it simply will not be available to them for the cognitive work necessary to transform input into something that is known and available for productive use.
3 For a detailed overview and discussion of CLA models, see Timpe-Laughlin, Wain, and Schmidgall (2015).
4 For a more detailed discussion of the language skills and components in instructed SLA, see Loewen (2015) and chapter 6 in this volume.

3

LEARNER INDIVIDUAL DIFFERENCES—STATIC

The next two chapters review key concepts and research findings on the long-standing observation that learners vary in language development and achievement due to factors unique to individuals. Although there are some known language learning universals that impact all learners in more or less the same way (e.g., orders of acquisition for certain morphosyntactic features), factors such as personality and aptitude are examples of characteristics or traits that are relatively stable within an individual but vary from one learner to the next and influence differential outcomes in how quickly the target language is acquired and what levels of proficiency are ultimately achieved. According to Dörnyei (2005), individual differences (IDs) are those dimensions of relatively "enduring personal characteristics that are assumed to apply to everybody and on which people differ by degree" (p. 4). A common distinction made in ID research is to categorize differences in terms of characteristics that are (to some degree) amenable to change or instructional intervention and those that are not (Loewen, 2015). This chapter considers the latter—important learner variables that are relatively stable at any given moment of instruction or learning experience, including age, proficiency, aptitude, personality, educational experience, cognitive or learning style, and working memory (WM). The mostly fixed nature of these constructs limits the ability of instruction and materials to impact or change a given learner's predispositions, though knowledge of such differences can be important both for generating learners' own self-awareness and metacognitive abilities and for tailoring of instruction and materials development to meet different learner needs. As with chapter 2, the coverage here is intentionally theoretical in orientation, with the objective of sketching out the landscape of what is known in relation to learner variables vis-à-vis second language acquisition (SLA), though implications for L2 instructional design are drawn in the conclusion to the chapter.[1]

Age

The impact of age on SLA is a long-established applied linguistics research concern. Research on age-related effects has developed out of a historical debate over the existence of a "critical period" or unique window of opportunity for language acquisition in human beings within which language learning must occur for normal adult language ability to develop. Couched in these terms, most researchers agree that evidence for a critical period in human language development is not strong, yet it is clear that younger learners enjoy considerable language learning advantages.

The overarching finding from age-related effects on L2 learning is that younger learners generally reach higher levels of ultimate attainment (i.e., maximum level language proficiency achieved) than older learners[2] (DeKeyser, 2012). For example, negative correlations between age of arrival (i.e., the point at which learners are first exposed substantially to input in the target language) and various measures of language ability support the claim that early L2 exposure or immersion results in higher attainment. However, a number of qualifications to this general finding bear attention given their implications for language instruction and materials development. First, when comparing the language achievements of older versus younger learners, researchers make a distinction between speed or rate of learning versus ultimate attainment. That is, children, or early learners, have a greater likelihood over the long term of reaching advanced or native-speaker-like (NS-like) levels of ability, whereas adults have an ability (initially) to learn discrete aspects (e.g., morphosyntactic rules) of the linguistic system faster (Jia & Fuse, 2007; Larson-Hall, 2008). A second, related distinction has to do with formal versus natural learning and explicit versus implicit learning. For example, older learners seem better able to learn grammar rules and lexicon via explicit, "tutored" instruction (with metalinguistic reflection) compared to younger learners. By contrast, adults do not learn as well naturalistically via communicative interaction and without reflection or other kinds of focus on morphosyntactic form. Children on the other hand can typically progress to high levels of ability via substantial amounts of social interaction alone.

Another qualification of the "earlier is better" notion relates to how age-related learning effects can depend on a particular mode of language ability. For example, age-related effects appear to be strongest for pronunciation, with only those learners who begin acquiring the L2 at a very young age able to reach NS-like levels of L2 pronunciation and accent (Abrahamsson & Hyltenstam, 2009). In addition, learning of morphosyntax (particularly more marked forms) seems strongly impacted by age effects, though perhaps less so when compared to phonology (DeKeyser, 2012). Finally, lexicon or vocabulary learning seems least impacted by age-related effects, with research showing little or no relationship between vocabulary learning and age of arrival (excepting knowledge of idioms; Abrahamsson & Hyltenstam, 2009).

A widespread (and erroneous) conclusion drawn from age-effects research is that children benefit from starting language instruction in schools as early (young) as possible. Current evidence does not support this claim and finds advantages (excepting pronunciation) for waiting until learners are older and have developed a certain amount of L1 literacy (Muñoz, 2008). Moreover, DeKeyser (2012) observes that a declining capacity for language learning associated with late arrival may be partly explained by a qualitative, cognitive shift from implicit to explicit learning during adolescence and early adulthood. That being the case, studies have shown the benefits of age-appropriate focus on form (J. White, 2008) and in particular the benefits of metalinguistic awareness and explicit learning in older children (Tarone, Bigelow, & Hansen, 2009).

Generally speaking,[3] the primary upshot for pedagogic design directed at adult learners is that it should emphasize or take advantage of

- explicit instruction and metalinguistic information, which adults will be better able to process, understand, and incorporate into learning;
- learner strategy training (see next chapter) and explicit attention to the rationales underlying a particular approach to pedagogy (e.g., precourse explanation of what it means to learn a language following a task-based approach; see chapter 5); and
- activities that appeal to or draw upon the adult learner's already considerable knowledge of the world, knowledge of other languages (at least the first), and cognitive capacities to learn via diverse channels (e.g., literate, oral-aural, visual-spatial).

Aptitude

Another long-established research interest in SLA has been the idea that certain individuals have a special capability or talent for language learning (termed *language learning aptitude*) compared to other learners of similar ages or learning circumstances. From a pedagogical perspective, however, research on language learning aptitude (LLA) has been of limited interest (and waned) because LLA appeared initially to be a static construct relatively unaffected by instruction. More recently, however, LLA research has been revived due to an interest in the possibility of aptitude-instruction interactions, looking for the benefits of L2 instruction matched to L2 learning strengths (see the section on aptitude-treatment interactions in this chapter).

Language learning aptitude has been conceptualized in a number of different ways, though current models have been derived from the seminal formulation proposed by psychologist J. B. Carroll. Carroll's (1965) research identified four components of language aptitude that predicted high levels of language attainment (in classrooms): (a) phonemic coding ability (the capacity to code and retain unfamiliar sounds); (b) grammatical sensitivity (the ability to identify grammatical functions of sentence constituents); (c) inductive language-learning ability (the ability to extract—and use creatively—syntactic and morphological patterns from discourse); and (d) associative memory (the ability to associate L1 and L2 vocabulary).[4] Despite its wide-ranging influence, Carroll's model and the associated assessment, the Modern Language Aptitude Test (MLAT) targets capabilities that are (a) related to formal learning and success in language learning classrooms, and (b) responsive (or not) specifically to a primarily audio-lingual instructional method that was popularized at the time of Carroll's original research (Skehan, 2012).

SLA research has since investigated whether aptitude can predict success in different learning contexts, such as in naturalistic settings outside of classrooms or in instructional contexts emphasizing communicative, implicit teaching methods. For example, studies suggest that language learning aptitude remains the strongest predictor of achievement even in informal, naturalistic learning situations (Reves, 1982). Research likewise finds that aptitude is moderately predictive of achievement across teaching methods. Learners with high levels of LLA achieve higher attainment via either explicit, deductive instruction, or implicit, communicative instruction (DeGraaf, 1997; Erlam, 2005; Kormos & Sáfár, 2008; Robinson, 1995; Skehan, 1996, 2012).

Despite the broadly predictive relationship between aptitude and L2 learning, because early research conceived of aptitude in terms of success in formal learning environments (and thus a somewhat narrow range of language and learning abilities), more recent aptitude research has also sought to understand aptitude as it relates specifically to various theoretical conceptualizations of SLA processes (see an overview in Doughty, 2013). For example, recent LLA models informed by SLA theories propose "complexes" of aptitude capabilities, which, when grouped together in different configurations, support specific L2 learning phenomena. Skehan (2002), for example, has put forward a model composed of primary macro-processes, including (a) noticing (attentional focus), (b) patterning (rule detection), (c) controlling (using new knowledge accurately), and (d) lexicalizing (chunking), each of which benefit uniquely from different combinations of aptitude types. Noticing, for example, requires focusing attention in robust ways and is aided by aptitudes in attention management, WM (see the next section), and phonemic coding; patterning requires aptitudes for grammatical sensitivity and inductive language-learning ability; controlling is aided by retrieval and proceduralization aptitudes; and lexicalization involves the ability to chunk language, which requires robust WM.

Another SLA-specific aptitude framework is Robinson's (2007a) aptitude complex hypothesis. At the most detailed level of conceptualization, Robinson's framework involves a number of "primary cognitive abilities," including perceptual speed, pattern recognition, phonological working memory (PWM) capacity, speed of PWM, analogies, capacity to infer word meaning, memory, speed of memory for text, grammatical sensitivity, and rote memory. Robinson groups these various aptitude components into superordinate ability categories, each composed of various combinations of primary cognitive abilities. For example, perceptual speed and PWM capacity are grouped together in support of "noticing the gap," whereas "memory for contingent speech" comprises PWM capacity and speed of PWM. Moreover, Robinson categorizes each of the superordinate aptitudes implicated in different learning contexts. For example, "learning via recasting" relies on noticing the gap and memory for contingent speech, whereas "incidental learning in the oral mode" relies on memory for contingent speech and deep semantic processing (additional contexts are "incidental learning in the written mode" and "explicit rule learning"). Robinson's aim is to capture the more complex nature of aptitude and the interactions of different cognitive abilities in different contexts such that it is possible to conceptualize certain learners doing well in one context and not in another (see also Skehan, 2012).

A key goal of aptitude research has been to use LLA research findings and diagnostic aptitude assessment tools to inform and support pedagogical practice and, in particular, to tailor instruction to learners' strengths (or remediate weaknesses). That means, of course, the identification of learners who are likely to succeed for selection and admissions purposes. On the other hand, Skehan (2012) makes a number of speculative recommendations for how aptitude diagnosis might be applied in any language education setting, proposing three main uses: (a) counseling, (b) remediation, and (c) instructional modification.[5] These recommendations provide useful food for thought in terms of pedagogic design considerations based on aptitude:

- Counseling involves using aptitude testing to inform learners about their strengths and weaknesses so that they can plan their own language education paths accordingly.
- Likewise for remediation, in which certain weaknesses in aptitude are identified, a language program can supply precourse instruction that is articulated to the development of distinct areas of need, such that the learner might benefit more from subsequent mainstream instruction.
- Lastly, instructional modification can be undertaken on the basis of aptitude assessments, such that learners with different aptitude profiles can be matched with appropriate instructional methodologies (see the section on aptitude-treatment interactions in this chapter).

Of course, a key concern for acting upon learners' aptitudes in pedagogically relevant ways is the (lack of) availability of an easy-to-use assessment that produces instructionally relevant information that can be turned into accurate decisions about what might be best for a given learner "type." Research has yet to identify such relationships to a sufficient degree for pedagogic decision making, nor is any such assessment readily available.

As a final note on aptitude, we should point out that research and development efforts are currently underway to resolve some of these challenges. Cutting-edge work undertaken recently at the Center for Advanced Study of Language (see Doughty, 2013), in the U.S., has produced new aptitude assessment batteries that focus on predicting ultimate attainment in foreign language proficiency, thereby advancing the field considerably in terms of the nature of aptitude constructs that can be measured. These assessments are intended to be used in identifying language learning candidates who, based on cognitive and perceptual abilities, have a high likelihood of achieving quite advanced to native-like proficiency in the target language, despite beginning the language learning process as adults (i.e., post-critical-period age). Of course, for a majority of language learners, such assessments may not prove particularly helpful. In these cases, the less modest goal of understanding their aptitudes will most likely be to identify and match them to instructional opportunities that can benefit learners during the early stages of L2 acquisition.

Working or Short-Term Memory

A key component of language learning aptitude noted briefly previously is a differential memory capacity between individual language learners that manifests after adolescence. Memory appears to be one of the main predictive variables of adult L2 attainment. As Skehan (2012) points out, many of the processes known to underpin language acquisition—noticing, input processing, pattern identification, response to feedback, lexicalization, and so on—are all impacted by a learner's ability to store and retain L2 input. Moreover, learners seem to differ in their ability to immediately retain and process L2 input, with research showing a clear learning advantage for postadolescent learners with stronger memory capacities.

Working memory (WM) is the specific aspect of cognition that involves temporary storage. According to Williams (2012), WM is the system of thought used for "temporary maintenance of task-relevant information whilst performing cognitive tasks" (p. 427). WM research in SLA has focused primarily on verbal or phonological WM, a component of WM derived from Baddeley's seminal model, postulating a "phonological loop" that is used for the short-term storage of information (also known as phonological-short-term memory, PSTM, or phonological working memory, PWM) and a subvocal rehearsal process. Traditional measures of verbal short-term memory involve "span task" performance and repetition of sequences of random digits, words, nonwords, or sentences—at varying lengths—and in the order of presentation (Williams, 2012).[6]

PWM has been found to correlate consistently with various aspects of L2 learning. According to a recent meta-analysis of the relationship between WM and measures of L2 proficiency development, Linck, Osthus, Koeth, and Bunting (2014) found an average correlation of $r = .26$ over some 700+ studies, reflecting a relatively moderate strength of association. Of course, the relationship varies by distinct targets of language learning. For example, studies have found relationships between PWM and (a) morphological learning and agreement rules (Ellis, 1996; Ellis & Sinclair, 1996), (b) grammar learning in artificial languages (Williams & Lovatt, 2003, 2005), (c) vocabulary learning (French & O'Brien, 2008; Service & Kohonen, 1995), (d) listening proficiency (Call, 1985), (e) overall proficiency or test performance (Harrington & Sawyer, 1992), and (f) the ability to benefit from feedback during interaction (Mackey et al., 2002; Mackey & Sachs, 2012). The overall conclusion drawn from WM research is that there is a consistent, if moderate, relationship between memory span and performance on various language development measures and that WM is thus a central component of language aptitude.

This general finding notwithstanding, a number of important qualifications help understand more precisely how WM interacts with different aspects of language learning and different types of learners (Ortega, 2009c). For example, studies have shown that WM is predictive of vocabulary learning at beginning levels of proficiency but wanes in effect at higher ability levels (Masoura & Gathercole, 2005). Moreover, WM may benefit learners at different proficiency levels in different ways. Although WM capacity aids vocabulary learning at lower levels of proficiency, it seems to aid grammatical learning at more advanced levels (O'Brien et al., 2006). In addition, WM may be an advantage for learning particular grammatical items and not for others (Williams, 2005). Finally, Mackey and colleagues (2002) found that the benefits of a robust WM capacity may manifest over the long term rather than in immediate posttreatment performance measures. In their study, low-memory speakers outperformed high-memory speakers on an immediate posttest, whereas high-memory speakers were superior on a delayed posttest. Although it is clear, then, that WM has a relationship with language learning, and that greater WM will be more conducive to learning than less WM, the precise nature of the relationship is likely to be considerably more complex than a simple one-to-one positive relationship across all dimensions of the language system and for all types of learners. One pedagogic ramification is that learners will definitely differ in terms of their WM capacities, and this difference might account for considerable variability in how they respond to instruction. As such, it is likely that different learners will require different amounts of time and different types or frequencies of input and other activities to acquire the same target L2 phenomena, and therefore pedagogic design should incorporate options for "differentiated" instruction based on this reality.

Aptitude-Treatment Interactions

Aptitude-treatment interaction refers to studies that look for evidence of whether different instructional treatments impact learning in different ways depending on a learner's cognitive aptitude (Doughty, 2013; for related general education research, see Cronbach & Snow, 1977; Snow, 1989; Snow, Frederico, & Montague, 1980).

The purpose of this research is to design and tailor training that will suit students' abilities best. Although research of this kind is relatively new in language learning, a number of studies suggest that the effectiveness of instruction depends on learners having certain abilities.

A review of aptitude-treatment studies by Vatz and colleagues (2013) summarizes findings that have (potentially) different practical implications for language learners and instructors. First, a group of studies show that learners with differential levels of aptitude (particularly WM) improve performance when different treatments are *matched* to their abilities (Brooks, Kempe, & Sionov, 2006; Perrachione et al., 2011; Wesche, 1981). For example, a well-known study from Wesche (1981) found that matches between aptitude profile (analytic vs. memory-oriented learners) and instruction (analytic vs. situational) resulted in higher levels of student satisfaction and achievement, as well as the reverse in which there were mismatches.

A second pattern of findings shows a single treatment having a similar impact on the performance of two aptitude groups, but with the higher aptitude group benefiting more. A study from Goo (2012), for example, on corrective feedback, shows that learners with greater WM capacity seem better able to benefit from recasts, whereas learners with low WM are helped much less by recasts (see also Hautpman, 1971; Li, 2013; Robinson, 1997; Sheen, 2007).

Finally, other studies suggest that a particular treatment "levels the playing field"— that is, a treatment produces superior results for all aptitudes and leads to *similar outcomes* for different aptitude groups. For example, Payne and Whitney (2002) showed this kind of effect, studying chat room interventions, which appeared to result in improved, and similar, outcomes for all aptitude levels (see also Erlam, 2005). Fundamentally, then, it is too soon to state unequivocally that there is a benefit from pedagogic designs that match aptitude profiles with instructional approaches or techniques. The current best knowledge would thus suggest that a mix of *treatments*, or intentionally varied pedagogic practices, might be called for in order to appeal to the needs of diverse learners who are learning in the same time and setting (i.e., in a single classroom). Additionally, it may be that pedagogic approaches based on tasks or projects, which themselves allow for variability in how learners approach and complete the learning and performance work involved, might offer preferable conditions for dealing with the realities of differences in learner aptitudes.

Learning Styles

Second language acquisition is known to be impacted by specific cognitive dispositions that impact how a learner approaches or engages in language education (Brown, 2007). *Learning style* denotes the tendencies of how learners process information during learning situations in specific ways (Dörnyei & Skehan, 2003). A number of such tendencies have been identified (e.g., a global vs. analytic orientation to processing language input) and are known to vary between individuals, thereby potentially impacting how language learning proceeds. Given the diversity of learning-style models, and the somewhat nascent research in this area, practical implications for language instruction are quite unclear. Still, a number of general recommendations may be made considering the possibly broad implications for instructed SLA.

Research on learning style and SLA has generated a number of models and constructs. Arguably the most researched conceptualization has been field dependence (FD) versus field independence (FI). FD denotes a learner preference for holistic processing of information and an orientation toward sociality and the ability to work well in groups. FI learners, by contrast, process information in analytic ways, separating information into component parts, and are distinguished in their social interactions by aloofness and a preference for learning alone (Dörnyei & Skehan, 2003). FD versus FI is one of many such conceptualizations in SLA research, each intended to capture specific cognitive approaches to processing new linguistic information during language education activities (see Table 3.1).[7]

TABLE 3.1 Taxonomies of Language Learning Styles

Oxford and Anderson (1995); Cohen, Oxford, and Chi (2001)	Ehrman and Leaver (2003)	Reid (1995)	Skehan (1998)
• FD versus FI	• Random (nonlinear) versus sequential (linear)	• Visual preference	• Analysis oriented versus memory oriented
• Global versus particular		• Auditory preference	
• Synthesizing versus analytic	• Global versus particular	• Kinesthetic preference	
• Sharpener versus leveler	• Inductive reasoning versus deductive reasoning	• Tactile preference	
• Feeling versus thinking	• Analog versus digital	• Group preference	
• Impulsive versus reflective	• Concrete versus abstract	• Individual preference	
• Intuitive-random versus concrete-sequential	• Impulsive versus reflective		
• Closure oriented versus open oriented	• Sharpening versus leveling		
• Extroverted versus introverted	• Synthesizing versus analytic		
• Global versus analytic			
• Visual versus auditory versus hands on (tactile-kinesthetic)			

Research on language learning styles is important because mismatches between style and instruction are proposed to be the cause of learning difficulties (Ehrman, 1996). Accordingly, the position advocated by learning-style researchers is that principled tailoring of instruction to different learning dispositions should be conducted (whenever possible) in order to improve learning effectiveness. Various types of mismatches can occur. There can be a mismatch between a student's learning style and (a) the teacher's teaching style, (b) a syllabus (e.g., insufficient coverage of grammar for analytic learners), (c) a language task (e.g., a visual learner participating in a task that involves receiving auditory input only), (d) a learner's own beliefs about learning (e.g., an analysis-oriented learner desiring rote learning, which is better suited to a memory-oriented learner), and (e) learning strategies (e.g., when a FI learner tries to apply social strategies, or a global learner uses bottom-up reading strategies; Dörnyei, 2005).

However, the practical application of cognitive or learner styles to language instruction and curriculum development is not straightforward (Dörnyei, 2005). On the one hand, Dörnyei (2005) and others suggest it is premature to develop pedagogy on the basis of learning styles research because the various constructs and models have been insufficiently researched and validated. Moreover, from a purely practical point of view, tailoring instruction to the numerous learning-style types that are bound to arise in heterogeneous classrooms would be unfeasible (Dörnyei, 2005). Still, researchers provide some general, speculative pedagogical guidelines given what is known about learning styles at this stage. One commonsense recommendation is that teachers should teach in a way that does not disproportionately favor one learning style over another and design or *differentiate* tasks and activities that accommodate multiple styles (Peacock, 2001, p. 15). In addition, Yates (2000) recommends an appealingly simple strategy: provide students with different time requirements to accommodate those learners whose dispositions are unsuited to a given task or activity. A second suggestion from Peacock (2001) is for teachers to involve learners in planning lessons and tasks and, more generally, to provide students more autonomy and control over their own learning such that students can adapt tasks to their preferred learning styles; similarly, assessments might enable learners' choice of modality or medium for demonstrating their learning and abilities. Finally, Dörnyei (2005) points out that schools might adopt some sort of an individualized consultation and diagnosis process to inform students about their learning styles, increase their meta-awareness, and thus choose learning experiences better suited to their learning dispositions.

Personality

According to Pervin and John (2001), personality denotes the characteristics of an individual that "account for consistent patterns of feeling, thinking, and behaving" (p. 4). In language acquisition it has long been held that different personality types (e.g., extroversion vs. introversion) impact language development in important ways, with certain traits conferring unique language learning advantages (and others, unique disadvantages).

Like research on learning styles, personality in language acquisition research borrows theoretically from psychology. Accordingly, the most widely used construct in language acquisition research has been the "big five" framework developed by Goldberg (1992, 1993) and McCrae and Costa (2003). The big five model consists of five subordinate constructs: (a) openness to experience, (b) conscientiousness, (c) extroversion vs. introversion, (d) agreeableness, and (e) neuroticism vs. emotional stability.[8] In addition to the big five model, Ellis (2008) identifies a number of additional personality constructs known (or proposed) to impact SLA, including risk taking, tolerance of ambiguity, empathy, self-esteem, anxiety, and inhibition. Of the various personality traits of interest in language acquisition research, extroversion vs. introversion and anxiety have received the most attention.

A number of observations have been made about how extroversion impacts language learning and use. For example, one speculation is that extroverted learners should enjoy certain advantages because, given their sociality, they are more likely to participate in class activities, engage in communication and interaction, generate more input and feedback, and produce more output (Skehan, 1986). Research studies have not fully corroborated this view (see Dörnyei, 2005, for a discussion). Nevertheless, despite historically mixed results for the advantages of extroversion, more recent research suggests extroverts do appear to have advantages in speaking ability, demonstrating more fluency than introverted learners, for example, in formal situations and in situations characterized by interpersonal stress (there do not seem to be any extroversion benefits for writing ability, however; Dewaele & Furnham, 1999). Introverts, by contrast, would seem to benefit less from learning opportunities and speaking practice that require participation in communicative tasks and situations (Dörnyei, 2005).

Related to broader notions of personality types, the impact of *anxiety* on language learning has also received considerable research attention. A distinction made in anxiety research is between trait versus state anxiety. *Trait anxiety* refers to a stable predisposition of anxiousness in different situations; *state anxiety* is the transient, moment-to-moment experience of anxiety as an emotional reaction to the current situation (Dörnyei, 2007). Anxiety specifically due to language learning is defined by MacIntyre (1999) as "the worry and negative emotional reaction aroused when learning or using a second language" (p. 27). Similarly, *foreign language classroom anxiety* is defined by Horwitz, Horwitz, and Cope (1986) as "a distinct complex of self-perceptions, beliefs, feelings and behaviors related to classroom learning arising from the uniqueness of the language learning process" (p. 128). Studies consistently report negative effects of language anxiety on various measures of L2 performance (Dewaele, 2007; Horwitz, 2001; Lu & Liu, 2011; MacIntyre, 1999; MacIntyre & Gardner, 1991; Saito, Horwitz, & Garza, 1999). To report one illustrative example, low-anxiety learners seem better able to benefit from corrective feedback and produce more modified feedback during L2 inter-action (Sheen, 2008).

In addition to these broad findings, language anxiety can be unique to par-ticular language modalities and also associated with particular educational back-grounds and cultures (see the next section). Speaking in classrooms, for example, is known to be especially stressful for certain learners (Dewaele, 2013; Pae, 2013). Moreover, it may be that anxiety is more acute at lower proficiency levels, with higher proficiency students potentially developing strategies and other resources to combat anxiety's debilitating effects (Révész, 2011). Finally, it is possible that the mode of communication may mitigate language anxiety. Computer-mediated chat, for example, may reduce anxiety by creating less threatening environments for interaction compared to face-to-face communication (Loewen, 2015). Other strategies (see Horwitz, Tallon, & Luo, 2009) for creating pedagogic environments that are less threatening and more amenable to diverse personalities include

- planning lessons from the point of view of learners and considering the pos-sible anxiety involved and personality types favored by different activities;
- making extensive use of group work and other "staging" opportunities to give students practice in speaking before asking them to perform individually and publicly;
- recognizing learners' anxious feelings, addressing them explicitly as an impor-tant learning topic in class, and helping learners realize that anxiety is a wide-spread phenomenon; and
- helping learners concentrate on communicative success rather than formal accuracy and realize the difference (e.g., through provision of criteria for task success, examples of successful communication).

Language Learning and Educational Background

An important and more recent vein of ID research has investigated the impacts of prior education and L1 literacy on L2 learning. Research suggests that level of schooling has crucial effects on how SLA proceeds, particularly for those who have little L1 literacy. Such learners are known to make slower progress in lan-guage classrooms and other formal learning contexts (Bigelow & Watson, 2012).

Adult language learners with limited or entirely lacking L1 literacy have unique disadvantages when learning languages, particularly in school or formal environ-ments where instruction—even at beginning levels of proficiency—is conceived and delivered assuming L1 writing or reading ability, as well as familiarity with the structures and cultures of classroom instruction (Bigelow & Watson, 2012). First, for learners without any experience with formal instruction, classroom tasks and content can be unlike anything in a learner's prior experience, and prelit-erate learners may react and interpret classroom activities and discourse differ-ently from literate learners and in ways that will hinder performance (Bigelow &

Watson, 2012). Second, literacy seems to confer a number of cognitive advantages. For example, research shows that fundamental aspects of oral learning and oral input processing are easier for learners with alphabetic literacy.[9] Low-literacy learners are known to have difficulty manipulating new phonemes and syllables, whereas high-literacy learners perform better because alphabetic knowledge provides a framework for visualizing—and manipulating—new oral, phonemic input (Tarone, Bigelow, & Hansen, 2009). In addition, "average-literacy" language learners perform better than low-literacy learners on WM digit-span tasks (Kurvers & van de Craats, 2007). Low-literacy learners also experience various input analysis disadvantages such as less ability to mark word boundaries accurately or recognize beginning words (Kurvers, 2007).

Research also suggests that literacy aids the ability to benefit from participation in classroom oral tasks. For example, high-literacy learners appear better able to perceive and repeat corrective recasts. A general finding along these lines is that where language learning requires analysis and manipulation of morphemes, grammar, or syntax, literacy is an advantage. Thus, some research suggests that provision of metalinguistic information is a particular benefit to low-literacy learners who often lack the conceptual framework for language analysis and language awareness (Kurvers et al., 2006).

It is also likely that the introduction of new learning materials, activity types, and pedagogic approaches to specific learner populations will require attention to the educational experiences—and particularly to the language learning experiences—that learners have had. For example, it may be that learners have developed considerable antipathy or reticence toward language learning as a result of negative experiences in previous classes. Or it may be that "cultures" of education, such as those prevalent in western societies versus those typical of East Asian societies and Confucian approaches to education, contribute differently to assumptions regarding the nature of learning, classroom behavior, and teacher and learner roles (e.g., learners being positioned in more receptive roles). Strategies for introducing pedagogic innovation into diverse educational cultural environments are addressed in detail in chapter 10 of this volume.

Summary and Recommendations

In sum, research is clear that the potential for language education is constrained by a number of relatively immutable dispositional and background factors that learners bring with them to any educational experience. A key implication of this overarching finding is that instruction—if unmindful of these differences—stands a good chance of disadvantaging particular groups of learners while advantaging others. Language teachers and materials developers, then, must have some sense of the likely set of IDs in a given target audience and tailor instruction accordingly (which calls for planning on the basis of needs analysis and other diagnostic strategies). In the event that the ID profile of a target audience is not fully known, educators should assume diverse individual learning differences among any set of learners. Accordingly, instructional design should thus avoid creating materials or educational sequences in ways that unduly favor one set of learner dispositions and aptitudes to the exclusion of others.

The following recommendations offer points of consideration in the design of language educational materials and experiences based on the likely influence of static learner IDs.

3.1. *Assess learner IDs prior to planning instruction.*

To the extent possible, it will be beneficial to understand learners' profiles in a given program, classroom, or other language learning environment through the use of both:

a. existing assessment batteries for variables like anxiety, aptitude, WM, and so on; and

b. locally meaningful observations, interviews, questionnaires, and other methods that offer a sense of what dispositions, assumptions, propensities, and likely capacities learners bring into the learning setting.

3.2. *Match instruction with learner IDs.*

Research generally supports the view that learners with a particular aptitude, learning style, or personality trait will learn better when matched with instruction that accentuates (or does not conflict with) a given trait or disposition (though it may be essential at times to raise learners' awareness that communicative events in reality may not always accommodate to their particular styles).

3.3. *Adapt instruction in ways appropriate to learner ages.*

a. Age is an important predictor of ultimate L2 attainment. Younger learners are more likely to reach L2 native-speaker levels of ability, particularly in the areas of phonology and morphosyntactic accuracy (whereas there seems to be less of an age-related impact for learning of vocabulary or lexicon).

b. Adult learners do not learn from naturalistic interaction in the same way children do and appear to need instructional strategies that draw their attention to linguistic form. Moreover, adult learners are better able to benefit from metalinguistic information and instruction compared to children.

3.4. *Consider L1 literacy levels in instructional design.*

L1 literacy is an important aid in L2 learning, both for early L2 learning in children and for adults who have relatively little L1 schooling. Learners without L1 literacy will progress more slowly than literate L1 peers.

Thus, it may be better to allow children to develop L1 literacy prior to L2 instruction. Likewise, adults with low L1 literacy will need instruction that specifically targets literacy deficiencies.

3.5. *Use instructional techniques appropriate to learners with different levels of aptitude or WM.*

    a. Language learning aptitude is an important predictor of L2 achievement when learning starts after childhood.

    b. Language learning aptitude predicts achievement in all learning context studies to date (e.g., naturalistic vs. instructed) and also when using different teaching methods (implicit-inductive-synthetic vs. deductive-explicit-analytic).

    c. Working memory is typically considered a component of language learning aptitude and likewise an important predictor of L2 achievement when learning begins after childhood. Aptitude and WM, however, do not confer advantages all the time and for all types of learners; benefits of aptitude or WM will depend on factors such as learner age, proficiency level, linguistic mode, linguistic form, and type of corrective feedback.

3.6. *Incorporate tasks and activities that accommodate a variety of personality types and learning styles.*

    a. Numerous learning styles have been identified, though their distinctness from personality constructs is perhaps a bit unclear.

    b. Extroverted learners appear to have certain advantages over introverted learners given their propensity for sociality and willingness to engage in communication.

    c. Anxiety has been shown to have consistently detrimental impacts on language performance.

3.7. *Make students aware of their ID profiles.*

    a. Making students aware of their particular ID profiles can help with metacognition, learning awareness, and the learners' abilities to plan their own language study.

    b. Addressing IDs, such as anxiety, explicitly as topics of instruction may help learners understand them and develop better learning strategies and dispositions.

3.8. *Allow students autonomy in their learning.*

    a. Allowing and encouraging greater learning autonomy will allow students to learn in ways that suit their ID profile best.

    b. Soliciting student involvement in instructional planning will help students learn in ways suited to their ID profile.

Notes

1 The coverage in this chapter is primarily conceptual in orientation; because static ID variables are somewhat immutable to intervention, we seek to introduce them here, rather than present detailed research findings about them in relation to language instruction. In chapter 4, turning to mutable ID variables, we attempt to synthesize key research-based findings about the extent to which such factors may be beneficially influenced in relation to language educational outcomes.
2 There are a number of studies, however, identifying exceptional adult learners able to perform at levels of L2 ability indistinguishable from native speakers (Birdsong, 1992, 1999; Coppieters, 1987; Ioup et al., 1994; White & Genesse, 1996).
3 Because this volume is focused on adult—that is, postadolescent—language learners, age arguably plays less of a role in pedagogic design considerations than other individual difference variables do, for our current purposes.
4 Carroll and Sapon's (1959) Modern Language Aptitude Test was the first of a number of subsequent instruments designed to capture language aptitude. Other notable tests include the Pimsleur Language Aptitude Battery (PLAB, Pimsleur 1966), the Defense Language Aptitude Battery (Peterson & Al-Haik, 1976); the CANAL-F test (Cognitive Ability for Novelty in Acquisition of Languages—Foreign); and the LLAMA, which is delivered online (Skehan, 2012).
5 In fact, Skehan proposes four applications of aptitude testing, the fourth being "selection" of candidates for admission into language programs; however, he notes that this is not an optimal use in most typical circumstances.
6 WM measures used in SLA research include digit-span recall tasks, word-span tasks, nonword-repetition-span tasks, and sentence-repetition tasks (Ortega, 2009c). Note Williams' observation that given the differences of the tasks between the assessments, they are likely to be measuring different components of WM.
7 Each of these constructs are operationalized in Cohen, Oxford, and Chi's (2001) *Learning Style Survey*, Ehrman and Leaver's (2003) *Learning Style Questionnaire*, and Joy Reid's (1995) *Perceptual Learning Style Preference Questionnaire*.
8 The "big five" personality is model is commonly operationalized using the NEO Five-Factory Inventory (Costa & McCrae, 1992). Another well-known personality model is the Myers-Briggs Personality Type, captured via the Myers-Briggs Type Indicator (MBTI, Myers & McCaulley, 1985).
9 Although when the target language involves a distinct alphabet or writing system, the challenges are compounded.

4

LEARNER INDIVIDUAL DIFFERENCES—DYNAMIC

Chapter 3 summarized concepts, theories, and research on individual differences (IDs) that are more or less static in the language learner. This chapter introduces IDs that are relatively dynamic and therefore amenable to change via instruction or some intentional educational strategy. Language learning motivation, for example, is seen as a conative variable (i.e., related to volition or effort) that can be manipulated by educational planning, instructional techniques, materials design, and formative assessment strategies such that a student can be encouraged to engage in language study. As with the various constructs in the previous chapter, numerous dynamic ID variables have been identified and researched (some conceptualizations overlapping and constituting variations of one another), each put forward as explanations of how learners vary in their language learning dispositions and conative orientations. Of these differences, we consider the following as the most current, relevant, and extensively researched IDs to date: motivation, willingness to communicate (WTC), learning strategies, learner beliefs (LBs), and learner identity.

Motivation

Motivation has arguably been the most researched dimension of individual variance in language learning. Broadly defined, *motivation* refers to the desire of a learner to initiate and sustain language learning (Dörnyei, 2005) and is arguably one of the most highly predictive variables of language learning attainment (Ortega, 2009c). Given its centrality in second language acquisition (SLA) and language education research, a large portion of this chapter is dedicated to reviewing motivation theories and research, as well as the most relevant pedagogical applications of findings and related instructional advice.

Current motivation research has its origins in social psychology and the seminal work of Canadian researchers Robert Gardner and Wallace Lambert. Gardner and Lambert framed language motivation in terms of a "socio-educational model," a conceptualization that was dominant in the field up to the 1990s (Gardner, 1985; Gardner & Lambert, 1972). The socioeducational model is centered on the idea that motivation has a social dimension. That is, a desire to learn a language is the result of learner attitudes toward, and relationships with, speakers from the L2 community. Thus, according to Gardner and Lambert (1972) motivation was composed of two main orientations: an *instrumental* orientation "reflecting the practical value and advantages of learning a new language" and an *integrative* orientation "reflecting a sincere personal interest in the people and culture represented by the other group" (p. 132). Of the two, Gardner regarded integrative motivation as the most facilitative type of orientation needed for successful L2 learning. A highly integrative orientation toward language learning involved positive attitudes toward L2 speakers, low ethnocentrism, and a desire to interact with individuals in the L2 community.

Starting in the 1990s Gardner and Lambert's framework came under criticism for casting motivation as a stable and static trait, and the model gave way to conceptualizations that conceived motivation as a more fluid, dynamic construct that fluctuates over time in different learning circumstances (Loewen, 2015). Nevertheless, the socioeducational model has had a lasting and prolonged influence on SLA research, not the least of which was to set a precedent for research methodology still used by motivation researchers today. Motivation research typically employs multi-item questionnaires, a legacy of Gardner's (1985) Attitude/Motivation Test Battery (A/MTB), which operationalized motivation in three dimensions, each via a different subset of survey items. Many different batteries have been developed since the A/MTB, but each has used the same method of capturing a motivational subconstruct or trait using multiple items, which respondents rate for agreement using a Likert rating scale (e.g., "I love learning French" 1 = *strongly disagree;* 7 = *strongly agree*).

The next important reconceptualization of motivation was developed by Dörnyei and Ottó (1998), who took into account the situated nature of motivation within the classroom. Dörnyei and Ottó (1998) proposed a dynamic model that attempted to account for how, on the one hand, motivation can derive from antecedent goals, reasons, decisions, and so on but, on the other hand, wax and wane within the context of a classroom from moment to moment depending on how the learning experience unfolds (Ushioda & Dörnyei, 2012). Dörnyei and Ottó's "process-oriented" approach delineates this temporal aspect by dividing motivation into three stages: (a) the preactional phase, (b) the actional phase, and (c) the postactional phase. The three stages refer to points in time before, during, and after a given classroom task, within which learner motivation can vary. The preactional phase refers to the motivation that learners carry with them prior to the task (e.g., their learning goals and intentions). The actional stage, or *executive motivation*, refers to motivation increasing or diminishing during the learning task. The postactional phase refers to the motivation that ensues after the learner reviews and evaluates the learning experience.

The most recent conceptualization of motivation—and one driving much contemporary research—is Dörnyei's (2005) L2 motivational self-system, a model that retheorizes motivation in terms of the potential for learners to imagine "possible selves" and, in particular, imagine future selves with the language abilities to which the learner aspires (Ushioda & Dörnyei, 2012). More specifically, Dörnyei suggests that motivation results from the learner closing the gap between the current self (and current language abilities) and either (a) the *ideal* self, which represents the attributes the learner would like to have in the future (i.e., personal aspirations, wishes, goals); or (b) the *ought-to* self, which signifies the attributes that the learner believes they ought to possess in the future ("representations of someone else's sense of duty, obligations, responsibilities"; Ushioda & Dörnyei, 2012, p. 400). The main mechanisms of the L2 motivation self-system are (a) that the learner is motivated by a future ideal self or future ought-to self that is L2 proficient, and (b) there is a psychological desire to "reduce the distance between current and future self-states" (Ushioda & Dörnyei, 2012, p. 401). In addition, both types of self-concepts are conditioned by the situational dynamics of the learning environment (though this aspect of Dörnyei's framework has received little research attention to date).

Numerous empirical studies have been conducted looking for relationships between the various theorizations of motivation and SLA. In almost every instance, motivation is related to L2 achievement to some, though quite variable, degree. For example, Masgoret and Gardner (2003) conducted a meta-analysis of 75 studies (all using the A/MTB) and found that of the various attitude and affect variables of interest, motivation had the strongest relationship with L2 proficiency (average correlations for distinct learner groups ranging from $r = .25$ to .50) Moreover, studies also show that particular teaching strategies can influence student motivation within L2 classrooms. Guilloteaux and Dörnyei (2008), for example, studied 27 teachers and 1,381 students in South Korea, investigating whether teachers' motivational strategies impacted student motivation. The study focused on motivational teacher discourse, student participation patterns, and encouragement of positive retrospective self-evaluation (the study used Dörnyei and Ottó's "process-oriented" framework). Results showed strong correlations between teachers' motivational strategies and student motivation (see also Moskovsky et al., 2013, for a study with similar results found in Saudi Arabia). Thus, current research does suggest that manipulation of the learning environment by teachers can increase student motivation to some extent, which, in turn, has an empirically established, if moderate, relationship with level of L2 achievement.

As noted previously, the research on motivation has generated a number of practical strategies and recommendations for teachers looking to increase learner motivation in L2 classrooms. Three of the most well-known and current frameworks—all devised by Dörnyei based on his evolving conceptions of motivation—are described next.

First, Dörnyei and Csizér (1998) asked 200 Hungarian teachers of English to rate the importance of 51 motivational teaching strategies based on Dörnyei and Ottó's (1998) process-oriented motivation framework. On the basis of the study findings, Dörnyei and Csizér compiled a set of 10 motivational macrostrategies (a distillation of the 51 strategies from the study), which they termed the "10 commandments for motivating language learners" (see Table 4.1).

Second, as noted previously, Guilloteaux and Dörnyei (2008) looked for evidence of motivational strategies used by Korean teachers of English and whether this would increase the motivation levels of Korean EFL students. Teachers were trained using Dörnyei's (2001) framework of motivation in foreign language classrooms (also based on the process-oriented model). Table 4.2 presents an abbreviated representation of Dörnyei's (2001) model indicating the main macrostrategies associated with four dimensions of his framework (derived from more than 100 specific motivational techniques; see Dörnyei, 2001). Moreover, these strategies were used as a basis for teacher observation in the Korean EFL study, all of which, again, contributed to increases in learner motivation in that context.

The third and most recent strategy framework comes from Hadfield and Dörnyei (2013) and was developed on the basis of Dörnyei's (2005) L2 motivational self-system. This system recommends practical pedagogical techniques for helping learners (a) construct and maintain a vision of their future L2 selves using visualization techniques; (b) develop action plans, use goal-setting techniques, and implement self-regulation techniques in order achieve that vision; and (c) counterbalance the ideal self with a feared self ("i.e., the consequences of not learning the language or failing in one's aspirations") in order to stay committed to their L2 learning goals (Ushioda & Dörnyei, 2012, p. 405). Hadfield and Dörnyei (2013) provide an entire volume devoted to practical classroom activities for teachers and learners, which include visualization techniques and other protocols

---

TABLE 4.1 10 Commandments for Motivating Language Learners (Dörnyei & Csizér, 1998)

---

1. Set a personal example with your own behavior.
2. Create a pleasant, relaxed atmosphere in the classroom.
3. Present the tasks properly.
4. Develop a good relationship with the learners.
5. Increase the learners' linguistic self-confidence.
6. Make the language classes interesting.
7. Promote learner autonomy.
8. Personalize the learning process.
9. Increase the learners' goal-orientedness.
10. Familiarize learners with the target language culture.

TABLE 4.2 Macrostrategies for Motivating Language Learners (Guilloteaux & Dörnyei, 2008)[1]

Creating Basic Motivational Conditions	Generating Initial Motivation	Maintaining and Protecting Motivation	Encouraging Positive Retrospective Self-Evaluation
• Adopting appropriate teacher behaviors • Establishing a good teacher-student rapport • Creating a pleasant and supportive classroom atmosphere • Generating a cohesive learner group with appropriate group norms	• Increasing the learners' expectancy of success • Increasing learners' goal-orientedness • Making teaching materials relevant • Developing positive attitudes toward the language course and language learning in general • Creating realistic learner beliefs	• Promoting situation-specific task motivation (via stimulating, enjoyable, and relevant tasks) • Providing learners with experiences of success • Allowing learners to maintain a positive social image • Promoting learner autonomy • Promoting self-motivating learner strategies	• Promoting adaptive attributions • Providing effective and encouraging feedback • Increasing learner satisfaction • Offering grades in a motivational manner

used toward enabling learners to realize their ideal self-image. Their basic idea is that learners should be encouraged to recognize their own self-visions and then to develop short- and long-term goals that are realistic and concrete. Thus, for example, learners can be encouraged to compare their visions with the goals and organization of a course syllabus, develop their own self-study strategies for the semester, identify methods to monitor their own progress, and compare ideas with other learners and teachers on effective language study, practice, skill development, and so forth. A variety of techniques and activities can be utilized to enable this visioning process, including group brainstorming, individual questionnaires, checklists and ranking of learning activities, and so on (see details in Hadfield & Dörnyei, 2013).

Finally, motivational constructs have been used to better understand student performance, specifically within a task-based language teaching (TBLT) pedagogical framework. One notable example, again from Dörnyei (2009), examines how a TBLT pedagogical approach can stimulate motivation given the common use of group- and pair-work activities. The study found a relationship between co-constructed motivation arising between interlocutors during instructional dyads and task engagement. Results suggest that TBLT and other methodologies emphasizing student interaction and communication uniquely create the conditions needed for students to work together and motivate one another, creating an environment that potentially encourages many of the recommended strategies and conditions listed previously.

Willingness to Communicate

A recent factor considered in conjunction with motivation (and at times subsumed within it) is a learner's WTC during L2 classroom instruction or other opportunities for using the target language. It is by now well known that both child language acquisition and adult multilingual learning—either in naturalistic or educational settings—is an inherently social process that requires communicative interaction. However, it is not uncommon to find individuals who avoid L2 communicative situations (Dörnyei, 2005). WTC, then, refers to the likelihood of a learner engaging in L2 communication when free to do so. Research on WTC investigates situational factors and other variables that impact the desire to interact in the target language.

The primary WTC framework of note in SLA research has been developed by MacIntyre, Clement, Dornyei, and Noels (1998). According to MacIntyre and colleagues (1998), WTC is defined as "a state of readiness to engage in the L2, the culmination of processes that prepare the learner to initiate L2 communication with a specific person at a specific time" (quoted from MacIntyre, Burns, & Jessome, 2011, p. 82). MacIntyre and colleagues' (1998) WTC framework is a multicomponent construct combining psychological, linguistic, educational, and communicative dimensions of language. The model is conceived as a pyramid with six layers or sections, starting from the most "distal" WTC variables (relative to the moment at which the learner might communicate) and culminating in the most "proximal" components of the interactive situation itself. The three distal levels of the framework describe the more enduring aspects of the L2 speaking context and learner, such as the learner's personality, his or her communicative competence, and his or her L2 confidence, as well as factors influenced by the learner's prior experience, such as intergroup attitudes and degree of affiliation between the speaker and the L2 group. The three proximal categories have more to do with aspects of the immediate speaking situation. For example, WTC is conditioned by a learner's desire to communicate with a specific person, as well as the learner's state of self-confidence at the moment of interaction. If all of these factors align in helpful ways, the theory suggests, then a "behavioral intention" develops in the learner, "freely chosen, to speak if one has the opportunity" (p. 84). Note that the system is dynamic, and any one of the components in the pyramid model can hinder or help WTC as speaking opportunities or injunctions arise.

Note also that two of the various subconstructs in this model, communication anxiety and perceived communication competence, are the strongest predictors of WTC (Dörnyei, 2005).

WTC is regarded as an important L2 ID because it apparently influences communication (Loewen, 2015). If a learner is unwilling to communicate, he or she may miss out on the known benefits to L2 development resulting from communication and social interaction (see chapter 2). This general observation aside, some studies show how WTC may vary for learners in different contexts. For example, results suggest there is variation in WTC depending on the learning situation. In a study from Baker and MacIntyre (2000), immersion students displayed higher WTC and more frequent communication in the L2 than their nonimmersion counterparts. In addition, a more recent study from MacIntyre, Burns, and Jessome (2011) used a qualitative research methodology (diaries), asking middle school L2 learners of French (in an immersion context) to list situations in which they were most and least willing to communicate in French. The most frequent situations where students were willing to communicate included during class, with other immersion students, for class projects, to follow a speaking norm, with friends, with immersion friends, to show off to friends, with family, with the French-speaking family, to showcase skills learned, with a friend, to exclude others, with a teacher, and especially with a noncritical teacher. Students were least willing to communicate when it is easier to communicate in English, when classwork is difficult, when unsure of an answer, when put on the spot, when afraid of mistakes, with a friend who corrects excessively, to strangers in public, and in front of family at home (for the full list of situations, see MacIntyre, Burns, & Jessome, 2011).[2]

Learning Strategies

Related to the notion of learning styles in chapter 3 is the idea that there are conscious psychological and behavioral procedures that learners employ in order to improve or gain control over their learning (Ortega, 2009c). Oxford (2011) defines learning strategies as "the learner's goal-directed actions for improving language proficiency and achievement, completing a task, or making learning more efficient, effective, and easier" (p. 167). Ortega (2009c) points out that learning strategies suffer to a certain extent (like many of the ID constructs reviewed in this chapter) from a certain fuzziness of conceptual boundaries. Learners may have preferences for certain learning strategies based on cognitive or learning styles, personality attributes, or aptitudes. Nevertheless, Loewen (2015) recommends that teachers help learners become more aware of their own strategies, use them more effectively, and possibly employ new strategies to enhance their language learning in ways they had not imagined.

The most influential research on learner strategies has been conducted by Rebecca Oxford (2011), whose learning strategy framework is operationalized in the Strategy Inventory of Language Learning (SILL). The SILL is a questionnaire with 32 items that identify the particular strategies a learner prefers. Strategies are categorized in terms of (a) cognitive (e.g., "guessing from context," "making notes"), (b) metacognitive (e.g., "having clear goals for improving one's own skills," "noticing one's own mistakes"), (c) affective (e.g., "encouraging oneself when afraid to speak"), (d) social (e.g., "practicing the L2 with other people"), (e) memory related (e.g., "connecting word sounds with a mental image or picture"), and (f) compensatory dimensions (e.g., "using circumlocutions").

A key interest in research into learning strategies—due to their auxiliary potential and teachability—has been to ascertain the degree to which they help learners improve their language achievement.[3] Studies have found moderate relationships between L2 achievement and teaching of learning strategies, on the order of half a standard deviation of benefit for learners who receive strategy training (average Cohen's $d = .49$; Plonsky, 2011). However, where studies have used groups-comparison designs (Cross, 2009; Vandergrift & Tafaghodtari, 2010), results have been mixed. In Vandergrift and Tafaghodtari (2010), as expected, the experimental group receiving strategy training (metacognitive listening strategies) outperformed the control group without strategy instruction. By contrast, Cross (2009) also trained an experimental group in listening strategies; however, the trained students improved in listening proficiency at a roughly equal rate compared to the control group participants. Moreover, studies show (again contradictory) evidence of moderator variables conditioning the impacts of strategy training. In Vandergrift and Tafaghodtari (2010), less proficient learners seemed to benefit more from listening strategy training than more proficient learners, whereas Plonsky's (2011) meta-analysis study found high proficiency learners benefiting more. Plonsky also found that (a) learning strategies have more impact on learners in second language (L2) contexts compared to foreign language educational contexts, (b) strategy training had more impact in laboratory settings than in classrooms, and (c) training in cognitive and metacognitive strategies had the greatest impact when only a few strategies were taught consistently over a long period of time (Loewen, 2015).

The inconsistency of findings in learning strategies research—as well as ongoing conceptual and theoretical critique of learning strategy constructs—has led some researchers to abandon the notion of learning strategies altogether, most notably in favor of self-regulation theory (e.g., Dörnyei, 2005; Dörnyei & Skehan, 2003; Tseng, Dörnyei, & Schmitt, 2006). Research on self-regulation and language learning is most prominently associated with Zoltán Dörnyei (and colleagues) who has argued that learners have a self-control capacity that underlies a variety of "personalized strategic learning mechanisms" (Tseng, Dörnyei, & Schmitt, 2006, p. 79). In Tseng, Dörnyei, and Schmitt's model, self-regulation is composed of various types of personal "control"—emotion control, commitment control, metacognitive control, satiation control, and environment control—that involve either consciously suppressing or enhancing psychological processes (or environment factors) that impact learning in negative or positive ways (Tseng,

Dörnyei, & Schmitt, 2006).Tseng, Dornyei, and Schmitt claim that the historical catalog of learning strategies from past research is in fact various manifestations of self-regulation brought to bear in different ways in the language learning problem or task (see, however, Rose, 2015, for a defense of learning strategy research).

Although development of learners' strategies has produced mixed evidence regarding effectiveness in terms of language learning achievements (and might usefully be reconceptualized as issuing from self-regulation), it may nevertheless be the case that explicitly addressing strategies is a sound pedagogic activity. Perhaps the key implication here is that learners and teachers should consider how learners are approaching language learning in general, as well as how they are approaching specific language tasks and skills, such that comparisons can be made between learners' a priori assumptions about how to "do language learning" and other possibilities that might be more beneficial.

Learner Beliefs

Language learning research on LBs attempts to explore the commonly held view that learner opinions about aspects of the language learning experience can influence learning outcomes. The first prominent investigation and measurement of LBs was Horwitz's (1988) seminal framework operationalized in the Beliefs About Language Learning Inventory (BALLI).The BALLI is a questionnaire instrument consisting of 34 self-report items that gauge student beliefs in five major areas: (a) difficulty of language learning (e.g., "grammar is the most difficult part of learning a foreign language"), (b) foreign language aptitude (e.g., "some people have a special ability for learning a foreign language"), (c) the nature of language learning (e.g., "some languages are easier to learn than others"), (d) learning and communication strategies (e.g., "the most important part of learning a foreign language is learning vocabulary words"), and (e) motivation and expectation (e.g., "people in my country feel that it is important to speak the language that I am studying").

Two additional models of LB that have developed out of Horwitz's initial work utilize the notions of *metacognitive knowledge* developed by Wenden (1999) and *epistemological beliefs* developed by Mori (1999). Metacognitive knowledge refers to what learners know about (as well as their attitudes toward) language learning (Wenden, 1999). Mori's (1999) framework of epistemological beliefs—or beliefs about the nature of knowledge and learning—includes five dimensions: beliefs about (a) the fixedness of language ability, (b) whether linguistics knowledge is simple or complex, (c) whether L2 learning is quick or gradual, (d) whether L2 knowledge is changeable, and (e) the trustworthiness of various sources of L2 knowledge. It should be pointed out, however, that not all researchers regard LBs as a viable vein of ID research given the lack of conceptual distinctness of LB constructs (Dörnyei, 2005). As such, a number of researchers have incorporated LB-type ideas into their models of motivation. Guilloteaux and Dörnyei

(2008), for example, include beliefs within the "process-oriented" motivation framework. Moreover, there is little research evidence of a clear link between LBs and measurable gains in student performance. Many of the claims of the impact of beliefs are speculative. For example, Kormos (1999) has found that learner orientation to accuracy and communication is moderately related to speech production, which would imply a learning advantage given the likely relationship with interaction and output. Moreover, studies show that learners can be guided to think in ways ostensibly conducive to language learning; however, there is little support for actual learning gains resulting from these interventions (Kartchava & Ammar, 2013; Pawlak, Mystkowska-Wiertelak, & Bielak, 2015; Sato, 2013). As with learning strategies, and perhaps even more so in the case of beliefs about language learning, it may be that the primary pedagogic implication is that some attention should be given to understanding LBs prior to instruction, so that learners and teachers can consider possible mismatches with pedagogic designs and materials. Where learners believe that language learning is primarily a process of explicit rule explanation, for example, it may be that their beliefs can and should be further developed through meta-level consideration of the implications of such beliefs for communicative language ability, especially in the context of introducing innovative materials that focus on the latter.

Identity

A recent and quite different theorization of how individual characteristics (within particular social situations) impact learning has been conceived in terms of *identity*, or, roughly speaking, the various processes by which the self is defined. Duff (2012) points out how terms such as "bilingual," "heritage language learner," "generation 1.5," "advanced," or "non-native speaker" are the results of politicized "naming" processes that have particular consequences for language learning, not the least of which being that they can disempower and marginalize multilingual individuals: "naming practices position people and their abilities and aspirations in particular ways, which itself has become a topic of critical reflection and theorizing in applied linguistics" (p. 410).

Traditionally, identity studies in SLA have been explored within the field of sociolinguistics, wherein categories such as gender, first language (L1), and ethnicity were examined for their impacts on language learning and use (though in such a way that these constructs were viewed as static and relatively immutable over time). More recently, identity research has looked to disciplines such as philosophy, cultural and literary studies, critical theory, feminist theory, LGBT studies, hermeneutics, and phenomenology to theorize how the individual defines him or herself through language, within social contexts, and in contrast with competing interests who possess differential access to power (Duff, 2012). Accordingly, the nature of identity has been understood as "discursive"; that is, it is constructed through language and thereby created within a system of representation that is dynamic and unstable and that relies on relational differences to produce meaning (Pennycook, 2001). Moreover, identity is realized through a continual struggle of rejecting and resisting, as well as claiming certain self-defining signifying categories (e.g., female, immigrant, beginner, language learner), especially as contested by powerful, often political interests.

Given that self-identification for language learners and users is often a contested struggle between speakers with different access to power, identity research has advanced an overtly social justice political agenda that seeks to investigate and redress the inequities of language learners and users who are marginalized because of their linguistic or socioeconomic status (Pennycook, 2001). Within this agenda, agency has been a key notion capturing how "learners are not passive, complicit participants in language learning and use, but can also make informed choices, exert influence, resist, or comply, though their social circumstances may constrain" their ability to do so (Duff, 2012, p. 413). Agency studies, then, have shown learners and speakers asserting themselves in language classrooms and other social situations where teachers, classmates, or other powerful interlocutors have positioned them in stereotypical, racist, classist, or gender-biased ways (e.g., Norton, 2000; Siegal, 1996).

Given the struggles many multilingual individuals experience in their attempts to learn or use a new language, certain language teaching approaches have been designed specifically to address the political, power-laden aspects of language teaching and learning. Critical language teaching and radical language teaching are just such approaches. Their aim is to organize language teaching in such a way that instruction redresses inequities in power and opportunity caused by race, culture, gender, proficiency, sexual orientation, expert-novice status, non-native or native-speaker status, legitimacy, and so on (Crookes, 2009a). Critical or radical language teaching is characterized by pedagogical practices that (a) are mindful of how language teaching is associated with concentrations of power; (b) are concerned with values opposed to the mainstream or elites; (c) are opposed to oppressive forces in society; (d) incorporate critical feminist ideology; (e) employ the teaching methods of Paulo Freire (e.g., developing student literacy, posing problems to students, "conscientization" of students to social issues); (f) empower and foster freedom of students; and (g) transform students into agents, makers, and "remakers" of the world (Crookes, 2009a). For one example of how such ideas can be implemented in a language teaching setting, Konoeda and Watanabe (2008) report on the implementation of "critical TBLT" in a middle school EFL class in Japan, where learners themselves identified the particularly salient social themes of stereotypical gender roles and bullying in school. The teachers created an "advice-giving" lesson, in English, wherein learners were encouraged to explore different identities through diverse (gender-related) perspectives on an event and then to provide written advice to all of the parties involved. Not only did the lesson allow for considerable language learning—in particular, how to express opinions and give advice—but the fact that the lesson was in English seemed to create a "safe" space where learners could address social issues and express distinct identities that were otherwise deemed innappropriate topics for attention in other class settings.

Summary and Recommendations

Although none of the ID research to date provides definitive evidence regarding a clear causal relationship of a certain magnitude with learning outcomes, on balance it does indicate that these learner variables are important in playing some kind of a role in moderating what and how learners learn. In sum, research findings on the aforementioned group of IDs suggest that language educators should strive to create learning materials and experiences that are as motivating and engaging as possible, and there is substantial empirically based guidance to help educators do so in terms of identifying specific factors at play and strategies that are likely to influence them. Moreover, and as noted at the end of chapter 3, having a good sense of the ID profiles within a targeted learner group (via needs analysis, learner intake assessments, etc.) will help inform strategies that can address likely LBs, learning styles, and identities in ways that effectively support instructed language acquisition. Overarching recommendations include the following.

4.1. Design instruction and materials to be maximally motivating.

    a.   Motivation is arguably the most important ID variable yet investigated, given its apparent strong relationship with language learning achievement and its susceptibility to instructional intervention.

    b.   Motivation research has identified a number of empirically supported techniques and features of language education that are known to increase language learning motivation.

The most recent set of instructional techniques and strategies—based on Dörnyei's L2 motivational self-system—is from Hadfield and Dörnyei (2013). It involves organizing instruction via tasks and activities such that learners (i) create a vision of the ideal L2-proficient self; (ii) plan, set goals, and identify learning strategies to achieve the vision; and (iii) sustain the vision via identity formation, visualization techniques, and performance of simulations.

4.2. Design instruction to increase learners' WTC.

    a.   A learner's WTC is an important predictor of language learning achievement, given the known importance of interaction and communication in L1 and L2 development.

    b.   A complex set of factors will impact a learner's desire to engage in communication. Aspects to consider in instructional design include characteristics of the individual and the context (e.g., the learner's personality and proficiency), as well as more dynamic aspects having to do with the immediate speaking situation (e.g., the interlocutor, the speaker's confidence in the moment).

4.3. Train students in relevant learning strategies.

a. Research on the efficacy of teaching types of learning strategies has been mixed, but a trend seems to suggest that, at least some of the time, instruction on learning strategies has a positive impact on L2 learning.

b. Learning strategies seem to impact different groups of learners in different ways. Efficacy of learning strategy instruction can depend on proficiency level, context of learning (foreign vs. L2; laboratory vs. classrooms), and number of strategies taught.

4.4. Understand learners' beliefs about language learning.

a. Learner beliefs appear to impact learning; as such, understanding what learners believe (e.g., through needs analysis) should provide a critical starting point for educators to raise learners' self-awareness and understanding of their own perspectives in comparison with the particular language instructional point of view adopted in a given educational setting.

b. Encouraging the "right" beliefs is perhaps less important (for adult learners) than (i) establishing clarity about the extent to which learners' beliefs match the instructional approach adopted and (ii) establishing a common foundation between learners, teachers, and materials regarding assumptions about how language learning will proceed.

4.5. Design instruction that empowers students.

a. Language instruction has the potential to assign marginalizing identities to students that prevent them from realizing personal goals. Avoid this eventuality.

b. Organize instruction that reflects the realities of students' lives and allows students agency, equality, decision-making power, and the realization of personal goals.

Notes

1 We note that such lists of strategies may not provide a coherent or organized basis for motivational actions in all circumstances, and at times some of these strategies may conflict with each other. For example, linking grades with performance and motivation may or may not have a positive effect on all learners, regardless of how the grades are presented, and grading per se may conflict with or override other strategies such as learner satisfaction or attention to positive feedback. These and other strategies are provided here simply as possible points of access to learner motivation and not necessarily as a comprehensive or holistic approach to motivating learners.

2 The role of the communicative situation in affecting WTC raises intriguing possibilities with regard to language learning in a technology-mediated environment, where it

may be possible to suspend or alter some of the affective concerns that learners have in face-to-face interaction. For example, some learners may be more willing to perform in an online and somewhat anonymous chat environment versus in front of a classroom of peers.

3 See Oxford (2011) for a description of the SILL learning strategy model, as well as numerous recommended techniques for strategy training and assistance. See also Chamot and colleagues (1999).

PART 2

Second Language Instruction, Assessment, and Educational Design

5

LANGUAGE PEDAGOGICAL APPROACHES

The previous chapters (and considerations explored in later chapters as well) make clear that the acquisition of languages other than the first depends considerably on a variety of individual, contextual, psychological, and social factors. In addition, a fundamental assumption in this volume, and in the field of language education broadly speaking, is that successful language acquisition can, at least to some extent, be engineered through the exposure of learners to particular types, sequences, and frequencies of carefully crafted language learning opportunities. That is, although certain dimensions of second language acquisition (SLA; e.g., developmental sequence orders; see chapter 2 and chapter 9) may proceed regardless of instruction, and although certain learner characteristics (e.g., individual memory capacity; see chapter 3) may be somewhat immutable to intervention, it is nevertheless the case that a well-designed learning context, or what we might call a pedagogy, can and should lead to efficient and effective language learning outcomes for a majority of language learners. This chapter reviews key features of contemporary approaches to language pedagogy for postadolescent learners,[1] with an emphasis on educational practices that foster simultaneous acquisition of both target language knowledge and communicative competence. The chapter summarizes ideas and issues related to the following broad aspects of language pedagogy: (a) why languages are taught and learned, (b) the recent history of approaches to language teaching, (c) current trends and practices in language pedagogy, and (d) the potential contribution of task-based language teaching (TBLT) as a synthesis of best practices.

Why Teach and Learn Language?

Languages are taught and learned for a variety of reasons, ranging from elective language study for humanistic purposes in economically privileged societies to de facto multilingualism for survival, trade, and cultural purposes in many other societies and sectors. It is by now a truism that economic globalization, human mobility, and participation in the worldwide information society (increasingly via the Internet) have brought people, cultures, and languages in contact with each other on an unprecedented scale (Kern, 2014; Kramsch, 2014). As a consequence, the associated need to communicate in mutually comprehensible ways has become the driving force behind most language learning and teaching today. People learn language, among many other reasons, in order to (a) access goods, services, and rights associated with immigration and participation in new societal circumstances; (b) avail themselves and their families of educational opportunities and improved career trajectories; (c) engage in communication (frequently via the Internet and other forms of mass media) for both work and entertainment purposes (including, e.g., appreciating literature); and (d) understand, appreciate, and sustain their own, other, and hybridized cultures (Della Chiesa, Scott, & Hinton, 2012; Kumaravadivelu, 2008; Lo Bianco, 2014).

National and pan-regional standards for language learning offer a window into the values and purposes attributed to language learning by societies across the globe. A cursory look at such standards indicates that, despite diversity in possible settings and reasons for language use by distinct learner groups, the core competences targeted by all are *functional* in orientation. Thus, for example, the Common European Framework of Reference (CEFR; Council of Europe, 2001) describes six levels of proficiency—from basic to proficient—that attempt to account for how language users engage in and accomplish a wide array of communication tasks:

> They draw on the competences at their disposal in various contexts under various conditions and under various constraints to engage in language activities involving language processes to produce and/or receive texts in relation to themes in specific domains, activating those strategies which seem most appropriate for carrying out the tasks to be accomplished.
>
> *(p. 9)*

The detailed descriptions of each proficiency level in the CEFR then spell out what learners *can do* with their language knowledge and related competences; clearly, language is learned in order to be used. Similar descriptions reveal the apparent functional orientation of other English-specific proficiency standards; for example, the TESOL Pre-K–12 Proficiency Standards Framework (TESOL, 2006) states that at the highest or "bridging" level of ESL proficiency,

> [...] students can express themselves fluently and spontaneously on a wide range of personal, general, academic, or social topics in a variety of contexts. They are poised to function in an environment with native speaking peers with minimal language support or guidance. Students have a good command of technical and academic vocabulary as well of idiomatic

expressions and colloquialisms. They can produce clear, smoothly flowing, well-structured texts of differing lengths and degrees of linguistic complexity. Errors are minimal, difficult to spot, and generally corrected when they occur.

(np)

As a last example, the Canadian Language Benchmarks (CLB, 2012) for English as a Second Language outline what adult language users can do across a diverse array of community, work, and study settings by emphasizing the target tasks (TTs) that learners should be able to successfully engage in, stressing that

> [t]he notion of the language task—a communicative "real world" instance of language use to accomplish a specific purpose in a particular context—is central to the CLB. When instructors or assessors describe communicative language ability, they are describing a person's ability to accomplish communicative language tasks for particular contexts. Accomplishing communicative tasks provides the learner, instructor or assessor with demonstrable and measurable performance outcomes.

(p. IX)

The key and common value, reflected in these and similar proficiency standards, is that language teaching and learning should lead to functional abilities to use the target language. As the CLB quote makes clear, the link between functional proficiency standards and implications for instruction and assessment is intentional: how we teach language, and how we assess it, must in turn be directly related to and supportive of the functional targets that professional and international organizations seem to be endorsing in the form of high-impact language standards such as these.

In terms of a philosophy of language teaching (see Crookes, 2009b), this orientation might best be described as pragmatic and socially progressive. Language is taught and learned in order to foster the ability to communicate (though clearly for a variety of purposes), and communication in turn is essential for participation in an idealized global democratic society (though clearly in a variety of ways). These tenets have obvious antecedents in the work of 20th-century philosophers of education, in particular John Dewey (1938), and they are associated most directly with an approach to pedagogy that is experiential, integrated, and holistic (Norris, 2015). Of course, it may be argued that such an orientation is decidedly "western" (Kumaravadivelu, 2012), and other philosophies of education might suggest alternative rationales for language learning and implications for language teaching (e.g., Confucianism). It is also possible that an explicit focus in such standards on developing communicative abilities to "get things done with language" may be misconstrued to indicate that those things do not include quite complex, advanced, large-scale, or esthetic and humanistic dimensions of language use (e.g., appreciating and creating art and literature, but compare with notions of "content-based" and "genre-based" pedagogy that follow). Nevertheless, given the predominant discourse of globalization and associated functional language learning targets, the assumption here is that socially progressive pragmatism, if broadly conceived, offers a useful foundation for making decisions regarding what may work as a preferred approach to language pedagogy.

How Has Language Pedagogy Developed Over the 20th Century?

Although contemporary proficiency standards point to language pedagogies that result in functional communicative abilities, this emphasis is relatively recent in the history of language teaching (though less so in mainstream educational design), and it is only very recently that language pedagogical theory has coalesced to some extent around a common set of principles. Summarizing considerably here, language pedagogy has developed over thousands of years (Musumeci, 2009), and, in particular, the past century has witnessed substantial evolution in the prevailing wisdom regarding best practices (see Richards & Rodgers, 2001; Stern, 1993). Without a doubt, the classical tradition of emphasizing explicit vocabulary and grammar-rule explanation and memorization, in connection with the reading of important texts in the target language (i.e., the grammar-translation approach), defined much of what constituted language teaching prior to the Second World War, and a review of published language materials today indicates its considerable staying power. However, the unprecedented degree of cross-cultural interactions that occurred during the world wars highlighted the reality that language teaching as such was not particularly effective at enabling communication, particularly in the oral-aural modalities. Thus a paradigm shift ensued, spurred not only by national security interests in the U.S. and elsewhere but also by the emergence of new international economies and opportunities. Drawing in part on new psychological learning theories (e.g., behaviorism), a first wave of post-war language pedagogy innovation took the form of the Army Method, Audio-Lingual Method, and similar techniques, all emphasizing spoken production and massive amounts of repetitive pattern drilling. Positive learning outcomes of these initiatives included good pronunciation and fluency development in particular, though at the expense of the ability to communicate creatively in nonrehearsed settings; interestingly, when it came to grammatical accuracy, associated teaching materials also reverted to explicit rule explanation as the default approach. It was also during this era that many of the language method schools were born (e.g., Berlitz, Lado), and these early methodological innovations persist today in the form of numerous commercial self-study courses.

Similar to the influences of behaviorism, interest in the possibility of psychological theory as a font of pedagogical inspiration led to the development of numerous other "methods" for language teaching in the 1960s and 1970s, all concerned with the role of affective factors (see chapters 3 and 4) in determining learning possibilities and outcomes. Hence, branded methods such as Suggestopedia, Silent Way, Total Physical Response, and others were born, more as psychoinstructional experiments than fully designed language educational approaches. However, the assumption that the individual learner was, or should be, at the heart of language teaching coincided with developments in linguistic theory to inspire the second major wave in postwar language pedagogy.

Perhaps the most readily identifiable turning point occurred when sociolinguist Dell Hymes (1966) observed that language competence was determined not only by mental representations of linguistic rules (i.e., the prevailing focus of Chomskyian linguistics) but also by performance with language in actual social interactions, thereby giving rise to the new notion of *communicative competence*, or the ability to do things with language. This performative orientation not only called into question the utility of grammar-translation approaches to instruction but also raised the more fundamental question of how the ability to communicate actually develops (in first or second languages). In a full pendulum-swing response, prominent second language (L2) researchers in North America (see Krashen, 1982) suggested that individual SLA was similar, if not identical, to first language acquisition, that individual variability and language development were both largely impervious to explicit teaching about rules or patterns in the target language system, and that instruction therefore should seek to simulate the conditions of first language acquisition. Language pedagogy, then, shifted its orientation primarily to the provision of large amounts of authentic input and the creation of opportunities for learners to process input that was just above their current level of ability (e.g., the natural approach; see Krashen & Terrell, 1983).

A parallel development in the emerging pan-European context also emphasized the importance of putting the learner in focus, though for a very different reason. Namely, the increasing demands for communication among the European Union member states inspired the earliest attempts at identifying the actual, specific communication needs of language users through a large-scale needs analysis (NA; Trim et al., 1973). The results were then stipulated in the form of the *Threshold Syllabus*, which highlighted various functions, situations, and language demands at different levels of communicative competence, inspiring in turn several new pedagogic methods, such as the notional-functional, situational, and lexical syllabi (e.g., Wilkins, 1976). As with the natural approach, instruction in these pedagogies was primarily about the presentation of authentic language *input* that had been categorized according to one or another dimension of language use. How precisely learners developed as a result of exposure to input (e.g., in terms of grammatical accuracy) was a detail left to the materials developers to adjudicate.

The ensuing period, from the late 1970s through the 1980s, witnessed a rapidly unfolding series of events, new ideas, and implications in relation to language pedagogy. First, the outcomes of Canadian language immersion education— arguably the best test to date of naturalistic L2 acquisition over sustained periods of time—suggested that, although learners could achieve very high fluency in the target language, their grammatical accuracy, lexical sophistication, and other dimensions of native-like performance fell short, even after some 12 years of schooling in an immersive environment (see Swain & Lapkin, 1982); input alone, it seemed, was not enough, even with quite young learners as the starting point. Second, the relatively new field of SLA research began to yield empirical evidence that suggested a variety of possibilities for focusing learners' attention on distinct forms (grammar, vocabulary, etc.) within the context of overall communicative meaning making (e.g., Long, 1983). Hence, ways of manipulating input, interaction (among learners and with the teacher), feedback, and output were all subjected to experimental studies, leading to new theories about how language pedagogy might encourage the development of basic performance abilities (fluency, etc.) while also fostering learner development of targeted levels of knowledge about language forms (grammar, etc.). Third, the first attempts at full descriptions of communicative competence appeared, highlighting the fact that language ability is composed of numerous interrelated subsystems (Bachman, 1990; Canale, 1983a; Canale & Swain, 1980) and suggesting that language instruction would need to address all of these if the outcome were to be full-blown L2 competence. Indeed, one very challenging upshot of these new understandings was the acknowledgment that language skills or types of knowledge do not, in reality, occur in isolation (e.g., just "grammar" as a system that is somehow independent of actual, purposeful language use, or just "speaking" as a skill that can occur independently from listening to or otherwise engaging with interlocutors). That is, a learner's or user's communicative competence had come to be best understood as an *interaction* of knowledge, skills, and strategies, all of which combine to result in the ability to use language for communication. The pedagogic implication was that teaching needed to address these interactions if it was to develop learners' communicative abilities that depended on them.

Conjointly with these developments, then, the third wave of language pedagogy emerged in the form of communicative language teaching (CLT). Rather than methodological prescriptions, CLT represented a loose set of general principles for guiding teaching practice, including the following recommendations: (a) emphasize communicative interaction in the classroom, (b) work with authentic texts, (c) enable a focus on learning targets and the learning process, (d) personalize language learning, and (e) establish some kind of link with nonclassroom language use (e.g., Nunan, 1991; Savignon, 1983). On the one hand, such an approach transcended both prescribed and proscribed classroom practices associated with earlier teaching methods, leading to the notion that language pedagogy had entered into a "postmethod" condition (Kumaravadivelu, 1994). It also simultaneously placed a considerable burden on the teacher to figure out just what to do in the classroom, and it opened the door for a hugely lucrative materials publishing endeavor to fill the lacunae.[2] On the other hand, although the focus on communication was widely celebrated, it also quickly became clear to some that simply "doing communication" in the classroom was not sufficient to support efficient language learning that led to sufficient levels of ultimate attainment. Indeed, the flexibility of CLT often seemed to deteriorate into a prescriptive method: *present* a target form (word, rule, etc.), *practice* it in repetition drills or comprehension exercises, then *produce* it in pair or group oral-interactive activities (hence the widely used acronym "PPP"). Furthermore, although this approach might provide sufficient opportunities for acquiring some dimensions of L2 competence for beginning to intermediate learners, it was clear neither how advanced language learning would ensue nor how competence for distinct, nonoral modalities (i.e., reading, writing) would be developed. Finally, typical characteristics of CLT—primarily oral communication, pair and group work, fluency development, learner- versus teacher-centeredness, apparent disorder in the classroom, and so on—triggered at least the perception of considerable resistance in nonwestern educational settings, where teachers and learners supposedly did not want to, or could not, alter their traditions of teaching and learning (see, e.g., Butler, 2011; Littlewood, 2004; but for counterevidence, see Shintani, 2011, 2012).

What Are Current Trends and Practices in Language Pedagogy?

In the final decade of the 20th century and the first of the 21st century, language pedagogy (at least in theory) has transcended methodological prescriptivism and embraced the postmethod condition to a large degree, focusing on general principles for teaching and learning and on variegated implementation models rather than a one-size-fits-all approach. A major theoretical development has been the recognition that language learning is inherently an interaction between the individual learner's cognition and the social contexts and communicative interactions the learner experiences. Of course, such constructivist foundations for general education have been in evidence throughout the 20th century (e.g., Bruner, 1973, 1975; Dewey, 1938; Piaget, 1967), but the introduction of social constructivism and sociocultural theory (SCT) into thinking about language pedagogy has raised renewed awareness about the important roles played by the learning environment and the actors within it (e.g., Lantolf & Poehner, 2008; Lantolf & Thorne, 2006; see also Vygotsky, 1978; Wertsch, 1997). From this perspective, language pedagogy should first enable learners to socially construct new knowledge via interaction before it can become available for acquisition (i.e., a cognitive change in the individual's evolving interlanguage system). Associated pedagogic practice is informed by principles such as (a) the diagnosis of learner backgrounds, needs, and interests, followed by the embedding of instruction in relevant and interesting content; (b) the persistent exposure of learners to tasks just beyond their level of knowledge or ability (the Vygotskyan "zone of proximal development," or ZPD) to both build on prior experience and motivate new learning; (c) the replication of target communication-task complexity in the instructional setting, such that learners develop ownership over language use in reality and not just in the abstract; (d) mentoring or apprenticing of learners through sustained interaction with expert "others" (e.g., the teacher, other learners) who are able to provide language input and feedback appropriate to the communicative act, as well as the learners' immediate needs; (e) the use of scaffolding, or temporary learning supports, to bridge gaps between learners' current knowledge or abilities and proximal language competence targets (and to stave off de-motivation), such that learners become increasingly self-regulating in their language behavior; and (f) dynamic or formative assessment through perpetual observation of current levels of performance, achievements, and gaps, provision of relevant feedback by the teacher or peer, and learner actions upon feedback for subsequent improvement. Note that one of the key implications of social constructivist and sociocultural perspectives on learning is the heightened pedagogical importance of assessment at all stages of the educational process, from the determination of target needs, to the identification of immediate gaps in knowledge or ability, to the provision of formative feedback to teachers and learners as a means for focusing their work (see chapter 7 for more on assessment as an essential component in instructed learning).

A variety of contemporary language pedagogic approaches have embraced some or all of these ideas in addition to emphasizing particular learning trajectories, environments, or targets. For example, content-based (Brinton, Snow, & Wesche, 2003) and content-language-integrated learning (Dalton-Puffer, 2011) highlight the potential advantages of concurrently teaching language and otherwise required or meaningful curricular subject matter, including establishing inherent linkages between language form and meaning making as they occur within particular discourse communities; addressing the realities of language development toward very advanced competence targets (i.e., envisioned participation in targeted communities of practice that call for various types of ability, e.g., reading and writing); and most basically, providing a motivating, engaging learning environment that enables development of holistic language competence in relation to the development of valued subject-matter knowledge (and the associated efficiency of integrated language and content learning). However, like their immersion education antecedents, content approaches tend to either suffer from a lack of guidance regarding the development of certain dimensions of the language (e.g., grammatical accuracy)—or even how to focus on language per se beyond simply "sink or swim" teaching of content in the target L2—or incorporate other pedagogic principles in a blended approach that reinforces a focus on language development.

A closely affiliated approach of the latter variety is that of genre-based pedagogy (e.g., Hyland, 2007), where language, content, and context are combined in an effort to develop learners' abilities to comprehend and create (often quite advanced) texts that are reflective of particular ways of making meaning in particular discourse communities. Drawing heavily on social constructivism and functionalist notions of language (systemic functional linguistics in particular; see Halliday, 1993), though dating to early theories of English for specific purposes pedagogy (Swales, 1990, 1991), genre-based pedagogy focuses primarily on exposing learners to multiple samples of particularly representative texts (e.g., exemplars of e-mails, letters, or other types of professional writing within a given discipline), followed by close analysis of the typified rhetorical structures within them, related language features, and the accomplishment of particular communication purposes. This approach has been applied nearly exclusively in the context of literacy or writing development, and it is as yet ambiguous to what extent "text" or "genre" may adequately encapsulate diverse communication targets (e.g., conversation) or serve equally well the needs of different learners (e.g., beginners, younger vs. adult learners). Nevertheless, its popularity for literacy instruction is widespread, and it has been implemented in the development of a handful of full-scale language curriculum design projects (e.g., Byrnes, Maxim, & Norris, 2010).

Still other recent trends in language pedagogy have reflected the desires of educators to foster something more than just learner *language* acquisition by integrating a variety of unique outcomes and processes into language teaching practice. Critical language pedagogy (e.g., Crookes, 2013), for example, aims to reorient language instruction to the redress of social injustices through the radical reenvisioning of learner and teacher roles, learning purposes, and related instructional constraints and affordances—here, transformation of the circumstances of the disempowered becomes an explicit outcome targeted by language teaching. In a second example, intercultural language teaching (e.g., Liddicoat & Scarino, 2013) underscores the interrelatedness between linguistic and cultural phenomena, and it emphasizes communication tasks, interactions, and experiences that lead explicitly to awareness raising about cultural assumptions, expectations, and consequences of language use—here, intercultural communication competence is the goal. For a third, increasingly popular example, self-access or autonomous language learning (e.g., Benson, 2011) seeks to develop learners' independence, capacity for self-regulation (rather than other-regulation), and individually effective, lifelong learning strategies through the provision of maximally flexible and supportive resources (increasingly via technology mediation). In addition, it emphasizes the development of learners' capacities to self-manage, self-monitor, and self-assess—here, the target is encouragement of individual learner engagement, choice, and decision making in the language learning endeavor.

What each of these examples reflects is the increasing integration of language learning with other domains of education and human development. Indeed, it may be that a hallmark of contemporary, 21st-century language pedagogy is that it is no longer merely about *language* per se—we do not only teach the lexis, phonology, syntax, morphology, and semantics of a given language system in the abstract. Rather, language pedagogy in the modern world (a) builds on the realization that language form (grammar, vocabulary, etc.) is always determined by the communicative uses to which it is put, for a variety of purposes, in a variety of social contexts; therefore it (b) inevitably incorporates other knowledge and ability competences into the design of language learning experiences; and (c) promotes language learning for a variety of individual and societal purposes. One contemporary approach to language pedagogy in particular has sought to embrace this diversity of expectations while providing clear guidance for practice: Task-Based Language Teaching.

What Is the Contribution of Task-Based Language Teaching?

Emerging from the rise of Communicative Language Teaching in the late 1980s, TBLT presents one possibility for the comprehensive design and delivery of language pedagogy that seeks to promote functional communicative competence toward a variety of possible valued targets (see Van den Branden, Bygate, & Norris, 2009). TBLT is perhaps unique in the history of language teaching in that it synthesizes multiple theoretical and empirical foundations (see Samuda & Bygate, 2008), including constructivist, experiential, and pragmatic philosophies of education (Bruner, 1975; Dewey, 1938; Kolb, 1984; Piaget, 1967), cognitive-interactionist SLA research (Long, 2015; Robinson, 2001b; Skehan, 1998), socio-cultural and situated learning theory (Lantolf & Poehner, 2008; Lave & Wenger, 1991), and many other sources in outlining recommendations for designing language education. It also provides a basis for conceiving of multiple aspects of educational programs, including curriculum, materials, teachers, instruction, and assessment, as these core elements interact in determining language learning possibilities (Norris, 2009). Rather than a fixed set of prescribed practices, TBLT has been described recently as a constantly evolving *researched* language pedagogy, one that builds upon empirical knowledge available to date regarding best practices but simultaneously subjects its ideas to ongoing empirical investigation and verification (Bygate, Norris, & Van den Branden, 2015). Thus, although early notions of TBLT focused on the design of primarily oral-interactive classroom tasks for use in promoting comprehension, negotiation, feedback, and output modification (e.g., Pica, Kanagy, & Falodoun, 1993), more recently task-based pedagogy has been extended to all skills and modalities, multiple learner proficiency levels, diverse societal domains and educational sectors, and ultimately to the full-scale design and delivery of language educational programs (Long, 2015; Norris, 2015; Van den Branden, 2006b).

TBLT utilizes the concept of a task—an activity in which students are required to use language with a primary focus on meaning in order to achieve some communicative outcome—as a heuristic for organizing instruction. Relevant Target Tasks are first identified via NA of the specific learners who will benefit from a particular language course or curriculum or set of materials, thereby establishing a critical link to interesting and important content, as well as providing clear targets for language learning outcomes (also known as TTs). Target tasks are typically organized into categories of similar tasks, or task types, sharing certain linguistic features and representing prototypical language use in communities with which learners will need to interact. These task types form the basis for language instructional sequences (i.e., at the curricular or syllabus level), which generally move from lesser to greater cognitive complexity, comprehension to production, and greater to lesser scaffolding for performance (see Long, 2015; Robinson, 2011; Skehan, 2014).

Task-based instruction follows (though with considerable flexibility) a cycle of pedagogic stages that draw upon methodological principles for promoting L2 acquisition (Bygate, Norris, & Van den Branden, 2015; Long, 2015; Norris, 2009).[3] Learners are initially schematized to the content, context, and purpose of a task through consciousness-raising activities (occurring in the L1 as needed) including brainstorming, discussion, prediction, and so on. Authentic TTs are then presented holistically, where possible in the form of multiple audio-video recordings or other samples of authentic performance products, such that learners have the opportunity to "scope out" the situation and participants of the task; get a sense of what accomplishment looks like "in the real world" (potentially including exposure to the criteria that will be used for assessing the success of performance under real-world conditions); identify known language, as well as possible gaps; and begin to learn new language through association. Language input from the task models may be analyzed by learners themselves or otherwise brought to learners' attention via enhancement or elaboration techniques, such that learners are focused increasingly on language form as it is used to create meaning in the particular task and context (i.e., often holistic chunks of language rather than specific grammatical features in isolation). Learners then move through a series of pedagogic task stages in which they begin to process the language for meaning and functionality, for example, by initially answering comprehension questions or otherwise responding receptively, then engaging in low-stakes work with task content and language in interactive sessions (e.g., with peers) that allow for considerable trial and error, as well as the opportunity or demand to negotiate meaning and language form in getting the task done. As collaborative learning proceeds, opportunities for a focus on form (Long, 2015) will ensue as learners circumlocute, question, argue, and otherwise encounter the need to express meanings in a particular way that they may not quite be prepared to do. It is at these moments that selective intervention by the teacher (or other source of expertise, including even a well-trained computer) can prove the most beneficial, primarily through the provision of feedback. The focus of feedback is derived either through teachers' or learners' own informal assessments of what is transpiring in the task or possibly through more formalized assessments that are interspersed intentionally throughout task work to create opportunities for focusing on specific learning gaps (see more in chapter 7). It may also be that, appropriately embedded within an overall focus on meaning and task accomplishment, explicit instructional techniques that help learners understand the use of a particular language form—at the point in time when that language is most needed—will prove fruitful as a kind of scaffolding toward acquisition.

Ultimately, the pedagogic task sequence comes full circle by having learners perform or produce at least simulations of the full TT under conditions similar to those beyond the learning environment. Here, performance assessment, rubrics and criteria, and feedback offer additionally critical formative opportunities for learners and teachers to reflect on what has developed as a result of the planned task-based lesson or instructional unit and to consider what still needs to develop. Crucially, by finishing a task cycle with the authentic TT, learners also make connections between the learning of language and its ultimate purpose in use for communication. Subsequent tasks will, of course, build on the learning that has occurred thus far, and recycling of tasks toward increased complexity, accuracy, fluency, and other dimensions of language performance is also common.

Summary and Recommendations

In sum, TBLT may solve a number of key problems in contemporary language pedagogy. It treats language as a holistic, authentic subject that must be acquired as such if it is to retain any meaning for learners' lives. It also allows for an embedding of intentional language learning within the teaching of content for various purposes and in relation to various domains of language use. It enables a focus on diverse language forms as they become important for learners to acquire, including not only structural features of the language but also pragmatics, rhetorical and discourse phenomena, pronunciation, interactional competence, and so on. It emphasizes form-function-meaning relationships within an overall effort targeted at developing communicative competences across modalities and proficiency levels. It builds intentionally upon assessment-derived evidence at various stages in the instructional process, from determination of learners' needs, to identification of learning gaps, to provision of critically important feedback for learning—and eventually to the testing of learners' abilities to use language under real-world performance conditions. Ultimately, TBLT harvests key aspects of distinct movements within the history of education, broadly speaking, and the evolution of language pedagogy specifically, and combines them into an approach to thinking about the big picture of language educational design, as well as the specific practices of teaching and learning. The following recommendations suggest key associated principles for the design of language educational experiences and materials.

5.1.   *Emphasize functional learning targets by teaching with tasks.*

Create lessons, units of instruction, and materials on the basis of target tasks or task types that provide a clear purpose for communication and demonstrate the ways in which language is actually used to accomplish meaning making in various discourse settings and communities.

5.2. Embed language learning within interesting, relevant content.

    a.   Language is used to make meaning about something; content that is interesting to learners and relevant to their needs provides a stimulating learning environment and heightens awareness about the fundamental connections between language form, function, and meaning.

    b.   Needs analysis articulates what gets taught with whom is going to be taught; NA may contribute prior to teaching (in determining what the overall goals of instruction may be, as well as what TT types should be represented in materials) and during teaching and learning (as an awareness-raising technique for both teachers and learners).

5.3. Schematize learners to the purpose, setting, and procedures of communication.

    a.   Generate learner motivation and familiarity by introducing the parameters of the communication setting, event, or task prior to focusing on language; raise learners' interest and awareness via observation, description, brainstorming, prediction, and other activities.

    b.   Modeling of task procedures may free up cognitive resources for a greater focus on language form in meaning; facilitate learning through demonstration, explanation, and illustration of steps that constitute a task or lesson, as well as through exemplification of particularly relevant learning dimensions of a task (e.g., modeling focused feedback practices to be employed during task-based peer-to-peer interaction).

5.4. Provide frequent, substantial, authentic language input.

    a.   Offer learners ample, low-pressure opportunities to view, hear, and otherwise engage with actual language use in the context of communication (e.g., video and audio recordings, writing samples); seeing and hearing language used for accomplishing TTs emphasizes the functional purpose of using language and begins to establish parameters for what constitutes effective language performance.

    b.   Authentic input allows learners to direct their attention to the scope, procedures, and elements that make up a complete communication task and to begin building new form-function-meaning relationships; multiple input examples demonstrate the variety of ways in which successful (or not successful) language use ensues in a given discourse setting.

5.5. Engage in comprehension-oriented analysis of language input.

    a.   Working on comprehension of new, authentic language input fosters important learning processes, including consolidation of what is already known, building of new knowledge through associative learning, identification of gaps in understanding, and awareness raising of unknown forms and functions.

b. Comprehension can be facilitated through a variety of input-enhancement techniques, including focused emphasis of particularly salient forms (e.g., highlighting, stressing the form), input elaboration (e.g., glossing), comprehension exercises (e.g., questions about meaning that are established through new forms), search and discovery activities (e.g., finding definitions and examples of other uses for targeted vocabulary), and so on.

5.6. *Incorporate opportunities for interaction with peers and expert others.*

a. Having learners engage in meaning-focused interactive communication (across a variety of media) with other learners encourages low-stakes work on language form in meaning, negotiation of comprehensible input and output, coconstruction of language knowledge, and opportunities for feedback about their language use.

b. Having learners engage in meaning-focused interactive communication with expert others (e.g., teachers, native speakers) enables modeling of effective and accurate L2 use, enhanced opportunities for timely feedback that is focused on particularly needed forms, bootstrapping of learner performance with language to advanced levels, and embedded assessment.

5.7. *Utilize a variety of scaffolding devices and feedback to fill gaps in learner knowledge.*

a. Numerous didactic techniques, ranging from implicit to explicit, may be deployed to focus learners on particular dimensions of language use and facilitate their learning during the overarching focus on meaning-oriented communication.

b. Implicit scaffolding includes both implicit feedback (e.g., recasts in spoken interaction, identification of errors without correction in writing) and planned consciousness-raising techniques (e.g., providing a table to fill in with information regarding a trip that occurred in the past, thereby encouraging use of past tense).

c. Explicit scaffolding includes form-focused activities such as grammar-rule explanation, metalinguistic discussion, language-focused pedagogic tasks (e.g., dictogloss), and other techniques that foster awareness and understanding of formal properties of the target language system.

5.8. *Design pedagogic tasks to encourage negotiation.*

Opportunities for negotiation (of meaning and form in meaning) provide crucial impetuses for language development, including the need to express ideas clearly, to comprehend ideas clearly, to circumlocute, to question, and to otherwise engage in the give and take of human interaction. Pedagogic tasks can be designed to enhance or even force such negotiation to occur, primarily by establishing information gaps between participants (shared vs. unshared information) and a common goal for completion of the task (e.g., jointly narrating a story for which each interlocutor has a portion of the storyline to contribute).

5.9.   *Select, design, and sequence tasks to enable balanced language development.*

    a.   Different communication tasks naturally emphasize different qualities of language use; tasks should be analyzed and understood regarding the language comprehension and production demands they authentically entail prior to selection for deployment in pedagogy.

    b.   Task features (e.g., complexity of the language code required, degree of "online" or spontaneous communication required, cognitive demands) and conditions (e.g., number and type of interlocutors) emphasize distinct qualities of language use, from grammatical or lexical complexity, to fluency, to accuracy. Tasks can be designed to vary such features and conditions in order to encourage the balanced development of language competence and develop learner awareness of the need for multiple qualities in language performance (e.g., not just grammatical accuracy).

    c.   Target and pedagogic tasks should be sequenced intentionally by, for example, moving from cognitively simple to complex, from highly structured to less structured, from familiar to unfamiliar, or following a natural order of task procedures (e.g., literature review prior to research question formulation). Tasks may be repeated and otherwise recycled to encourage skill development via practice, as well as awareness raising about and improvement in performance.

5.10.   *Finish with language performance.*

Pedagogic sequences regularly culminate in the doing of a simulated or real-life TT by the learners under authentic performance conditions. Finishing with TT performance reiterates the primary goal of language learning for use, and it enables critical reflection on the extent to which language development has occurred and identification of what might still need to occur.

Notes

1 Technically, for adult learners the correct Greek terminology would be *andragogy*; however, pedagogy (*ped* = child) has become the accepted cover term for any attempt to understand and describe the teaching of any kind of learner.
2 By far the highest selling language textbooks came out of the CLT movement. For example, David Nunan's *Go for It* English learning series has sold multiple billions of volumes, and Jack Richards's *Interchange* series has enjoyed similar popularity.

3 Note also that similar stages have been proposed within non-language-specific approaches to pedagogy, such as *Backwards Design* (Wiggins & McTighe, 2005) and *Assessment for Learning* (Black & Williams, 2012). Key to these approaches, and to TBLT, is a fundamental role for formative assessment as a means of generating actionable and immediately relevant data as a basis for learners, teachers, and curriculum designers to make decisions about how to focus learning-oriented activities.

6

TEACHING LANGUAGE SKILLS

Although some instances of language use may draw primarily upon a single skill, such as reading a book or listening to music, the majority of communicative situations require language users to employ multiple skills and to integrate various types of knowledge into their communication efforts. For example, when conversing with a coworker about a job task, one typically needs to be able to interpret, express, and negotiate meaning, orchestrating various language skills (minimally listening and speaking) simultaneously to achieve successful communication. In an effort to bring instructed language development in line with real-world communication, then, L2 educators have increasingly adopted integrated or multiskill instructional approaches. Certainly, the description of TBLT in the preceding chapter presumes that much of language teaching and learning will be concerned with complex, skills-integrated communication tasks rather than teaching toward the disarticulated parts of a holistic language competence one at a time.

Nevertheless, theory and research on the teaching and learning of the four language skills does have much to offer by way of implications for instructional design, even where associated techniques are embedded within an overall approach to language learning that is fundamentally skills integrated in orientation. Therefore, this chapter provides an overview of trends and current practices in the teaching of the four individual skills—reading, writing, listening, and speaking. Attention will be paid to relevant research that elucidates how L2 learners can develop those skills and how they can benefit from particular instructional techniques designed to help improve the four skills across different domains and communicative contexts. First, we will briefly consider the overall relationship between L2 knowledge and skills as a point of departure for the subsequent review of each skill and corresponding instructional approaches.

Language Knowledge Versus Language Skills

As a multifaceted construct, language consists of two fundamentally distinct but overlapping domains: (a) mental representations and (b) language use skills (VanPatten, 2013; VanPatten & Benati, 2010). Mental representations refer to "the abstract, implicit, and underlying linguistic system in a speaker's mind/brain" (VanPatten, 2013, p. 4). This abstract linguistic system includes syntactic, morphological, semantic, phonological, lexical, and functional rules of language use. Although language users may not be aware of the different mental representations they possess, they tend to derive certain rule-like or patterned behaviors from them. Thus, a language user may have a feeling about or even be able to state explicitly what is possible and OK in a language and what is not. That is, mental representations of language underlie all manifestations of language use and are thus fundamental to communicative language ability. Although grounded in mental representations, all surface (i.e., performative) manifestations of language are the product of some form of language use skill. That is, skills can be regarded as the mechanisms for the execution of communicative ability.

Generally defined as "the speed and accuracy with which people can perform certain actions or behaviors" (VanPatten, 2013, p. 10), skills can be either general (e.g., learning or problem solving) or context and domain specific (e.g., solving *The New York Times* crossword puzzle). In the case of language, L2 educators traditionally distinguish between four basic language skills that are essential for successful communication—listening, speaking, reading, and writing.[1] These language skills are related to one another by two underlying parameters: mode of communication (i.e., literacy vs. oracy) and direction of communication (i.e., interpreting vs. expressing or producing). For example, speaking is considered an oral, productive skill. However, of course, that single skill still reflects a vast potential domain of ability: speaking to a friend over coffee is different from speaking to a large audience when giving a lecture, and so on. Similarly, reading a scientific article differs from reading an advertisement while waiting for a train. Given these context-specific deployments of the four language skills, VanPatten (2013) maintains that L2 educators need to ask themselves a key question: "Language as skill for what purpose and in what context?" (p. 11).

In the field of L2 teaching, most professionals take it for granted that instruction is based on discrete skill sets, at least to some extent. The structural division of language teaching (indeed, a typical breakdown of language classes by their corresponding focus) into four distinct skill areas aims at the superordinate teaching goal of communicative competence with the often accompanying goal of native-speaker-like competence (Hinkel, 2006). Although language pedagogy in many parts of the world has been witnessing a shift toward more intercultural and integrated aspects of communication (Spencer-Oatey & Franklin, 2009; Timpe, 2013; chapter 5, this volume), the "continual separation of the four skills lies at the core of research and testing in speaking, listening, reading, and writing" (Hinkel,

2010, p. 110). Accordingly, in the following sections we review key ideas that have issued from this literature as a way of motivating instruction that seeks to promote a given skill focus.

Reading

Reading is generally understood as a multifaceted, goal-oriented, active, and mental process of meaning construction. To derive and construct meaning from the written words of a text, the reader draws upon information from the text itself, including schemata of textual organizations, as well as prior background knowledge, feelings, opinions, and expectations. In short, reading is conceived as an interactive process that involves both bottom-up and top-down cognitive processing strategies to achieve L2 reading comprehension.

Interactive information processing is perhaps the most widely acknowledged theory today that describes the cognitive, psycholinguistic processes involved in (L2) reading (see Birch, 2007, or Koda, 2005, for further models). Given that the skillful reader needs to be adept at both bottom-up and top-down strategies (Bernhardt, 2011), the interactive model suggests a balanced or integrated approach that includes both types of cognitive processes to derive and construct the comprehensive meaning of a text. Top-down processing can be described as the prediction of information based on prior world knowledge or perceptions. The reader approaches a given text "with expectations of meaning developed before and during the process [. . .] making use of just as much of the visual information on the page as they need to confirm and extend their expectations—a process of predicting, sampling, and confirming" (Eskey, 2005, p. 564). By contrast, bottom-up processes constitute the reader's strategic interaction with information derived from the text, which involves a variety of subskills such as word recognition, orthographic and phonological processing, and morphosyntactic parsing, as well as lexical access and recognition (see, e.g., Birch, 2007; Eskey, 2005; Hinkel, 2006). Hence, as Birch (2007) argues, a core assumption of the interactive information processing perspective on L2 reading is that "there are important bits of linguistic knowledge and different strategies that must be developed in order for a reader to become an expert at reading an alphabetic system" (p. 9).

Several scholars have criticized the field of L2 reading for its still-predominant focus on top-down processing despite the prevalence of interactive models, arguing that reading should concentrate on bottom-up strategies (Birch, 2007; Eskey, 2005). Given L2 readers' comparatively lower target language proficiency, Eskey (1988) argues that L2 educators must not "lose sight of the fact that language is a major problem in second language reading, and that even educated guessing at meaning is not a substitute for accurate decoding" (p. 97). Hence, researchers have highlighted that L2 reading instruction needs to maintain a focus on language in L2 reading instruction, accounting for and attending more to bottom-up processes than is the case in L1 reading pedagogy (Birch, 2007; Hinkel, 2006; Koda, 2005).

Reading and L2 Instruction

As a competence consisting of multiple components, "L2 reading is an ability that combines L2 and L1 reading resources into a dual-language processing system" (Grabe, 2009, p. 129) that differs from L1 reading in three main areas: (a) linguistic-processing, (b) developmental-educational, and (c) sociocultural-institutional. Adult L2 learners who are literate in their respective L1s already have, based on their L1 socialization, as well as prior educational and developmental cognitive experiences, a large amount of L1 reading experiences, higher order reading skills, strategies, and metalinguistic awareness that they may draw upon when reading L2 texts. However, although literacy in one language has been found to strongly predict corresponding literacy skills in the L2 (see Grabe, 2009, for a discussion of the interdependence hypothesis), L2 readers also face a number of challenges.

Without doubt, the main challenge for L2 readers is L2 linguistic knowledge and related processing abilities. Although factors such as background knowledge and motivation also play considerable roles in the L2 reading process, it is knowledge of the language that constitutes the main prerequisite for successful L2 reading. In other words, learners have to have developed sufficient L2 proficiency to successfully process L2 reading schemata (Birch, 2007; Eskey, 2005). Hinkel (2006) notes that to employ their L2 proficiency in bottom-up processing, L2 readers need to "gather visual information from the written text (e.g., letters and words), identify the meaning of the words, and then move forward to the processing of the structure and the meaning of larger syntactic units, such as phrases and sentences" (p. 120). Thus, potential limitations in linguistic knowledge representations, including phonology, orthography, grammar, and vocabulary, may provide challenges for L2 readers in decoding written text in the target language. Although overlaps or similarities between the L1 and L2 systems may facilitate L2 reading comprehension (e.g., similar cognates or syntactic structures), transfer effects may appear at any or all levels of linguistic knowledge, which makes them quite difficult to predict. Birch (2007), Grabe (2009), and Kato (2012) provide a range of practical activities intended to foster lexical subcomponents in the context of promoting accuracy and fluency in L2 reading skills.

Words and lexical knowledge constitute the fundamental building blocks in text-meaning construction in the L2 reading process (e.g., Birch, 2007; Grabe, 2009; Nation, 2001, 2005, 2011; Schmitt, 2008). In a somewhat reciprocal relationship, reading is recognized as a means of building new vocabulary, which in turn is essential for L2 reading—or as Eskey (2005) put it, a "classic chicken and egg situation" (p. 567). Given that researchers have noted that successful reading in English among adults, for instance, requires a large vocabulary of about 8,000 to 9,000 words (Grabe, 2009; Schmitt, 2008), a primary concern for L2 instructors when promoting L2 reading skills is to develop their learners' vocabulary. Thereby, it is essential that L2 instructors not reduce reading to a mere guessing game by immersing their L2 readers in texts that are lexically beyond their grasp but that they prepare them lexically for a text that ideally meets "Krashen's $i+1$ standard for comprehensibility" (Eskey, 2005, p. 567). Nation (2005) proposed that in order to learn new vocabulary, "unknown vocabulary should appear at a density not more than 1 unknown word in every 50 running words" (p. 587). Moreover, the new vocabulary should also recur at fairly regular intervals and with some degree of novelty, such as by means of using it in new linguistic contexts (e.g., the same word presented in multiple morphological manifestations). Although graded readers have been criticized by teachers for a lack of authenticity (e.g., Honeyfield, 1977), well-written, simplified reading materials for less proficient learners may be a good choice because they can be strategically composed to include repetitions and a certain degree of generative use.[2]

In addition to graded reading materials, three pedagogic approaches have been proposed that facilitate the development of vocabulary, accuracy, and fluency in L2 reading: (a) extensive reading, (b) intensive reading, and (c) speed reading. Rooted in the principles of L1 literacy instruction, extensive reading refers to reading large amounts of L2 texts for pleasure, which is considered conducive to vocabulary acquisition through exposure to meaning-focused input. Moreover, it is thought to establish, enrich, and develop fluency with known vocabulary while providing opportunity for the uptake of new words (see Eskey, 2005; Grabe, 2008; Nation, 2005). By contrast, intensive reading requires learners to interact with a text that contains a rather heavy vocabulary load (i.e., learners are familiar with less than 95% of a text's vocabulary). Intensive reading often involves a prereading plan facilitated by the teacher to prepare students for the reading experience. Vocabulary learning during intensive reading is a form of language-focused learning, requiring the learner to pay particular attention to lexical items. There are also multiple exercises and activity types to aid vocabulary learning during intensive reading such as preteaching words, matching words, glossing, finding collocations, and word-part building and analysis (see Nation, 2001, for an extensive list). Moreover, several studies have provided evidence that the use of dictionaries can facilitate comprehension and vocabulary acquisition if students are properly trained in using dictionaries (e.g., Knight, 1994; Prichard, 2008).

In contrast to extensive and intensive reading, speed reading specifically aims to facilitate fluent access to word meaning. Whereas trained native speakers can read up to 500 words per minute, untrained native speakers read about 250 words per minute. By contrast, beginning L2 learners tend to read "around 100 words per minute" (Nation, 2005, p. 588). To accelerate the reading pace and automatize the process, learners should read texts consisting of 500–1,000 words under time constraints. Moreover, it is essential that all words be known to the learners, that texts be accompanied by comprehension questions, and that the process be repeated frequently. In sum, four conditions need to be met in order to foster fluency and automaticity in L2 learners' reading skills: (a) no unfamiliar language features in the text, including vocabulary; (b) a focus on content and information encoded in the text; (c) some pressure to perform at a fast pace; and (d) quantity of practice (Nation, 2005, p. 588).

To summarize, reading (comprehension) on its own is an invisible process. It does not generate a product that a teacher can see, read, or hear. Although L2 instructors often give L2 activities such as written or oral comprehension questions, these product-oriented activities do not necessarily teach L2 reading (Eskey, 2005). Moreover, L1 reading skills do not necessarily transfer to L2 reading. They have to be developed in compliance with L2 proficiency. So in order to provide high-quality L2 reading instruction, it is suggested that teachers need to "start with work on the visual appearance of words" (i.e., a sight-word approach) and the development of word recognition fluency before beginning instruction on top-down processes (Hinkel, 2006, p. 121). Moreover, teachers should gradually promote different aspects such as vocabulary, grammar, and fluency in order to help learners develop the ability to convert written language automatically into meaningful information, combining the information from the text with background knowledge in order to construct a meaning for the L2 text.

Listening

Similar to reading, listening constitutes a skill area in performance, as well as a means of acquiring the target language. As such, it also includes bottom-up and top-down processing. That is, both in the L1 and L2, listeners utilize receptive, constructive, and interpretive aspects of cognition to derive meaning while drawing upon prior knowledge schemata and expectations to guide the listening process. In doing so, they are required to process spoken texts in real time, integrating and processing pace, pauses, and other linguistic elements that are unique to spoken language (e.g., ellipses, repetitions, false starts). This simultaneous processing takes place at various levels: phonological, grammatical, lexical propositional, and discursive (Farrell & Mallard, 2006; Rost, 2005). Processing at all levels contributes to evaluation of the input and identification of the salient information or intended meaning conveyed. Thus, Vandergrift (1999) summarized listening as "a complex, active process in which the listener must discriminate between sounds, understand vocabulary and grammatical structures, interpret stress and intonation, retain what was gathered in all of the above, and interpret it within the immediate as well as the larger sociocultural context of the utterance" (p. 168). Hence, listening is anything but a passive or merely receptive process.

Given that "adults spend 40–50% of [oral] communication time listening" (Vandergrift, 1999, p. 169), they tend to have particular ways of mediating the cognitive processing load. As Vandergrift (2015) observes, listeners "do not pay attention to everything; they listen selectively, according to the purpose of the task" (par. 5), thus determining the way in which they approach aural input. Richards (1990), for example, distinguishes between two purposes or ways of listening:

interactional and transactional. Interactional purposes, such as in greetings or small talk, aim at establishing harmonious relationships between interlocutors rather than conveying information in an accurate and orderly format. By contrast, transactional functions are information oriented and, thus, used primarily to convey a message, such as in news broadcasts or lectures. Based on this distinction, Vandergrift (2015) contends that knowledge about the communicative purpose of a listening task guides and aids L2 listening processes given that it reduces the cognitive processing load when, for instance, listeners may only need to focus on and, thus, listen for specific information.

Although L1 and L2 listeners employ the same underlying cognitive processes, L2 listening is fundamentally different from L1 listening. Just as L2 readers are faced with a number of language-based challenges when reading in the L2, L2 listeners face a number of obstacles when decoding, comprehending, and interpreting spoken text in the target language. Goh (2000) provides an overview of these challenges, including the inability to recognize lexical meaning, keeping the meaning of the message in working memory (WM), and mapping literal word-level meanings with the actual (intended) meanings or ideas a given spoken text is conveying (see also Shintani & Wallace, 2014). In addition to achieving accuracy of comprehension, processing speed constitutes a further challenge. L2 learners have to achieve efficient processing capacity in order to be able to focus attention on the "relevant part of linguistic information and to select, coordinate, and integrate information in real time, which eventually leads to a performance that appears fluent and effortless" (Taguchi, 2008, p. 36). Especially when L2 listeners cannot control the speed of the aural input, they are required to access the linguistic knowledge and perform form-function mapping processes in real time (Farrell & Mallard, 2006). Moreover, in most cases L2 learners acquire an L2 after they have already developed cognitive processing skills and language use habits in their L1 (Rost, 2005; Thomas, 1983). Hence, if two languages operate under different language use conventions, comprehension processes such as inferencing may pose additional challenges for L2 listeners (Cohen, 2008; Taguchi, 2008). A final challenge for L2 listening has to do with the diversity of task types within which listening is required, each with its own unique characteristics and problems. For example, interactive, face-to-face listening involves considerable contextual support in the form of gestures, body language, and the opportunity to negotiate comprehension (e.g., through questioning, requests for repetition). However, listening to a radio broadcast entails none of these possibilities (although a recorded podcast might be stopped and replayed, of course), and listening to a public announcement in an airport may occur in the context of considerable distortion and interruption by other sounds. Developing listening skills, thus, requires more than merely language knowledge and aural processing abilities; it must also attend to the other types of input involved in comprehension and to strategies for managing the listening activity in context.

Listening and L2 Instruction

In a historical overview, Vandergrift and Goh (2012) identify three types of listening instruction: (a) text oriented, (b) communication oriented, and (c) learner oriented. Prevalent primarily before the 1990s, the text-oriented approach typically involves the L2 teacher reading written texts out loud while L2 learners are required to complete dictation exercises or cloze-type activities. With the rise of communicative language teaching (CLT), L2 pedagogy witnessed a shift toward more communication-oriented, authentic materials. Thus, teachers often activate L2 learners' topical background knowledge prior to the listening task and then expose L2 learners to authentic aural input before engaging them in tasks such as information-gap activities. However, several scholars have noted that neither approach has proved to be very successful (e.g., Hinkel, 2006; Vandergrift, 2004). Summarizing the issue, Hinkel (2006) remarks that L2 learners who only "rely on linguistic processing often fail to activate higher order L2 schemata, and those who correctly apply schema-based knowledge tend to neglect the linguistic input" (p. 117). Since the 1990s, L2 listening instruction has shifted toward an increased focus on cognitive and metacognitive strategies, thus adopting a learner-oriented approach (O'Malley & Chamot, 1990; Rost & Ross, 1991; Vandergrift, 1999, 2004).

Current L2 listening pedagogy focuses mainly on listening practice in tandem with (meta)cognitive listening strategies (Hinkel, 2006; Shintani & Wallace, 2014). Shintani and Wallace (2014) divide L2 listening practice further into (a) listening exposure (i.e., extensive listening without any support or scaffolding) and (b) listening support, including linguistic or contextual aids. In their meta-analysis, Shintani and Wallace (2014) found that (a) in comparison to extensive listening, listening support increased the effectiveness of listening practice more; and (b) linguistic support showed a larger effect size than contextual support. They argued that "providing linguistic information about the text in the form of vocabulary teaching, grammar explanations, or a transcript of the text was more beneficial in developing listening comprehension ability than assistance in the form of pictures, videos, and background information" (Shintani & Wallace, 2014, p. 90). Moreover, they found listening training was more efficient when the learner had control over the listening materials and the speed of the aural text, thus allowing the learner to control the processing load associated with listening while training their L2 aural abilities.

Along with providing listening practice, current L2 instruction also focuses on nurturing the development of listening skills by helping L2 learners develop and utilize cognitive and metacognitive strategies. Unlike skills, strategies are under an L2 learner's conscious control (see chapter 4). In listening, they constitute a means of comprehending and storing aural input in WM for later retrieval; aid the approach to listening; and compensate for potential "incomplete understanding, missed linguistic or schematic input, or misidentified clues" (Hinkel, 2006,

p. 119). In line with research on listening strategies, which has generally found that skilled L2 listeners employ a broader range of metacognitive strategies than unskilled learners (Goh, 2000, 2002; O'Malley & Chamot, 1990; Rost & Ross, 1991; Vandergrift, 2003), studies on the effectiveness of listening-strategy training have provided evidence that metacognitive strategy instruction can facilitate L2 learning and listening task performance (Vandergrift, 1999). Although Plonsky's (2011) meta-analysis revealed only a small effect size for listening-strategy instruction, Shintani and Wallace (2014) observed that Plonsky's modest findings may have been due to the lack of support materials used in the intervention studies included in the meta-analysis. In addition to positive effects for listening-skill training, some studies have found metacognitive strategy instruction (including planning for listening, self-monitoring of one's comprehension process, evaluating comprehension, and identifying comprehension difficulties)[3] to be more effective than work on listening skills alone (e.g., Graham & Macaro, 2008; Hinkel, 2006; Jin, 2002; Vandergrift, 2004).

Both L2 listening practice and (meta)cognitive strategy training have been increasingly applied in current integrated approaches to L2 instruction, such as task-based or content-based language teaching (Hinkel, 2006; Snow, 2005). Listening practice can be incorporated in a number of ways that engage a range of linguistic and schematic variables in authentic contexts, allowing for "frequent occurrences of target syntactic and lexical structures in the context of a meaning-focused task" (Hinkel, 2006, p. 119). For example, low-proficiency learners may benefit from tasks with emphases on bottom-up and top-down processing, in combination with selective strategy training, all included in "listening-to-do tasks" (Hinkel, 2006, p. 118). Such tasks might take the form of repeated opportunities to follow directions on a map, including simply pointing to landmarks provided orally, tracing directions on a simplified map as provided by the teacher, and following directions on an actual city map as provided by target language speakers (and many live variations of the same using portable, Internet-connected devices). More advanced L2 learners may benefit from integrated tasks, such as academic note taking during a lecture, which may feature specific (cultural) topics with distinct grammar, vocabulary, accent, and discourse demands, as well as strategy training, including summation, discourse organization, inferencing, and elaboration.

Speaking

Speaking is often used as a generic term to describe an individual's skill of producing oral speech. Thus, speaking is often considered as something an individual does. Although it may help for educational purposes to view speaking as an individual's skill, it is also important to remember that people use the skill when communicating with others. That is to say, one needs to also consider speaking as *spoken interaction* in which speakers create and convey messages in real time, drawing upon a range of features such as vocabulary, spoken grammar, formality, speed, pauses, hesitations, volume, pitch, and intonation, thus supporting and enhancing what they are saying to their interlocutors in a given context. Moreover, a speaker rarely speaks in complete sentences (except for more written-like planned speech, such as presentations). Unplanned oral speech consists of what Luoma (2004) has called "**idea units**," short phrases and clauses that are either connected by conjunctions or are simply spoken sequentially (p. 12; emphases in the original). Idea units tend to be two seconds or seven words long (Chafe, 1985); they are primarily interconnected thematically and would often be considered ungrammatical in written language (see Luoma, 2004 for a discussion of features such as topicalization or tails). To summarize, speaking or spoken interaction is a skill that draws upon a range of features to tailor the message to a particular communicative context.

A number of component models have attempted to identify the broad range of competencies involved in oral communication (see Timpe-Laughlin, Wain, & Schmidgall, 2015 for a detailed review of these models). For example, Bachman and Palmer (1996) proposed the "Model of Communicative Language Ability," which stipulates several interrelated knowledge components that constitute (second) language ability, including higher order skills such as pragmatic, organizational, and sociolinguistic competencies. Although their framework (similar to other models, e.g., Canale, 1983a; Celce-Murcia, Dörnyei, & Thurrell, 1995; Usó-Juan & Martínez-Flor, 2006) identifies key components of declarative knowledge, fundamental cognitive and metacognitive processes, and important tasks or contextual characteristics that should be considered when teaching or assessing speaking ability, it does not specify in any level of detail as to how individual competencies or knowledge components are interrelated or how processing is performed—something provided by cognitively oriented models.

A widely recognized psycholinguistic model of L1 speech production is Levelt's (1989, 1992) schematic representation of the different autonomous processing components involved in speech production. The components include (a) a conceptualizer, the component responsible for generating and monitoring messages; (b) a formulator, a component in charge of then encoding the message grammatically and phonologically while drawing upon the mental lexicon; and (c) an articulator, which provides motor execution for the articulation of overt speech. The productive part is complemented by a speech comprehension system that permits the parsing and processing of both self-generated and other-generated messages (see Gilabert, 2004; Levelt, 1989, 1992).

Adapting Levelt's model for bilingual processing to account for phenomena in L2 speech such as accents and codeswitching, de Bot (1992) hypothesized that at the preverbal stage the conceptualizer performs a type of macroplanning, determining the language that is to be used. Subsequently, during microplanning, the formulator for a given language then encodes the message at a phonological and grammatical level while retrieving lexemes and lemmata from the mental lexicon. With regard to lexical retrieval, de Bot hypothesized that L2 speakers probably have one mental lexicon with sublexica that store lexical elements from the different languages. Finally, the phonetic and articulatory plan produced by the language-specific formulator is then sent to the articulator, which employs a set of motor plans to articulate overt speech.

Based on considerations proposed in models of speaking ability, Poulisse (1997) and Gilabert (2004) noted that L2 speaking instruction needs to accommodate three fundamental distinctions. First, L2 knowledge representations may not be— indeed, will not be among beginning L2 learners—as complete as L1 knowledge. For example, lexical items may not be completely developed in terms of morphological, semantic, syntactic, or phonological information, thus resulting in error. Second, different processing components may lack automaticity. That is, lengthier processing may result in hesitations, pauses, and a slower rate of speech. Third, L2 speech may show traces of a speaker's L1. Drawing upon Gilabert (2004), Poulisse and Bongaerts (1994) provide a number of reasons for this, arguing that "one particular lexical item may be missing; there may be greater availability of L1 words; the speaker may wish to emphasize his or her identity; a change of subjects is intended; the speaker wants to specify a particular addressee, to express an emotion, or simply to mark asides from the ongoing discourse" (p. 41). Hence, from a psycholinguistic perspective alone, L2 speaking is a much more complex process than L1 speech production.

Additionally, L2 speaking always takes place in a particular communicative situation that "requires speakers to make decisions about why, how and when to communicate depending on the cultural and social context in which the speaking act occurs" (Martínez-Flor, Usó-Juan, & Alcón Soler, 2006, p. 139). Therefore, L2 learners must not only develop knowledge representations of linguistic forms but also become aware of their appropriate application(s) in different communicative contexts to fulfill a variety of communicative functions. Tarone (2005), for example, distinguishes between three superordinate communicative functions: (a) interactional functions, when establishing and maintaining social relationships; (b) transactional functions, when language is used to convey information; and (c) ludic functions, when language is used for entertainment purposes. Across the three functions, the ability to "imagine the world from the receiver's point of view is central to successful referential communication" (Tarone, 2005, p. 487). That is, the speaker needs to precisely encode information so that the listener can understand it. Thus, L2 learners need to be able to evaluate the communicative situation (including interlocutor constellations), conceptualize the message they intend to convey, and encode and formulate it linguistically in an appropriate and accurate way, before articulating overt speech.

Speaking and L2 Instruction

Often considered the most complex and challenging skill to master, speaking can be regarded as "an interactive, social and contextualized communicative event" that involves dynamic interaction between interlocutors, requiring the L2 learner to orchestrate a number of subskills for successful performance (Martínez-Flor, Usó-Juan, & Alcón Soler, 2006, p. 139). In real time, they need to attend to a variety of knowledge representations, including content, morphosyntactical, lexical, phonological, and discourse information, as well as register, prosody, and pragmalinguistic elements (see Tarone, 2005, for a detailed discussion). Thus, L2 pedagogy is faced with two core decisions: (a) which speaking skill to focus on, and (b) what type of environment and opportunities to create in order to promote a given feature or function of speaking.

To develop fluency, accuracy, and a broad linguistic repertoire, research has long argued that exposure to and interaction in an L2 context provides an ideal learning environment. However, mere immersion is not a panacea for fluent and accurate L2 speaking ability. Hinkel (2006), for example, notes that although "immersion learners can [often] speak fluently and with ease, their speech contained [*sic*] numerous grammatical, lexical, and pragmalinguistic errors" (p. 115). Thus, L2 pedagogy has to provide for an educational environment that permits a triple focus on accuracy, appropriateness, and fluency—that is, on form, function, and the development of automaticity of retrieval and mapping processes (Ellis, 2003; Long, 2015; Van den Branden, Bygate, & Norris, 2009). Generally speaking, such an environment can be built around oral-interactive tasks of various kinds, based on target tasks that have been identified as relevant for learners and pedagogically manipulated such that a focus on form is enabled in the context of meaningful communication. A simple example might be ordering food at a specific fast-food restaurant, the pedagogic task sequence for which might work as follows: (a) modeling of spoken interactions typical of the task (e.g., repeated viewing and analysis of authentic videos); (b) comprehension-oriented work with selected parts of the input (e.g., menu sections, vocabulary items, turn-taking strategies), enabling learners to focus on discrete parts of the language that they have already seen holistically in the input; (c) interactive work between learners where they try out new language in order to accomplish meaning-focused tasks (e.g., information-gap exercises); (d) reflection by learners and teacher on what they understand and do not understand, and the provision of feedback of various kinds focused on learner spoken production during the pedagogic tasks; (e) doing of the target interactive task in a simulated or actual situation, along with outcomes assessment; and (f) repetition of the task cycle in other similar settings.

Three specific dimensions of speaking—formulaic sequences and chunks, pronunciation, and pragmatics—have recently witnessed burgeoning research interest, providing a number of suggestions and implications for L2 speaking instruction. It is estimated that formulaic sequences or multiword lexical items (i.e., idioms, phrasal verbs, and chunks) constitute the majority of spoken English (Nation, 2013; Schmitt, 2004). As a key feature of producing fluent, competent spoken language (Garnier & Schmitt, 2016), formulaic sequences should also be central to L2 English instruction. However, researchers have repeatedly argued for more empirical research on best practices for teaching formulaic sequences given that idioms, phrasal verbs, and chunks are often not accurately represented in learning materials (Meunier, 2012; Rossiter, Abbott, Kushnir, 2016). A particular resource that teachers can utilize to inform their teaching would be lists of frequent formulaic expressions such as the "*PHRASal Expressions List*" (PHRASE list) put forth by Martinez and Schmitt (2012) or the "Academic Formulas List" (AFL) by Simpson-Vlach and Ellis (2010). Based on the British National Corpus (BNC), the PHRASE list presents the 505 most frequent formulaic sequences in English, whereas AFL outlines the empirically derived, most common three-, four-, and five-word formulaic sequences in academic speech and writing. Lists such as the PHRASE list and AFL can be used in L2 pedagogy to prioritize the inclusion of particular formulaic sequences into L2 instruction and assessment.

In addition to research on spoken vocabulary use and instruction, pronunciation has received considerable interest in L2 research. Given that the majority of communication in English takes place between non-native speakers who use English as an international language or a lingua franca (Canagarajah, 2007; Jenkins, 2000; Seidlhofer, 2011), pronunciation teaching has shifted from targeting native-like accents to a concentration on mutual intelligibility—that is, the degree to which interlocutors understand one another's utterances (Hinkel, 2006; Loewen, 2015; Moyer, 2013; Tarone, 2005). Therefore, L2 instruction has to address "issues of segmental clarity (e.g., articulation of specific sounds), word stress and prosody, and the length and the timing of pauses" (Hinkel, 2006, p. 116).

Considering pronunciation priorities in light of achieving intelligibility when using English in international contexts, Jenkins (2000) even goes a step further. Based on several studies and a rigorous corpus analysis, she identified a phonological baseline, the *Lingua Franca Core* (LFC), which identifies a number of phonological features that are typical and need to be mutually understood in order to ensure intelligibility (core features) whereas accurate pronunciation of other sounds is not as necessary (noncore features). Whether these features, which have become known in English as "ELF pronunciation," should be the target of instruction is a contentious issue, however, principally because they represent norms that might be particularly and stereotypically marked within western English-L1 societies and that might also lead to misinterpretation and decreased intelligibility in the same settings (for a detailed discussion, see Jenkins, 2000, 2003; Low, 2014).

To summarize, although teachers and developers of curricula cannot be expected to address pronunciation training for all possible phonological environments (e.g., across registers and dialects), they may still profitably take into account the speech-production difficulties that can be predicted, broadly speaking, as well as the essential features to promote mutual intelligibility in L2 speech. Although L2 instruction has traditionally taught target language pronunciation in an explicit and decontextualized manner by means of phonetic transcripts, minimal pairs, repetition drills, and imitation of role models, current skill acquisition theory makes the argument for "repetition and practice as a means of developing procedural knowledge, but it places this practice in a larger context that has more concern with semantic content" (Loewen, 2015, p. 121; see also Bygate, 2006, for a discussion on the use of repetition to teaching L2 oral production).

In line with the international perspective on pronunciation instruction, sociocultural aspects of L2 speaking have increasingly gained attention in language education. Hinkel (2006), for example, notes that "current oral pedagogy has the objective of enabling nonnative speakers to communicate effectively and to negotiate cross-cultural interactional norms successfully" (p. 116; see also Ishihara & Cohen, 2010; Kasper & Roever, 2005; Timpe, 2013). To reach this superordinate goal, L2 pedagogy increasingly targets pragmatic phenomena such as speech acts, routine formulae, and discourse organization (see Ishihara & Cohen, 2010, or O'Keeffe, Clancy, & Adolphs, 2011, for an overview of pragmatic phenomena and practical applications for L2 instruction). Although several studies have highlighted deficiencies in textbooks and other commercially available materials (e.g., Crandall & Basturkmen, 2004; Vellenga, 2004), L2 pragmatic instruction has repeatedly been found to be successful, both with regard to sociopragmatics (the social norms and "rules" that guide communication, such as notions of what is and is not polite behavior in a given situation) and pragmalinguistics (the specific forms that realize these norms, such as the use of subjunctive in English to soften requests, e.g., "could you . . . "). Furthermore, and generally speaking, explicit instruction has been found to be more effective than implicit instruction, resulting in more accurate and appropriate language output (Jeon & Kaya, 2006; Takimoto, 2009).[4] Takimoto (2009) summarized what seems to have been the key pedagogic implication from such research thus far, arguing that "effective learning occurs when the tasks provide learners with opportunities for processing both pragmalinguistic and sociopragmatic features of the target structures" (p. 22). Thus, raising L2 learners' awareness about the contextualized use of speech, including power relationships, social status and distance, register, and politeness, may facilitate deeper processing, resulting in more appropriate and accurate L2 speech production. For example, a typical lesson sequence might involve the following steps: (a) awareness-raising activities, such as demonstrations of intercultural communication situations and settings, that help schematize learners to the sociopragmatic context and the pragmatic "problem" at issue; (b) authentic input, in the form of video and audio recordings of both native-speaker and L2-speaker engagement in tasks that call for specific pragmatic behaviors; (c) analysis and interpretation activities that encourage learners to identify social dimensions of the observed interactions (e.g., power relationships between the interlocutors), as well as to become aware of the use of specific language forms (e.g., routings, greetings, politeness markers) that are typical of the situation; (d) explicit instruction in the apparent, or frequently not readily apparent, underlying "rules" of behavior at work and the formal pragmalinguistic features of language use in the task and interaction; and (e) opportunities for learner practice of the new forms and norms in simulated or real-world tasks that call for their application, along with formative feedback regarding relative success in pragmatic terms.[5]

Writing

Writing, both in the L1 and L2, is a unique process. Unlike the relatively fast and ephemeral nature of speaking, writing tends to be slow and permanent (although text-based communication via new technologies is increasingly blurring these previous clear-cut distinctions; see chapter 13). As Kormos (2012) put it, "[p]roducing 100 words orally might take about a minute in an L2, whereas writing a composition of 100 words might take 30 minutes" (p. 390). Moreover, given the production of written text, writers can revisit the actual product. Several researchers have identified the constitutive components or stages of the multilayered writing process that are hypothesized to be universal across languages (Kormos, 2012; Williams, 2003): (a) planning; (b) translating or drafting ideas into linguistic form; (c) execution; and (d) monitoring, including pausing, (re) reading, revising, and editing. Across all stages, writers can "pause, ponder, plan, trace back their words in mind or text, and revise [. . .] without the pressure for fluent delivery that is felt when speaking" (Ortega, 2012, p. 406). Moreover, a number of factors, including time commitment, self-efficacy beliefs, WM capacity, and motivation, influence the writing process at all stages. Hence, writing is a complex task that requires determination, concentration, and time commitment.

Although the writing process is widely considered to be the same across languages—which may explain the long tradition of L1 writing research versus the "short biography" of L2 writing scholarship (Hedgcock, 2005, p. 597)—researchers have found that there are considerable differences between L1 and L2 writing, including divergent preferences for arranging and sequencing textual elements, differences in constructing arguments, distinctions in terms of integrating source materials, differences in anticipating reader expectations and schematic knowledge, and divergent uses of linguistic elements to structure a text and convey information (Ferris & Hedgcock, 2014, p. 23). Thus, L2 writing not only means potentially learning a new orthographic system but also acquiring new social and discourse practices, as well as cognitive schemata.

Research has provided a number of insights into factors that may influence the development of L2 writing skills. For example, L2 writing studies have revealed that if L2 learners were already proficient writers in their L1, they can effectively transfer L1 strategies such as planning, interpreting, organizing, and revising their written texts (Cumming, 1989; Ferris & Hedgcock, 2014; Ortega, 2009a). With regard to L2 proficiency, it has been found that high L2 proficiency is a necessary, but not sufficient, condition for L2 writing ability (Leki, Cumming, & Silva, 2008). However, transfer of knowledge "cannot explain all phenomena in interlanguage development" (Ortega, 2009c, p. 53). Hence, it is hardly surprising that research has not found a uniformly strong and positive relationship between a learner's L1 and L2 writing abilities, and that there are mixed findings regarding educational, cognitive, attitudinal, and social influences on L2 writing ability over time (Ferris & Hedgcock, 2014).

Additionally, it is crucial to consider the actual target learner population in terms of writing needs. Although much research in L2 writing has been conducted on and with fairly proficient L2 learners (i.e., on L2 composition for largely academic purposes), cultivating low-proficient L2 learners' writing skills may pose different and greater challenges. As Hedgcock (2012) observes, fostering learners' literary capacities in an L2 "can impose even greater psychocognitive and sociocultural demands on learners whose L2 oral and aural proficiency may be emergent and whose literate knowledge in L1 may be limited" (p. 221). That is to say, different L2 learner populations may have divergent L2 writing needs. In the context of English language learning, Ferris and Hedgcock (2014), for example, identify four subgroups of L2 writers, including international EFL learners, ESL students, resident immigrants, and generation 1.5 learners (i.e., children of first-generation immigrants who are educated in the target language context). These groups vary considerably in terms of L1 literacy, knowledge of the L2 culture, L2 proficiency, and motivation to develop and master L2 writing skills. Hence, to borrow Hinkel's (2006) words, "L2 writing pedagogy requires special and systematic approaches that take into account the cultural, rhetorical, and linguistic differences between L1 and L2 writers" (p. 123).

Writing and L2 Instruction

Given that "[n]o unitary theory or model of L2 writing has yet emerged on which to build a coherent disciplinary identity" (Hedgcock, 2005, p. 610), much of L2 writing instruction was and is based on L1 writing research and pedagogy (see Matsuda, 2003, for a historical overview). In particular, three instructional approaches—product oriented, process oriented, and learning oriented—can be tracked with regard to developing L2 writing capacities. Mainly rooted in L1 composition instruction, product-oriented approaches have informed L2 writing pedagogy for a long time. Accordingly, students are expected to produce a number of written text forms such as narratives, interpretations, argumentative essays, and so on. That is, teachers would introduce a given genre such as a narrative, then students would be given a literary narrative text (potentially for interpretation), before they would be asked to imitate the previously introduced rhetorical pattern and discourse structure.

In contrast, process-oriented L2 writing instruction, as a more recent pedagogical approach, places its emphasis on the writer and the process of producing a written text. Williams (2003), for example, argues that the goal of a process-oriented approach is to "modify student behaviors to match those of good writers" (p. 101). Thus, compared to a product orientation, process-oriented pedagogy is characterized by a more comprehensive and inclusive approach, including free writing, as well as discovery and articulation of the writer's own voice, and continuous feedback and response by peers and teachers, situating writing in meaningful contexts so as to "develop [L2] writers' sense of audience and reader expectations" (Hedgcock, 2005, p. 605). A process orientation also implements writing tasks with meaningful source content materials; promotes writing-focused recursive practices such as revising, editing, and rereading; and provides for content integration and the representation of ideas (see Hedgcock, 2005, for a detailed discussion). Note that little is known about individual differences (IDs) with regard to writing processes (Kormos, 2012)—an area that is crucial to inform process-oriented L2 writing instruction.

The third, or learning-oriented, approach is a field of much more recent genesis that can be regarded as a further development or spin-off of the process-oriented tradition. Situated at the increasingly active interface of L2 writing and second language acquisition (SLA), learning-oriented writing views the process of writing in an L2 as a site for learning and development (e.g., Manchón, 2011; Ortega, 2012; Williams, 2012). Scholars in this tradition contend that writing in the L2 supports learners in noticing and internalizing new linguistic knowledge. It provides output opportunities and thus promotes automatization, knowledge consolidation, and hypothesis testing. Moreover, feedback on L2 writing also aids SLA processes and L2 learning (see Bitchener & Ferris, 2012; Hanaoka & Izumi, 2012; Kormos, 2012; Polio, 2012).

Although the field still "lack[s] a definite understanding of optimal methods for enhancing the composing skills of L2 writers" (Ferris & Hedgcock, 2014, p. 87), the three traditions outlined previously have given rise to a number of central pedagogical interventions and practices in the current dialogue around L2 writing instruction, including feedback and integrated tasks. Although the scope of research on teacher feedback is quite limited, with most research conducted in the area of error correction (Bitchener & Ferris, 2012; Ferris, 2011), findings across studies suggest that students value clearly delivered, constructive, and encouraging teacher feedback at various levels (i.e., regarding lexical, grammatical, discursive features), perceiving it as helpful and important for the development of L2 writing skills (e.g., Ferris, 2003; Ferris & Hedgcock, 2014; Montgomery & Baker, 2007).

To account for the procedural nature of L2 writing and the development of multiple-language literacy, scholars have highlighted the centrality of integrated or multistage writing tasks. Current approaches that feature integrated task instruction in L2 writing not only combine vocabulary and grammar but also combine reading with writing instruction (Hedgcock, 2005; Hinkel, 2006). To facilitate learners' noticing strategies regarding particular linguistic devices or particularities of target language texts, L2 instructors often draw upon authentic, written, target language texts, embedding the written text in the context of reading, content-based, or form-focused instruction. Practice in text analysis can facilitate an awareness of grammar, lexis, routine formulae, register, and politeness features or other situational variables of language in context, as well norms of specific academic or professional genres (e.g., Swales, 1991; Swales & Feak, 2012). Highlighting the reciprocal relationship between reading and writing, Grabe (2001) outlines five literacy interactions: "reading to learn, writing to learn, reading to improve writing, writing to improve reading, and reading and writing together for better learning" (p. 15). Given the often highlighted parallel cognitive operations of reading and writing (Ferris & Hedgcock, 2014; Grabe, 2009; Grabe & Stoller, 2011; Hudson, 2007), tasks such as reading for gist and details, inferencing, critical reasoning, predicting, skimming, scanning, and reacting—that is, tasks that require L2 writers to read like writers and write like readers—have been reported as particularly useful in fostering L2 writing skills.

Summary and Recommendations

The review presented in this chapter has traced key dimensions of the four traditional skills and outlined strands and trends in current L2 research and instruction, presenting a variety of empirical findings and research-based ideas that can inform the design of language learning environments. Although skills have been the basic unit of L2 instruction and assessment for a long time, there are a number of propositions that may underscore and potentially redefine more integrated approaches to L2 instruction, as covered in chapter 5 and elsewhere in this volume. Nevertheless, some specific recommendations issuing from a particular focus on individual skills are presented next.

Before outlining recommendations for each of the four macroskill areas, two overarching aspects need to be highlighted.

6.1. *Keep language learning in the focus of any type of L2 skill development.*

Although it may sound obvious, compared to L1 speakers of a given target language, L2 learners face different challenges when developing and employing skills in an L2. Although L1 speakers have a "relatively mature mental representation of language in place prior to skill onset" (VanPatten, 2013, p. 11), L2 learners do not necessarily have complete mental representations for the given target language at their disposal. That is to say, when children learn to read and write, they tend to have a fairly developed mental representation of the language system in place. By contrast, adult L2 learners are asked to read, write, listen, and speak before a mental representation is in place—that is, they are asked to use language that is far beyond their underlying representation (VanPatten, 2013). In other words, L2 skill acquisition must occur while "linguistic sophistication is still limited" (Koda, 2005, p. 38). Thus, a focus on L2 learning during skill development in the L2 must not be forgotten.

6.2. *Identify sequences of real-world language use situations to develop different L2 skills by means of integrative task-based instruction in holistic contexts.*

Based on the premise that skill constitutes accuracy, appropriateness, and speed, how a language skill develops in any given domain depends on the tasks in which L2 learners actively engage. As Burns (2006) notes, given that "the four macro-skill areas of speaking, listening, reading and writing are not discrete" (p. 249), L2 instructors may—in cooperation with their students—identify sequences of real-world language use situations to develop segments or syllabus specifications for more authentic learning contexts in order to gradually foster the development of various L2 skills. For example, Burns (2006) proposes a sequence of tasks that engage learners in a number of successive speech events in different constellations, requiring a variety of (integrated) skills: (a) discuss a good travel agent with friends, (b) consult directory pages for a telephone number, (c) make an initial request for brochures by phone or in person, (d) read brochures, (e) consult the travel agent on cheaper options, (f) fill in booking forms and make the payment, and (g) describe plans to family, friends, or neighbors. Integrating multiple foci, the L2 instructor can prepare learners for a role-play activity by introducing vocabulary and routinized expressions used in service encounters or, in L2 contexts, even encourage learners to visit a travel agency and bring materials back to the classroom (Burns, 2006).

Reading:

6.3. *Focus on bottom-up.*

Reading relies essentially on the decoding of written text. L2 learners' potential limitations in linguistic knowledge representations, including phonology, orthography, grammar, and vocabulary, may provide challenges for L2 readers in decoding written text in the target language. Thus, depending on the learners' L2 proficiency and L1 literacy skills, phoneme-grapheme relationships and processing may need to be addressed before lexical information can easily be extracted based on visual, graphic representations of words.

6.4. *Select texts that are challenging yet not beyond the learners' lexical grasp.*

Words and lexical knowledge constitute the fundamental building blocks in text-meaning construction in the L2 reading process. In a somewhat reciprocal relationship, reading is recognized as a means of building new vocabulary, which in turn is essential for L2 reading. To avoid reducing a reading task to a mere guessing game for L2 readers, "unknown vocabulary should appear at a density not more than 1 unknown word in every 50 running words" (Nation, 2005, p. 587). Otherwise, as research has shown, L2 reading may become a frustrating endeavor. Three pedagogic approaches have been proposed that facilitate vocabulary, accuracy, and fluency in L2 reading: extensive reading, intensive reading, and speed reading.

6.5. *Foster L2 reading strategies and reading speed.*

Reading materials differ in style, content, and purpose, requiring readers to adjust their approach to a text accordingly. Thus, raising learners' awareness of reading strategies and supporting the development of effective use thereof has shown to facilitate (speedy) reading comprehension of potentially diverse, distinct, and unknown texts (see Janzen & Stoller, 1998, for an overview of L2 reading strategies and suggestions for incorporation into instruction). Generally speaking, helpful strategies include having a purpose for reading; predicting ideas; previewing structure; asking and answering questions about a text; relating new reading to other bodies of knowledge or readings; synthesizing and summarizing; multiple, repeated reading; and others.

Speaking:

6.6. *Eschew simply immersing students into the target language context to promote L2 speaking skills.*

Although research has shown that exposure to and interaction in an L2 context provides an ideal learning environment for fluency, mere immersion is not necessarily a panacea for accurate L2 speaking ability. L2 pedagogy has to provide for an educational environment that permits a triple focus on accuracy, appropriateness, and fluency (i.e., on form, function, and the development of automaticity of retrieval and mapping processes). Carefully planned tasks should provide built-in opportunities for practicing different speaking-related skills. For example, problem-solving tasks can include mechanisms that foster contextualized uses of specific grammatical structures. Deliberately incorporated repetitions can provide articulatory practice or transfer and deployment of vocabulary across different language-use situations.

6.7. *Base pronunciation instruction on realistic, rather than idealistic, language models.*

Research has shown that for the majority of L2 learners, native-like proficiency is neither a realistic nor a desirable goal. To avoid frustration in learners and having them strive for the mostly unattainable goal of the highly controversial "native-speaker pronunciation," L2 pronunciation pedagogy should enhance learners' intelligibility and attend to L2 speakers' sociocultural identity rather than attempt to drastically change their pronunciation. For English, Jenkins (2000) has identified a phonological core that features sounds whose accurate pronunciation is particularly relevant for mutual comprehension.

6.8.   *Foster segmental clarity in pronunciation practice.*

To enhance learners' intelligibility, pronunciation should begin at the microlevel (i.e., syllable structures, elisions, assimilations, reductions, and contractions) before addressing stress and intonation of words, sentences, and discourse (see Chun, 2002). Current skill-acquisition theory makes the argument for "repetition and practice as a means of developing procedural knowledge, but it places this practice in a larger context that has more concern with semantic content" (Loewen, 2015, p. 121). Thus, pronunciation practice should be embedded in a meaningful contextualized task, potentially in connection with listening activities.

6.9.   *Use materials that are authentic and appropriate in their portrayal of pragmatic norms.*

Given the dearth of appropriate material for L2 pragmatics instruction, it is incumbent upon L2 educators to develop practical materials that can guide effective instruction in promoting the appropriate application of pragmatic phenomena in L2 speaking. Given that the pragmatics input learners may receive often tends to be constrained in authenticity, frequency, and variety (Loewen, 2015), opportunities for exposure to and interaction with pragmatic input was found to enhance L2 pragmatic development in L2 instruction.

6.10.   *Provide explicit L2 pragmatics instruction.*

Although extensive input was shown to provide for exposure to and thus opportunities for noticing and uptake, research has repeatedly provided evidence that explicit pragmatics instruction is more beneficial than implicit teaching. Explicit instruction can include activities such as output practice and explicit correction, as well as the delivery and use of metapragmatic information in order to raise L2 learners' awareness of target language pragmatic conventions (see also Jeon & Kaya, 2006; Loewen, 2015).

Listening:

6.11.   *Enable learner control over the pace of the listening text.*

Speed of delivery of the aural text places a particular cognitive demand on L2 learners. Research has found listening training to be more efficient when the learner has control over the listening materials and the pace of the aural text, thus allowing the learner to control the processing load associated with listening while training their L2 aural abilities.

6.12. *Help L2 learners develop and utilize (meta)cognitive strategies.*

Research has shown that skilled L2 listeners draw upon a range of listening strategies. In addition to listening strategies, skilled L2 listeners employ a broader range of metacognitive strategies than unskilled learners. Studies on the effectiveness of listening-strategy training have provided evidence that metacognitive strategy instruction can "help students to capitalize on the language input they receive, and to improve their performance on listening tasks" (Vandergrift, 1999, p. 171).

Writing:

6.13. *Combine the instruction of L2 reading and writing.*

Given the reciprocal relationship of reading and writing, or what has been called L2 literacy, Grabe (2003) proposed 10 guidelines for designing effective, authentic L2 literacy tasks, including analyzing authentic literacy tasks; practicing and producing authentic genre tasks; developing learners' rhetorical stances; promoting awareness of text structure; teaching L2 learners to read and write strategically; collecting, understanding, and applying peer and expert response; teaching students to assemble and interpret meaningful information; focusing on effective strategies for writing from sources; teaching and practicing summary and synthesis skills; and integrating reading and writing in the assessment plan (see also Ferris & Hedgcock, 2014).

6.14. *Use genres that are realistic and relevant for the learner population.*

Especially in the field of genre pedagogy and task-based instruction, researchers have been arguing for the composition of texts relevant for the L2 learners. For example, Hyland (2007, 2009) provides a list of genres for academic and professional writing, including resumes, research articles, reports, book reviews, grant proposals, conference abstracts, and so on.

6.15. *Provide directed assistance for the specific dimensions that are to be promoted through L2 writing tasks.*

Consider the specific dimensions that are to be promoted through a given L2 writing task, including practical, procedural, and mechanical requirements; the socioliterate context and core content; available resources; and assessment criteria (see Ferris & Hedgcock, 2014, for a writing assignment checklist). Research has shown that L2 learners need targeted assistance in acquiring macrolevel features such as composition and text development strategies and knowledge of different text types and genres, as well as linguistic and rhetorical awareness, before microlevel features such as grammatical structures, word choice, register, and spelling (e.g., Ferris & Hedgcock, 2014; Olson & Land, 2007; Segalowitz, 2010). L2 learners and writers require extensive, assisted, and focused practice to facilitate different L2 writing abilities (see Matsuda et al., 2010, and Nation, 2009, for actual practice tasks).

6.16. *Provide continuous, focused, and constructive feedback during the writing process, not just for the final product.*

As a balance of praise and constructive criticism, feedback about a variety of features should be continuous and individualized during the writing process. Feedback should not be given for the final product only. With regard to the effectiveness of written feedback, research has warned extensively against expecting "one-size-fits-all benefits of written corrective feedback" (Ortega, 2012, p. 407). Five aspects need to be taken into account to provide individualized feedback: "(1) the nature of the information provided, (2) the frequency with which [learners] receive it, (3) the proficiency level of the learner, (4) the ability of the learner to relate it to other linguistic knowledge that s/he may also be processing and consolidating, and (5) the complexity of the linguistic focus" (Bitchener, 2012, p. 360).

Notes

1 Note that large-scale language proficiency assessments have, by and large, also maintained this four-skills distinction, reflecting some degree of apparent utility in breaking down language ability along these lines.
2 Drawing upon generative learning theory (Wittrock 1974, 1985), generative use refers to a means of learning and instruction that aims to help learners recognize certain language aspects, such as critical features and functions of words, by drawing connections between them. For example, when the word "justice" is taught, learners may be able to apply this knowledge to derive or generate the meanings of words in the text that had been unknown to them such as "just" or "justification" (see Lee, Lim, & Grabowski, 2008 for a more detailed discussion).
3 See Rost (2005) for a detailed list of pedagogical approaches for developing L2 metacognitive listening strategies.
4 However, the evidence is relatively limited in this regard. Very little research has been conducted that investigates the effectiveness of pragmatics instruction beyond the level of a single class or a few lessons and the immediate outcomes of whatever teaching techniques were utilized.
5 For numerous practical lesson ideas, see the "Teaching Pragmatics" website at the U.S. Department of State *American English* website: http://americanenglish.state.gov/resources/teaching-pragmatics.

7

ASSESSMENT IN SUPPORT OF LANGUAGE LEARNING AND TEACHING

An increasingly central dimension to language educational design and instructed language learning has to do with the uses for and roles played by assessments of various kinds in the context of classroom instruction, as well as at program, institutional, and societal levels. Assessments are powerful tools that may guide, focus, and constrain learning, as well as foster, enable, and promote learning. Thus, it is clear that assessments can be used to help make many different educational decisions, though those that come most quickly to mind likely involve an estimation of student language ability at the end of a sequence of instruction and typically without much intentional impact on individual learner development. That is, "summative"-type assessment is commonly undertaken in language education, for example, to make placement and admission decisions; award grades; award course credit; certify abilities; hold teachers, learners, and schools accountable to standards; and so on. However, assessment can also play a more direct role in enhancing teaching and learning, in integration with other educational activities. To this end, assessment information can be used "formatively" to identify learner needs, define learning expectations, modify instruction, focus students on their learning or study, motivate students, or make students aware of their learning progress and what they need to do to improve (among many other uses; see Bachman & Palmer, 2010; Brown, 2014; Norris, 2000, 2008). In this chapter we focus primarily on assessment purposes oriented toward understanding and improving learning and teaching—that is, assessment as it takes place mostly within the classroom—but including both formative and summative orientations. Additional uses for assessment in conjunction with program monitoring and evaluation are considered in chapter 12.

Formative Assessment

Formative-oriented assessment[1] can be distinguished roughly from summative in terms of (a) what assessment is focused on (e.g., gaps in student learning,

learning processes, effectiveness of instruction); (b) when assessment happens (after or during learning tasks, interactions, instruction); (c) types of assessment methods (e.g., traditional vs. "alternative" possibilities such as journals, logs, conferences); (d) the roles that students play (an active, participatory role vs. a more compliance-oriented, responsive role); and, most importantly, (e) types of assessment use (e.g., to make students aware of learning expectations, to motivate students, to engender self-regulation). Outside of the language teaching field this summative-formative distinction has been relabeled as "assessment of learning" (the equivalent of summative assessment) and "assessment for learning" (formative assessment). This terminology has come out of key developments in general education assessment (in the U.K. in particular) that have aimed to better understand how both types of assessment can contribute, albeit in distinct ways, to student development (Assessment Reform Group, 2002; Black & Wiliam, 1998, 2012). More recently, as captured in the work of Carless (2007, 2009), the term "learning-oriented assessment" has come into use, denoting a proposed collapse of the summative-formative distinction and a research agenda investigating how all assessments can be conducted to improve student learning. This latest term has also been taken up by Purpura and Turner (2014) to theorize "learning-oriented language assessment" in language education, particularly in language classrooms.[2]

Formative assessment in language education denotes using assessment as a vehicle for furthering language learning. According to Turner (2012), formative assessment (in classrooms) refers to strategies that both teachers and students engage in for collecting information on student language and then using that information to help make decisions to enhance teaching and learning. As with other assessment purposes, formative assessment involves the systematic elicitation or observation of evidence about student language performance of different kinds to make inferences about the L2 abilities or knowledge that learners have acquired. However, perhaps in contrast to other assessment approaches and uses, formative (learning-oriented) assessment "prioritizes the interpretation of L2 performance evidence on both learning outcomes and L2 processes, so that goal-referenced decisions can be made by individual classroom agents to further L2 processing and achieve target-like performance" (Turner & Purpura, 2016, p. 260). Thus, formative assessment approaches typically involve a systematic process of performance analysis for the purpose of instructional and learning modification on the basis of student learning evidence, both in terms of process of learning and product.

Feedback

Perhaps the key formative assessment aim is to provide *feedback* both to students to enhance their learning and to teachers as a means for tailoring their instruction. Students need to know where they are in their learning progression, where they need to be, and how to close the gap between what they can do and what they need to do to succeed. Raising learner awareness requires that teachers and students engage in a continual process of reflection and review of student progress.

High-quality feedback empowers students to improve their learning and enables teachers to adjust their plans in response to learning evidence (Qualifications and Curriculum Authority, 2001).

Formative feedback can be delivered to learners in a variety of ways (e.g., via verification of response accuracy, explanation of correct answers, hints, worked examples), from various individuals (instructors, peers, the student him or herself), and at various times during the learning process (e.g., during the assessment experience,[3] immediately after, after some period of time has elapsed; Shute, 2007, p. i). Although formative assessment feedback is in itself a large domain of educational research, a few important benefits and best practices are identified here (see Shute, 2007, for a review).

Wiliam (2010) identifies two characteristic features that define feedback in support of student learning. First, formative feedback should be "prospective" in that it informs learners how to improve, and not "retrospective," or merely telling them what they did wrong. Second, effective feedback is "descriptive" or competence related, not "evaluative" or judgmental. Additional general best practices are that feedback should be credible, specific and focused, not excessively frequent, transparent, and provided shortly after performance (Shute, 2007), with a key factor being that the focus of the feedback is relatable to the learning activities and objects immediately at stake—in other words, learners have to be able to relate feedback to something they are working on, otherwise its effectiveness will rapidly diminish. Much of this advice aims to increase the "mindfulness with which students engage in the feedback" (Wiliam, 2011, p. 111), which helps students develop awareness of targeted learning, aids memory of new information, and enhances learners' capacity to "notice" how their language compares with target language forms (Schmidt & Frota, 1986). Moreover, feedback helps stimulate *metacognition*—that is, it encourages thinking about learning and makes students aware of their learning processes (Anderson, 2012). Feedback also plays a role in *self-regulation* in that it encourages learners to set goals for learning and to monitor, regulate, and control their cognition, motivation, and behavior in order to reach their goals (Pintrich, 2000). Interestingly, it may be that other forces typical of assessment in schools can actually counter the potential positive benefits of feedback. One major challenge has to do with a tension between assigning grades for administrative, institutional purposes—that is, an "evaluative" or judgmental use typically associated with summative assessments—versus providing learning-oriented feedback; thus, some research (e.g., Butler, 1988) suggests that grades should be disarticulated clearly from formative feedback, such that learners (and teachers) understand the different intended uses of assessment.

Self- and Peer Assessment

Another critical dimension of formative assessment is the involvement of learners actively and directly in the process and uses of assessment. Having students reflect on their own and other classmates' educational experiences is an additional (and important) strategy that helps provide important feedback on learning and teaching and stimulates learning itself. For example, self-assessments (via can-do checklists, questionnaires, interviews, conferences, learning logs, or journals) can provide information on attitudes, affect, and motivation, as well as abilities, all of which impact learning (Purpura, 2009). In addition, students can be made aware of and sensitized to specific knowledge, skills, and dispositions, as well as performance criteria—for example, by providing learners with language-task rating scales, rubrics, and rich descriptors of different levels of performance—thereby enabling learners to "notice" for themselves how their language compares with relevant targets. Self- and peer assessment can also stimulate metacognition by having students think about how they learn, which can lead to greater awareness of preferred and possible learning styles (Anderson, 2012). Reflecting on one's learning and future learning targets can increase self-regulation in that students grasp what they need to do and achieve, plan their own learning goals, and take personal responsibility for their learning. Research suggests, however, that intentional student training is needed for peer and self-assessment to be effective (Anderson, 2012); at the same time, persistent engagement in these activities also seems to help learners acquire the ability to recognize quality in what they are doing, internalize criteria for success, and act on these understandings in improving their own performance. Finally, self-assessments are useful for collecting information on learning that might otherwise be difficult to capture via other behavioral assessments (e.g., appreciation of multiculturalism; Davis, 2013), and they are essential as a means of informing teachers about learner response to pedagogic activities.

Instructional Effectiveness

Formative assessment involves using assessment processes and findings to make impacts on teaching, as well as learning. One important aim of formative assessment is to provide feedback to teachers and administrators on their educational practices. Information on students' engagement in and outcomes of learning, as well as their affective responses, can be a barometer of the effectiveness of materials and resources, the coherence and articulation of course or module sequences, the effectiveness of teacher practices and instruction in general, the needs of students, and the appropriateness and adequacy of assessment itself. For example, periodic essays collected in a capstone course portfolio might reveal that students are not developing the intercultural competence and dispositional outcomes that a curriculum has been designed to engender. Assessment would seem, in this case, to have revealed a discrepancy between student learning and the desired learning targets of the program. Subsequent investigations could then be conducted to see why the desired learning has failed to occur, and appropriate instructional modifications could be made on the basis of what is discovered (Genesee & Upshur,

1996). Generally speaking, this use of assessment as a source of insight for instructional improvement falls within the purview of program evaluation. As such, we return to related considerations in chapter 12.

Key Aspects of Assessment in Support of Learning

In sum, formative assessment is characterized by a number of key features (Rea-Dickins, 2007):

1. Assessment tasks, activities, and criteria are linked to learning and teaching.
2. Assessment is integrated into everyday teaching and learning activities.
3. Learners are active participants in the assessment process.
4. Teachers adopt a more collaborative and interactive approach to assessment.
5. Various methods and tools are used to gain insight into teaching and learning.
6. There are sustained exchanges between teacher and learner and between learners.
7. There is rich teacher questioning and probing.
8. Assessment happens, and contributes to learning, during classroom talk-in-interaction.
9. Different types of meaningful, timely teacher feedback are provided.
10. There are opportunities for learners to self- and peer assess.
11. Summative tests are also used formatively.[4]

Summative Assessment (Assessment of Learning)

Another important use of assessment will have less to do with creating feedback loops on day-to-day learning and teaching and more to do with evaluative judgments about student achievement. As noted previously, assessment that provides information on student learning to teachers and educational authorities or other stakeholders—often to judge program quality or teaching effectiveness—is referred to as *summative assessment* (Weir, 2001). Summative assessment can be distinguished from formative assessment in a number of ways. For example, summative assessment will differ in focus in that it tends to capture final states of achievement or attainment (as opposed to learner development), or development on a large scale (such as at the end of a year of instruction). Summative assessment will also differ with respect to when assessment is administered, typically occurring at the end of a sequence of courses, a single course, or a module (or prior to instruction for placement or admission purposes). Most importantly, however, summative assessment is distinguished by the uses of information. Again, summative assessment is commonly used to make high-stakes decisions about students, as well as language educators and administrators entrusted with providing language instruction.

Criterion-Referenced Assessment

In situations where summative assessment for high-stakes decision making is called for, issues of assessment quality, reliability or dependability, and validity become especially pertinent, particularly as prescribed by recommended approaches to *criterion-referenced assessment*. A common distinction in language testing is the difference between norm-referenced testing (NRT) and criterion-referenced testing (CRT). Norm-referenced tests typically measure general language proficiencies, which—like other ability traits in large populations—are assumed to be normally distributed. That is, most individuals will score near the mean and progressively fewer individuals score at the extreme higher or lower ability ranges (Brown, 1995). By contrast, criterion-referenced assessment aims to measure how much an examinee knows or can do in terms of a specific domain of knowledge or set of educational objectives (Brown & Hudson, 2002). CRT captures learner performance in relation to an explicitly stated standard, such as course learning outcomes and objectives that describe the kinds of tasks the examinee can perform (Brown & Hudson, 2002). CRT will often be relevant in educational programs or modules where there is an interest in knowing what proportion of students have mastered course content at important program, course, or module learning junctures.

For any assessment endeavor—be it NRT or CRT—high-quality implementation will be a primary concern, particularly for high-stakes decisions. Ethical assessment practices demand that a test be used in a way that is accurate and fair for a particular group of assessment users in a particular context. Accordingly, a key consideration will be the appropriateness of test score inference given a particular assessment use. Establishing appropriateness of inference and use—both for NRT and CRT—involves empirical analyses of assessment processes, including demonstration of measurement reliability or dependability, evidence of construct validity, and post-hoc investigations into the adequacy of actual test use and other test consequences (these processes are termed *assessment validation;* see Chapelle, 2012b; Kane, 2012; Norris, 2008). Again, given the CRT aim of estimating student mastery of course content or domain knowledge, CRT emphasizes certain features in test design, implementation, and score interpretation that help support claims of appropriate score inference and use. Key aspects of high-quality CRT planning, administration, item analysis, and use follow:

- CRT tasks and items are closely integrated with, and reflective of, instruction, curricula, and learning outcomes of a program or module.
- CRT is deeply contextualized and integral to local educational processes and as such involves a diverse range of interested stakeholders (including students) in CRT design, administration, and use.
- Close links between the educational objectives of the program and CRT fosters positive washback on teaching and learning (i.e., CRT results in actions

by teachers and learners that contribute productively to educational delivery; Brown & Hudson, 2002).

- CRT task and item development is conducted using "test-specification" procedures, which describe the nature of the items and their rationale for use in a test; test specifications establish links between the assessment and the content of interest, increasing "item-objective" congruence (Brown & Hudson, 2002; Davidson & Lynch, 2002; Fulcher, 2010).

- Test tasks and items are designed (and scrutinized) to ensure they elicit the full range and types of knowledge, skills, and dispositions identified in student learning outcomes and objectives (Brown & Hudson, 2002; Genesee & Upshur, 1996).

- Interpretations of CRT scores are made with reference to how many of or how well student learning outcomes and objectives have been attained (Genesee & Upshur, 1996).

- Consistency (or "dependability") of measurement is determined via threshold-loss agreement and generalizability theory approaches that indicate the consistency of pass-fail (or "master"-"nonmaster") classifications (see Brown & Hudson, 2002).

- Traditional statistical item analyses provide an indication of how well items discriminate between masters and nonmasters of test material (e.g., difference index, B index, agreement statistic, item phi; Brown & Hudson, 2002).

- Scoring can involve the creation of rubrics or scoring guides used by raters to judge examinee performance (Brown, 2012a; Davis & Kondo-Brown, 2012). Systematic rubric development procedures and rater training contribute to increased rater reliability and accuracy (Fulcher, 2010).

- Specific procedures are used for standard setting and systematically determining appropriate "cut scores" or minimum levels of competency (Brown & Hudson, 2002; see also Livingston & Zieky, 1982, for various techniques).

Integrating Formative and Summative Assessment Into a Holistic Approach

Given the discussion so far, it is clear that assessments are intended to play a variety of supporting roles within language education, from providing useful feedback to learners and teachers, to indicating how well students in a class or school "mastered" certain bodies of knowledge. Given this array of purposes for assessment, how might language educators go about designing a systematic approach to assessment development and use? Furthermore, how can the fundamental value of "supporting learning and teaching" be achieved in a comprehensive approach to assessment? One way of putting the pieces together is to conceive of assessment as an integral part of educational design—to treat assessments "programmatically" (Norris, 2008)—with the ultimate goal of supporting and improving educational endeavors at the levels of the individual learner, the teacher, the classroom, and the school. Accordingly, a programmatic assessment cycle might involve (a) clearly articulating learning objectives and outcomes as a baseline frame of reference for all assessments, (b) determining the uses for and users of each assessment, (c) evaluating performance and attainment of objectives and outcomes or other targets of assessment, and (d) using assessment results to enhance individual learning and otherwise support teaching. This iterative assessment process (Davis, 2014) is implemented via the following steps:

1. State learning outcomes.
2. Identify the users and uses of assessment.
3. Create or select assessment tools.
4. Administer assessment and collect information.
5. Interpret information and evaluate performance and processes.
6. Use information to enhance learning and teaching.

Stating Student Learning Outcomes

The language education literature tends to conflate the terms *goals, objectives*, and *outcomes* in confusing ways in that each are used inconsistently to refer to student learning achievement targets or the various aims of teachers and administrators in delivering language education. Here we use the term "outcomes" or "student learning outcomes" to denote the specific articulations of knowledge, skills, and dispositions (values and attitudes) students are to develop as a result of their learning experiences in a program, course, or module (Watanabe, Davis, & Norris, 2012).

Language educators must be clear on what they want to know with respect to student performance and the relevant types of information needed, given a set of intended assessment or testing uses (Norris, 2000). A fundamental component of any assessment system, then, is the initial articulation of learning outcomes (e.g., "students will able to use modals to express different levels of certainty"). Numerous types of outcomes statements are possible, and they encompass the wide range of language abilities and related dispositions that constitute the targets of second language acquisition (SLA). For example, global proficiencies; abilities to use functions or notions; reading, writing, speaking, and listening skills; intercultural competence; capabilities to accomplish valuable, real-world tasks; vocabulary knowledge; and so on may all be identified as desirable targets.

Moreover, outcomes should be developed with their ultimate uses in mind and with input from relevant stakeholders who have an interest in student learning (Watanabe, Davis, & Norris, 2012). Thus, if a group of educators intend to use assessment in a particular way, their assessment efforts must proceed on the basis of a clear articulation of the students' language abilities—at various instructional levels (e.g., course, class, module, program)—relevant to the goals and mission of the educational program and therefore will serve as the backdrop to any and all assessment efforts.[5]

Identifying Assessment Users and Uses

Any endeavor using assessment to inquire into student learning must proceed on the basis of a specification of what assessment is trying to achieve. That is, at the very beginning of assessment planning there should be a clear articulation of the specific uses to which test scores or assessment findings or processes will be put. What people want to achieve via their assessment efforts (e.g., the aforementioned formative vs. summative purposes) will determine the specifics of how they go about achieving it, which will have implications for the specific questions that teachers, learners, and other decision makers want to ask and the information they will need in order to answer those questions. For example, a group of educators can use students' performance evidence to ascertain educational effectiveness of materials, demonstrate student learning to outside audiences, identify student needs, motivate students, or engage students in their own learning. Each of these uses may require different types of evidence and information, hence distinct assessment methods for eliciting student performances, scoring them, and reporting scores. Specifying use at the start of assessment efforts avoids collecting meaningless types of evidence and helps ensure that stakeholders get the information appropriate for their decisions and further actions (Norris, 2000, 2006, 2008; Patton, 2008). For a common example, assessing learners' mastery of a particular grammatical rule in English by use of a multiple-choice test (MCT) will likely indicate very little about the extent to which learners can actively and accurately use the rule in real-time communicative performance; if the assessment is intended to provide feedback to learners about their abilities to communicate on the basis of what they are learning, as in this example, then a different kind of assessment method would be needed (e.g., a task-based performance test). On the other hand, an MCT might be quite useful where the assessment is intended simply to provide teachers and learners with a quick determination of the grammatical rules that learners know passively (see the useful discussion with ample examples of different types of grammar-oriented assessments in Purpura, 2004).

In addition, different stakeholders will have different assessment aims and will seek to use assessment findings in different ways. Students, for example, are key users of certain kinds of assessment information (e.g., criteria for language task performance as a basis for interpreting and improving their own abilities), yet their needs differ considerably from other users (e.g., program administrators who need to understand student achievement of certain levels of language ability by the end of a course). If important stakeholder groups are overlooked when conceiving an assessment-based inquiry, assessment will be useful for some stakeholders and not others—alternatively, some uses and users will require fundamentally different types of information, leading to the demand for distinct assessment practices and instruments. Thus, one or more specific groups of intended users must be identified at the beginning of any and all assessment planning. The productiveness and ultimate usefulness of the enterprise, then, will depend on (a) identifying groups or individuals who will be responsible for doing something as a result of assessment findings and processes and (b) being clear about what those people want assessment to achieve (Norris, 2000, 2008).

Creating or Selecting Assessment Tools

Information on student learning can encompass any number of performances and processes of interest occurring within learning programs, courses, and modules. For example, educators may be interested in the development of intercultural dispositions, the effectiveness of materials or teaching, the level of student motivation, or the degree to which students are aware of intended learning outcomes, among many other "assessables." As such, in addition to specifying assessment uses, it is also important for educators to be clear about the specific aspects of student learning they want to know about (Bachman & Palmer, 2010; Norris, 2000). For example, educators may want to know whether students can produce particular grammatical forms during talk-in-interaction, in which case spoken performance assessments of some kind will be called for to elicit this type of ability. By contrast with this focus on accurate language output, it may be that an assessment is needed that can identify earlier stages of grammatical knowledge development, including (a) initial awareness of the need for a grammar form (e.g., assessing recognition of when the perfective tense is used in English, through comprehension-oriented true-false or multiple choice tests), or (b) the ongoing development of abilities to manipulate a form in various linguistic contexts (e.g., a gap-fill or cloze-type assessment that forces restructuring the system to deal with present vs. past perfectives). Teachers in particular will be able to use this information to guide individual learners with focused feedback that is relevant to their ongoing developmental needs (see additional discussion in Purpura, 2004).

In addition, educators may want to know whether a course or module responds to student language learning needs more generally and broadly. If so, likely sources of information might be students, teachers, likely employers, and existing research, and likely tools to collect that information will include questionnaires, interviews, tests, learning logs or journals, or document analysis (e.g., of course materials or research literature; Genesee & Upshur, 1996). Different assessment foci, then, will call for different assessment tools. Thus, a key consideration when choosing assessment instruments is for educators to be clear about the particular information they need, after which relevant assessments can be selected or created in order to achieve desired aims.

A number of sources provide advice on the variety of tools available to language educators, which readers are encouraged to review. A few general categories are described here to give a general sense of the possibilities. One well-established variety of assessments includes *standardized or other published language tests*, which measure broad language constructs and typically provide norm-referenced benchmarks of language abilities. These assessments are useful for a variety of purposes, including selection and admissions decisions, as well as large-scale achievement and accountability purposes, though they tend to be less indicative of short-term learning (Norris & Pfeiffer, 2003) and agnostic to educational processes (Davis, 2013). Another broad group of assessments are *locally developed or adapted language tests* (placement tests, diagnostic tests, exams, quizzes, etc.) that focus on the measurement of language constructs or language learning outcomes and objectives that have local, typically instructionally and curricularly embedded meaning (Davis, 2013). Learning-oriented assessment purposes make use of tests of this sort to some extent, though they may also call for less conventional assessment tools given the broader scope of inquiry into many different aspects of student learning and teaching. So-called *alternative assessments* (Brown, 2004; Brown & Hudson, 1998) may be better suited to these aims and can include methods such as portfolios, student questionnaires, interviews, focus groups, learning logs or journals, diaries, conferences, embedded course assignments, and teacher observation (among others). These types of assessments can be helpful for learning-oriented purposes in that they (a) are closely aligned and integrated with instruction; (b) can reveal aspects of educational processes (e.g., via student and teacher reporting); and, importantly, (c) aim to provide feedback to learners, teachers, and other stakeholders (Davis, 2013; Norris, 2009). Of course, each of these distinct assessment methodologies calls upon different types of resources, including variable amounts of training, time, commitment by teachers and learners, and so on, such that the resource demands of any assessment approach must also be considered carefully prior to adopting a particular practice (see Bachman & Palmer, 2010; Norris, 2008).

Task-Based Language Assessment

Within contemporary approaches to language education, an increasing proportion of assessment uses will call for evidence of student performances with authentic, contextualized assessment tasks, such as writing essays, giving presentations, or conducting any of the real-world activities students are likely to encounter in the target language community. As such, we highlight here a few key aspects of *task-based language assessment* (TBLA; see also Norris, 2016). TBLA is an approach to assessment emanating out of the principles and techniques associated with task-based language teaching (TBLT; see chapter 5) and the rise of performance assessment in education more generally (e.g., Wiggins, 1998). As such, TBLA uses the concept of "task" as the organizing principle of assessment design and use: "task-based language assessment takes the task itself as the fundamental unit of analysis, motivating item selection, test instrument construction and the rating of task performance" (Long & Norris, 2000, p. 600). TBLA involves estimating an examinee's ability to perform some discrete real-world activity (e.g., giving an academic presentation). TBLA thus requires setting the test taker a contextualized, goal-oriented challenge that requires the use of complex cognitive skills and domain-related knowledge (Norris, 2009, p. 586). For formative assessment uses, TBLA is able to illuminate a wide spectrum of learning and teaching processes because task-based assessments are embedded throughout the curriculum or module and are closely aligned with, and articulated to, curricula, instruction, student needs, and learning outcomes and objectives. Indeed, having learners perform target tasks (TTs) provides teachers, learners themselves, and others critical opportunities to see language ability at work, to identify performance gaps, to indicate learning needs, to elicit focused feedback, and so on (e.g., Adair-Hauck et al., 2006). Similarly, from a summative perspective, task-based performances shed light on the most prototypical of language learning outcomes: what learners can actually do with the language they are acquiring.[6]

Collecting, Interpreting, and Using Assessment Information

Once critical decisions have been made about users, uses, and fitting types of assessment, actions must be taken in order to collect, interpret, and do something with targeted information about student learning (or related phenomena). Several excellent guides exist for helping teachers and others engage systematically in these actions, both from a language education perspective (e.g., Brown, 2014) and from a broader educational perspective (e.g., Wylie et al., 2012). Here, we highlight just a few concerns with "following through" on language assessment in ways that will encourage assessment usefulness.

Key to the *collection* of useful assessment information on language learning is both the systematicity and openness of the process. To the extent possible, language assessments (even those used informally within a class for providing feedback to individual learners) should be planned in advance,[7] should adhere to well-conceived and clear guidelines for administration, and should be adequately introduced and framed such that all participants understand the "what," "why," and "how" of the given assessment. Indeed, where assessment is intended increasingly to promote awareness raising and ownership over learning (Carless, 2011), it is essential that the focus, procedures, and criteria for assessment be open to scrutiny by both language learners and teachers, which implies that various aspects of assessments (e.g., timing, format, rating scales) be made available in advance of their use. For example, prior to recording a weekly individual speaking assessment outside of class, learners might be introduced to the topic, task procedures, and assessment rubric or scale during class, they might be asked to engage in a trial run in which they and a peer assess informally on the basis of the rubric, and they might then record their individual performances for subsequent submission to the teacher. For another example, a teacher might model the useful provision of negative feedback (e.g., in the form of requests for repetition or recasts) prior to having learner peers perform tasks and assess each other during the process.

Interpretation of language assessment information involves careful and often collaborative reflection on the meaning of scores and other types of assessment data. With language assessments in particular, outcomes must be understood within a broader frame of reference to notions of language development, as well as to curricular and instructional expectations (e.g., the types of tasks learners are expected to be able to do). Given that language knowledge and ability are complex and long-term iterative phenomena, it is generally not the case that learners will exhibit change from no knowledge to absolute knowledge from one assessment to the next. Instead, patterns of performance (including non-native-like performance, often referred to as "errors") are best interpreted developmentally as indications of the current status of the learner's interlanguage system. Analytic scales with rich descriptors of expected knowledge and performance attributes at distinct levels of developmental ability can provide essential bases for improving the accuracy of interpretation and the meaningfulness of scores vis-à-vis teaching and learning foci. Especially where performance assessments are used to elicit language use (e.g., speaking and writing tasks), rubrics and criteria can provide a critical "common" space within which learners and teachers can individually and collaboratively review performances, consider progress, identify gaps or needs, and determine accomplishments. Indeed, the joint consideration by teachers and learners of various perspectives on performance is probably a key attribute of a "learning-oriented" assessment, with potential benefits in terms of awareness raising, the determination of differences in opinion and degrees of subjectivity, and the promotion of consensual work toward a valued (and explicit) target. For summative assessments, collaborative interpretation might take the form of multiple "experts" (e.g., teachers) independently scoring performances (or other assessment information) and then meeting to adjudicate outcomes in order to increase the reliability of their ultimate decisions, to identify ambiguities in rubrics and criteria, and as a basis for improving assessment (and associated instructional) practices per se.

Lastly, on the basis of interpretations about language knowledge and abilities, decisions and other actions are taken—that is, assessment findings are *put to use*. Where intended uses have been clearly specified, decision-making practices should be apparent, although it is often necessary to put in place various mechanisms to facilitate assessment-based decisions as well. For formative uses, it may be that teachers and learners simply plan times when they can sit together, reflect on the results of an assessment, and mutually agree on what the learner needs to work on next. For classroom-scale formative uses, teachers might benefit from tools and procedures that help aggregate assessment findings across a class of learners such as, for example, a computer-based analysis of written essays that not only provides descriptive statistics of holistic ratings but also identifies particularly common grammatical errors or points to the most and least frequent vocabulary items used by learners, thereby indicating areas in need of future instructional attention with the whole class. Where learners are expected to act upon assessment of their own accord, it is likely that they will need metacognitive assistance in doing so, given the reality that such activities are generally unfamiliar—teachers can explain and model learner use of assessment, for example, by sharing example essays and scores and then relating the outcomes to instructional materials, additional resources for learning, motivation or other dispositional characteristics of learners, and so on. For decisions and actions that depend primarily on summative assessments, more formalized standards of practice are likely necessary to ensure that scores and other information are turned into fair, reliable, accurate, and consequential uses. For example, assessments used for placing students into language curricular levels require explicit guidelines on cut scores and margins of error relating score ranges to corresponding classes; what to do in the case of competing implications from scores on different subtests (e.g., learners who score high on listening but low on speaking tests); and procedures for adjustments after placements have been made. Ultimately, ensuring useful (as opposed to useless) assessments, really requires forethought, planning, and guidance regarding just what the intended users will actually do, how they will do so, and what they will need in order to do so, on the basis of any given assessment. Similarly, procedures should be put in place to review the usefulness of assessments on a periodic basis, checking to see the extent to which they are living up to expectations and determining whether their use is inspiring the kinds of consequences that were anticipated (Kane, 2012; Norris, 2008).

Summary and Recommendations

In sum, assessment plays a number of important roles in support of language learning and teaching. Increasingly, in recent thinking about assessment, it is treated less as a separate process, typically associated with admissions, accountability, and grading, and more as an integral part of an educational environment that is designed holistically in pursuit of valued learning outcomes. That is, assessments of all kinds interact with curriculum scope and sequence, materials, teachers and teaching, and learners and learning. Assessments are therefore aligned with these dimensions of the educational environment and their use is articulated to specific purposes—or at least that is how assessments should be conceived, designed, and implemented. In reality, to date, assessment practices often function as the Achilles heel of language education, in that they are designed without much consideration of who uses them to do what and with what intended consequences. All too often, then, assessments serve to constrain or even undermine what is learned, given the undue weight that is attributed to success on assessments and a frequent lack of alignment between assessment practices and the kinds of understandings outlined in the preceding six chapters. In order for assessments to play a critical role in support of learning and teaching, we recommend the following points for consideration.

7.1.   *Establish language learning targets.*

    a.   In order for assessments to be aligned with and supportive of the fundamental instructional orientation of the particular educational setting, the valued targets of learning should be stipulated.

b. State student learning outcomes that are expected as a result of the educational experience, at the level of modules, courses, sequences of courses, and so on.

c. Consider what targeted outcomes actually look like, and the learning that they imply or require, when conceiving of all assessments used within the particular setting; assessments that are not aligned with the targeted outcomes will likely work to undermine effective learning.

7.2. *Specify intended uses of assessment.*

a. Conceive of each and every instance of assessment intentionally, and design assessments as programmatic endeavors.

b. Identify who will utilize an assessment (teachers, learners, others?), what information they need from the assessment (achievement, ability, materials effectiveness, affective response, etc.?), what specific decisions and actions should be taken (feedback to guide learners; feedback to teachers to guide teaching, grading, advancement, etc.?), and what consequences should ensue (increased learning motivation, greater learning efficiency, improved affective response, etc.?).

c. Consider what balance of assessment types (formative, summative) and proportion of assessment versus other activities is optimal in the given setting, as well as in light of available resources and possible constraints.

7.3. *Design formative assessment as an integral component of instruction.*

a. Embed assessment activities within the daily practices of learning and teaching, making it a routine component of instruction.

b. Involve learners in all aspects of assessment, from considering and selecting different assessment activities, to working with rubrics and criteria prior to performance, to judging assessment performances themselves.

c. Emphasize useful feedback that is descriptive and prospective, highlighting particular dimensions of learner performance that meets expectations, as well as those that might fall short, and identifying paths toward success.

d. Engage learners in assessment directly by having them assess their own and their peers' performances and learning activities, in order to increase meta-awareness, self-regulation, and involvement in their own learning.

e. Utilize a diversity of assessment methods in order to tap into not only learners' knowledge and abilities but also their perspectives on pedagogic effectiveness, their dispositions toward learning (and assessment), and other dimensions of the learning environment and learning process.

f. Consider carefully the relationship between grading (and other administrative or institutional uses of assessment) and formative assessment, as the potential benefits of formative assessment may be undermined by other emphases.

7.4. *Design summative assessment as an opportunity to reflect on educational effectiveness.*

a. Align summative assessments with the stipulated learning outcomes for a given sequence of instruction, such that assessments reflect what was intended to be learned.

b. Make clear the criteria by which "mastery" of taught content will be judged, including the scope of learning products in a given assessment, as well as descriptions of expected levels of performance (e.g., in the form of rating rubrics); criteria should be made available in advance of assessment as a mechanism for guiding learning.

c. Only assess that which has been taught; in other words, summative assessments should cover only those targets for which there has been an opportunity to learn.

d. Involve teachers and other assessment users in standard-setting exercises that determine legitimate expectations for performance on a given assessment in light of the actual opportunity for learning that students have.

e. Consider very carefully the likely consequences of summative assessments, especially where they are used for achievement or certification purposes, and choose assessment methods to maximize positive washback.

f. In addition to judgments made on the basis of summative assessments (e.g., pass-fail, grades), report assessment results such that they may be used formatively; for example, provide teachers with full analyses of students in their classes, showing proportions of scores at different levels of mastery, rich descriptions of performance that reveal areas of need, and so on.

7.5. *Select or create assessment instruments and procedures on the basis of intended uses.*

a. Choose from among the myriad alternatives in assessment those methods that will (a) yield specified, needed evidence; (b) within available resource constraints; (c) in a way that intended uses can turn into actual uses; and (d) with a high likelihood of bringing about desired consequences, all of which should be established prior to and separate from selection of specific instruments. Any of the variety of assessment methods, from selected to constructed response, from tests of knowledge to tests of performance, may be useful for some purposes at different times. Key is the alignment of the assessment method with the types of information needed in order to fulfill a given assessment purpose.

b. Formative assessment typically calls for instruments and procedures that do more than merely produce a score; consider assessment alternatives that provide rich descriptive evidence about specific aspects of student language learning.

c. Summative assessments typically have considerable washback effects on teaching and learning; consider instruments and procedures that encourage language-learning-related activities that align with the values and targeted outcomes of the educational setting.

d. In language education, there is much to recommend the use of authentic communicative tasks for many assessment purposes, both formative and summative in orientation: tasks encapsulate the valued expectations at the core of contemporary approaches to language learning, they have clear expectations for accomplishment and the use of language, they can provide rich sources of data for various analyses of language ability and development, and they can be scored in ways that encourage subsequent learning efforts.

7.6. *Follow through on assessment uses.*

a. Administer assessments and collect assessment information systematically such that findings can be trusted to reveal accurate information about student learning and related phenomena.

b. Interpret assessment findings on the basis of explicit expectations, rubrics, scales, and criteria to the extent these are available (and where not available, encourage their development). Consider collaborative interpretation of assessment findings, involving both learners and experts, to illuminate distinct perspectives and to enhance the meaning of assessment outcomes.

c. Act on assessments in nonarbitrary ways, making decisions that are justified and intended a priori and employing mechanisms and procedures for increasing systematicity where appropriate.

7.7. *Take steps to evaluate the validity of assessment uses.*

a. Regularly collect evidence regarding the ways in which assessments are actually administered, scored, reported, and especially acted upon in order to judge the extent to which they are accomplishing what they were designed to accomplish.

b. Systematically and empirically evaluate the extent to which assessment has resulted in intended impacts and, importantly, whether there have been any unintended negative consequences; in particular, pay attention to teacher and learner behaviors and opinions regarding assessments to elicit understandings of the effect that assessments have on the learning environment.

Notes

1 Although the terms formative and summative assessment may be dis-preferred by some language testing specialists, we include them here for three main reasons. First, the distinction is very common within mainstream educational assessment (e.g., Wylie et al., 2012) where it has been used to help teachers in particular to understand the relationship between different kinds of assessment practices and teaching/learning. Second, language educators are likely to have been exposed to these ideas at some point in their development, and it may be that such familiarity will help increase further understanding. Third, the emphasis in this chapter is on aligning assessments and the information they provide with clear uses for the same, and we believe that the formative/summative distinction helps to capture broadly differing categories of assessment information use.

2 Here we use the term *formative assessment* to encompass both "assessment for learning" and "learning-oriented assessment," but we also retain the term *summative assessment* to help focus on uses for assessment that mediate between classroom- and program-level decision making.

3 We have omitted discussion of "dynamic assessment," "interactive assessment," and similar assessment varieties that happen in situ during classroom discourse (typically) or via individualized tutoring sessions. The characteristic aspect of these types of assessment is their emphasis on unplanned, spontaneous feedback by teachers—typically during L2 interaction—that "scaffold" learners toward a heightened performance they could not have otherwise achieved on their own. For further information on this type of assessment we recommend Hamp-Lyons & Tavares (2011), Lantolf & Poehner (2004, 2011a, 2011b), and Rea-Dickens (2006).

4 For extensive research- and practice-based recommendations and examples of formative assessment (not specific to language education), as well as a coherent approach to developing formative assessments, see Wylie and colleagues (2012).

5 For information on how to develop language learning outcomes, see Brown (1995); Brown and Hudson (2002); Genesee and Upshur (1996); Graves (2000); and Watanabe, Davis, and Norris (2012). Outcomes statements can also be derived from benchmarks in established educational standards such as the American Council on the Teaching of Foreign Languages (ACTFL) proficiency guidelines, the Common European Framework of Reference (CEFR), or the Teachers of English to Speakers of Other Languages (TESOL) PreK–12 English Language Proficiency Standards.

6 For more information on TBLA, see Brindley (1994), Brown and colleagues (2002a), Byrnes (2002), and the collection of studies edited by Shehadeh and Coombe (2012).

7 Even so-called spontaneous assessments can be planned in that the assessor (teacher, learner, peer) approaches the activity from a frame of reference for whatever language event is occurring in the name of assessment. For example, feedback in the form of recasts of learners' utterances may be a very useful type of spontaneous assessment, providing critical information at precisely the moment when it is needed so that learners can fill a gap in their developing language. However, if the assessor is not cognizant of the context and purpose of the speaking task, the developmental needs of the learner, and the corresponding type of information that will be processable or that will simply be missed by the learner, then the assessment will not succeed in its formative intent. Planning, even for the possibility of immediate or spontaneous provision of learning-oriented feedback, will go a long way toward rendering any assessment activity useful.

8

APPROACHES TO CURRICULUM AND MATERIALS DEVELOPMENT FOR LANGUAGE EDUCATION

As part of a broader field in education known as curriculum development, inquiry, or studies, language curriculum development has its roots in early discussions of "best practice" teaching methods during the first half of the 20th century (Richards, 2001).[1] In fact, over the past century, second language (L2) instruction was largely preoccupied with and driven by the belief that a particular teaching method or approach was required for effective and meaningful L2 instruction (Larsen-Freeman & Andersen, 2011). Although methods such as the grammar-translation method or audio-lingual method primarily constituted prescriptions about *how* to teach an L2, they also implied specific assumptions about the content of instruction—that is, *what* should be taught—and were typically realized in the form of preset textbook materials. As language educators and researchers began to consider the interaction of methods with syllabus design, and became increasingly aware of the important role played by the learner per se in determining effective L2 acquisition, they came to realize that effective instructed SLA would require a more comprehensive and well-reasoned approach to providing learners with a useful educational experience, thus giving rise to the field of curriculum development in L2 instruction in the late 1960s (Marsh, 2009; Richards, 2001). Today, emerging from critical work over the intervening decades, language curriculum development addresses the interrelated processes of designing, goals setting, planning, revising, implementing, assessing, and evaluating in language education. Hence, early debates over teaching methods and syllabus types largely have been replaced by "a focus on the interlinked processes that compose curriculum development, of which methodology is simply one element" (Richards, 2001, p. 41).

Curriculum Design

A curriculum is generally understood as an active force of human educational experience that is provided by a given language program (Qi, 2013). In less philosophical terms, a language curriculum is composed of a range of different components including what L2 students learn, how they learn, how teachers facilitate learning, and the materials and learning aids they use, as well as the styles, methods, and assessments employed in planned L2 instruction. Thus, a curriculum encompasses the set of all interrelated activities included in the teaching-learning process of acquiring an L2.

Several models of language curriculum development or curriculum-planning frameworks have been suggested in both the applied linguistics and the mainstream educational literatures (e.g., Brown, 1995; J. D. Brown, 2009; Nation & Macalister, 2010; Richards, 2001; Wiggins & McTighe, 2005, 2011). For example, in his *Systematic Approach to Designing and Maintaining Language Curriculum*, Brown (1995; J. D. Brown, 2009) put forth a series of interrelated components that are applicable to a wide range of language programs, providing both "a set of stages for logical program development and a set of components for the improvement and maintenance of an already existing language program" (Brown, 1995, p. 19). He maintained that, regardless of the teaching techniques, syllabus design, or methods employed, five consecutive steps are needed to develop a viable, goal-oriented language curriculum: needs analysis, objectives, testing, materials, and teaching. All of these steps are also subject to consistent evaluation in order to provide for ongoing revisions and improvements. A similar framework, called *Language Curriculum Design* (LCD), was proposed by Nation and Macalister (2010, 2013) who refer to the process of developing and designing language learning curricula and materials as an activity that includes a number of triangulated, justifiable steps. Similar to Brown, their framework contains essential elements organized in concentric circles. Goals, as the driving force of all curriculum design, constitute the core of their model. Goals are surrounded and influenced by factors such as content, methods, and assessments, which are in turn determined by practical and theoretical considerations such as needs, principles, and environment. In line with J.D. Brown (2009), evaluation as a system of checks and balances constitutes the outer circle that encompasses all other LCD elements (see Nation & Macalister, 2013, p. 2, for a concise overview of the LCD model).

Although different in their organization, both models contain similar elements that have been proposed as crucial for curriculum design in general (Brown, 2012b; Richards, 2001; Wiggins & McTighe, 2011). Among these core components inherent in most frameworks are (a) needs analysis; (b) the development of goals and objectives to address those needs; (c) evidence-based instruction, including determining appropriate syllabi, course structures, materials, teaching methods, and principles; (d) testing and assessments; and (e) evaluations of the processes

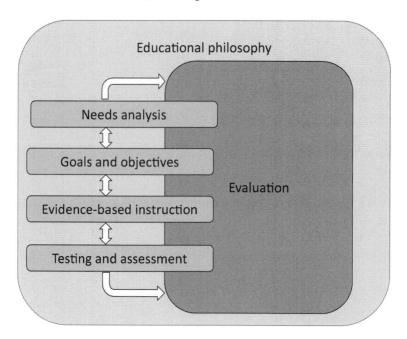

FIGURE 8.1   Basic approaches and practices in developing language curricula. Adapted from Brown (1995).

related to effective educational delivery. Hence, as depicted in Figure 8.1, these five core components, embedded into an educational philosophy, constitute a holistic conceptualization of, and practices for, the development of language curriculum, instruction, and materials.

Educational Philosophy

An educational philosophy or "school mission" (Wiggins & McTighe, 2007, 2011) is a long-term goal or purpose for which a language curriculum is generally designed. This superordinate expectation for student learning functions as a guide for the purposeful arrangement and implementation of all curricular components. Similar to a mission statement in the business world, it summarizes why the educational program exists, what it hopes to accomplish in society, and the particular values it holds. It may also stipulate more specific expectations for student learning and thus guide the development of educational experiences through the statement of student learning outcomes, or what "successful graduates [would] look like, be like, [and] be capable of doing well with their learning" (Wiggins & McTighe, 2007, p. 11).

Needs Analysis

The first step taken in developing or reevaluating an existing curriculum is typically (or ideally) a needs analysis (NA). Also called *needs assessment* (J. D. Brown,

2009), *situation analysis* (Richards, 2001), or *constraint analysis* (Kauffman, 2005), the concept of NA in L2 instruction refers to the processes involved in gathering information about the "learning needs of students, and then, once they are identified, needs are translated into learning objectives, which in turn serve as the basis for further development of teaching materials, learning activities, tests, program evaluation strategies, etc." (Brown, 2009, p. 269). Drawing upon the work of several other scholars (e.g., Graves, 2000; Jordan, 1997; Schutz & Derwing, 1981), Brown (2009, p. 270) defined 10 steps, subdivided into three general stages, for conducting a NA in L2 instruction. As summarized in Table 8.1, the first stage is primarily concerned with the conceptualization of the NA. Thus, it includes the identification of contextual factors that impact the given teaching-learning environment such as student body, mode of instruction (e.g., classroom based vs. autonomous, online learning), supplies and resources, teacher-related aspects (e.g., teachers' educational background), and political and national requirements. The situational factors and constraints constitute the basis of the data-collection procedures (for a detailed overview of sources and instruments, see J. D. Brown, 2009, and Long, 2005a). Stage II outlines the actual research procedures and activities, whereas the final stage is directed at the identification of objectives and content of a course, unit, or module that emerge out of the findings of the NA research. Hence, a NA is aimed at (empirically) identifying the (language) requirements and factors that will influence the objectives of the course or learning environment that is to be designed.

In reference to Hutchinson and Waters (1987), Nation and Macalister (2010, p. 24) differentiate between three types of needs that are to be identified in a NA: (a) necessities, (b) lacks, and (c) wants. Whereas *necessities* refer to the required knowledge—that is, what is necessary for a learner to know—*lacks* constitute the present knowledge of L2 learners in terms of what students already know and what they are lacking. Finally, *wants* refer to the subjective needs of learners—that is, what they wish to learn. Once identified, these different types of needs are

TABLE 8.1 Needs Analysis in L2 Instruction (Adapted From J. D. Brown, 2009)

Stages	*Steps*
I. Get ready to do NA.	1. Define the purpose of the NA.
	2. Delimit the student population.
	3. Decide on approaches and syllabi.
	4. Recognize constraints.
	5. Select data-collection procedures.
II. Do the NA research.	6. Collect data.
	7. Analyze data.
	8. Interpret results.
III. Use the NA results.	9. Determine objectives.
	10. Evaluate and report on the NA project.

translated into goals and objectives that guide what is being covered in the actual language learning course or module.[2]

Goals, Objectives, and Outcomes

Emerging from the NA, goals and objectives are at the heart of language education, driving and guiding the effort of designing language learning courses. As goals are typically presumed to be broader in scope, they describe general statements of what students need to learn. A particular type of learning goal that has become increasingly influential in L2 learning and teaching takes the form of educational standards. Generally intended to structure the learning-teaching process by providing clear guidelines for stakeholders as to which skills, knowledge, and competences L2 learners need to acquire, standards for L2 education have been proposed by a number of professional organizations and institutions. For example, the American Council on the Teaching of Foreign Languages (ACTFL) has put forth the "World-Readiness Standards for Learning Languages."[3] Applicable to learners at all levels, these educational standards, which are based on national and international trends, identify five goal areas for L2 instruction (i.e., communication, cultures, connections, comparisons, and communities). Whereas ACTFL has proposed standards applicable to all levels, other organizations such as Teachers of English to Speakers of Other Languages (TESOL) have proposed domain-based, as well as principles-based, standards that apply to specific L2 learner groups, professional educators, and areas of instruction.[4] Hence, standards may constitute goals for local, state, national, and international, as well as industrial educational, requirements. Goals may also simply present the broad targets for accomplishment that language programs are designed to achieve, thereby representing something of a values statement by the program "owners" (typically its teaching staff) regarding what the program contributes to learners and the world.

In contrast to goals, objectives are "comparatively precise statements of the content or skills the students will know or be able to use at the end of the course" (Brown, 2012b, p. 160). Thus, objectives are statements of which contents or skills L2 learners need to master in order to attain a specific goal. Although objectives come in many shapes and forms, which tend to vary in type and degree of specificity (even within a single course), they need to be clearly stated. Brown (1995, pp. 96), for example, provides six guidelines for designing teaching and learning objectives:

1. Objectives can range in type and level of specificity.
2. Objectives are not permanent. They must remain flexible enough to respond to changes in perceptions of students' needs and changes in the types of students served.
3. Objectives must be developed by consensus among all of the teachers involved.

4. Objectives must not be prescriptive in terms of restricting what the teacher does in the classroom to enable students to perform well by the end of the course.
5. Because of all of the above, objectives will necessarily be specific to a particular program.
6. Above all else, the objectives must be designed to help the teachers, not hinder their already considerable efforts.

A further distinction here may be helpful. Often, the larger scale targets of instruction might be usefully posed in the form of learning *outcomes*, stated in the form of what students will know or be able to do, or how they will act, as a result of an entire course, a sequence of courses, or a full program. For example, at the end of a two-year, college-level program in English for academic purposes, in the specific content area of academic writing, student learning outcomes might be stated as follows:

Student Learning Outcomes
   ELI Writing Curriculum Area—Undergraduate Level

After successful completion of ELI Writing courses, undergraduate students will be able to:

- Fluently generate sufficient written text, at the brainstorming and drafting stages of the writing process, in response to a writing assignment.
- Compose college writing that achieves a specific purpose and responds adeptly to an identifiable audience.
- Provide evidence of effective strategies for generating, revising, editing, and proofreading a text in order to produce finished prose.
- Compose an argument that makes use of source material that is relevant and credible and that is integrated in accordance with an appropriate style guide.[5]

Objectives or outcomes may also be stated at finer grained levels and with distinct purposes. Thus, within a given course, teachers may produce objectives for individual units of instruction, lessons within units, and even stages within a lesson. The focus of these objectives might be on expected learner activities and behaviors, teacher actions, intended use of materials, and so on. That is, at this microlevel, objectives might indicate how language teaching and learning processes are supposed to occur and what should happen as a result. Outcomes for a course, then, might point to learning products or achievements that are the targeted expectations for the end of a sequence such as a semester of instruction. Indeed, at this level, both objectives and outcomes are best presented in language that is understood by both students and teachers, that helps them orient to what the purpose is behind lesson activities and syllabus sequence, and that helps them reflect on or assess their own understanding and progress within the lesson and over a sequence of lessons. Goals, outcomes, and objectives, then, might be seen as ever narrower representations of what the curriculum seeks to accomplish and, to some extent, how pedagogic practices are intended to contribute to that accomplishment.

Evidence-Based Instruction

Second language educators are increasingly held accountable and, thus, required to carefully plan and document the teaching-learning process; that is, they need to provide reliable, trustworthy, and valid evidence that indicates that, through their instruction, L2 learners can be expected to make adequate gains in L2 acquisition.

Syllabus, Course Structure, and Sequencing

Although defined differently by different scholars, a syllabus is generally understood as "a specification of the content of a course of instruction and lists what will be taught and tested" (Richards, 2001, p. 2). Thus, syllabi constitute ways of organizing the course and materials insofar as they provide (a) a focus for what should be studied and (b) a rationale for how to organize, structure, and sequence the contents (Brown, 1995, 2012b; Richards, 2001; Robinson, 2009). Hence, a syllabus formalizes the content that needs to be learned in a domain of knowledge or skills and "arranges this content in a succession of interim objectives" (Widdowson, 1990, p. 127).

In general, four dimensions need to be accounted for in L2 syllabus and course development (see Richards, 2001, or Robinson, 2009, for in-depth discussions): (a) a course or unit rationale, (b) L2 proficiency entry and exit levels of learners, (c) content and materials selection, and (d) structure and sequence of contents. First, a *course rationale* specifies (a) the target population, (b) the content focus, and (c) the kind of teaching and learning that will take place. That is, perhaps in a few paragraphs, such a rationale clearly states the beliefs, values, and goals of the specific instruction module that is planned. Second, it is essential to have a clear understanding of *the entry and exit levels of the L2 learners* for whom the course is designed. Information on learners' proficiency levels in the target language may be obtained from their results on either large-scale tests, such as a TOEFL exam, or locally designed (diagnostic) assessments. Although they have also attracted controversy because they are not convincingly research based (Richards, 2001), guidelines such as the Common European Framework of Reference (CEFR) or the ACTFL proficiency guidelines provide useful domain-specific proficiency scales that may inform the design of band-level descriptors for assessments and course structures in different local settings. Third, the *selection of course content* is fundamental insofar as the content covers and operationalizes specific needs or sets of objectives. In cooperation with teachers and other language instruction experts, content selection should take into account subject-matter knowledge, learners' L2 proficiency levels, and current views on (instructed) SLA. Brown (2012b) maintained that typically the "selection of which structures, situations, topics, etc. to teach has been based on rationales like usefulness, salience, or importance" (p. 155). Fourth, the development of content usually takes place simultaneously with the *sequencing of content* because "[d]ecisions about course content also need to address the distribution of content throughout the course" (Richards, 2001, p. 150). Sequencing decisions that underlie the units of a syllabus tend to be guided by broad pedagogic orientations, as well as psycholinguistic positions (Richards, 2001; Robinson, 2009; see also chapter 9, this volume).

Several different approaches to syllabus design have been used to varying degrees in L2 education, including grammatical (or structural), situational, topical, notional, functional, skills-based, task-based, lexical, problem-solving, pragmatic, discourse-based, genre-based, and communicative strategies (for detailed discussions, see Brown, 1995, 2012b; J. D. Brown, 2009; Richards, 2001; Robinson, 2009). For example, contents in a grammatical syllabus tend to be organized on the basis of presumed difficulty levels, covering a series of increasingly complex grammatical structures. However, SLA research has shown that "the additive 'accumulation' of increasingly complex and accurate grammatical structures in a linear sequence is not what happens during second language development" (Robinson, 2009, p. 296). Therefore, grammatical syllabi have begun to be structured based on the frequency of occurrence of grammatical phenomena that can be identified by means of corpus analysis (Flowerdew, 2009; Gries, 2008). In a situational syllabus, materials tend to be presented chronologically, according to the order in which events or topics occur in real-life situations (e.g., at a restaurant, at a hotel). In problem-solving or task-based syllabi, for example, content organization can be determined by needs—that is, which problem-solving skills or target tasks learners most likely need outside of the classroom. As units of real-world activity involving language use identified on the basis of a needs analysis (see Long, 2005b), target tasks in a task syllabus are broken down into simpler versions, which are then subsequently presented in order of increasing complexity, so as "eventually to approximate the full complexity of the target task demands" (Robinson, 2009, p. 301). Although these different organization patterns will continue to prevail, other syllabi will likely surface as L2 education and research expand our knowledge about grading and sequencing units in L2 teaching and learning.

Teaching Methods and Principles

The current focus on methodological principles in L2 education has emerged from several decades in which prescribed "methodologies" dominated and guided L2 instruction. Historically, language teaching was conceptualized on the basis of a particular methodology employed in L2 instruction that was considered to be most effective for promoting target language learning by L2 students. Over the past century, L2 pedagogy has witnessed considerable fluctuations in methodological preferences, with different methods prevailing over others at different times. For example, grammar translation and the direct method primarily dominated the first half of the 20th century, whereas the audio-lingual method, silent way, suggestopedia, total physical response, communicative language teaching (CLT), and content-based instruction—to enumerate the more prominent "brand name" methods—emerged as responses to preceding methodologies over the second half of the 20th century (see Brown, 2007, Larsen-Freeman & Andersen, 2011, Long, 2009, or Richards, 2001, for detailed historical overviews; see also chapter 5, this volume).

However, current research has shown that a method-based design is a rather "inappropriate, even irrelevant, way of conceptualizing or evaluating LT [i.e., language teaching]" (Long, 2009, p. 375). First, teaching observations have indicated "considerable differences between what advocates of the methods prescribe or proscribe and what teachers actually do over time" (Long, 2009, p. 374). Second, different methods have been found to support very similar activities and procedures (Long, 2009; Richards, 2001). Third, there is no empirical evidence that one method is more effective or superior to another at all times for all learning goals and learners (Bartholome, 1994; Prabhu, 1990). Finally, the need for more situationally relevant L2 pedagogies has promoted a more critical stance and the flexible adaptation of methodological "techniques which realize a set of principles or goals" (Bell, 2007, p. 141). Thus, the "shift to localization" (Canagarajah, 2005) has given rise to a focus on the context-specific adaptability of principles underlying different methods (Hinkel, 2006; Larsen-Freeman & Andersen, 2011).

Given these findings, the focus on methodology has increasingly been replaced by a focus on L2 teaching and learning principles that motivate a particular educational agenda (Brown, 2000; Larsen-Freeman & Andersen, 2011; Long, 2015). These methodological principles constitute "universally desirable instructional design features, motivated by theory and research findings in SLA, educational psychology, general educational curriculum design, and elsewhere, which show them either to be necessary for SLA or facilitative of it" (Long, 2009, p. 376). For example, as shown in Table 8.2, Nunan (2004, p. 35) has identified eight teaching and design principles underlying a TBLT approach.

Although methodological principles such as the ones exemplified previously are often conceptualized as principles for classroom-based L2 teaching, they also constitute an important foundation for the development and design of learning materials.

Materials Development

Language learning materials have generally been defined as "any or all of the very wide range of resources capable of aiding language learning" (Waters, 2009a,

TABLE 8.2 Principles of Task-Based Language Teaching (Nunan, 2004, 2005)

Scaffolding	Lessons and materials should provide supporting frameworks within which the learning takes place. At the beginning of the learning process, learners should not be expected to produce language that has not been introduced either explicitly or implicitly.
Task Dependency	Within a lesson, one task should grow out of, and build upon, the ones that have gone before.
Recycling	Recycling language maximizes opportunities for learning and activates the "organic" learning principle.
Active Learning	Learners learn best by actively using the language they are learning.
Integration of Form and Function	Learners should be taught in ways that make clear the relationships between linguistic form, communicative function, and semantic meaning.
Reproduction to Creation	Learners should be encouraged to move from reproductive to creative language use.
Learning Strategies	Learners should focus on both the learning process and the language content.
Reflection	Learners should be given opportunities to reflect on what they have learned and how well they are doing.

p. 311). Thus, instructional materials and aids can be any resource available to an L2 educator, ranging from traditional textbooks to any kind of technology-enhanced multimedia application. Materials developers tend to distinguish between two perspectives and approaches in materials design. First, design of teaching materials should, to the extent possible, reflect advances in SLA theory and research concerning language, language learning, and education. Second, materials developers need to assume an audience-based perspective about materials design that makes primary reference to perceptions of the needs of end users (Waters, 2009a). Therefore, the relationship between applied linguistics research and practical language teaching experience should be a mutually informative, dialectical one (Widdowson, 2000).

The development of learning and teaching aids (materials) is generally intertwined with efforts in syllabus design. When anchored in SLA theories, clear-cut needs analyses, objectives, and syllabi, instructional materials have a direct impact on what is taught and how it is taught. Although they operationalize the given syllabus or syllabi underlying a particular course, module, or unit, current approaches to designing L2 learning aids tend to enable a number of different syllabi—that is, they include multiple forms of content organization. This "multisyllabus" approach (Swan & Walter, 1990) is nowadays the norm (McDonough, Shaw, & Masuhara, 2013; Waters, 2009a)—that is, each unit consists of multiple foci such as topic and vocabulary; strategies; communication skills, functions, or formulae;

tasks; and so on. While seeking to ensure that all "market needs" are accounted for, this "cover all bases" approach also constitutes a recognition of the complex, multilayered, and situated nature of language learning (Waters, 2009a, p. 320).

Particular methods and principles such as CLT or task-based language teaching (TBLT) increasingly have shaped the design of recent L2 learning materials (Brown, 2012b; Lee & VanPatten, 2003; McDonough, Shaw, & Masuhara, 2013). Since the 1970s, CLT has given rise to communicative design criteria in L2 learning aids, primarily implementing and covering specific L2 skills and functional categories of language use. The ramifications and general principles of CLT are still predominant in L2 materials design today, featuring a combination of structural and functional components (McDonough, Shaw, & Masuhara, 2013; Richards, 2001).

Approaches to task-based learning (TBL) can be seen as "a significant further evolution of CLT, both in terms of views of language in use and the development of classroom methodology" (McDonough, Shaw, & Masuhra, 2013, p. 41). With an emphasis on communication and interaction, TBLT adopts a holistic perspective of language in use, focusing on integrating both accuracy and fluency. Generally, task-based teaching is envisioned to entail three key phases (e.g., Nunan, 2004; Willis & Willis, 2007): (a) a pretask phase, (b) the task cycle itself, and (c) the language focus (though see considerable complexification of this simple idea in Bygate, Norris, & Van den Branden, 2015; Norris, 2009). The first phase typically includes schematizing work on the content and topic covered, phase two contains the actual task cycle, whereas the final phase requires a focus on language to "avoid the risk of learners achieving fluency at the expense of accuracy" (Willis, 1996, p. 55).

Based on a particular approach, curriculum and material developers are faced with having to make a number of decisions. First, they need to decide whether they should adopt or adapt existing materials or develop new materials from scratch (Brown, 1995; McDonough, Shaw, & Masuhara, 2013; Tomlinson, 2001). Whereas CLT language learning materials tend to be available and are often freely accessible,[6] TBLT-oriented materials based on target and pedagogic tasks are not as abundant yet (see Byrnes & Manchón, 2014; Long, 2015, p. 248). Indeed, Long (2015, p. 298) maintains that the "best task-based (or any other type of) materials are usually locally written and adapted by the teacher to make them suitable for use with his or her students"—be it for face-to-face instruction, blended learning, or computer-mediated learning environments (Brett & González-Lloret, 2009; Thomas & Reinders, 2010).

Moreover, material designers have to make a decision regarding two key aspects: (a) the authenticity of materials used in learning aids (e.g., Mishan, 2005) and (b) input elaboration (Long, 2015). In TBLT, for example, Long (2015) argues that in a time "when 'authenticity' is a buzz word in LT [language teaching] materials design, TBLT involves use of *modified* materials in the early stages" and beyond, depending on the skill, domain, or purpose of instruction (p. 297). Elaborated input—that is, input fitted to learners' current processing capacity—has been shown to be more appropriate than either genuine or simplified texts (Long, 2015). In task-based materials, elaborated input is theoretically motivated and empirically supported to count as a methodological principle in TBLT (see, e.g., Doughty & Long, 2003b; Long & Norris, 2000). Hence, Long (2015) concludes that the "[t]raditional belief in the value of so-called 'authentic' LT materials needs rethinking" (Long, 2015, p. 298)—and should thus be carefully weighed against the purpose and objectives guiding instruction.

In the end, given the potential for materials to play a decisively influential role in determining the "what" and "how" of language learning, careful attention should be paid both to supporting teachers and learners in their engagement with materials (see chapter 11, this volume) and to evaluating the outcomes and effectiveness of materials as they are used.

Assessment and Evaluation

Formative and summative assessment of language learning is a key feature of every curriculum, not only to provide evidence of language learning outcomes and, thus, meet accountability demands, but also to support teachers and learners in their ongoing learning-oriented efforts (see extended discussion in chapters 7 and 12). Assessing objectives or outcomes is "an essential part of monitoring students' progress and providing feedback, but also a crucial part of determining the degree to which the objectives are appropriately defined" (Brown, 2012b, p. 160). Thus, well-designed courses and language programs should include "short-term achievement tests in the curriculum design" (Nation & Macalister, 2010, p. 10), as well as longer term, broader scope outcomes assessment (see chapter 12). At the same time, insights gained from ongoing formative assessment (e.g., employed daily within the classroom environment by both teachers and learners) can be used to provide feedback to students, which will allow them to improve the quality of their language use, and to teachers, enabling them to tailor their instructional efforts. Moreover, summative assessment can also inform the evaluation of the learning experience as it provides insights into a course's effectiveness and L2 learners' progress.

Finally, although outlined in a seemingly chronological order, the components of a language curriculum enumerated previously are all interconnected and grounded in the never-ending, ongoing process of evaluation. As a systematic process of gathering and synthesizing information about different aspects embedded in a given language curriculum, thorough evaluations should ideally be conducted at all stages in the curriculum development and implementation process in order to inform and provide for potential adaptations, revisions, enhancements, and improvements (Brown, 1995, 2012b; Nation & Macalister, 2010). The evidence accumulated and identified by evaluations can either serve summative or formative purposes, depending on the time and goal of the evaluation conducted (for detailed discussions and guidelines for L2 program evaluation, see, e.g., Brown, 1995; Nation & Macalister, 2010; Norris et al., 2009; Patton, 2008). Hence, evaluation is a fundamental component of curriculum development that constitutes the essential means of monitoring and maintaining the language curriculum by providing "meaning to all the other elements" (Brown, 1995, p. 217; see also chapter 12, this volume).

Summary and Recommendations

The components enumerated in this chapter constitute basic concepts, issues, and practices in language program and curriculum development. Although curriculum design is highly context dependent and will therefore vary in relation to the (local) situation, target language and learner population, purpose of L2 learning, and so on, a number of key factors can be identified that facilitate the planning and decision making that is involved in developing effective language learning experiences of all kinds, including the following.

8.1. *Consider the (local) context and environment in which the curriculum will be implemented.*

Often viewed as a step that precedes a needs analysis (e.g., Nation & Macalister, 2010), language curriculum planning should start with a consideration of the situational factors—related to learners, teachers, or the context of instruction—that may impact a given language course that is about to be designed. This initial brainstorming can be guided by a number of questions constructed to identify the constraints and effects of environmental and situational influences (see Nation & Macalister, 2010, p. 16; see also chapter 10, this volume).

8.2. *Implement ongoing needs analyses.*

As part of the philosophy of educational accountability, any educational program or language curriculum should be based on a thorough analysis of learner needs, which include, but are not limited to, learning goals, language requirements, L2 standards, societal demands and potentially other considerations. A needs analysis identifies what learning outcomes need to be targeted in the language curriculum in a particular context of L2 education.

8.3. *Determine and formulate clear goals and objectives.*

Goals and objectives are driving and guiding the effort of designing and implementing language learning experiences.

a. Goals are generally broader in scope, as they typically describe general statements of what students need to learn. Educational standards constitute a particular type of learning goal that needs to be accounted for.

    b. Objectives are precise statements about which contents or skills L2 learners need to master in order to attain a specific goal, often also including activities—that is, how learners will be enabled to reach specific targets. Objectives can range in type and level of specificity: (i) they are not permanent manifestations of aims, but need to remain flexible for potential changes; (ii) they should be developed jointly by all educators involved in the teaching-learning process; (iii) they must not be prescriptive in the sense of restricting the teacher; and (iv) they need to be articulated context specifically—that is, in reference to a specific program.

8.4. Provide evidence-based instruction.

    a. In cooperation with teachers, stakeholders, and other language instruction experts, compose a syllabus that articulates and formalizes the selection of contents based on the goals and objectives identified through the needs analysis; content selection should take into account subject-matter knowledge, learners' L2 proficiency levels, and current views on (instructed) SLA.

    b. Select the underlying syllabus design, and organize the presentation and sequence of content items based on the goals of the learning course, SLA research, and (methodological) principles. As language learning experiences should provide the best possible coverage of language in use, consider the inclusion of items that occur frequently in the language (e.g., through corpus analyses) so that learners get the best return for their learning efforts (Nation & Macalister, 2010).

    c. Ground L2 learning aids, materials, and activities in instructional design features to implement a broad methodological basis, supportive of the goals and objectives guiding the learning experience; accommodate for L2 use in a variety of language contexts and include activities based on "local and international situations that are recognizable and applicable to the students' everyday lives, pertaining to both NS-NNS [native speaker–non-native speaker] and NNS-NNS interactions" (Brown, 2012b); adapt the amount of authentic texts and elaborate input to the specific skills and developmental levels of the target population.

8.5. Implement meaningful assessment procedures.

    a. Document the teaching-learning process by providing reliable, trustworthy, and valid evidence that indicates that, through the intervention, learners can be expected to make adequate gains in L2 acquisition.

    b. Implement both summative and formative assessments, such as diagnostic, classroom-based, and achievement tests, to monitor, record, report, and provide feedback to L2 learners, teachers, and others in response to particular needs related to learner engagement, instructional design, and curricular effectiveness.

    c. For all assessments, establish the intended uses and users, such that information needs, decision-making procedures, and eventual consequences contribute to the overall learning endeavor (see chapter 7).

8.6. *Conduct ongoing evaluations on all parts of the language curriculum.*

Thorough, continuous evaluations should ideally be conducted at *all* stages in the curriculum development and implementation process in order to inform and provide for potential adaptations, revisions, enhancements, and improvements. Ensure that fundamental areas for evaluation inquiry are being adequately addressed: implementation, processes, and outcomes. Evaluations should be utilization focused; that is, they should be carried out in ways that enhance the utilization of findings to inform decisions and improve performance, thus being useful to the (primary) intended users (see chapter 12).

Notes

1 The terms "curriculum" and "syllabus" are used by different discourse communities to mean either the same or different things. Curriculum design in North American English, and syllabus design in British English, both generally suggest a comprehensive way of conceiving of an approach to language education, from theory to structure to practice, as it is intended to be carried out within a given instructional setting. Alternatively, in some varieties, "syllabus" is often understood to mean just the specific plan for a given course of instruction, laying out the daily schedule of teaching objectives and materials that will be covered in arriving at targeted learning outcomes.

2 See Long (2005a, b) for considerable methodological detail on the conduct of NAs, as well as case studies of NAs in relation to a range of language learning contexts.

3 World Readiness Standards for Learning Languages, https://www.actfl.org/publications/all/world-readiness-standards-learning-languages

4 Standards, http://www.tesol.org/advance-the-field/standards

5 This example is from the publicly available student learning outcomes at the University of Hawaii English Language Institute. For more examples and information, see http://www.hawaii.edu/eli/

6 See the UCLA Language Materials Project, http://www.lmp.ucla.edu/Default.aspx, or the Center for Advanced Research on Languages Instructional Materials, http://www.carla.umn.edu/lctl/materials/index.html for overviews of language learning materials.

9

INSTRUCTIONAL SEQUENCING AND LANGUAGE LEARNING PROGRESSIONS

A particularly challenging dimension of second language (L2) curriculum design has to do with the question of what aspects of the target language to teach in what order—that is, on what basis can we sequence language learning experiences? This chapter considers available rationales for sequencing language learning experiences at distinct levels of decision making, from language courses, units, or modules, to individual lessons. Although widely agreed to be a fundamental requirement for maximizing the efficiency and effectiveness of language instruction (Richards, 2001), sequencing of language learning content remains largely intuitive, theoretical, and minimally investigated (Long & Crookes, 1992). Numerous proposals do exist, and there is some consensus regarding very basic recommendations; however, empirical evaluation of sequencing approaches for language teaching and learning has proven largely untenable to date, hence any suggestions forwarded here should be considered tentative.

In this chapter, we first introduce the roles of sequencing decisions in instructional design, and we refer briefly to approaches typical of contemporary education. Next, the chapter reviews options for instructional sequencing emerging out of specific traditions of language pedagogical research and practice. These pedagogy-driven rationales have focused on ordering diverse components (grammar, lexis, notions, functions, tasks, etc.) associated with specific language teaching approaches such as grammar translation, situational-functional language teaching, and task-based language teaching (TBLT). The discussion then probes deeper into research on developmental sequences and orders of acquisition in L2 learning, popularized starting in the 1980s as a putative scientific basis for organizing language instruction (particularly by Ellis, 1993, 1997a; Pienemann, 1998). Despite the appearance of immediate applicability of such "language learning progressions" to language teaching, we discuss a number of problems that arise when trying to sequence planned instructional interventions in terms of patterns in interlanguage development. The chapter concludes by reviewing three more recent proposals for instructional sequencing in language learning: (a) those based on proficiency scales and standards; (b) those derived from theories of cognitive task complexity; and (c) those informed by the integration of systemic functional linguistics with TBLT and using the notion of *genre* as the primary unit of instructional design (terminology to be defined later in the chapter).

In the end, the overarching recommendation we put forward is that approaches to instructional sequencing should be mindful of interlanguage research on learning progressions, as well as phenomena such as frequency and prototypicality of language forms to be targeted by instruction, but without depending on strict adherence to their use as a basis for designing and ordering learning experiences. Additionally important will be the employment of activities and tasks that accommodate different learning trajectories, styles, and strategies, while attending to immutable and inevitable variability in certain learner individual differences (IDs), like age, and in particular to the language learning needs targeted by instruction. Approaches that consider the cognitive, textual, or perceived complexity of learning activities holistically might prove the most amenable for sequencing decisions that account for these distinct challenges.[1]

Instructional Sequencing

Instructional design is traditionally conceived in terms of the interaction of two dimensions: the *scope* of what needs to be taught and the *sequence*, or order, in which it should be taught. In most cases, scope decisions are made prior to sequencing decisions, and they depend on both the time and resources available (so, what needs to be taught to whom in what amount of time and with what intensity of instruction?), as well as the needs of the learners that are addressed by the course, curriculum, or program (so, what will learners need to learn by the end of the available sequence?). Sequencing decisions depend in turn on the parameters established by scope decisions—without a good sense of the scope of instruction, there is not much point in trying to sequence learning experiences, as the sequence begs the question of efficient and effective learning toward what ends (Wiggins & McTighe, 2005). Given an established scope (e.g., in the form of targeted learning outcomes, see chapter 8) the sequencing of learning content can be divided helpfully into macro- (or curricular-) level decisions and micro- (or lesson-) level decisions. Macrolevel decisions suggest the order in which larger scale units of analysis are taught and hopefully achieved, including, for example, content to be covered, skills to be mastered, principles to be understood, and so on, at the level of sequential years, semesters, courses, or other units that constitute the building blocks of coherent curricula. Microlevel decisions posit the order in which teaching occurs within individual lessons or modules, where new ideas are introduced, taught, and learned to some degree. Typically, microlevel design depends primarily on a theory of instructed learning or, in other words, how the minute-to-minute acquisition of new material takes place within whatever content is being taught; as a result, the design of lessons following a particular instructional approach often adopts a certain similarity regardless of the point at which it falls in a larger order sequence. For example, a presentation, practice, production (PPP) approach to language teaching (see chapter 5) will tend to follow that pedagogic sequence from one lesson to the next, without a lot of variation. Macrolevel design, on the other hand, addresses the idealized ordering of fundamentally distinct elements (i.e., the new ideas themselves) and calls for some kind of rationale for doing so (e.g., what gets taught in each PPP lesson will vary, of course, and that depends on a rationale for ordering learning targets in a particular way).

Macrolevel Sequencing

Summarizing considerably, prevailing educational design approaches to macrolevel sequencing have been characterized primarily, and historically, according to "simple-to-complex" trajectories, albeit with distinct ways of defining relatively simple or complex phenomena depending on the particular learning domain. Building from Tyler's (1948) objectives-based educational model, where learning targets are first defined at the broadest level and then iteratively divided into ever more detailed and specific components down to unit- and lesson-level expectations, numerous proposals have been put forth over the years for ordering learning objectives (e.g., Ausubel, 1963; Bruner, 1966; Merrill, 1978; Reigeluth, 1999). Perhaps the most iconic and still relevant—if somewhat simplistic—example of a simple-to-complex sequence is Bloom's (1956) taxonomy of educational objectives, which established six levels of cognitive complexity for typical learning activities, from lowest to highest demand, focusing in turn on knowledge, comprehension, application, analysis, synthesis, and, finally, evaluation. The basic sequencing argument, then, would be to analyze whatever learning objectives have been identified according to their fit with a particular level of cognitive complexity (i.e., what do they expect the learner to do or focus on, mentally) and to order the objectives accordingly, because the expectations of each subsequent level are dependent on mastery of the content of the previous. An important adjustment to this idea was proposed by Bruner (1966), who suggested that complex cognitive domains require more than a linear progression through stages of mastery, from zero to full competence, given the interrelationships among different components of the system being learned and the likely extended time needed for development of certain capacities. Thus, he proposed a spiraling approach to sequencing whereby sets of ideas were introduced at one level of complexity and then revisited periodically at subsequent levels of complexity (e.g., from one school grade to the next).

A variety of other sequences have been proposed and implemented for educational design in accord with the particular demands of distinct learning situations (see Reigeluth, 1999), including the following:

- *Chronological, job, or natural order:* follow a logical set of interrelated steps that occur in a particular order in the "real world" (i.e., outside of the classroom).
- *Priority, need:* Teach, in order of critical demand, what is needed first by the learners.
- *Build from the known:* Introduce new content on the basis of known content.
- *Prior mastery:* Build from most basic ideas to those that are dependent on them.
- *Transfer:* Arrange objectives together according to commonalities, such that learning is transferred from one objective to the next.
- *Advance organizers and anchoring:* Introduce general ideas followed by specific details.
- *Shortest path:* Teach the most direct solution or route followed by problems, details, and complications.
- *Elaboration:* Start with the big picture and key ideas that epitomize it, followed by increasing elaboration of details, nuance, and sophistication.

Ultimately, these kinds of proposals must be translated into practice in discipline- or domain-specific ways, and the determination of simple versus complex learning activities (or other orders suggested previously) depends considerably on the understandings of educational designers or teachers about the subject matter at hand. For example, Bloom's original taxonomy has been adapted to reflect the ways in which it is actually used by educators in a variety of domains, such that it is now presented as a multidimensional model consisting of the interaction between cognitive processes (remembering, understanding, applying, analyzing, evaluating, creating) and the types of knowledge they require (factual, conceptual, procedural, metacognitive; see Anderson & Krathwohl, 2001). This revision in turn has been adapted to specific educational domains as a framework for guiding learning activities such as, for example, technology-mediated learning and education for the digital world (e.g., Churches, 2009).

Microlevel Sequencing

As introduced previously, micro- or lesson-level design depends considerably on the specific instructional approach adopted. However, 20th-century educational researchers have coalesced around a basic set of instructional strategies that seem to function well as a principled learning sequence. Perhaps best captured initially in the work of Gagné (1968) and later with his colleagues (e.g., Gagné & Briggs, 1979; Gagné et al., 2005), a prototypical lesson sequence might feature the following nine instructional events:

1. gaining learners' attention to activate their interest and readiness;
2. identifying the new objective and its importance or relevance to their learning;
3. stimulating recall of previous, relevant information to encourage associative and cumulative learning;
4. presenting new material as stimulus for new learning elements;
5. guiding the learning (or interaction with stimulus material) that ensues as needed by the individual learner or learners;
6. eliciting performance that exhibits desired learning;
7. providing feedback on performance and encouraging improvement or adaptation;
8. assessing performance at the end of the learning sequence to determine effectiveness and need for subsequent revision; and
9. enhancing retention and transfer through reflection, linking activities, expansion, and mechanisms to aid in recall.[2]

Depending on the particular learning objectives targeted, or the domains of learning (e.g., cognitive vs. motor skills), the specific strategies adopted within each of these stages or the amount of time spent on each stage would clearly need to be adjusted. However, as a generalized lesson sequence, there is much to recommend about this approach, as indicated by its adoption in numerous instructional domains, the development of textbooks, and, more recently, the design of technology-mediated learning environments (e.g., Becker, 2007; Richey, 2000).

Language education has adopted these ideas for macro- and microlevel sequencing to some extent over the years (e.g., Nunan, 1988; Richards, 2001; Skehan, 1998). However, language learning also presents unique challenges, including substantial age and environmental effects, disagreements regarding fundamental assumptions about how an L2 develops and might best be taught, the feasibility of expectations about language learning outcomes, and the interrelationship between language learning and other domains of education and cognitive development. Therefore, we turn now to consideration of sequencing decisions from an explicitly language-pedagogy perspective.

Pedagogy-Driven Approaches to Language Instructional Sequencing

Language pedagogical approaches to sequencing are conceptualized depending on their association with a particular theory of instructed second language acquisition (SLA). One fundamental SLA debate broadly divides approaches to pedagogical design along a continuum between two positions: the extent to which instructed learners acquire language via an explicit focus on discrete linguistic features (e.g., intentional teaching of grammar rules, vocabulary words); and, whether learning is largely implicit and proceeds via incidental exposure to features of the

L2 input during communicative interaction (Long & Crookes, 1992; Robinson, 2009). Privileging one or the other (or adopting a middle road; compare with "focus on form") leads to particular instructional strategies, as well as specific conceptualizations of the "units of analysis" adopted to organize sequences of instruction. *Unit of analysis* refers to instructional "building blocks" employed to construct and order episodes of language teaching. Units can be linguistic features (e.g., notion, function, grammar point, vocabulary, skill) or types of communicative activity (e.g., a real-world task).

Language pedagogy research typically situates and discusses the sequencing of instructional units in terms of their organization within a syllabus (Robinson, 2009).[3] Language learning syllabi thus have been categorized in terms of how a language learner engages with a specifically chosen instructional unit. Two important categorizations of syllabi have emerged on this basis: the *synthetic syllabus* and the *analytic syllabus* (Long & Crookes, 1992; Robinson, 2009; White, 1988; Wilkins, 1974, 1976). A synthetic syllabus denotes a type of instructional design in which the learner is first taught and then presumed to compile discrete linguistic components (e.g., lexical items, morphosyntactic structures) with the aim that these will eventually coalesce into target-like language ability given enough time and practice. It is therefore situated at the intentional and explicit end of the SLA continuum. An analytic syllabus, by contrast, organizes instruction via units of holistic language input (e.g., tasks, texts, genres) typically within meaningfully communicative activities, whereby students are encouraged to analyze the holistic input, primarily by inducing rules and patterns, and thereby develop functional language ability. Analytic syllabi are at the opposite end of the continuum, emphasizing as they do the implicit learning of language form as needed for communicative purposes, through incidental exposure. Each syllabus type has different rationales for selecting and ordering instructional units (discussed next) based on theoretical, as well as practical, considerations.

Synthetic Syllabi: Grammatical, Lexical, and Notional Units of Analysis

Arguably the most widespread strategy of syllabus design, of a highly explicit and intentional orientation, has involved the reliance on morphosyntactic structures or other grammatical elements as the unit of analysis. Such an approach issued out of the earliest teaching approaches emphasizing explicit grammar knowledge, translation, and reading and writing abilities (see chapter 5). The *grammatical syllabus* and its widespread use in language instruction was based on the long-held assumption that discrete grammar items are best learned by presenting forms to learners in isolation and having them practice with the new input in controlled activities building toward target-like performance. However, the gradation of forms in grammatical syllabi was not systematic and relied mostly on teachers' or materials writers' intuitions of importance, frequency, or difficulty (Brown, 1995).

A more contemporary variation on the grammar syllabus is the *structural sylla-bus*, which is equally based on morphosyntactic forms though using more system-atic methods and rationales for determining pedagogical sequences. The structural syllabus approach is perhaps most closely associated with the research and peda-gogical advice from Rod Ellis (1993, 1997b). Ellis justifies a morphosyntactic unit for syllabus design on the basis of a psycholinguistic theoretical claim that declarative linguistic knowledge (knowledge that learners are consciously aware of) can eventually become automatized language ability with enough practice and under the right learning conditions (Ellis & Shintani, 2014). Ellis thus takes the view that there is some degree of interface between explicitly learned input and implicit language ability and as such adopts findings from acquisitional order research to advocate a syllabus design approach structured around the learnability of morphosyntactical elements (see the following discussion on learning progres-sions; Ellis & Shintani, 2014).

The emergence of communicative language teaching gave rise to instruc-tional approaches that aimed to enhance learners' communicative competence. Key linguistic concepts within this approach were based on a reconceptualiza-tion of language ability, beyond Chomskyian linguistic competence that focused on the grammar of a language, and toward a wider range of language abilities needed to communicate in social situations. Thus, concepts such as "notions" and "functions" were introduced as units of syllabus design, as these were thought to be more useful targets within an instructional paradigm aiming for functional communicative abilities. According to Wilkins (1976), *notions* are categories of communicative aims that a proficient L2 speaker should be able to accomplish, including semantico-grammatical categories (e.g., time, quantity, duration, qual-ity), modal meanings (e.g., expressing certainty, intention, or obligation), and communicative functions (e.g., suggesting, giving information, interrupting). However, little advice has been provided for how to sequence notions or func-tions within communicative instructional syllabi. Apart from selecting language needed in programs of English for specific purposes and other approaches to spec-ifying communicative needs (see Munby, 1978), there appears to be no systematic rationale for instructional sequencing of notions and functions apart from instruc-tor (or textbook publisher) intuitions about logical chronology, relative difficulty, or communicative usefulness (Brown, 1995; Nunan, 1988; Robinson, 2009).[4]

An additional approach to syllabus design is based on Willis's (1990) method of using lexical or collocational items as the unit of instructional analysis. A *lexi-cal syllabus*, according to Willis, is constructed by conducting corpus analyses to select the most frequent lexical items—for example, at 700-word, 1,500-word, and 2,500-word levels—and then focusing instruction first on the usage, syn-tactic patterns, and collocations that accompany the most frequent lexical items. Despite the frequency-based method of selection, the lexical approach does not provide much of a rationale for instructional sequencing beyond addressing the most frequent forms first. Moreover, Willis's recommendation is to choose topics of interest for particular groups of learners, identify texts and tasks related to those topics, and then conduct corpora analyses of relevant texts to identify the most frequent lexical and collocational items within them (for an example of this process, see the Collins Birmingham University International Language Database, or COBUILD, Course described in Willis and Willis, 1989; see also Willis, 1990). However, certain issues arise when using frequency as a criterion for item selection. Ellis and Shintani (2014) point out that frequency counts identify the most frequent linguistic "tokens" (unique, individual lexical items), which may not be the most optimally learnable elements in a given corpus compared to the most frequent lexical item "types." Linguistic "types" are lexical or collocational items that function as generalizable categories that learners can use to identify L2 lexical-syntactical patterns (e.g., *going to* + *verb*). In addition, the most frequent tokens can commonly have abstract meanings, which may not be developmentally appropriate for particular learners, especially those at beginning proficiency levels, compared to more concrete—and less frequent—uses of the same item (Flowerdew, 2009).[5]

Selecting and sequencing instructional units on the basis of discrete linguistic constituents has arguably been the dominant method of pedagogical design, even though current language education research (on the whole) finds a number of drawbacks with such approaches. In addition to lacking rationales for sequencing, a primary objection has been that at the heart of a synthetic syllabus approach is a dubious assumption that language learning proceeds in a piecemeal fashion of explicit learning and accretion toward target language ability (see the following section). Yet, if linguistic elements are to feature as the privileged organizing unit, it might be best to use these (a) in a principled way (using frequency analyses, focusing on linguistic "types," etc.), and (b) in a subordinate role within instructional approaches that view language learning as fundamentally emanating from engagement with communicative texts or tasks (not linguistic isolates) and that sequence language instruction on the basis of related instructional units (texts, tasks, genres, etc., discussed next).

Analytic Syllabi: Task-Based Units of Analysis

In addition to the shortcomings mentioned previously, Long (2000) has observed that synthetic syllabi lead to the creation of inauthentic, linguistically impoverished materials that fail to provide the range of input learners can use in personalized ways to satisfy different developmental levels and learning styles (see also Robinson, 2011). By contrast, and assuming largely implicit and incidental learning processes, analytic syllabi present learners with holistic texts, without linguistic interference or control, and by so doing offer opportunities for individually varied learning, as well as the use of innate inductive learning mechanisms that respond to frequencies and regularities of extended linguistic input (Long, 2015).

The most current instructional approach adopting an analytic syllabus paradigm has been developed within the research agenda of task-based language teaching (TBLT). As introduced in chapter 5, TBLT uses the notion of "task" as the primary unit of analysis around which instructional sequences are built and ordered. The notion of task operationalized within TBLT is commonly distinguished in two ways: (a) *target tasks*, or TTs, which are the real-world activities identified via learner needs analysis that spell out the accomplishments students must be able to perform in the target language at the conclusion of the program of study; and (b) *pedagogic tasks*, or PTs, which are simpler versions, components, or other didactic manipulations of TTs used to scaffold learners toward successful TT accomplishment (Long, 2015; Norris, 2009). Broadly speaking, TTs provide a unit of analysis for macrolevel sequencing, and PTs play the primary role in microlevel sequencing, as defined previously.

With the exception of structural and lexical syllabus methodologies (and TBLT), historical approaches to syllabus design do not offer much empirical rationale for sequencing instructional units in particular ways, though all provide some justification for unit *selection*. TBLT is conspicuously different in that theories of instructed SLA are advanced to justify the selection and sequencing of task units in ways that optimize the learning potential for students in L2 classrooms (Robinson, 2001b, 2001c, 2003, 2007b, 2009; Skehan, 1998, 2001, 2003; Skehan & Foster, 2001). The established method of unit selection in TBLT is to identify TTs on the basis of student needs, which are then abstracted into "target task types" or generalized tasks that share features common to a set of similar TTs. Once TT types are selected, they are analyzed for their constitutive subcomponents or processes that form the basis for designing PTs, the building blocks and units of analysis of the TBLT syllabus. For example, a subprocess of a TT type involving the completion of a job application might involve communicating various types of personal information (Long, 2015).

Instructional sequencing in TBLT, then, involves grading at two distinct levels. On the one hand, TT are typically set as the intended outcomes of units and longer term periods of instruction (e.g., courses, semesters, years). Although much attention has been devoted to the identification of TTs through needs analysis, and the development of resulting task types, much less is available in the way of recommendations for large-scale sequencing decisions answering the question of which TTs to teach in what order. Some possibilities—all of which depend on the overall scope and instructional time of the course or curriculum, as well as the needs of the learners—include (a) order of priority (e.g., survival TTs first for immigrant education; safety TTs before shop floor TTs in vocational settings); (b) natural chronological ordering (e.g., planning and packing for a trip, at the airport, finding your hotel, going to dinner, and so on, for a tourism course); (c) proficiency or standards sequences (e.g., TTs associated with distinct levels of the Common Core State Standards or the CEFR); (d) simple-to-complex ordering based on the cognitive demand of the tasks (e.g., in an immigrant literacy program, filling out information forms, writing letters and e-mails, writing a report); and others.

More ideas have been generated on the microlevel sequencing of PTs within TBLT. On the one hand, a standardized instructional sequence popularized by Willis (1996) suggests that task-based lessons should follow a three-stage cycle. In the pretask stage, learners are introduced to the topic or task, schematized to the possible language and communication demands, and provided instructions on the coming task procedures. In the task stage, learners carry out (typically interactive, group-based) tasks first, then plan with each other how they will report on what happened, and finally report back to the full class and teacher on their observations of the task. In the final, posttask stage, based on what happened during the task and what learners observed, a variety of (typically teacher-led) activities are used to analyze language use issues, reflect on performance, and engage in consciousness raising through feedback, as well as additional practice with the language forms implied in the task. Although this PT cycle has proved very popular with teachers (e.g., Leaver & Willis, 2004), its application is clearly limited to certain kinds of largely oral, group-based tasks, and it is unclear to what extent other kinds of TT types might be similarly didacticized (e.g., extended writing tasks). Still, the pre-during-post cycle has been widely adopted as a typical pedagogic sequence in various task-based courses and programs.

On the other hand, a distinct and more complicated approach to sequencing within lessons and units suggests that PTs should be ordered on the basis of their complexity such that learners move through a sequence of increasingly complex PTs until they reach the full complexity level of the TT type (Long, 2015). The precise nature of task complexity is not a straightforward matter in current TBLT research (Long, 2015), and neither is determining language task complexity for pedagogical or assessment purposes. Nevertheless, a considerable amount of advice is provided on how to estimate task complexity, which is supported by gradually accumulating instruction-related research into the relationship of task complexity with language performance and potentially learning. The theoretical rationales undergirding such studies have been primarily provided by Peter Robinson and Peter Skehan. Skehan (1998, 2001, 2003) defines complexity in terms of the demands a task places on attentional control. Task attention can be taxed in three areas: (a) by *code complexity* (i.e., the morphosyntactic and lexical density of task input); (b) by *cognitive complexity* (i.e., the procedural thinking required to do a task); and (c) by *communicative stress* (i.e., the conditions under which the task is performed). Robinson's (2007a, 2009) approach likewise involves classifying tasks in terms of their cognitive demands, though differing in that task complexity is determined by the degree to which task elements are either resource directing (i.e., focusing attention on linguistic elements) or resource dispersing (i.e., dividing attention on aspects of task procedures). Robinson's claim is that resource-directing demands focus attention on linguistic features in ways that stimulate language development.[6] A key research agenda in TBLT, then, has been to explore the dimensions (and validity) of Robinson's and Skehan's rationales, looking for the specific ways in which task complexity impacts L2 learning. Out of this research has emerged a taxonomy of PTs and related investigations into the relationships between a particular PT type (open tasks, planned tasks, one- or two-way tasks, etc.), their dimensions of task complexity, the learning conditions of PT performance, and the impacts of these variables on performance quality and learning (Long, 2015).

For one example of a prototypical PT sequence, moving from simple to complex, Chaudron and colleagues (2005) provided the following "direction-getting" task-based lesson:

1. *The real thing:* The teacher explains the focus of the lesson on obtaining and understanding street directions; learners then listen to three authentic tape-recorded examples of native speakers providing directions.
2. *Fragments:* The teacher displays a simplified street map and gives oral directions while following along and pointing to the directions taken; learners follow along on their own maps, tracing the directions as the teacher provides them.
3. *Fragments, part 2:* The teacher repeats directions multiple times, with multiple sets of directions, gradually increasing the distance, routes taken, mention of landmarks, and so on; learners continue to follow receptively.
4. *Where are you now?:* The teacher begins questioning learners at different points during the directions, asking them to describe where they are at a given moment on the map, thereby checking that they are following directions accurately.
5. *Asking the way:* Learners work in pairs, practicing asking for and giving directions, first on the previous simplified maps and subsequently on three new maps with new destinations.
6. *Following the route:* Using authentic tourist maps, learners listen to multiple new tape-recorded dialogues and follow the routes described, checking their arrival against a key.
7. *Unknown destinations:* Again using authentic maps, learners are given new starting points and sets of directions, and they have to determine where they are supposed to have arrived; questions are interspersed to check progress (where the learner is at a given point in the directions, based on landmarks).
8. *On your own, assessment:* Learners have to follow new sets of directions to unknown destinations, with check questions only at the end to confirm whether they have arrived as intended.

These kinds of pedagogy-driven approaches to sequencing for language learning have been utilized to varying degrees in the development of materials, courses, and programs. For example, using task as the basic unit of analysis for both macro- and microlevel sequencing has been explored in English for business purposes materials such as *Widgets* (Benevides & Valvona, 2008), whereas numerous examples of structural and lexical syllabi have been produced over the years. However, one additional challenge faced by all language pedagogy designers has to do with the nature of interlanguage development and the extent to which attempts at engineering learning actually match up with how L2s emerge, evolve, and are eventually acquired by individuals. Therefore, we turn in the next section to considerations of L2 acquisition orders and the extent to which they may play a role in sequencing decisions, prior to concluding with a focus on three recent examples of sequencing at work in pedagogic design.

Interlanguage and Language Developmental Progressions

The claim that learners pass through fixed sequences of L2 development has resulted, in part, from the foundational concept of *interlanguage* and the idea that L2 learning is characterized by consistent patterns of development related neither to the learner's particular L1 nor to the rules or patterns of the target L2. *Interlanguage* refers to a specific state of L2 competence characterized, on the one hand, by features of both L1 knowledge and internalized L2 input, and on the other, by elements that are unique, systematic, and independent of either language (Selinker, 1972). Three observations about linguistic development have led to the identification of interlanguage as a key concept in L2 acquisition (Ortega, 2009c): (a) learners build quite different (i.e., non-target-like) models of L2 knowledge compared with those in the ambient L2 input; (b) many L2 errors cannot be explained in terms of interference or transfer from the L1; and (c) monolingual children also display unique, non-target-like "interlanguage solutions" when acquiring their first language (Ortega, 2009c, p. 83). Thus, a fundamental concept in certain approaches to SLA theory and research is that L2 learners form interim systems of linguistic knowledge during L2 learning and, importantly, that these systems may follow universal patterns of development (Ortega, 2009b). By "universal," it is meant that all L2 learners apparently proceed through the same sequence of developing and deploying the particular patterns in a particular order, though rate of acquisition may vary considerably depending on the learning context and learners' individual factors (see Meisel, Clahsen, & Pienemann, 1981).

Learning Progressions in Adult Interlanguage Development

The earliest research on L2 interlanguage development identified acquisitional orders for morpheme development in English (Bailey, Madden, & Krashen, 1974; Dulay & Burt, 1973, 1974). This important finding has since been replicated in a number of studies indicating the same morphological sequence irrespective of L1, learning setting (Pica, 1983), or mode of production (and in this case, also irrespective of age, e.g., Lee, 1981; Makino, 1980; see also Ortega, 2009b). A consistent English morpheme order was first proposed by Dulay and Burt (1973), who observed that Spanish-speaking children initially learned English plural -s, then developed progressive -ing, followed by copula be, auxiliary be, definite and indefinite articles (a, the), the irregular past tense, regular past -ed, third person -s, and, finally, possessive -s. Moreover, early research also identified patterns of L2 syntactical development (Schumann, 1979; Stauble, 1978). Stauble (1978), for example, observed that acquisition of English negation starts with preverbal negation (no/not + verb), followed by preverbal use of don't, then postverbal negation in certain contexts (AUX + don't), terminating with postverbal negation in all contexts.

Although groundbreaking, these early studies were mostly descriptive—researchers had yet to supply systematically theorized rationales for why orders emerged in specific ways. The challenge for SLA research has since been to explain and delineate the factors—both cognitive and environmental—that account for consistent patterns of development. Anderson and Shirai (1994), for example, have advanced the aspect hypothesis to explain acquisition of temporal expression. Communicating temporality (in English) is proposed to have three phases, each characterized by lexical resources available at a given stage. The beginning stage is limited to the use of pragmatic resources (e.g., simple narrative sequencing of events); the next stage involves the use of lexical elements (e.g., use of time expressions such as "yesterday"); and in the final stage, time is expressed grammatically using morphological forms, such as past-tense -ed (Schumann, 1987). The aspect hypothesis accounts for learning patterns in the third stage in which certain grammatical forms appear earlier than others, the explanation being that grammatical tense and aspect are acquired initially via prototypical lexical items with especially salient temporal meanings, whereas grammatical markings for items with less salient meanings are learned later (Anderson & Shirai, 1994).

The systematic nature of L2 input as a determiner of interlanguage development has also been applied to the English morpheme orders initially identified by Dulay and Burt (and others). For example, Goldschneider and DeKeyser's (2001) meta-analytic study found that morpheme development is mainly determined by five input factors: (a) perceptual salience, (b) semantic complexity, (c) morphophonological regularity, (d) syntactic category, and (e) frequency. Frequency has also been put forward to explain the sequential learning of relative clauses in Keenan and Comrie's (1977) noun phrase accessibility hierarchy. They hypothesized that acquisition of relative clauses follows a pattern determined by clause *markedness* such that a less marked clause type (i.e., a more frequent type) is learned before a more marked (less frequent) type. Thus, in English and German, subject relative clauses (e.g., "The boy who goes to the school . . . ") are learned first, followed by direct object relative clauses, indirect object, object of a preposition, genitive, and finally object of comparison relative clauses (Keenan & Comrie, 1977). Moreover, although other languages are known to have fewer clause categories, none show L2 learning patterns that deviate from Keenan and Comrie's hierarchy.

Another very influential theorization of acquisitional orders is based on Pienemann's cognitive theory of processability (see also O'Grady, 2015). Derived from early observations of naturalistic L2 learners that identified a stable pattern of interlanguage development for basic rules of word order in German (Meisel, Clahsen, & Pienemann, 1981) and questioned development in English (Pienemann, Johnston, & Brindley, 1988), Pienemann (1998, 2005) conceptualized acquisitional orders in terms of processability theory and a "processability hierarchy." According to Pienemann, L2 development proceeds through six universal levels of processability for particular morphological and syntactic features. Pienemann's central claim is that the structure of the human language processor determines developmental trajectories and that the capability of a learner to process L2 input is constrained by proficiency (Pienemann, 1998). That is, structures requiring complex processing (e.g., exchange of grammatical information across constituent boundaries) cannot be accomplished at beginning proficiency levels due primarily to limitations in working memory (WM). The stages of Pienemann's (1998, 2005, 2015) processability hierarchy are listed in Table 9.1.

TABLE 9.1 Pienemann's Processability Hierarchy (Adapted From Lenzing, 2015, p. 94)

Stage	Defined	Example
1. Word or Lemma	The learner can access individual words, but these do not vary morphologically and are not assigned a grammatical category.	Formulaic expressions: "Play volleyball"; "Play soccer"
2. Category Procedure	The learner can assign lexical items to syntactic categories; morphology begins to emerge, as well as S-V-O word order, but there is no exchange of grammatical information between phrases.	Canonical word order (S-V-O): "The mouse play volleyball"
3. Phrasal Procedure	The learner can produce noun phrases and unify the components within the phrase.	Determiner + noun agreement: "The mouse have **two** ears"
4. Verb Phrase Procedure	The learner can unify components within verb phrases and use inversion to produce questions.	*Wh*-copula S(x): "What **is** your number?"
5. Sentence Procedure	The learner can process subject-verb agreement and questions with inversion.	S-V agreement: "**The mouse plays** volleyball"; "Where is the mouse?"
6. Subordinate Clause Procedure	The learner can process main and subordinate clauses, as well as generate cancel inversion structures.	Cancel inversion: "I wonder what the mouse wants?"

Finally, evidence exists for predictable patterns of L2 pragmatic interlanguage development. For example, Achiba (2003), Ellis (1992), and Kasper and Rose (2002) have identified a five-stage process for the production of English requests. The stages include prebasic (context-dependent requests without verbs, e.g., "Sir"), formulaic expressions (reliance on unanalyzed chunks of speech learned as holistic units, e.g., "Let's eat breakfast"), unpacking (elaborating on formulaic expressions, e.g., by adding politeness markers, "Can you pass the pencil please?"), pragmatic expansion (greater complexity, mitigation, e.g., "Can I see it so I can copy it?"), and fine-tuning (adjusting requestive force to participants, goals, and contexts, e.g., "You could put some blue tack down there"; see Kasper & Rose, 2002). Research from Chang (2009) on English apologies further confirms the five-stage hypothesis, the exception being that formulaic pragmatic apologies (e.g., "Sorry") precede prebasic communication. In addition, Bardovi-Harlig (2013) has proposed that pragmatic development is intrinsically tied to morphosyntactic-lexical development. Bardovi-Harlig observes that pragmalinguistic resources become available as particular lexical and grammatical structures emerge. For example, the relatively late emergence of the English modals *could* and *would* results in delayed pragmatic development, in contrast with the earlier appearance and acquisition of *maybe* and *I think* (Bardovi-Harlig, 2013).[7]

Learning Progressions and Curricular Design

The discovery of acquisition orders by SLA researchers seemed to hold great promise for language pedagogy because it appeared that curricula and materials could be designed to accommodate known progressions in interlanguage development. For example, early observations of fixed developmental sequences in naturalistic German word order acquisition (precursors of processability theory) led Pienemann (1984) to propose the "teachability hypothesis," which stipulated that "an L2 structure can be learnt from instruction only if the learner's interlanguage is close to the point when the structure is acquired in the natural setting" (p. 201). The teachability hypothesis implied that because students need to be developmentally ready for learning to occur, teachers should tailor their instruction to the student's developmental stage by strategically introducing (or delaying) input as prescribed by known learning progressions. In English, for example, this might involve focusing instruction on S-V-O word order first, leaving question word order until later, and not emphasizing third person -*s* until much later, given its very late stage acquisition (recommendations from Cook, 2001; see also, Ellis, 1993). The teachability hypothesis is further supported by many failed attempts to teach learners end-state or more advanced forms that seem to be beyond students' developmental levels (Ellis & Shintani, 2014). Indeed, some studies of instructed L2 acquisition have shown that learning of certain structures appears to happen in the orders predicted by the kinds of theories outlined previously (e.g., Ellis, 1989; Lightbown & Spada, 2013).

In practice, however, several challenges have prevented the widespread adoption of acquisitional order theory and research into instructional practice. First, there is currently an incomplete (and relatively limited) description of developmental sequences, in a handful of languages only, and primarily for English and German. In addition, known progressions focus predominantly on rules of morphosyntax, and language learning obviously involves mastery of many different linguistic elements including vocabulary, pragmatics, phonology, and so on, about which considerably less is known with respect to developmental trajectories (Ellis & Shintani, 2014; Ortega, 2009b). Moreover, Ortega (2009b) points out that there is likewise an incomplete understanding of how different developmental sequences interact with one another (e.g., pragmatics and morphosyntax). More practically, a further difficulty is that teachers must be adept at diagnosing learner readiness, and they would likely need to do so in classes with mixed ability levels, with a lack of ready-made developmental inventories and tools, and so on. Given that initial knowledge of particular L2 forms may emerge for different learners at different points in time and in distinct linguistic environments, it appears to be a particularly daunting task to both detect the "opening of developmental windows" for different learners and then provide each with individually tailored instruction and materials that build upon his or her initial experimentation with the form. How long each learner takes to fully acquire the form also is not posited by most developmental sequences (where acquisition typically means initial emergence, not end-state or native-like ability), especially when "fully acquire" means the development of ability to use a form in diverse circumstances to accomplish a full range of associated functions and with pragmatic sensitivity. In certain instructional settings, it may also be that initial emergence of acquisition orders happens quite rapidly (e.g., Ellis, 1989), whereas sustained instructional attention is required for high levels of accuracy to be mastered.

The most problematic issue for application to planning language learning experiences, however, is the variation in learning trajectories typical within language classrooms and across individual learners (Robinson, 2009). A well-known feature of language learning is the occurrence of "U-shaped" interlanguage development or the gradual, nonlinear acquisition of a new form. Learners—at beginning levels in particular—commonly demonstrate target-like use of a new form, initially within only one or two functional linguistic contexts, then regress to non-target-like production as they experiment with the form, and subsequently return to a prior state of target-like ability once the full systematicity of the form has been realized. This variability—arising in complex ways at the individual-learner level—is lost in acquisitional order research findings when learning patterns are generalized for large groups in empirical studies (Lowie & Verspoor, 2015). Recent empirical evidence of a more qualitative orientation supports the observation that there is considerable variability in learning progressions for individual learners, presenting nontrivial challenges for instructional design

(Ellis, 2015; Eskildsen, 2015; Lowie & Verspoor, 2015; Zhang & Lantolf, 2015). Indeed, some of the earliest research on developmental sequences (e.g., Clahsen, Meisel, & Pienemann, 1983; Meisel, Clahsen, & Pienemann, 1981) also observed that individual naturalistic learners varied considerably in the amount of time required to develop certain target forms, as well as their ultimate attainment after considerable time in the target language environment, to the extent that separate sociolinguistic theories of the interaction between learner and environment were developed to account for such differences (e.g., the "multidimensional model").

Finally, an important critique of order-based instruction is that using isolated, discrete linguistic components for instructional design leads to the creation of "synthetic syllabi," discussed previously (Long & Crookes, 1992). Again, designing instruction on the sole basis of linguistic elements operates under an assumption that L2 learning proceeds by acquiring "isolates" and the synthesis of these into ever more complex combinations that eventually coalesce into target-like ability. This assumption has been thoroughly challenged because it fails to account for the importance of inductive learning mechanisms applied to holistic input (Long, 2015; Long & Crookes, 1992). It also strays far from the original naturalistic language learning settings (and associated benefits, like massive input and interaction with native speaking interlocutors) in which most of the acquisition orders were first attested.

The previous critiques notwithstanding, findings on acquisition orders offer one of the few empirically backed sources of evidence for sequential language learning progressions. That being the case, if instructional design calls for focus on particular linguistic forms—ideally as a featured component of a particular text or task, for example—instructors and course designers might well present the form in a way mindful of the sequences presented previously, or at least in ways that do not overtly violate them. Conversely, analytic instructional units might be ordered in ways that not only are responsive to a variety of criteria (e.g., student needs, complexity) but also include known acquisition orders for elements that feature prominently in a particular task (e.g., the use of questioning behaviors within service encounters). We thus tentatively put forward the view that although acquisition orders by themselves do not constitute a basis for instructional sequencing, they may profitably inform other superordinate—especially analytic—approaches.

Examples of Integrated Language Instructional Sequences

Several approaches to sequencing language instructional content and objectives have emerged recently that combine multiple perspectives and integrate distinct components of the target language system into recommendations for instructed learning progressions. Here we review three proposals as examples that may prove useful for inspiring design decisions in distinct educational environments.

Proficiency Scales and Standards

Larger scale instructional sequences can be based on the orders implied within language proficiency scales, frameworks, and standards of various kinds. To the extent that they depend on consensus-based professional judgment, these may prove to be particularly salient for instruction that meets broad expectations for corresponding learner populations, and as such they should be carefully considered for any design efforts that have a public audience or dimension. For example, in the U.S., age- and grade-specific English language proficiency development standards have been created to guide teachers in helping K–12 learners achieve abilities associated with the content learning expectations in other domains of learning, such as math, science, and language arts (e.g., CCSSO, 2012; WIDA, 2012). For adult foreign language learners, again in the U.S., the American Council on the Teaching of Foreign Languages Proficiency Guidelines (Swender, Conrad, & Vicars, 2012), and the Interagency Language Roundtable (ILR, 2012) Proficiency Guidelines have served as the basis for curriculum design and sequencing decisions for many years (e.g., Omaggio Hadley, 2000). Worldwide, perhaps the best-known approach to guiding language curriculum and instruction is the Common European Framework of Reference (CEFR, Council of Europe, 2001), one explicit intended use of which is the provision of advice on what aspects of the language should be taught in what order. Organizations associated with the teaching of specific languages have in turn developed detailed guidelines regarding what should be introduced, reviewed, and mastered at each of the six CEFR levels (North, 2014). For one example, the British Council (2011) has developed the "EAQUALS Core Inventory for General English" as a guide for teachers of adult ESL learners, based on a consensus-development process that asked expert teachers to judge various language learning targets for different levels of proficiency. This guide spells out the precise language learning expectations for each CEFR level in terms of the functions, grammar, discourse markers, vocabulary, and topics that should be covered, and it provides instructional scenarios to help teachers understand how the different categories might be integrated into lesson sequences. Although potentially useful for making macrolevel decisions (e.g., those associated with distinct semesters, years, or courses of instruction), no recommendations are provided for sequencing learning within each CEFR level, nor is there much guidance regarding how much time might be required for progression from one level to the next. For these decisions, the general recommendation is that teachers or curriculum developers should conduct a thorough needs analysis of their actual learners and the learning context (including time and resources available for what ultimate scope of learning), prior to selecting and sequencing specific learning targets.

SSARC Model

Emerging out of considerable recent interest in task-based instruction, Robinson's (2011) SSARC (stabilize, simplify, automatize, restructure, complexify) model provides an important iteration in possibilities for designing language learning sequences that seek to build upon the inherent properties of communication tasks for directing learners' attention toward distinct aspects of language and performance. Fundamentally, Robinson has been interested in developing a universal set of parameters by which language task complexity can be manipulated as a means for optimal sequencing of tasks, and considerable research has been conducted under the guidance of his "Triadic Componential Framework" of task complexity, seeking to verify the complexity effects of manipulating the posited parameters, as well as the results, on learner performance. More recently and specifically (see Baralt, Gilabert, & Robinson, 2014), the SSARC model operationalizes two basic principles: (a) sequence according to the cognitive (i.e., conceptual and processing) complexity of tasks, not the variety of other factors that might affect difficulty (e.g., IDs, interactive or interlocutor variables); and (b) increase resource-dispersing dimensions of tasks (i.e., those that challenge attentional resources by introducing extraneous load) first, followed by resource-directing dimensions (i.e., those that focus attentional resources on the specific uses of language in accomplishing task performance). In practice, the combination of these basic ideas leads to the following typical instructional sequence that increases cognitive task complexity in a principled way. Note that the starting point for any given set of tasks in this sequence should be the current interlanguage state of the learner or learners (hence some judgment is required from teachers or materials designers to first select the given task or task type).

1. *Stabilize:* Task variables are all set to "simple" conditions, including, for example, allowing planning time before the task along with low cognitive demand in terms of task familiarity, number of elements, reasoning demands, and so on. This stage allows learners to recall and mobilize their existing interlanguage resources in attempting to do the task without additional pressures for performance.
2. *Simplify:* Gradual introduction of resource-dispersing dimensions (e.g., by the reduction of planning time) encourages learners to work more efficiently in deploying the language they already know.
3. *Automatize:* Additional increase in resource-dispersing dimensions, such as no planning time and working with novel input, maximizes the consolidation and automatic retrieval of existing interlanguage resources in fluent task performance.
4. *Restructure:* New challenges are introduced in the form of resource-directing variables, such as reasoning demands, that cause the learner to have to reanalyze language use in performing the task; the objective here is destabilization of the interlanguage system, but in specific directions that induce the learner to make adjustments and ultimately expand on the system (e.g., addition of new characters in a picture narrative will call for new ways of signifying who is being referred to by the learner).

5. *Complexify:* Additional challenges are provided to expand the cognitive demands of the task such that it approximates the task in authentic conditions, including both resource-dispersing and resource-directing dimensions; the objective here is to maximally "stress" the interlanguage system repeatedly, such that the learner is forced to make adjustments by incorporating new forms or by rearranging presumed relationships (e.g., past-time marking), to otherwise optimally push the learner to develop the need to communicate meaning in new ways and contexts, and to develop the awareness of possibilities for doing so.

The SSARC model has only just begun to be investigated as a means for sequencing tasks in actual pedagogic circumstances, and the primary focus has been on discrete, lesson-level sequencing decisions (i.e., the microlevel addressed previously), though a few studies have explored the possibility of using the SSARC stages in a more extended fashion to motivate the use of tasks over multiple weeks and up to a semester of instruction (see collected studies in Baralt, Gilabert, & Robinson, 2014). Clearly, a key challenge for applying this model has to do with the nature of tasks being taught and whether they can be conceptualized in terms of the dimensions of task complexity that Robinson has proposed (i.e., it is questionable whether a set of extended writing tasks might also be amenable to complexification in the ways envisioned for largely oral-interactive tasks typical of this research domain; see Byrnes & Manchón, 2014). Still, the possibility of sequencing certain kinds of PTs by resource-directing and resource-dispersing factors may prove particularly useful in making design decisions about the kinds of tasks that are often in focus in communicative and task-based approaches.

Genre-Based Pedagogy

A third approach to sequencing content for language instruction that has garnered attention in recent years is that of genre-based pedagogy (Johns, 2002; Paltridge, 2001; Swales, 1990). From a language use point of view, genres are typified ways of using language under specific social circumstances in order to achieve certain communication goals that are common to a given discourse community. Genres may occur within any of the four skills, and they may range from brief utterances (e.g., the genre of small talk or chatting) to extended discourse (e.g., giving a presentation at a conference). They are perhaps most closely associated with L2 writing instruction (e.g., Hyland, 2004), though they are by no means limited to literacy development. What is perhaps most useful about genres is that they occupy a "middle space" that integrates notions of audience and voice, discourse conventions and typicality of language use, task goals and procedures, and ultimately the linguistic features that are deployed in realizing communication. It is this integrated nature that has led to genres being proposed as a means for identifying major sequences and objectives within L2 curricula, and several curriculum development and implementation projects have been carried out utilizing genre as the basis for sequencing decisions (e.g., Byrnes, Maxim, & Norris, 2010; Swaffar & Urlaub, 2014; Yasuda, 2011).

Drawing heavily on systemic functional linguistics (Halliday, 1993), a variety of continua have been identified for distinct types of genres in various educational and professional discourse settings, with a primary emphasis on the relationships between communicative purpose and features of the texts produced. Such continua offer apparent means for ordering instruction at the macro level, including, for example,

- *Primary to secondary:* moving from a primarily oral modality in familiar circumstances with known interlocutors to a primarily literate modality in unfamiliar and institutionalized circumstances with a potentially unknown audience;
- *Personal to public:* moving from "me-oriented" to "other-oriented" language use;
- *Informal to formal:* moving from relatively unrestricted to carefully selected language use (i.e., in following conventions associated with distinct discourse communities); and
- *Congruent to metaphorical:* moving from clearly indicated and unambiguous cause-effect relationships to increasing abstraction and nuance in language use.

These continua can be used to map particular rhetorical domains or disciplinary communities in terms of how they use language to get communication done. For example, genres typical of historical communication (see Coffin, 2006) might reflect the following four stages: historical autobiography (telling my history), historical biography (telling someone else's history), historical retelling (providing a multiperspectival background and narration of events), and historical account (providing an evaluation and judgment from a particular perspective on past events). Clearly, each of these genres calls for distinct language features in their realization, thereby also implying what might need to be learned, and in what order, to be able to successfully participate in the corresponding discourse community.

For sequencing purposes, then, the delineation of meaningful genres might offer a macrolevel design strategy that also implies quite microlevel learning objectives. For example, Byrnes, Maxim, and Norris (2010) outlined how four sequential years of a university German studies curriculum were motivated primarily through a cline of genres moving from the primary, personal, routine, and informal during the first year of instruction (e.g., focusing on genres such as casual conversation, personal narratives, reading advertisements, negotiating travel arrangements, and conducting service encounters), to the secondary, public, formal, creative, and abstract during the fourth or final sequenced year of instruction (e.g., focusing on genres such as academic articles, public speaking, editorializing, and profession-specific formal encounters). These macrolevel objectives led to the identification of more specific PTs that characterized the realization of each genre, as well as the language performance features called upon in successfully transacting the tasks to the expectations of the genre. Whether a genre-based approach proves appropriate for sequencing decisions in diverse language learning contexts depends on the sophistication of the designer in understanding (or finding out about) the intimate links between discourse communities, their rhetorical practices, the genres that typify them, and the task and language requirements that provide communicative substance. Where that is the case, this approach offers some promise for structuring language education that deals holistically with form-meaning-function relationships in an integrated and highly meaningful manner.

Summary and Recommendations

This review of both recent and influential historical thinking on approaches to language instructional sequencing presents a myriad of options and possibilities. Nevertheless, it seems fair to say that there is still a somewhat nascent understanding of how best to order instructed language learning experiences, and the field awaits more empirical investigation into the recent sequencing alternatives emanating out of synthetic and analytic syllabus approaches alike. What is clear, however, is that no single method currently emerges as a universally superior choice over others in all instances. This state of affairs arguably reflects the intrinsically dynamic and context-specific—as well as long-term developmental—nature of language instruction, where different circumstances and stakeholder needs will require tailored instructional design. We thus generally advocate for a principled hybrid approach to instructional sequencing that combines elements of the aforementioned approaches in response to the particular needs of learners and specific aspects of the educational setting. The following recommendations elaborate this general proposition.

9.1. Avoid isolated, structural linguistic elements as the sole unit of instructional analysis.

    a.   Research evidence does not strongly support the long-held, traditional approach to language teaching in which learners acquire input in a piecemeal fashion, slowly accumulating linguistic items and combining these into ever more complex combinations that eventually approximate target-like accuracy and fluency.

    b.   Rather, instructed SLA research suggests that an important aspect of language learning involves engaging with holistic, textual input during meaningful interaction and allowing learners to utilize natural learning mechanisms and sensitivities to input frequency and regularity.

    c.   Utilize, then, analytic units that accommodate holistic, inductive learning processes (task, text, genre) as the privileged unit of instructional sequencing.

9.2. *Consider research on acquisitional orders (where relevant) in instructional design.*

    a.   For some languages and linguistic elements, there is evidence of consistent patterns of linguistic development in the areas of morphosyntax, tense aspect, and pragmatics.

    b.   Studies show that instruction has little effect on the route of L2 development (for a given acquisition order) and can even be counterproductive when it ignores developmental readiness.

    c.   Avoid sequencing instructional units in ways that violate known orders of acquisition.

9.3. *Structure learning experiences to accommodate different learning trajectories.*

    a.   Note that the nature of language learning development, although progressing through known acquisition orders, is nonlinear within stages and may vary in terms of rate between individuals.

    b.   Therefore, design instruction (and select instructional units) that provides sufficient flexibility and autonomy such that students can progress in ways amenable to their differing learning styles, needed time frames, and stages of developmental readiness.

9.4. *Use "analytic" units of analysis for instructional sequencing.*

    a.   Although different types of instructional units may be effective, we advocate *analytic* instructional units (task, text, genre, etc.) as being superior for instructional organization.

    b.   Analytic units have the advantage of providing holistic input that learners need in order to acquire language effectively.

    c.   The analytic approach of TBLT calls for needs analysis and the identification of tasks that respond to learners' learning goals; doing so increases the likelihood of providing learning opportunities and activities more closely attuned to learners' developmental readiness.

    d.   A TBLT instructional approach—and the use of task units for instructional design—offers one of the few theory-based rationales for instructional sequencing (on the basis of task complexity).

9.5. *Adopt a principled, hybrid sequencing approach, where appropriate, within a superordinate, analytic syllabus approach responding to student needs.*

    a.   Selecting analytic instructional units in response to student needs appears to be the best supported method for addressing issues of unit selection, scope, and sequencing, as well as learner developmental readiness and variability in rate and direction of learning.

    b.   Within this overarching structure, use principled, hybrid approaches—taken from the knowledge base of the field—to sequence instruction at micro and macro levels as appropriate.

Notes

1 Note that, as a design science, instructional sequencing has tended to be the purview of researchers and/or curriculum developers more than language teachers or materials designers per se. We are aware that the discussion in this chapter may at times be conceptually challenging, also in light of its theoretical and research origins, yet that is precisely where any substantial consideration of sequencing decisions has tended to occur. As such, although we have attempted to make this chapter's contents as "accessible" as possible, we have also tried to reflect accurately the type of attention that has been paid to related issues.

2 Steps (f), (g), and (h) exemplify what might be considered a typical formative assessment cycle, whereby learner performances with the learning material (e.g., a communication task) are first elicited, then judged by the teacher or other observer against criteria for development (e.g., standards that describe language ability on the task at the corresponding level of instruction), then feedback is given in ways that are specific to the learning at hand, and finally opportunities for improved performance and subsequent assessment are provided.

3 Robinson (2011) points out that syllabi are not always planned prior. Syllabi can also be conceived and implemented dynamically as instruction proceeds (Breen, 1984) or even constructed after instruction has occurred (Candlin, 1984).

4 Long and Crookes (1992) and Widdowson (1978) categorize notional syllabi as a synthetic, not analytic, syllabus type given that notions are essentially "isolates" to be accumulated and combined to develop language ability.

5 Note that assessments of vocabulary size have been found to correlate relatively strongly with overall proficiency, and as such, lexical frequency bands have been further promulgated as one basis for syllabus design and sequencing (e.g., Nation & Beglar, 2007).

6 See Long (2015) for more detailed discussions on how task-based teaching materials (i.e., pedagogic tasks) can be classified and sequenced on the basis of the complexity criteria described previously.

7 See also Bardovi-Harlig (2000) for a morpheme-based explanation of emergent temporal expression ordered as follows: (a) simple past, (b) past progressive, (c) present perfect, (d) past perfect.

PART 3

Second Language Educational Innovation and Support

10

LOCALIZING LANGUAGE EDUCATION

Curriculum design—and within it especially materials development—provides an essential starting point for integrating diverse decisions and actions that determine an overall approach to language education, with the ultimate goal of helping learners achieve valued language learning (and other) outcomes. Of course, curriculum and materials often begin as idealized representations of what learning achievements are thought to be possible, and what teaching practices are likely to accomplish them, whereas the local realities of teachers and learners may present a variety of important factors that will alter the appropriateness, efficiency, and effectiveness of initial plans. Critical to maximizing the utility of educational materials and designs, then, is the careful consideration of such factors and the provision of mechanisms whereby adjustments can be made. Perhaps the key factor in a majority of educational settings is the teacher per se (e.g., in terms of preparation, experience, language proficiency), hence major issues related to supporting *teachers* are considered in chapter 11. The current chapter summarizes likely challenges and proposes possible solutions related to the local realities of *language educational contexts*. First, distinct approaches to the uses of educational materials are considered, including the determination of users, medium of instruction, and articulation to curriculum standards; in addition, implications for effective delivery of materials to users are addressed. Next, two key dimensions of local context are introduced. On the one hand, the *local language learning context* is critical in establishing the instructional parameters within which materials and pedagogy must function, including factors such as the institutional setting, relative heterogeneity of learners (e.g., different first languages [L1s], proficiency levels, relative literacy), and class size, as well as distinct educational philosophies, traditions, and cultures of the particular society where materials are to be adopted. At the same time, the *local language use context* plays an important role in the setting of language learning norms and standards, perceptions about the value of language learning, access to language input and exposure to distinct varieties, and ultimately the determination of meaningful learner needs to be addressed via education. The interaction of such factors, then, will call for considered adoption or adaptation of language learning materials in situ, and recommendations are provided to guide educational designers in facilitating this inevitable process of localization.

Approaches to Delivering Language Education

A first dimension of context has to do with the ways in which educational designs and materials will actually be used by learners, teachers, educational authorities, and potentially others. Depending on the features of the local delivery model, specific characteristics will be required within the materials themselves and distinct affordances will be called upon to facilitate implementation in ways that are meaningful to the local users. An initial cautionary example helps illustrate this key contextual concern. Llosa and Slayton (2009) report on their evaluation of the large-scale and expensive adoption of a computer-based instructional program for reading skills development within the Los Angeles Independent School District. Results of experimental comparisons between kindergarten and grade 1 students in classes that received the program versus those that did not revealed rather dismal findings after the first year of implementation: there was either no perceptible difference or an actual detriment for students in the experimental classes, with particularly disappointing outcomes for the large proportion of ESL learners in the schools. However, extensive qualitative analysis of the ways in which the program was delivered revealed substantial challenges to the *potential* for materials to be effective, including (a) uncertainty on the part of teachers and principals regarding the use of the program in addition to the standing (required) curriculum and textbook, (b) lack of time available for use of the program as a supplement to the curriculum, (c) lack of learner guidance in using the program on an individual basis, and (d) lack of affordances (e.g., instructions in the L1) for ESL learners to be able to understand or benefit from the program. This example highlights the essential need to align new materials with the local context by articulating a delivery model in terms of who will use the materials, in what medium, and with what relationship to an overall curriculum or program design.[1]

Users

Users of language learning materials include, of course, learners and teachers, but the central issue here has to do with the degree of learner autonomy versus teacher or other guidance that is assumed in how materials will be accessed, engaged, and completed. At one end of the continuum, learners may be fully autonomous, making all decisions about what they learn, when, how, with what frequency, toward what goals, and so on. Key to the delivery of such self-access language materials (see Curry & Mynard, 2014; Sullivan & Collett, 2014) are considerations regarding what will be expected of learners, as well as the kinds of support needed for fully independent learning, such as (a) language of instructions provided to learners (e.g., L1s of learners); (b) clarity of materials design and structure for identifying appropriate learning paths (e.g., unit of analysis for learning, sequencing of materials); (c) technological sophistication required (e.g., for using software packages, Web-based tools); (d) learner maturity and self-awareness (e.g., ability to articulate needs, interests, ability to identify weaknesses); (e) learners' learning strategies (e.g., assumptions regarding the role of memorization or drill activities); and (f) provision and uptake of learning feedback (e.g., through self-assessment). Ultimately, learner training in self-directed learning may have to be built into successful language learning materials that are intended to be accessed in a fully learner-independent approach.

Moving away from a fully independent learning model, much more typical is the assumption that materials are most effective when some form of guidance is provided to the learner; who, or what, provides that guidance is another key question to be addressed in the delivery model. Fully automated scaffolding of language learning is, of course, increasingly common in the form of highly structured language learning software that incorporates computerized assessment, diagnosis, and feedback to facilitate learning progress through a predetermined sequence of lessons or modules.[2] Less restrictive forms of learner guidance (i.e., with more flexibility in terms of decisions regarding which materials to use with which learners, how, for what outcomes) involve peers, learning communities, or advisors and tutors in the role of mentor, helping learners to determine their goals, make intelligent choices about learning materials, assess their progress, and sustain interest and motivation (e.g., Curry, 2014; Manning, 2014; Mok, 2013). Important in the delivery of such semiguided learning materials are concerns with (a) frequency and type of guidance needed (e.g., during-lesson learning feedback vs. end-of-unit assessment and diagnosis of subsequent needs); (b) awareness and sophistication of support providers (e.g., advisor training in interpretation of assessment results); and (c) availability, sequence, and organization of materials (e.g., indication of clear paths to choose from based on what materials would be of most benefit next).

At the far end of the materials-user continuum, an individual teacher is posited traditionally as the primary user of materials, engaging in regular and sustained decision making about what learners should do, when, and how. Where the teacher is assumed to guide learning fully by judicious use of materials (McGrath, 2013), consideration should be given to issues of (a) teacher preparation and sophistication (e.g., understanding of intended learner roles and activities within lessons); (b) teacher choice (e.g., availability of alternatives, among which teachers can select the most appropriate for diverse learners); (c) teacher adaptation (e.g., flexibility of lessons to incorporate a variety of content in response to learner interests); and (d) teacher assessment (e.g., the provision of feedback to teachers that facilitates making decisions about what to do next). Fundamentally, then, who will be using materials and making decisions about language learning is a critical consideration for determining how materials will be delivered and, in particular, the types of user-oriented affordances or supports that should accompany materials.

Medium

A second, increasingly important delivery consideration has to do with the medium or media in which materials are to be encountered, as well as the number, location, and types of participants. Traditionally, textbooks and related materials have been designed to be used by individual teachers with a fixed number of relatively homogenous students all present in a single, physical classroom setting and working toward the same goals (Richards, 1985). Where that is the case (as it arguably may still be in many language learning contexts worldwide), there are considerable assumptions about the roles of materials, such as (a) a primary provider of target language input and model of language use; (b) a facilitator of critical acquisition processes such as focus-on-form and interaction; (c) a pedagogic guide and learning sequence organizer; (d) a reference tool for grammar rules, vocabulary, and so on; and (e) an assessor of language learning development. The delivery of materials that meet these assumptions involves the prepackaging of essentially everything that might be needed to foster language learning, from a textbook per se, to accompanying student workbooks, teacher manuals, audio-video supplements, tests, and other related resources (McGrath, 2007). Localization for a given language learning context, then, occurs primarily during the evaluation and selection process, as adopters decide which prepackaged materials will best meet the needs of their learners within the constraints of the teaching context.

Increasingly, however, assumptions regarding learning spaces and participants are becoming more diverse and disperse, as physical classrooms within schools give way to all possible permutations of technology mediation and distributed learning. The new default, in many language learning contexts, is that teachers and learners spend part or all of their "classroom" time outside of an actual classroom, they may be geographically distant from each other, there may be few or many participants (including L1 speakers of the target language), and a majority of their communication may transpire through the medium of the Internet and a variety of tools that facilitate synchronous or asynchronous, visual, audio or textual interactions. The primary medium of language instruction, then, is increasingly "blended" or "hybridized" as physical class meetings cede instructional time to virtual spaces and tools (Mishan, 2013). On the one hand, at least in those regions where unrestricted access to the Internet is available (which definitely is not the case worldwide at this point in time), technology enables the ultimate localization of materials in that authentic target language content and communication is essentially limitless and free—industrious teachers and learners can avail themselves of all manner of input and interaction via Web 2.0 applications in the design of language learning experiences that are maximally meaningful (e.g., González-Lloret & Ortega, 2014a), and Web 3.0 applications are beginning to provide automatic localization of a sort, in the tailoring of the Internet to patterns of individual engagement with it (as Orwellian as that might sound to some, it is the nascent reality; see details in chapter 13).[3] On the other hand, the burden on whomever designs language learning experiences—at least those that involve something more than simply surfing the Internet or participating in gaming—has increased exponentially over recent years and continues to do so as newer technologies emerge and available resources to choose from become ever more vast. Among critical concerns for the design and delivery of technology-mediated language teaching materials (see Kiddle, 2013) are (a) the choice of digital platform and associated restrictions on accessibility and sustainability; (b) the array of devices that may be used by learners and teachers to work with materials (e.g., from iPhones to tablets to computers, each with its own constraints); (c) the distribution of resources within a learning environment, from one central device to individualized access on personal devices; (d) the provision of connection, interaction, and feedback opportunities with or without mediation by a teacher; (e) the degree of technology automation (e.g., computerized feedback on L2 speech or writing) in terms of desirability, feasibility, and reality of expectations; (f) the personalization of learning spaces (e.g., with various detection, archiving, design, annotation, and other affordances for learners) and individualization of learning activities (e.g., learner- or teacher-specified goals, sequences, or preferred learning styles); and (g) the administration, scoring, and reporting of learner assessment for diagnosis and tracking, for individual- and criterion-referenced achievement, and primarily for learning-oriented feedback purposes. The effective localization of learning materials thus depends critically on decisions regarding the medium of learning that is most amenable or feasible to the specific users and targeted uses within a given context, and once the learning media have been identified, the corresponding array of possibilities and constraints must also be considered as part of the delivery model.

Relation to Curriculum

A third dimension of the delivery model addresses the relationship between materials and an overall curricular or program design. The key concern for localization here is the determination of the intended roles for materials assumed by local users, with possibilities ranging from supplemental uses to a full course-book approach. In the course-book approach, which is the traditional model for commercial materials development, the materials are assumed, by and large, to operationalize the curricular goals, scope, and sequence (Byrd, 2001). From another perspective, course books often become the default curriculum in situations where their use is mandated, where teachers and learners have limited access to other resources, or where little thought has been put into the determination of curriculum in the first place (see chapter 8). Where materials are intentionally adopted or mandated to play this primary role, key considerations include their alignment with existing curriculum, standards, policies, or other representations of the "what" and "how" that is expected by local educational authorities or decision makers, including (a) learners' needs; (b) desired learning outcomes; (c) accountability standards and mandated assessments of progress, achievement, and so on; (d) pedagogic principles, philosophies, cultures, and traditions; and (e) time and resources available. The overarching concern for materials such as course books is the extent to which they are fully capable of providing comprehensive language learning experiences that lead to desired outcomes in situ. Materials delivery should include information that is relevant for evaluating their suitability vis-à-vis these kinds of local expectations (Tomlinson, 2011, 2012). Where such expectations do not exist, it may be that materials delivery can facilitate awareness raising about the importance of curriculum and program design through the provision of frameworks for thinking about the scope, sequence, and outcomes of language learning. Indeed, the entire process of adopting new course books can be seen as a type of language teaching innovation, which may be more or less feasible and effective depending on how the innovation is enacted (Carless, 2013; Markee, 1997; see also the following chapter).

Another possibility is that materials will be adopted to supplement existing materials and pedagogy as a way of enhancing whatever teaching and learning is already taking place. Generally speaking, supplementation takes place when there is a perceived gap in what is currently available and a need to add to the educational experience (McGrath, 2002). Such additions may take a variety of forms, from new content and language input to new activities or tasks to new ways of assessing learning, and supplementation is itself often a common type of localization that occurs as teachers or others seek materials that better suit the needs of their learners or expand their learning opportunities (Carless, 2011; McGrath, 2013; Samuda, 2005). Key considerations for the adoption of supplemental materials include (a) the specificity of the perceived gap to be filled; (b) the clear purpose of the materials; (c) the general fit in terms of articulation to the existing curriculum, as well as particular components of lessons or units of instruction; (d) the flexibility of use as stand-alone content and pedagogy, typically in the form of self-contained instructional modules; and (e) the efficiency or feasibility of use in light of existing curricular expectations, teacher preparation, and so on. Supplementary materials work to the extent that they add something useful and new, above and beyond what is already being experienced, but they can only prove effective where they are carefully matched with what is in fact already being experienced and when there is time and support allocated for their use.

In sum, a first pass at localizing educational materials and designs calls for the careful consideration of what exactly will be done with materials, including who will be using materials and responsible for decisions about learning, what media and participation structures are assumed, and what roles the materials will play in relation to overarching curricular structures and pedagogic emphases. Delivery models should incorporate frameworks for facilitating local decision making about materials in light of these concerns.

Language Learning Context

A second and closely related dimension of educational context has to do with several prominent characteristics of the language learning environment per se, or those factors commonly represented as "challenges" to innovation in language teaching. It is a certainty that not all language classes across the globe are equivalent in terms of the composition and backgrounds of learners and teachers, the physical environment and educational affordances, the institutional and cultural settings, the resources invested and outcomes expected, and many other factors that characterize each environ within which language learning is supposed to take place. The effective localization of language learning materials and designs, then, must take such factors into consideration and, ideally, provide heuristics for articulating and adjusting proposed educational experiences in light of local realities. Here, three of the most commonly cited challenges are considered briefly: large classes, learner heterogeneity, and educational cultures.

Large Classes

A factor commonly cited for nonadoption of new materials and resistance to language teaching innovation is the perceived or actual challenge of class size—that is, the number of students being taught within a single class at any given time (Hess, 2001; Loo, 2010; Shamim, 2012; Watson Todd, 2013). Classes range in size for a variety of reasons, from availability of teachers, to institutional resources, to regional norms (to the increasing use of massive open online courses, or MOOCs), and what is considered large is always a relative determination. Indeed, large classes in one setting (e.g., private language institutes with multiple class meetings per week; advanced proficiency university courses; academic writing classes) may be small by comparison with another setting (e.g., public K–12 schools where language classes meet once a week; beginning language training for general education requirements in college). Still, commonly cited figures suggest that language classes with a single teacher and more than 40–50 students are typically considered to be large. Language classes are also perceived to present an especially sensitive case for student-to-teacher ratio, due to the presumed emphasis—at least in teaching oriented toward communicative competence—on pedagogic features such as interaction and group work, focused attention by the teacher on individual learners, provision of tailored and meaningful feedback across multiple skills (especially speaking and writing), individualized learning assessments, expectations of proficiency development and performance ability (i.e., vs. mastery of mere knowledge), and the cumulative nature of learning with subsequent lessons predicated on learning in previous lessons. Challenges of large language classes, then, include primarily (a) the sheer logistic and pedagogic practicality of making acquisition-rich experiences happen with greater numbers of learners; as well as related concerns with (b) learner affect, including attention, interest, participation, and motivation; (c) classroom management issues such as discipline, noise, and organization; and (d) classroom climate and associated physical, as well as rapport, limitations (LoCastro, 2001; Watson-Todd, 2013). In terms of localization, then, the typical, minimum, or expected range of class size would need to be determined for a particular context, given the likelihood that certain materials and designs will prove more or less feasible with distinct numbers of learners.

Where classes are expected to be large, a variety of possible strategies may be incorporated into materials design and delivery (also, as strategic guidance provided to teachers), such that they may be effectively adapted (see Sarwar, 2001; Shamim, 2012; Watson Todd, 2013), including the following:

- Reconceptualize the "classroom" (virtual or physical) as a time and locus for *organizing* a variety of learning activities that are subsequently undertaken by learners, individually or in groups, primarily outside of class meeting time; this distributed learning model emphasizes in-class actions such as providing instructions, schematization, review, and feedback, all based on learner work that is done independently, prior to and following class meetings.
- Emphasize collaborative and cooperative learning, project-based learning, and task-based learning, where learners are provided highly structured and extended activities that they can undertake successfully with each other and without extensive intervention by a teacher.
- Incorporate learner awareness raising and strategy development that enables learners to engage effectively in self-access, autonomous, and peer-supported learning.
- Establish explicit rules for classroom behavior; regular routines for efficient use of class time; and advance organization of goals, objectives, and procedures for each lesson or unit.
- Develop small-group learning communities within classes accompanied by a teacher rotation strategy for managing observation and feedback opportunities, such that groups of learners are regularly monitored despite the limitations of time and number of learners to be observed.
- Adopt structured and supported self- and peer assessment and feedback (and learner training in the same) incorporated into pedagogic task design, so that students regularly benefit from both giving and receiving feedback and are not reliant solely on teacher feedback, along with teacher strategies for rotating among students to provide individualized assessment and feedback on a regular, if not constant, basis. For self- and peer assessment in particular, the

focus should always be on reflection and feedback, and not grading, and this aspect should be made clear to learners from the outset.
- Use automated technology to manage and monitor pair, group, and individual work and to provide fine-grained feedback on students' performance samples, which can be complemented by delayed or distributed feedback from teachers.[4]

Learner Heterogeneity

Another potential challenge in effective localization of materials has to do with the composition of language classes in terms of learner characteristics. Learners may differ from each other in numerous ways (see chapters 3 and 4, this volume), though typical observations of L2 classroom heterogeneity (e.g., Bell, 2012; Millrood, 2002; Ur, 2005) tend to focus on language proficiency levels, degrees of literacy and educational background, and multiplicity or difference of L1s. However, many other types of heterogeneity may play important roles in determining classroom dynamics and interaction with materials and designs (e.g., gender, age, religion, aptitude, intelligences, personalities, motivation, learning "styles"). Heterogeneous classes occur in distinct settings for different reasons, though often they are a result of resource and economic demands such as, for example, when adult immigrants from distinct backgrounds are placed together into available language support classes where individually tailored curricular tracks and sequential levels of instruction are not feasible (Bell, 2012). Challenges resulting from heterogeneous constellations of learners include (a) learner de-motivation and lack of interest, imbalanced participation, differential development and achievement, and fundamentally diverse needs (e.g., distinct skills profiles for different educational backgrounds); and (b) teacher and teaching constraints in terms of demands on instructional individualization, monitoring of learning progress, provision of effective feedback, and maintenance of a positive, learner-oriented environment.

Localizing materials and designs in response to the possibility of learner heterogeneity may be accomplished through a variety of procedures and affordances included in materials, all building on the fundamental notion of *differentiated instruction* (Tomlinson, 2014; Ur, 2005), such as the following:

- Utilize initial needs analysis for determination of the important dimensions according to which learners within a class actually differ, such as language skills self-assessments, educational background protocols, interviews, and brief speaking and writing performances, all geared toward helping identify distinct profiles of learners.
- Establish individualized and personalized learning targets and trajectories to encourage learner awareness and autonomy and to enable identification of individual-referenced achievements.

- Select content (linguistic and cultural) that is capable of addressing identified learner needs and interests, including, in particular, activities that build upon learners' own background knowledge and experience.
- Deliver instruction in multiple modalities (graphic, digital, audio, literate) to enable access for learners with distinct linguistic and educational profiles.
- Provide options to enable individual choices within a given unit of instruction, such that learners maintain interest and can work within their individual capacities to achieve success; choices may involve content (what is being learned or talked about), as well as task procedures (e.g., medium or style of accomplishment) and language modality (e.g., literate vs. oral).
- Vary task designs, such that all learners are completing the same tasks, but with distinct levels of scaffolding or at different hierarchies of successful accomplishment (or degrees of task difficulty), to accommodate different proficiency levels; similarly, structured but open-ended tasks generally allow for different types of success to be achieved.
- Adopt diverse and systematically shifting collaborative structures in pair or group work, including grouping by both different and similar proficiencies, interests, or L1s and revolving assignment of specific and meaningful roles within group work (manager, note taker, informant, decision maker, etc.), all to encourage legitimate participation by all learners.
- Use jigsaw and information-gap activities that enable or require participation by all learners and the design of support structures for such participation through increase or decrease in scaffolding provided to different learners.
- Train learners (through substantial modeling, guidance, etc.) in socially appropriate and useful collaboration, interaction, feedback, and peer-teaching techniques.
- Use visual (nonlinguistic) cues, L2 models, and other kinds of rich input, especially in multilingual classrooms to enable associative, inductive, and implicit learning without reliance on explicit grammar explanation, rule presentation, and similar activities that require advanced proficiency in a common language of instruction.
- Develop individualized homework and self-access assignments that enable learners to pursue their own learning needs in depth and with the opportunity to receive highly focused feedback from the teacher or peers.
- Apply varied assessment techniques (e.g., knowledge tests, performances, best works portfolios, interviews, blogs) to maintain motivation, encourage engagement, recognize accomplishments of different kinds, and especially to provide opportunities for individualized feedback.[5]

Which of these recommendations will prove the most appropriate depends largely on the nature of the educational setting, the constellation of learners, and the purposes of instruction. Certain strategies for localizing materials and educational designs will make considerably more sense for some occasions than for others. For example, Ntelioglou and colleagues (2014) report on a superdiverse, highly multilingual elementary school class for immigrant English language learners (ELLs) in Canada, where literacy development was the primary and immediate priority of instruction. In that context, a focus on individual learner identities (within the classroom, as well as at home), diverse opportunities for learner self-expression (e.g., across modalities, across languages, across "literacies"), and a mix of collaborative and individualized tasks led to substantial development of descriptive writing abilities among the individual learners. Learner heterogeneity, in this case, became the core identity of the class and the focus of pedagogic practices, suggesting intriguingly that heterogeneous learners may provide rich opportunities—not just challenges—for diversified learning to take place.

Educational Cultures

A third major concern in the local language learning context has to do with the systemic and philosophical characteristics of educational cultures within which new materials and designs are being adopted. Language teaching takes place in a variety of institutional (and extrainstitutional) settings across distinct regions of the world, and diverse traditions of education play a considerable role in determining expectations (of teachers, learners, the public) for what language teaching "looks like" and what it hopes to achieve (Crookes, 2009b). Where new materials are being considered or delivered, however, change is inherently at stake, and change implies the potential departure from familiar traditions of practice that may lead to resistance on the part of different stakeholders, teachers in particular (Laime, 2005; Shamim, 2013). Indeed, even where new materials or approaches to pedagogy are not perceived to be linguistic imperialism enacted by empowered western societies (Canagarajah, 1999; see next section), the past several decades have witnessed substantial resistance to innovation in language teaching due to purported mismatches between local educational cultures and the new ideas being introduced (e.g., Carless, 2013; Van den Branden, 2009; Waters, 2009b; Wedell, 2009). For example, much has been made about the extent to which Communicative Language Teaching does not fit well with the prevailing philosophies and traditional learner and teacher roles in Confucian-oriented educational cultures, especially in China and Hong Kong. In these settings, it is argued, teaching traditionally involves the transmission of knowledge from teacher to learner, classrooms are thus highly teacher and not learner centered, classroom behavioral norms do not allow for "chaotic" interaction or individualization, oral communication is devalued, learners are differentially motivated, and high-stakes form-oriented examinations exert tremendous influence on what is taught and learned (e.g., Carless, 2011; Cheng & Dörnyei, 2007; Hu, 2002, 2005; Littlewood, 2007).[6] Though resistance to innovation is, therefore, often attributed to a mismatch between "western" notions of language teaching and East Asian traditions of education, similar observations have been made for other regions of the world (e.g., Africa; see Weidemann, 2002), as well as for other domains of education (e.g., resistance to adopting technology in the classroom; see Hu & McGrath, 2011). These observations thus call into question somewhat the attribution of resistance to specific educational philosophical tenets (e.g., of Confucianism) versus other situated factors (e.g., teacher workload, teacher training and support, intransigence of educational authorities, textbook-driven market economies). Moreover, the successful integration of new approaches to language education in the same contexts (e.g., Task-Based Language Teaching in East Asia; see Adams & Newton, 2009) suggests that inherent cultural traditions need not be assumed as de facto barriers.

Nevertheless, perceived or real or somewhere in between, local educational cultures will exert an influence on reactions to new materials and educational designs, hence efforts should be made to enable their localized consideration and adaptation (e.g., Carless, 2013; Hyland & Wong, 2013; Shamim, 2013; Van den Branden, 2006a, 2009), such as the following:

- Consider prevailing teacher and learner beliefs (e.g., through questionnaires, observation strategies) regarding effective language teaching and learning, teacher and learner roles, the need for change, and constraints on innovation with the objective of raising awareness about why innovation might be called for and what is possible.
- Provide teacher development (e.g., workshops related to new materials, online teacher support services) that anticipates reactions or resistance and offers explanations, solutions, and especially examples of practice with new materials in relevant situations.
- Provide examples of research studies (appropriate to the audience) that illustrate the positive impact of these potentially new practices on student learning.
- Provide learner development in the form of explicit awareness raising about the goals of language learning, roles played by the learner, metalearning strategies, and new and different expectations for the classroom environment, as well as the intended positive impact they will have on learning.
- Identify practical dimensions of the educational culture that may influence innovation (e.g., teacher workload, mandated examination systems, availability of resources), and suggest the ways in which new materials respond to or may be adapted in light of likely constraints.
- Recommend strategies for the gradual adoption of new materials and associated innovations, including appropriate time scales for change, stages of change, suggestions for managing change, and procedures for ensuring multidirectional communication about change (e.g., between teachers, principals, educational authorities, the public).

Language Use Context

Localizing materials will also call for a careful consideration of the social, economic, political, and cultural forces that are always at play in a given learning context. Moreover, global flows of capital, people, and information have created conditions in which language education is impacted not only by local circumstances but also by global modes of communication within (and between) communities of multilingual speakers. As such, particular pedagogic strategies are needed in contexts where languages must be used both locally and globally in productive ways.

English, Globalism, and Multilingualism

The prototypical example of how instructional techniques and materials interact with a local learning culture is found in the global spread of English. Historically, the global expansion of English has been understood in terms of Kachru's (1986) model of world Englishes and his concentric framework of English language use within (a) *inner-circle* nations (the U.K., the U.S., etc., where English norms originate), (b) *outer-circle* nations (e.g., established English varieties in postcolonial contexts), and (c) *expanding-circle* contexts (nations starting to learn and use English as a foreign language). Kachru characterizes theses domains as norm dependent (in the expanding circle), norm developing (outer circle), and norm providing (inner circle). The prevailing conceptualization (until recently) of how these circles interact with one another is one in which speech norms and pedagogical models originate in U.S. and British communities and, in worst-case scenarios, are imported to outer and developing-circle communities in ways that are tied to colonial aspirations and cultural and economic exploitation (typically on the part of "western" nations; see Phillipson, 1992). The result has been the denigration and devaluing of local cultures, languages, and indigenous approaches to language education. On the other hand, English has been adopted and promoted in outer and developing circles for the economic and social advancement of citizens, though even in instances with such noble intentions, English has nonetheless reinforced structures of inequality and failed to provide educational and economic opportunities across all societal levels (Ramanathan, 2005). In what might be seen as best-case scenarios, English pedagogical approaches have been localized and adapted to contexts in ways that mitigate the harmful and exclusionary ideologies latent within exported English teaching techniques and materials and try to instantiate teaching practices more culturally appropriate for local communities.

As Canagarajah and Ben Said (2010) have argued, however, the aforementioned conceptualizations no longer fully capture contemporary English forms and functions that have emerged from the societal conditions brought about by globalization. Technology, primarily, has forged a new set of relationships between communities, diasporic groups, indigenous groups, and nation-states such that the way English communication happens in complex multilingual contexts does not wholly conform to the "centre/periphery stratification" of Kachru's schema noted previously (Canagarajah & Ben Said, 2010, p. 158). Rather, the use of English throughout the world has been transformed by "transcultural flows" of people and information such that there are now nonhierarchical, multilateral interactions in and between communities during which English is used in novel, hybrid, and situationally specific ways. That is, globalized communication in English now happens in expanding- and outer-circle varieties (even within "inner-circle" contexts), using norms and grammars that do not conform to inner-circle pre-scriptions, and all of this is brought about by ever-increasing numbers of English speakers in multilingual communities that outnumber speakers in monolingual communities and nation-states.

A Pedagogy of Globalized Multilingualism

The consequence of these developments is the claim that conceptualizations of English language learning (e.g., notions of "proficiency") must be adapted to account for new modes of globalized English communication and applied in new approaches to language pedagogy that respond productively to the many hybrid uses of English, in different settings, for a variety of local and global purposes. Contemporary English must, then, be reconceptualized as a "heterogeneous language with multiple norms" (Canagarajah & Ben Said, 2010, p. 159). In addition, language ability and proficiency must likewise be redefined in terms of skills and competencies needed to negotiate communicative encounters in which novel varieties of English are used by multilingual speakers.

A number of key competencies have been proposed to accommodate these new exigencies for English language use in the 21st century (captured in the term "meta-cultural competence" coined by Garton & Graves, 2014). For example, research on English as a lingua franca suggests that learners need to develop abilities of communicative analysis—that is, they should be able to analyze, recognize, and process the features and systems of language varieties used by speakers from diverse English-speaking communities (Seidlhofer, 2004). Learners will also need to develop sociolinguistic sensitivities to different norms of politeness, considerations of identity, and other contextual communicative constraints that arise in situations where linguistic variety and diversity are the norm. In addition, successful interaction with multilingual English speakers requires particular negotiation skills that involve crossing, codeswitching, and speech accommodation, as well as interactional strategies (repair, rephrasing, clarification, etc.) and attitudinal stances (patience, tolerance, humility, etc.) conducive to intercultural communication (Canagarajah & Ben Said, 2010).

These conceptions of global multilingual language ability now call for novel approaches to language pedagogy. A "globalized English language teaching (ELT) pedagogy" thus emphasizes the social praxis of communication—interactional and pragmatic competence, in particular—over traditional, conventional empha-ses on knowledge of morphosyntax or lexis. Table 10.1 captures some of the pro-posed conceptual shifts in pedagogical practice that enable speakers to develop the needed skills for communication in situations of linguistic diversity and English multilingualism.

TABLE 10.1 Shifts in ELT Pedagogy (Adapted From Canagarajah & Ben Said, 2010)

From	To
"Target language"	Repertoire
Text and language as homogeneous	Text and language as hybrid
Joining a community	Shuttling between communities
Focus on rules and conventions	Focus on strategies
Correctness	Negotiation
Language and discourse as static	Language and discourse as changing
Language as context bound	Language as context transforming
Mastery of grammar	Metalinguistic awareness
Text and language as transparent and instrumental	Text and language as representational
First language or community as problem	First language or community as resource

Pedagogic Materials for Globalized Multilingualism

The aforementioned proposals notwithstanding, that English is now a language learned locally but used globally presents special challenges for pedagogic applications, as Modiano (2009) points out,

> While there is agreement that English is now "global" and as such is best defined as a heterogeneous entity, few practitioners have as yet been able to devise methods and curricula that can act as a basis for teaching with such understanding as the guiding principle.
>
> *(p. 59)*

This challenge is especially daunting when we consider one of the primary channels through which English pedagogy has spread internationally: language teaching materials and textbooks.

An important feature of the global spread of English has been the use of English language course books, with differential impacts on local communities depending on the circumstances of their implementation (in situ sociopolitical circumstances, student needs, teacher adaptation methods, etc.). Given the issues of linguistic imperialism noted previously, the promotion of "global" course books in outer and expanding nations is understood as problematic. Influenced by market considerations, western publishing companies create course books that can be used in as many international contexts as possible. The universal applicability of global course books has the effect of serving the profit needs of publishing companies, though possibly less so the needs of local learners and teachers (Masuhara & Tomlinson, 2008). Moreover, course books from international publishers will often reflect ideologies and pedagogical approaches that are inner-circle centric, are alien to local cultures and educational practices, and do little to promote the learning and teaching of English as an international language or lingua franca.

Of course, a key strategy in localizing language instruction is for teachers (and materials designers) to adapt course books to better suit local teaching and learner needs. Part of this process will involve making materials more relevant to a particular locale. To these ends, López-Barrios and de Debat (2014)—commenting on localizing practices in Argentina—suggest key features of local and localized English educational materials. Their proposals are theorized within a political orientation toward critical language pedagogy (see chapter 4) and global multilingualism.[7] For Lopez-Barrios and Debat (2014) localization of materials involves four main components: (a) contextualization, (b) linguistic contrasts, (c) intercultural reflection, and (d) facilitation of learning. *Contextualization* involves personalization of content by reflecting local places, personalities, and facts; creating content that is sensitive to sociocultural norms of the local culture where materials are to be used; and ensuring pedagogical fit such that approaches to teaching match the local educational culture and curriculum. *Linguistic contrasts* refers to the pedagogic use of contrastive analysis and drawing learners' attention to similarities and differences between their L1 and the target language system. *Intercultural reflection* involves designing and tailoring course-book content in ways that ask learners to analyze linguistic relations between target and local cultures, with the aim of fostering an understanding of diversity, otherness, and appreciation of differing world views. Materials need to make learners aware of the ways in which their language use represents values and assumptions drawn from their L1 systems. Finally, *facilitation of learning* refers to the inclusion of pedagogic elements that emphasize learning autonomy such that students benefit from actively reflecting on intercultural interaction and cultural modes of linguistic expression within local and global language varieties.

The current view, then, from language teaching research and commentary is that there are new imperatives for language teachers, policy makers, and publishing companies when designing and implementing language materials within specific communities. Educational decision makers must take into account, on the one hand, the political and sociocultural exigencies of language use in particular locales, especially those where language education may have ties to periods of colonial rule (e.g., India, Bangladesh, Algeria, and numerous island nations of the South Pacific, to name a few). Materials should thus represent local people, concerns, contexts, practices, and topics of interest because these will be more relevant to local language learning needs and modes of use (Garton & Graves, 2014). On the other hand, educators and publishers need be mindful of the ways in which languages are used internationally and globally, untethered to any central authority prescribing linguistic norms and standards. Materials should thus represent a range of global contexts and speakers and provide a variety of strategies for communicating with multilingual speakers via lingua franca and international forms.

Summary and Recommendations

In sum, this chapter has emphasized the importance of considering various dimensions of local context in the development and dissemination of appropriate and useful language learning materials and related educational designs. Key dimensions for consideration include the actual delivery model (in terms of users, media, and relationship to curriculum), potentially challenging features of the local learning context (e.g., class size, learner heterogeneity, and educational traditions and cultures), and characteristics of the local language use context (e.g., the influence of globalization, assumptions regarding multilingualism, norms and standards of the target language, and the effects of language teaching on the local context). In responding to these important concerns for localization, it is likely that a needs-driven (vs. universalist) approach to materials development and educational design will be called for. For example, Jolly and Bolitho (2011) advocate the following steps in a contextually responsive approach to materials development and evaluation: (a) identification and exploration of needs for materials, (b) contextual realization of materials in locally meaningful ways, (c) pedagogic realization of materials in learning-oriented ways, (d) materials production and delivery in locally feasible ways, and (e) use and evaluation of materials in situ.

A mechanism or set of procedures whereby good ideas (i.e., new materials or educational designs) can be converted realistically into good local practice should include consideration of the following recommendations.

10.1.   *Align new materials with the local context by articulating a specific delivery model.*

    a.   Who will use the materials? Users may range from autonomous learners in self-access settings to distributed learners and teachers in technology-mediated settings to teachers in traditional classrooms. Materials should be accompanied by support structures that help actual users understand and benefit from the attendant educational designs.

    b.   In what medium will materials be accessed? Materials may consist of course books, computer programs, Web-based modules, and so on. Depending on the primary medium of use, guidance for implementation and utilization will be required.

    c.   How will materials be articulated to existing curriculum? Materials may be supplementary, intended to fill specific gaps in existing educational practice, or they may be intended to fully replace and innovate existing (or nonexisting) curriculum. Depending on intended uses, frameworks for evaluating the fit of materials to local curricular expectations will facilitate their appropriate adoption.

10.2.   *Take into account likely challenges in the local language learning context.*

    a.   For large classes (e.g., >50), provide strategic guidance to teachers, pointing to possible alternatives in implementing materials, including adaptations to classroom structures, learner dynamics and responsibilities, individual versus group or project work, self- and peer assessment practices, and so on.

    b.   For heterogeneous classes (e.g., mixed proficiency or L1), build flexibility and differentiation into materials such that, based on an initial understanding of learner composition, tasks and other educational activities may be diversified according to content, modality, choice, scaffolding, personalization, learner roles, feedback, and so on.

    c.   For encouraging innovation in distinct educational cultures (e.g., Confucian oriented), materials should be accompanied by heuristics for clarifying their rationales and purposes and for adaptation to local traditions of practice, as needed, including the identification of teacher and learner beliefs, local *means analysis* (i.e., of situational affordances and constraints on innovation), teacher and learner development in learning approaches, and strategies for gradual adaptation and change.

10.3.   *Use various strategies to make instruction relevant in the local educational context.*

    a.   Materials and instruction should reflect aspects of local cultures including depictions of local people, concerns, contexts, practices, and topics of interest, as well as, where relevant, local modes of L2 language varieties.

    b.   Ensure that teaching approaches and methodologies are relevant to and not in conflict with local values, morals, and other cultural traditions.

10.4.   *Integrate a range of linguistic varieties into materials, as well as strategies for interacting successfully with multilingual speakers.*

    a.   Instruction should provide examples of different language forms spoken by multilingual speakers in a variety of communicative situations.

    b.   Provide instruction on communicative strategies for interacting with multilingual speakers and using the target language as an international lingua franca.

10.5.   *Provide opportunities for students to analyze and reflect on different aspects of multilingual communication.*

    a.   Instruction and materials should provide opportunities for analysis and reflection on culturally based communicative differences between target language varieties and the student's L1(s).

    b.   Ask learners to analyze linguistic relations between target and local cultures in order to foster understanding of diversity, otherness, and appreciation of differing world views.

Notes

1 Of course, the example also points to the critical need to provide for teacher professional development whenever such innovations are introduced, but such development begs the initial question of how new materials are supposed to be used in the first place.

See the following chapter for suggestions regarding teacher professional development in conjunction with the introduction of new materials.

2 Though it should be noted that the accuracy and effectiveness of such automated guidance remains relatively undetermined.

3 For one example, an individual learner might be prompted automatically upon entering a particular type of store with key phrases related to shopping in that store, and even related to shopping for particular items in that store related to the learner's shopping history, all based on the detection of the store by a GPS-integrated application that was downloaded to the learner's mobile phone.

4 See chapter 13 for additional discussion of the incorporation of automated technologies into educational design for a variety of purposes.

5 Note that many of these recommendations may be usefully augmented or fully facilitated by computer technologies that automatically process information about the diverse characteristics of learners in order to tailor learning experiences. Further discussion on this topic can be found in chapter 13.

6 Interestingly, developments in national curriculum policies and large-scale language testing suggest that these claims are shortsighted. For one example, in China, the College English Test has introduced both writing and speaking performances as a standard part of assessment since the early 2000s, and the College English Curriculum has encouraged innovation toward communicative and learner-oriented language teaching for some time (see, e.g., Zheng & Cheng, 2008).

7 The Lopez-Barrios and Debat proposals appear in a collection of essays edited by Garton and Graves (2014) describing various approaches to localizing English language teaching (ELT) materials in Bahrain, Argentina, Algeria, Albania, Thailand, Bangladesh, Portugal, South Korea, and Japan.

11

SUPPORTING TEACHERS IN UTILIZING LANGUAGE LEARNING MATERIALS

In addition to context-, program-, and curriculum-related localization of innovative language learning materials, in most instructional settings worldwide the primary arbiter of language learning is the teacher (though see increasing interest in self-access approaches to language learning, e.g., Watkins, Curry, & Mynard, 2014). Depending on characteristics of the institutional setting and other factors, language teachers may take responsibility for any and all of the following actions: determining teaching objectives and learning outcomes; crafting syllabi and unit and lesson plans; selecting and sequencing materials; providing target language input and modeling learning and language behaviors; introducing learning tasks and schematizing and motivating learners to engage with them; monitoring learner behavior and development via ongoing formative assessment; providing crucial feedback articulated to learners' emerging language needs; assessing learner progress and achievements; and generally managing the classroom or other learning environment. What teachers do with materials in any of these dimensions will depend, to some extent, on what they are asked or required to do. Teachers may be expected to "teach" the textbook strictly and fully, they may be held accountable to student performance on standards-based or materials-related exams, they may feel compelled to align instruction with cultural traditions of education, or they may be encouraged to act autonomously in utilizing materials as they see fit. Teachers' actions also depend considerably on who they are, where they come from, and what their experiences have been. Language teachers vary in important ways, including, in particular, their level of general education and teaching-specific preparation; their proficiency in the target language; their familiarity with recent developments in language pedagogy and assessment; their own language learning backgrounds and assumptions regarding effective language instruction; and their professional, social, and economic circumstances. All of these factors, then, will conspire to determine the particular demands on, and possibilities for, how teachers utilize language learning materials. In this chapter, several of these key factors are explored from the perspective of the teacher, in order to identify practices that may best support diverse language teachers in working with new, innovative, and potentially challenging language learning materials.

Although sustained teacher professional development—and "lifelong learning"—are considered increasingly to play a critical role throughout teachers' careers, the focus here is not on language teacher preparation or ongoing development per se. That topic should be the focus of another volume and, of course, addressed in teacher education programs. Rather, the focus in this chapter is on what kinds of support might also be provided to teachers as innovative educational materials and designs are introduced into their working contexts. In other words, what is the responsibility of the producer of the materials in terms of helping teachers in diverse circumstances to work with new ideas effectively? Materials producers probably should not be held responsible for teacher development programs in the first instance, but they do have a responsibility to enable innovation as teachers work with their products and new ideas.

What Are Teachers Expected to Do With Language Learning Materials?

As a fundamental starting point, it is important to consider what it is that language teachers actually do with materials. Though it may be the case in some circumstances that teachers feel compelled, for a variety of reasons (e.g., Zheng & Davison, 2008), to let the materials be the syllabus and do the teaching, most contemporary approaches to language learning materials development (see, e.g., Gray, 2013; McGrath, 2013; Tomlinson, 2013) presume a language-teacher-user who has undergone training and development to some extent, who assumes the rights and responsibilities of a professional, and who is provided a degree of autonomy in decisions regarding classroom practice. Indeed, language teachers are often likely to be materials developers themselves, if not the local translators, of materials that must be tailored for use with specific learners in particular settings. Most basically, teachers use materials as a means for organizing and implementing the instructed language learning process, including providing language, cultural, and other content input; engaging learners in pedagogic activities that require the processing and use of input; creating opportunities for reflection and feedback; and assessing learner development and achievement. Teachers also use materials to sequence instruction within the time and resources available and toward expected learning outcomes. Rather than merely delivering materials, then, teachers are generally assumed to (a) interact with materials in making planned and spontaneous, immediate to long-term decisions about how instruction will occur and (b) work with materials and learners in creating ongoing learning opportunities.

A common model describing how language teachers work with materials (McGrath, 2013) suggests several stages. First, teachers engage in course planning and design, setting out a sequence of instructional units and lessons within available time toward the achievement of certain learning outcomes by their particular learners; of course, any or all of this planning work might be mandated to greater or lesser extent (e.g., by national standards, district or school curriculum), yet all but the most disenfranchised teachers will think to some extent about the design of the courses they teach. Second, teachers analyze materials according to a variety of possible criteria in order to select those materials that will most effectively align with the course plan and promote the achievement of targeted outcomes; analysis and selection happens both during long-term planning (e.g., what to cover in a semester) and in more immediate decision making (e.g., what to cover in tomorrow's lesson or how to adjust in real time what is happening in today's lesson). This analysis implies, on the one hand, a good understanding of the learning context and the learners themselves and, on the other hand, a sense of the qualities of effective learning materials. Numerous guides are available for the preadoption evaluation of materials by teachers (e.g., McDonough, Shaw, & Masuhara, 2013; McGrath, 2002; Mukundan & Ahour, 2010; Tomlinson & Masuhara, 2004), though they all recommend analyses of factors like learning and pedagogic theory; alignment with research findings on instructed language learning; interest and relevance; motivational potential; flexibility of use; pedagogic guidelines; built-in teacher development; inclusion of multiple dimensions of language and culture; treatment of diverse learning styles; focus on learner affect and emotion; opportunities for language input, output, and feedback; development of learner awareness and approach to language learning; useful assessment strategies; and logistical requirements (including cost, technology, and other resource demands).

Once selection and adoption decisions are made on the basis of such criteria, teachers allocate materials to corresponding portions of the syllabus, and they begin working with materials and learners to enact instruction. As teachers transition from the selection of materials to their use in specific settings, they inevitably engage in adaptation—that is, they tailor materials to better meet the needs of their learners, to function within the constraints of their educational settings, and otherwise to improve the fit and effectiveness of materials (Saraceni, 2013). Adaptation may involve a variety of processes, including reduction, rearrangement, supplementation, expansion, development, and editing (Tomlinson, 2003), and it typically occurs for purposes such as (a) localization (aligning with cultural and linguistic concerns, eliminating taboo topics, adjusting targets of learning); (b) modernization (updating of usage, vocabulary, stereotypical content, authentic communicative situations,); (c) personalization and differentiation (articulating topics, content, skills focus, etc., to learner interests and needs); (d) leveling (simplification, elaboration, reordering of language teaching according to learners' proficiencies and need for appropriate challenge); and (e) balancing of skills (integration of multiple skills, addition of productive to receptive materials and vice versa). It is also typically the case that teachers evaluate materials in use, either informally or formally, in order to make spontaneous adjustments during instruction, as well as to inform longer term considerations regarding materials' effectiveness and the need for additional adaptation or selection and development of new materials. Evaluations of materials in use may take a variety of forms, though they typically focus on both learner and teacher reflections about specific phenomena (e.g., clarity of instructions and explanations, topic interest and learner engagement, time requirements) and more general concerns (e.g., value, fit with learning theory, attractiveness; see various criteria and checklists in McGrath, 2013). They may also focus on observations regarding what specifically transpired during pedagogic tasks or other parts of lessons, as contrasted with what had been planned (e.g., Ellis, 2011; Jolly & Bolitho, 2011).

In sum, then, teachers may be expected to (and they do) interact with language learning materials in a variety of ways, ranging from merely following instructions in a textbook or pressing play on a computer program to engaging deeply with the content and pedagogy of materials in order to make important decisions as they are selected, adapted, and evaluated for use. The implications for a reflective, well-informed teacher practice—or simply for the appropriate use of most materials—are considerable. Teachers must (a) understand materials, their rationales, the techniques they employ, and the goals they target and (b) be prepared to work with materials in terms of the demands they make (e.g., on teachers as models, guides, facilitators, explainers, providers of input and feedback). Teachers must know how to evaluate materials according to criteria that are meaningful within their educational circumstances. Accordingly, teachers must understand their contexts, the societal and curricular standards to which they are held accountable, the constraints and affordances within their classrooms (or other learning spaces), and in particular their learners (and the variety of ways in which learners can vary, from educational background, to proficiency in the target language, to learning styles, to interests, and so on). Teachers must also be able and willing to make decisions about materials on the basis of these understandings, and they must learn from materials along the way. If these are the expectations for how teachers work with language learning materials, then the reverse is also at least desirable if not to be expected: *language learning materials themselves should be designed in ways that facilitate all of these teacher actions.* The following sections explore several ways in which teachers can be supported by materials and accompanying practices, such that they may work jointly toward creating effective language learning experiences.

Analyzing Teacher Needs in Using Materials

One way in which teachers can be supported is through the provision of tools and procedures for analyzing their own needs and matching the results with options in language learning materials. Thus, it is clear that language teachers' beliefs, training, experience, and confidence affect how they work with materials and what effects the ensuing instruction has on language learners (e.g., Nel & Müller, 2010), and it is simultaneously true that aspects of the teaching context (e.g., national policies, standards, institutional expectations, mandated curricula, exams, learners) will constrain the possibilities for using innovative materials (e.g., Goto Butler, 2011; Johnson, 2006). Needs analysis techniques (e.g., Huhta et al., 2013; Long, 2005b) can be used to raise teachers' (and others', like supervisors', curriculum designers', etc.) awareness about these factors and provide a basis for making decisions about materials selection and adaptation. Methods for eliciting data might range from existing questionnaires on established constructs (e.g., Foreign Language Teaching Anxiety Scale, Beliefs About Language Learning Inventory; see Horwitz, 1985) to surveys designed to access teachers' backgrounds, abilities, and perspectives on language teaching. Interview and focus group protocols might help tap deeper into the dispositions of teachers in specific settings toward the teaching, learning, and materials therein. Checklists and related inventories might also enable teachers to consider the influence of contextual variables on what is possible and desirable, versus not feasible, in their materials-related teaching endeavors.

Teachers themselves would form a particularly high-priority focus for an analysis of needs related to using materials. Teacher beliefs about the nature of effective language pedagogy, the role of grammar instruction, the possibilities for learner autonomy, the roles played by formative and summative assessment, and the use of technology in the classroom, among other factors, have received extensive attention as sources of influence on whether and how teachers work with innovative materials in diverse contexts worldwide (e.g., Basturkmen, 2012; Borg & Al-Busaidi, 2012; Farrell & Ives, 2015; Goto Butler, 2011; Mama & Hennessy, 2013; Mills, 2013; Underwood, 2012). Other prominent factors that have been shown to affect teacher practice include proficiency in the target language (Braine, 2013; Chambless, 2012; Eslami & Fatahi, 2008), knowledge of the language system (Lantolf, 2009), language learning experiences (R. Ellis, 2007), and pedagogical knowledge (Gatbonton, 2008). Additionally important would be considerations of teaching experience, training, and qualifications; specific skills or expertise (e.g., with technology); familiarity with contemporary developments in language pedagogy and assessment and with associated materials; and affective factors such as morale, anxiety, stress, and motivation (Jacobs & Farrell, 2001; Richards, 2001; Tsui, 2003). Finally, teachers' personal and professional situations may play a pivotal role in whether materials innovation is even possible, including questions regarding how many contact hours they teach per day or week, how many different teaching positions (or other jobs) they hold, whether they have time and support for experimenting with new materials or developing new capabilities, and fundamentally whether they are open to or capable of change in the first place (Markee, 1997; Richards, 2001).

Teachers' beliefs and behaviors may also be interpreted at least in part as reflections of the contexts within which their educational work takes place. Without a doubt, factors external to the teacher will exert considerable force on what they are able, encouraged, required, or supported to do, including what materials they work with and how they do so (see, e.g., Carless, 2011; Pan & Block, 2011; Richards, 2001; Zheng & Davison, 2008). Key contextual factors with a bearing on the use of materials might be the following:

- *Societal and governmental:* roles of the target language and other languages, social status of education, cultural traditions of education, language and education policies and mandates, national exams and traditions of assessment, public perceptions of language learning and teaching, economic demands on language education, media attention, pressures to conform, and so on;
- *Professional:* certification or other requirements for teaching, opportunities for teacher development, standards for language learning and education, perception of teaching as a profession, and so on;
- *Institutional:* leadership, physical and technological resources, curriculum and targeted learning outcomes, mandated assessments, available instructional time, class size, role of textbooks and other materials, instructional staff, esprit de corps, openness to innovation, teacher autonomy, and so on; and
- *Learners:* beliefs and attitudes toward language learning, educational and linguistic backgrounds, reasons for study, affective variables (motivation, styles, etc.), interests and needs, heterogeneity, access to learning outside of the classroom, and so on.

It is very likely that some or all of these external variables will interact with teachers' own internal variables to condition the possibilities for innovation via materials, never mind the day-to-day uses of materials by teachers. The implication for supporting teachers, then, is that such factors first need to be understood before materials can be effectively selected, evaluated, adapted, and utilized. On the one hand, large-scale materials development and innovation initiatives might first undertake analysis of these kinds of teacher-internal and teacher-external needs comprehensively like, for example, the needs analysis described by Mody (2013) in conjunction with school innovation and teacher development initiatives in India. Here, needs analysis would require considerable time and effort, be multimethodological, engage a variety of stakeholder perspectives, and likely be facilitated by an evaluation expert. On the other hand, and more amenable to actions by individual teachers or schools, materials publishers might endeavor to provide simplified tools for use by prospective teachers in identifying particularly salient dimensions of these kinds of needs, as well as recommendations regarding which materials to adopt or how to adapt them, depending on the specific profiles that result from needs analysis. Here, needs analysis would encourage awareness raising among teachers of the factors that enable or constrain their teaching in particular ways; at the same time, materials developers would also be encouraged to confront the challenges of aligning innovative pedagogic products with diverse potential users and educational contexts. The outcome of both approaches to needs analysis would be a basis for selecting and adapting materials according to local teacher circumstances, not only in recognition of what might not work, but also as a means for introducing appropriate changes into their language teaching practices.

Supporting Teacher Use of New Materials

Once materials have been adopted, teachers interact with them in several ways to create language learning opportunities. With the introduction of new, innovative materials, teachers must come to understand the pedagogic rationale underlying their design, learn to work with the materials as designed, engage in ongoing adaptation of materials in ways that are appropriate to their learners and settings, and evaluate materials for effectiveness and improvement. Helpful for teachers, then, is the provision of a variety of built-in or supplemental support structures that facilitate their learning about and use of materials; in this sense, teachers working with new materials and adapting them to their own needs may be conceived as an awareness-raising and professional development process (e.g., Bolitho, 2003). In other domains of educational materials and teacher research, this orientation toward an explicit awareness-raising function has come to be referred to as "educative curriculum materials" development (e.g., Davis & Krajcik, 2005), though evidence (at least in the published literature) is scant that such a movement has been taken up within large-scale language materials publishing. Perhaps a more modest target is achievable in the short term for language learning materials, where, according to Saraceni (2013), " [. . .] materials developers should produce materials with the specific aim of facilitating the evaluation and inevitable adaptation process: materials purposely designed to be adapted later by their users" (p. 56).

Research into how language teachers around the world work with new materials (e.g., Bell & Gower, 2011; East, 2012; Masuhara et al., 2008; McGrath, 2013; Tomlinson, 2008) suggests that the following kinds of support, provided by materials publishers and developers, may be beneficial to facilitating teacher understandings and actions:

- *Comprehensible introduction to teachers* about the language learning and pedagogic theory underlying the design of materials, accompanied by clear examples of how learning is supposed to take place in relation to key materials components (e.g., input processing activities, interactive tasks, performance assessments, homework assignments) and what observable learner behaviors might indicate (e.g., uptake, comprehension, confusion, de-motivation).
- *Comprehensible introduction to learners* about the nature of language learning, how it is addressed in the materials, and what the implications are for them in terms of learning behaviors.

- *Annotated teaching guidelines* for each unit and lesson, or *learning object*, providing suggestions for classroom implementation, ongoing formative assessment, and expected learning processes and outcomes that should occur.
- *Sample lesson plans* that illustrate how materials might be used and adapted, including core or baseline versions and possible variations based on learner proficiency levels, needs and interests, styles, and so on, as well as factors such as time available (e.g., extending or reducing content covered), class size (e.g., teacher-individual vs. teacher-group interactions), and so on.
- *Suggestions for (and examples of) adaptation* based on known factors that influence learner engagement, such as personalization of topic or content addressed in each lesson or localization of tasks to those relevant for particular settings or learner types (e.g., vocational vs. academic courses).
- *Recommendations for differentiation of pedagogy*, particularly in terms of challenge presented to learners, such as the inclusion of input options (e.g., texts of differing levels of difficulty) or task-procedural options (e.g., scaffolded task performance vs. learner choice in how to complete a task).
- *Customization of materials according to the learning context*, including (a) modular materials, which present self-contained (i.e., not prepackaged into a course book or sequenced in a fixed order) lessons or units covering particular content, language, and task learning targets and which may be selected and sequenced as determined by teachers or local curriculum designers; or (b) local materials designed with a specific group of learners and expectations in mind.
- *Additional resources* that may be used to augment, supplement, or replace materials, including alternative content, tasks, assessments, sources of linguistic and cultural input (e.g., video, audio, and textual artifacts), and so on.
- *Tools and procedures for evaluating materials*, including learner surveys, teacher self- and peer-observation protocols, outcomes assessments, and a variety of informal assessment practices that may be incorporated into daily use of materials.

Depending on the delivery model for the materials in question, much of the aforementioned suggestions may be provided in a teacher textbook manual, though increasingly the locus of materials themselves, as well as support structures, tends to be on materials-related websites. With web-based materials delivery, the possibilities for teacher support expand considerably, as do the possibilities for the design of materials themselves and types of learner support. For one example, a quick review of the Oxford University Press English Language Teaching website[1] indicates the following affordances provided to teachers in relation to any of a wide array of language teaching materials: teachers' club website (a portal into teacher support opportunities); teaching blogs; webinars and instructional videos; examples of teachers using materials; supplementary input, activities, and tasks; assessment tools; research publications related to materials and teaching; downloadable interactive applications (e.g., iTools) for teachers and learners; and others. For each set of materials, there is also considerable product information provided, as well as specific pages on "teacher resources" and "learning resources." Clearly, Web-based platforms such as this one offer tremendous possibilities for supporting teachers in the use of language learning materials, though with several attendant challenges. One, of course, is the variable accessibility of the Internet and associated technologies to possible teachers in diverse situations worldwide; many English teachers probably would not be able to take full advantage of what is made available. A second issue has to do with the potential for information overkill and the ability to navigate and filter through what is available to arrive at what is needed for understanding and utilizing certain materials. A third issue, or question, is whether the various support structures are oriented toward facilitating the kind of careful, reflective teacher practice that is involved in the inevitable adaptation of commercial materials to local needs, as opposed, perhaps, to the selling of more materials.

Supporting Teacher Use of Assessments

Assessments may present a special case of new materials, calling for additional considerations in terms of what kinds of support teachers will need in order to make the most of them. Although assessment is likely best conceived as one among several integrally connected components that constitute an educational context (see chapters 7 and 8), it is also the case that teachers often distinguish assessment as a unique activity, separate from pedagogy, materials, and syllabus design (e.g., East, 2015; Winke, 2011). Language teachers may also lack the necessary knowledge and abilities for understanding, interpreting, and utilizing assessments, leading to the recent rise in attention being paid to "assessment literacy" and its development among language teachers (Fulcher, 2012; Malone, 2013). In addition, in many contexts, it is clear that the traditional role for assessment has been to enact external policies set by educational authorities, frequently delimiting, rather than contributing to, innovations or improvements in teaching and learning (e.g., Carless, 2011, 2013). Clearly, then, teachers may require a variety of types and degrees of support when it comes to using assessments and assessment-based information in new or innovative ways.

Where assessments are intended to play a primarily internal, formative role within the classroom, Wylie and colleagues (2012) provide a systematic approach to helping teachers develop their own capacities to work with such assessments. Their approach includes the following stages:

1.   Considering characteristics and practices typical of good formative assessment and selecting a target among these for self-study and improvement;
2.   Identifying individual strengths and weaknesses in the target area through self-evaluation and then setting manageable goals for immediate improvement;

3. Working toward improvement by trying out new ideas, reflecting on how they worked, revising the approach, and trying things out again; and
4. Looking for evidence of the effectiveness of personal change and deciding when to move on and work on new challenges of formative assessment.

For example, in an educational setting where new emphasis is being placed on students' abilities to speak English, a teacher might identify the provision of feedback on authentic speaking tasks as a key use of formative assessment in need of attention in her own practice. She might then set about studying how others (peers, or examples in the published literature) utilize assessments to provide meaningful and developmentally appropriate feedback to learners on their speaking abilities, and she might evaluate the extent to which she feels prepared to do the same with her own students. A next step would involve trying out a small-scale speaking feedback project, wherein a task is provided to students to perform in front of the class, and a rubric is used by the teacher to rate the performance according to key English-speaking criteria and offer suggestions for improvement. A final step in the cycle would see the teacher evaluating the extent to which she feels comfortable incorporating this dimension of formative assessment into her regular practice and then deciding to either work further on refining her approach to speaking feedback or move on to another dimension of formative assessment.

As is the case in this example, innovations in language assessment most recently have taken the form of introducing a performance orientation into educational situations that traditionally featured selected-response tests of knowledge about the language rather than a focus on ability to use the language for communicative purposes (e.g., East, 2012, 2015; Norris, 2016). Certain characteristics of performance assessment may provide an essential opportunity for helping language teachers develop their own understandings about both how assessments can and should work in the classroom, as well as what the implications might be for revising educational practices. Darling-Hammond and Falk (2013) suggest that, where the following practices are used in introducing performance assessments, teacher development and educational change will be maximized as a result:

*   Ensure that performance assessment is integral to the learning system.
*   Include performance tasks as part of assessments.
*   Ensure that rubrics for scoring assessments are clear and explicit.
*   Involve teachers in collaborative scoring of assessments.
*   Expand opportunities for teachers to engage in assessment.
*   Provide teachers with coaching and professional development around assessment.
*   Build communities of practice to inform performance-assessment work.

It may also be the case that assessments themselves can offer teachers considerable support in achieving new goals within the classroom and in enacting innovation or reform. Technology-mediated assessments are evolving rapidly, and

considerable possibilities already exist for the use of automation to scaffold learners by providing instantaneous and learner-relevant feedback (see the review of
possibilities and examples of technology-mediated language assessment in chapter 13). Such uses of assessment may free teachers' time for attending to other
dimensions of their work, or they may offer assistance in helping teachers achieve
deeper understandings of individual learners' progress, achievements, and needs.

Teacher Development and Educational Reform Through New Materials

Beyond facilitating teacher understanding, use, and adaptation of materials for
their particular needs, through the provision of various support structures that are
delivered along with materials, it may also be that adopting and working with new
materials (including assessments) implies a commitment to educational reform.
Such a commitment may be implicit or explicit, locally conceived by a teacher
or teachers versus mandated by an institution or government, but at some level
the notion of reform or innovation is inherent in the adoption of new materials.
Forward-thinking materials developers, perhaps those that work hand in hand
with local curricular authorities and language teachers themselves, might thus
conceive of their work as incorporating teacher development and reform of the
educational system, as suggested, for example, in relation to mathematics education by M. Brown (2009):

> If, however, developers appreciate that teaching involves a process of design
> and view materials as resources to support such a process, then the errand
> of such materials shifts from simply transmitting instructional ideas to
> transforming practice by serving as a catalyst for local customization [. . .]
> Materials that support teacher design stand a better chance of engaging
> practitioners with the curricular ideas the reform intends to foster and thus
> have a greater potential to transform teacher practice.
>
> *(p. 18)*

Where transforming language teacher capacities and practices is the target, it
may be that additional kinds of support will be needed to foster ongoing development that leads to perceptible improvements in educational outcomes. Teacher
development and change is a robust domain of research and practice, both in
mainstream and language education, the details of which are beyond the scope of
this chapter (in reference to language teachers, see, e.g., Borg, 2003, 2006; Feryok,
2010; Johnson, 2006, 2009; Kubanyiova, 2007, 2009, 2015; Tsui, 2003; in mainstream education, see, e.g., Darling-Hammond et al., 2009; Garet et al., 2001).
What seems clear, though, is that teacher change—that is, transformations of what
teachers know, think, and believe (teacher cognition), as well as how they act in
teaching—is dependent on multiple factors, including the contexts and cultures

in which teachers work, possibilities and encouragement for change, opportunities for learning, motivation to change, individual visions of change and a new "teacher self," normative obligations, fear of change, and others. However, despite the possible complexities of teacher change, it is widely agreed that this factor is at the heart of language educational innovation (e.g., Adamson & Davison, 2003; East, 2012; Markee, 1997; Van den Branden, 2009), and teacher reactions, reinterpretations, and buy-in will determine much of what happens as a result of educational reform efforts. There is also evidence that language teachers can and do change even in what might be considered challenging environments worldwide (e.g., Hiver, 2013; Mushayikwa & Lubben, 2009; Xu & Connelly, 2009; Zhan, 2008), though change is not always to the extent or of the sort originally anticipated.

What, then, are the types of support that might accompany new language learning materials when what is at stake involves a transformation of teacher cognition and action? Generally speaking, research suggests that any approach to effective teacher professional development should be intensive, ongoing, and connected to practice; focus on the relationship between teaching and student learning and address the teaching of specific curriculum content; align with school (or other external) improvement priorities and goals; and build strong working relationships among teachers (Darling-Hammond et al., 2009). Within language teaching, one specific example will serve to illustrate some of the possibilities for materials-related teacher support and development. In the area of task-based language teaching (TBLT), several evaluations have been conducted related to the introduction of new materials as part of language educational innovation (e.g., McDonough & Chaikitmongkul, 2007; Towell & Tomlinson, 1999; Van den Branden, 2006a). Evidence that has accrued from these evaluations suggests that (a) teacher understanding and buy-in of materials is crucial to reform, (b) teachers do change, and (c) change is iterative and requires substantial time. One instance in particular, related to the introduction of TBLT into Dutch second language (L2) education in Flanders, Belgium, is particularly revealing of the kinds of teacher support that were necessary for teacher development and change to ensue. As described in Van den Branden (2006a), through a series of more or less trial-and-error efforts at bringing about language teaching reform in Flemish schools, materials developers and teacher trainers eventually identified several key types of teacher support, including the following:

- Provision of annotated and well-articulated examples of syllabi to accompany materials (textbooks, in this case), including examples of how the new materials accomplished certain objectives (like the teaching of grammar);
- Task-based teacher development workshops that demonstrated the use of actual materials via task-based methodologies (i.e., by having the teachers work through tasks from the point of view of both learners and teachers) and that were delivered repeatedly (not one shot);

- School-based TBLT expert coaches who were responsible for ongoing observation and feedback to teachers as they worked with the new materials, as well as for answering questions and providing ideas for materials use on an ad hoc basis (as requested by teachers);
- Persistent development and revision of materials themselves to meet teachers' expressed needs, including, in particular, materials that were flexibly adapted to diverse learners and teaching concerns; and
- Encouragement of teacher agency through sustained involvement of teachers in the selection and adaptation of materials; the evaluation of materials (and subsequent improvements); and collaborative sharing of observations, assessments, and reflections on the use of materials in the classroom.

In the Flemish TBLT case, over some 10 years of innovation efforts, it became clear that robust guidelines, explanations, demonstrations, and examples of how to teach with task-based materials were necessary but not sufficient. Profound teacher change only came about when teachers were involved as active agents in the process of materials use, adaptation, and evaluation. In particular, the availability of persistent and individualized support was highly valued by the teachers as a means for engaging in on-the-job professional development and educational reform simultaneously, all proceeding hand in hand with the use of innovative materials.

In light of this example, it may be that additional support structures and opportunities might be conceived in conjunction with the development and delivery of new language learning materials. Robust and repeated opportunities for engaging teachers with new materials and how they can be put to work seem essential (e.g., webinars, local workshops). Teacher networking for the sharing of "frontline" practices and observations may encourage teacher agency and disseminate alternatives for working with materials. Establishing a means for individualization and localization of materials evaluation, feedback, and improvement (e.g., Web-based or local mentors or coaches) may involve teachers in their own development, demonstrate a commitment to valuing of local teacher knowledge, and provide important input for the improvement of materials. Such practices may become eminently more feasible as Internet-based accessibility spreads to various regions and as materials developers reconceive the scope of their endeavors and responsibilities (see also Johnson, 2006; Santos, Darling-Hammond, & Cheuk, 2012).

Summary and Recommendations

In most approaches to language education, teachers play a central role in designing language learning experiences, typically in interaction with materials of various kinds, ranging from published textbooks to computer-based modules to in-house developed tasks and assessments. Beyond simply using materials, teachers engage with materials through processes of planning, adaptation, localization, and evaluation. Teachers may also develop their awareness and otherwise learn as a result of working with materials. In order for teachers to make the most of innovative language learning materials, several types of support may be recommended.

11.1.   *Acknowledge and support teacher agency with materials at different stages.*

Teachers work with materials as they plan and design syllabi, units, lessons, and teaching; select and adopt fitting materials; adapt materials to meet their local needs; evaluate the effectiveness of materials during and after use; and improve materials for subsequent use. Materials should be developed with an active teacher agent in mind who is engaged deeply with the materials in trying to present the most effective language learning experiences; materials should be considered inherently adaptable and designed as such.

11.2.   *Provide teachers with tools and procedures for analysis of their needs.*

In order to select and adapt materials appropriate to their circumstances, teachers must understand their needs. Materials that are accompanied with recommended tools and procedures for determining these needs can help raise teachers' awareness about what kinds of materials are feasible and appropriate, how materials might need to be adapted, what might need to change in their contexts in order to utilize particular materials, and so on. Critical needs include (a) teacher beliefs, backgrounds, experiences, language proficiency, expertise, affect, and professional situations; and (b) societal, professional, institutional, and learner variables that will constrain or enable the use of materials. Materials themselves should be presented in ways that can be easily articulated to particular profiles of teacher need, along with recommendations for ameliorating apparent discrepancies.

11.3.   *Offer information and resources that help teachers understand and implement materials.*

A variety of information types may help teachers engage deeply and usefully with materials, including teacher manuals and guidelines, learner guidelines, annotated sample lesson plans, suggestions for adaptation, and recommendations for possible differentiation of materials based on contextual factors. Additional resources that may facilitate materials utilization include the provision of modular or otherwise customizable materials, supplementary materials, and tools for evaluating materials. Web-based materials platforms may provide considerable additional support, including access to training, examples, communities of practice, downloadable applications, and so on.

11.4.   Encourage teacher development and educational reform through new materials.

The adoption of new materials involves, at some level, the inevitability of innovation, often calling for changes in how teachers think and act, along with expectations for reform of educational practices and outcomes. In order for teacher change to happen in conjunction with new materials, consider (a) sustained opportunities for teacher practice and development in the use of new materials; (b) accessible expertise in helping teachers understand and work with new materials (e.g., coaches, mentors); (c) involvement of teachers in ongoing materials evaluation and improvement to meet their local needs; and (d) teacher networking for sharing of best practices with materials.

Note

1   English Language Teaching, http://elt.oup.com.

12

MONITORING AND IMPROVING LANGUAGE INSTRUCTION

The preceding chapters in this section have described critical approaches to designing, delivering, and supporting innovative educational materials and language learning experiences proactively—that is, in anticipation of their use in actual teaching and learning circumstances. Of course, although proactive efforts along these lines may increase the likelihood of success, that is not ever a foregone conclusion. For this reason, it is essential to address the need for ongoing evaluation of whatever is undertaken by way of instruction and pedagogical innovation. This chapter builds upon chapter 7, with its focus on assessment of student learning, by articulating the relationship between the design and delivery of instruction and the need to monitor and provide feedback on learner development and progress. It summarizes primarily program evaluation practices that enable periodic insights into instructional effectiveness and learning outcomes for the main purpose of educational program improvement. One key idea developed throughout the chapter is that, as with the uses of assessment, the specific intended uses of evaluation must be clearly specified by those who intend to engage in evaluation for some educational purpose. Moreover, a system of checks and balances should be in place to ensure that evaluation (and assessment) findings and processes are actually used as intended and likewise monitored for any unintended or harmful consequences. In this chapter, an approach to conceptualizing and operationalizing useful evaluation is first sketched out, providing a guide for conducting evaluation in support of innovative educational design and delivery and as a means to monitor and ensure educational effectiveness in terms of student learning. Subsequently, several examples of program evaluation at work in language education settings provide insights into the diverse possible contributions of evaluation.

Evaluation and Instruction

Language education involves a number of interrelated components that work together to bring about changes in students' language knowledge, skills, or dispositions (see chapter 8). Genesee and Upshur (1996) provide a useful schema to conceptualize elements of a language educational program that combine to make learning happen. According to Genesee and Upshur, at the broadest level of conceptualization, language education involves (a) instructional purposes, (b) instructional plans, and (c) instructional processes. Instructional purposes represent the "why" of instruction: the objectives and goals that educators seek to achieve. Instructional plans represent the "how" of instruction: the means or resources for attaining learning outcomes and objectives. Instructional processes represent the "what" of education and instruction: the actual strategies, materials, activities, and tasks used by teachers and students during instruction. Genesee and Upshur also suggest that various "inputs" are needed (i.e., personnel and environmental factors) for the development of sound instructional purposes, plans, and processes (e.g., student needs, instructor abilities, facilities, technology, materials, resources, funding support).

The aforementioned delineation is one of a number of ways that a framework or "theory" of educational design might be conceived within a language program, course, or module. Within this (or any similar) paradigm, and as mentioned already in chapter 8, evaluation can be understood as a process and accompanying methods or tools that enable language educators to gather information about, better understand, and modify any of the educational elements listed previously or any others that constitute a program of instruction or study. Evaluation, then, is a systematic process of investigation that provides useful feedback on program functioning in support of educational design and decision making. Such decisions will focus on a wide array of programmatic elements, including administrative and educational processes, student needs, educational infrastructures and materials, human resources, the extent of educational impacts on student learning, and so on. Furthermore, decisions will be made for a range of purposes such as developing educational courses, materials, and programs; improving instructional delivery; holding teachers and schools accountable; judging program quality; and even generating knowledge about good practice.

Evaluation is thus understood, here, as a method of programmatic inquiry that makes many different types of educational decisions possible:

> Program evaluation is the systematic collection of information about the activities, characteristics, and results of programs to make judgments about the program, improve or further develop program effectiveness, inform decisions about future programming, and/or increase understanding.
>
> *(Patton, 2008, p. 39)*

In addition, because the scope of evaluation encompasses the full spectrum of educational functions and processes, a wide array of information sources and information collection techniques are possible. A key source of information, of course, will be student learning development and achievement, and a key tool to shed light on learning for program evaluative purposes will be student assessment, typically of the more "summative" type described in chapter 7. Thus, along a continuum of educational inquiry, in contrast with program evaluation broadly conceived, assessment is more narrowly focused in that it directs inquiry toward student learning specifically. In this sense, assessment is defined (here) as

> the systematic gathering of information about student learning in support of teaching and learning. It may be direct or indirect, objective or subjective, formal or informal, standardized or idiosyncratic, but it should always provide locally useful information on learners and on learning to those individuals responsible for doing something about it.
>
> *(Norris, 2006, p. 579)*

Evaluation information or data, then, can come from many different sources (including assessments of student learning), using different data-collection methods, and, importantly, collected for a variety of purposes. Whatever the purpose, a key methodological concept linking assessment and evaluation is that both need to be concretely *useful* endeavors that enable educators and other stakeholders to achieve desired aims. Accordingly, the productiveness and ultimate usefulness of evaluation will depend on (a) identifying the specific individuals who will do something with evaluation findings (or processes); (b) specifying what the evaluation uses of these individuals will be; (c) being clear about the specific educational elements evaluation will investigate; and (d) ensuring that evaluation uses have occurred as intended.

Operationalizing a Useful Approach to Program Evaluation

The contemporary delivery of language education calls for greater engagement in evaluation as political and funding entities heighten their scrutiny at all educational levels. However, the use of evaluation for program development, improvement, and accountability purposes has created unique challenges for language educators who are called upon to implement evaluation not only in response to external demands but also as a means for ensuring the effectiveness of their educational efforts. This state of affairs has given rise to a heightened focus— both in theory, research, and practice—on the efficacy of evaluation methodologies and the need for language educators to concretely use evaluation in desired ways. More specifically, the notion of evaluation *use* undertaken by key evaluation *users*—and the need to specify both in explicit terms—has become a key conceptualization in thinking about how evaluation practices can be mobilized by diverse groups of stakeholders to achieve various program development, improvement, and accountability aims.

Recent developments in program evaluation theory have thus centered on the notion of evaluation "use" as an important conceptual innovation and organizing methodological principle, which has led to a number of key implications for evaluation practice (Norris, 2006, 2008; Patton, 2008, 2012). An important observation about language program evaluation up to the early 1990s was that methodological quality and technical expertise were no guarantee that an evaluation would achieve its intended aims (Alderson & Berretta, 1992). Evaluation, it seemed, had a problematic tendency to be a fruitless, often useless endeavor that failed to live up to its formative or summative potential. Given that evaluation is a fundamentally practical activity that needs to have concrete impacts on program decision making, traditional debates about methodology—on the merits of quantitative versus qualitative epistemological orientations, for example, or the advantages of experimental versus nonexperimental evaluation designs, and so on—gave way to a realization that (a) evaluation is a fundamentally pragmatic undertaking, (b) "utility" should be the ultimate criterion of effectiveness and quality, and (c) any and all techniques should be made available to evaluators to ensure that evaluation leads to intended impacts (Norris & Watanabe, 2013).

Accordingly, a pragmatic orientation to language program evaluation methodology has been developed (derived largely from the work of Michael Quinn Patton) that involves organizing all aspects of evaluation projects—planning, data collection, reporting, and action—on the basis of how an evaluation will be used. The purpose of doing so is to increase the likelihood of an evaluation project's ultimate usefulness. For example, during evaluation planning, stakeholders can be asked to engage in role-play scenarios during which they are presented with fictional evaluation results and quizzed on the likely usefulness of the information. This strategy is one of many employed intentionally and systematically to increase the likelihood of evaluation use by ensuring that evaluation findings will be sufficiently relevant to meet stakeholders' decision-making needs (Patton, 2008). The key features of utilization-focused language program evaluation include the following:

1. Explicit identification of intended uses and users of evaluation, and the inclusion of intended users in decisions about evaluation.
2. Articulation of prioritized evaluation foci in the form of well-crafted questions that need to be answered about specific components of the program.
3. Systematic collection of evaluation data and information in appropriate, efficient ways that help ensure evaluation use.
4. Strategic reporting and follow-through that helps support evaluation use.[1]

Identifying Intended Evaluation Uses

According to Patton (2008), "evaluations must be focused in some way; focusing on intended use by intended users is the most useful way" (p. 571). A key premise of use-focused evaluation is that for evaluation to be meaningfully productive, intended evaluation use must be the superordinate priority and organizing principle throughout an evaluation project. Accordingly (and as noted previously), any endeavor inquiring into the various elements of language programs—be it teacher training, assessment, materials, cocurricular learning experiences, student learning, administrative processes, and so on—must begin with a clear specification (and prioritization) of what the evaluation project is trying to achieve. That is, at the beginning of evaluation planning, educators must articulate the specific uses to which evaluation findings or processes will be put. For example, language educators in recent formatively oriented evaluation projects—projects that were successful in making meaningful impacts from the point of view of the evaluation users—were clear from the outset that evaluation would be used to

- identify strengths and weaknesses in student learning outcomes for the purpose of improving program delivery (Grau Sempere, Mohn, & Pieroni, 2009);
- find out how well current new-teacher induction practices in an English for academic purposes (EAP) program are able to meet new teachers' needs and administrators' expectations (Yang, 2009);
- know if advertising is working effectively in attracting students and placing them in the right courses (Milleret & Silveira, 2009);
- understand what students in beginning classes need or want to learn (Milleret & Silveira, 2009); and
- judge the quality of undergraduate foreign language teaching by graduate teaching assistants and adjust teacher-preparation programs accordingly (Zannirato & Sánchez-Serrano, 2009).

By stating their uses up front, and planning the subsequent evaluation on the basis of those uses, language educators in each of the aforementioned instances mapped the trajectory of their evaluation toward known, explicit, and valued project outcomes. The evaluations undertaken in these examples were also all quite discrete—that is, highly focused in orientation; rather than evaluating the "program," each evaluation focused on a particular component of the overall educational design and more specifically on a high-priority question about the particular component under investigation. The importance of specifying intended uses in these ways (and users; see the next section) cannot be overstated. A survey of 991 members of the American Evaluation Association (Fleisher, 2007) found that the most influential factor in facilitating successful evaluation was "planning for use at the beginning of the evaluation" (cited in Patton, 2008, p. 570). Thus, evaluation efforts that articulate (and are guided by) intended evaluation uses greatly increase the chances that evaluation will have productive impacts.

Identifying Intended Users of Evaluation

Using evaluation in particular ways implies that actions must be taken by some individual or group of individuals. Although this may seem self-evident, the fact that people use evaluation is at the heart of making these processes as meaningfully productive as possible, an idea that Patton (2008) refers to as the *personal factor:* "evaluation research finds that personal commitments of those involved in an evaluation undergird use. Thus evaluations should be specifically user-oriented—aimed at the interests and information needs of specific identifiable people, not vague, passive audiences" (Patton, 2008, p. 571). As noted previously, those who are most likely to use evaluation must be brought into the evaluation project from the beginning and engaged to identify their priority uses of evaluation. This engagement might occur in the form of a series of meetings of the intended users (e.g., teachers, curriculum developers, and administrators of a given language program), on the basis of a survey questionnaire, or through individual and focus group interviews, for example, wherein the users' interests in the program and its evaluation are established and priority needs for focusing evaluation are elicited.

Additional aspects of evaluation users should be borne in mind in order to increase the likelihood of evaluation usefulness. Typically the primary intended users of evaluation in a language program will be educators themselves; however, other groups of users should not be overlooked and may be relevant for evaluation to have meaningful impacts. For example, students and parents may have a stake in evaluation findings, and their needs may require consideration if a project is going to be useful for all relevant parties (i.e., they may understand data-based findings in different ways from teachers, educational researchers, or administrators). Similarly, materials developers or curriculum designers may have a vested interest in the apparent "success" of their efforts, thereby rendering suspect any evaluation that is conducted solely by these users and without the consultation of other interested stakeholders with other investments on the line (e.g., learners, teachers, schools, school districts). Therefore, because excluding relevant users of evaluation can undermine usefulness in a variety of ways, a working group of stakeholder representatives will typically be called for in order to ensure that an evaluation project responds to the needs and interests of all who are primarily concerned. Such instances require inclusiveness, democratic representation, and involvement of diverse constituencies (Kiely & Rea-Dickens, 2005; Norris, 2006, 2008).

Inclusiveness notwithstanding, particular types of users are going to be more important than others and, crucially, better able to maximize the impact of evaluation through their influence or status. Prioritization of users may be called for in the interest of efficiency and increasing the likelihood of evaluation usefulness. Optimal primary intended users are those who have the greatest impact on decision making, are the most knowledgeable about the program, and care the most about program success.

Focusing Evaluation: Asking Evaluation Questions

An important aspect of successfully using evaluation in language programs is a clear articulation of what users want to investigate. Even if uses and users are identified, an amorphous or vague sense of what an evaluation project is supposed to find out runs the risk of targeting the wrong program element for attention. In evaluation methodology, being clear about a project's focus involves articulating an "evaluation question" (Patton, 2008). An evaluation question is similar to a research question in an academic study in that it creates a logic of argumentation and evidence that can be used to systematically know about an object of interest in a language program (e.g., "How well are pre-semester induction practices helping new teachers prepare for their teaching duties?"; see Yang, 2009). Such questions guide the evaluation process toward a clearly conceived goal and facilitate a rational process of data collection, interpretation, and reporting. Ideally, an evaluation question should be (a) something that intended users are interested in answering, (b) answerable in a reasonable amount of time and at a reasonable cost, and (c) empirically oriented such that data can be used to provide an answer (Patton, 2008).

Collecting Data

"Strategizing about use is ongoing and continuous [. . .] " (Patton, 2008, p. 570). Evaluation is useful when users get the information they need to take desired actions. Collecting information about the various elements of a program is an important aspect of an evaluation project and likewise one that should be governed by intended evaluation uses and with evaluation usefulness in mind.

A key decision in evaluation is choosing data-collection methods and tools. Part of this process involves users identifying the acceptably trustworthy types and sources of evidence that will enable them to answer their evaluation questions and realize their evaluation uses. Note that these sources of information (termed "indicators" in evaluation literature) are typically not the same thing as the data-collection tools themselves. For example, if a group of educators wants to ascertain the types of classroom activities and assessments most conducive to student learning, the information needed to answer this question might come from (a) students' opinions (i.e., their attitudes toward or satisfaction with class assessments and activities), (b) instructors' opinions (i.e., their perceptions of student learning gains, enjoyment, participation), (c) student classroom actions (i.e., observed levels of student participation, motivation, enthusiasm), or (d) student performances (i.e., demonstrated learning on assessments and assignments; Davis, 2011). Establishing relevant indicators or sources of information—separate from their method of collection—allows for a needed type of evidence to be systematically matched to an appropriate data-collection tool and heads off the possibility of choosing a wrong method prematurely (e.g., the "let's do a survey" approach) and collecting irrelevant information (Patton, 2008). In the previous example, depending on evaluation uses and questions, student opinions could be captured in a variety of ways including typical postcourse student evaluations, interviews, focus groups, observations, learning logs or journals, and so on.[2]

In addition, an important aspect of selecting data-collection tools—which will increase the likelihood of people using the information they gather—is that the primary intended users and other key stakeholders agree on methods choices (Davis, 2011; Patton, 2012). Methods need to be perceived by users and relevant stakeholders as appropriate and sufficiently accurate, or findings may be seen as untrustworthy, decreasing the likelihood that information will be used.

A further consideration in collecting evaluation data is the widely held view that use of *multiple* evaluation tools increases accuracy and trustworthiness (AAHE, 1994; Norris, 2006; Suskie, 2009). As noted previously, evaluation research has a history of debating the merits of quantitative versus qualitative epistemological orientations in data-collection design. Again, the resolution to this debate has been a practical synthesis such that any and all techniques are viable as long as they help lead evaluation to answering questions with accuracy and generating intended consequences (Norris & Watanabe, 2013). Likewise, current advice is that evaluation use is best supported when *multiple data-collection tools are used*. Thus, where appropriate, "mixed-methods" data collection is recommended (Norris & Watanabe, 2013).[3]

Finally, a use-focused approach to evaluation takes a particular position regarding reliability and validity of data collection (in the research sense of these terms). Prescriptions for methodological validity and reliability coming from academic discourses may need to be relaxed because the superordinate concern in evaluation is *use* of findings, as opposed to generating (and publishing) new scientific-theoretical knowledge as governed by the epistemological orthodoxies of research-based academic inquiry. Although methods should be as reliable as possible, stakeholders may need to come to a consensus about aspects of data-collection design and implementation that will lead to *sufficiently* trustworthy and accurate results. For example, in a situation where information is needed quickly or where informants are difficult to access, educators might relax the view that probability sampling of student survey respondents is required in order to generalize findings from the sample to the student population. Rather, because some action must be taken on the basis of survey findings, users might agree to tolerate a nonprobability sample (i.e., selected without randomization) because this may be the only way needed information can be gathered (Davis, 2011).

Evaluation Use

Finally, when the evaluation's information gathering has concluded, educators should systematically follow through on targeted uses, decisions, and actions (and ultimately investigate whether evaluation use has occurred as anticipated). For evaluation projects, Patton (2012) recommends a number of follow-up strategies to help ensure use of evaluation findings (or processes). For example, reporting should be adapted to different audiences; findings should be kept in front of evaluation users and reinforced when new opportunities for use emerge; misuse of findings should be anticipated and strategically headed off; and resistance from critical audiences should be countered (Patton, 2012). Typically, in educational settings where evaluation is conceived as an ongoing component of program practice focused on sustained improvement and quality control, uses of one evaluation project will generate ideas for subsequent projects focusing on new priorities in need of attention. Here, a systematic understanding of the overall program design can prove essential as a basis for maintaining a broad overview of the different parts of the program that interact in determining the "why," "what," and "how" of language education (see chapters 8 and 10 on program models).

Evaluation at Work: A Few Examples From Language Education

Clearly, evaluation may be undertaken for a variety of reasons in relation to language education programs, and the ultimate usefulness of evaluative endeavors will depend largely on the extent to which practices have been conceived along the lines outlined previously. Here, we provide a few brief, illustrative examples of program evaluations related to educational design, innovation, and delivery projects. These examples, from English-language education programs in distinct regions and settings, all highlight the importance of the characteristics of useful evaluation outlined previously, and they are suggestive of the critical contributions to be made by program evaluation in support of effective language education and innovation, in keeping with the overall theme of this volume.

Participatory Program Monitoring

In a large, multisite English language program in Indonesia, evaluation was undertaken in order to raise awareness among administrative and teaching staff about effective program delivery, to identify aspects of the program in need of improvement, and to provide a basis for sustainable monitoring of the program for quality control purposes.[4] Key to this large-scale evaluation initiative, which involved hundreds of participants at 25 different schools, was the involvement of program stakeholders (teachers and other staff) in the development—through a series of workshops—of a bottom-up model of the various factors involved in effective delivery of the English language program, as understood from their point of view, and including everything from finances and accounting to physical space to recruitment of students and, of course, teaching activities. In addition, evaluation participants identified performance indicators (specific, contextualized expectations) that would provide meaningful information on each factor included in the program model. This participatory process thus resulted in a model of the program and a set of performance expectations for each part of the model, which was then utilized as a basis for judging how well each factor was performing and where improvements were needed. According to Mackay and colleagues (1998), such a large and dispersed program setting called for "participative monitoring and evaluation activities initiated within the unit to facilitate periodic or continuous improvement by programme staff themselves" (pp. 111–112), which then led to awareness raising among staff and administrators about exactly how the language program was supposed to work, sharing of best practice ideas across program sites, and an increased sense of empowerment among the staff members at each site as they acted to make improvements on the basis of evaluative judgments.

Focus on Program Implementation and Opportunity for Success

In this example, an external, summative evaluation was undertaken in order to determine effectiveness of an innovative English-language extensive reading (ER) program for primary school students implemented across public schools in Malawi.[5] The summative evaluation was based on an experimental comparison of students who did not participate in the innovative program versus those who did, and findings from several independent reading comprehension assessments indicated that the ER program had no beneficial effects. However, and critically important, additional data were gathered about the actual implementation of the ER program across diverse school contexts, utilizing classroom observations, interviews, and feedback from teachers and students, leading to the equally important finding that there was considerable variability in delivery of the ER program—that is, the innovative program, by and large, did not have sufficient opportunity to be successful, given less than adequate efforts to implement it as intended. A variety of factors likely undermined appropriate implementation, including both extrinsic factors (e.g., low teacher morale, changes in public school student profiles due to growth of private schools) and critical intrinsic factors (e.g., insufficient teacher training in the new program itself). This evaluation illustrates not only the importance of collecting multiple types of information in order to situate and explain summative findings but also the essential need to focus on how educational practices implied by innovative materials are actually implemented (and especially how teachers are, or need to be, supported in doing so), if innovations are to be adequately attempted and accurately judged on their merits.

Internal Evaluation for Specific Improvements

In this evaluation case study, a utilization-focused evaluation was put into practice by a pair of teachers within a U.S. university academic English program in order to resolve a very specific set of concerns.[6] Namely, the two teachers were responding to their own and others' perceptions of insufficient teacher induction processes into the culture and expectations of working in the program, the result of which was a generalized sense of lack of preparation for the various tasks associated with teaching. The teacher-evaluators set out to better understand the problem and identify possible solutions via formative evaluation. They first recruited the involvement of program administrators as the key decision makers in the program context, and they worked closely with the administrators to design and implement an evaluation that would meet their needs and provide immediately actionable information. Initial interactions with the administrators led to the development of a set of expected outcomes for teacher induction within the program, and these were then used to explore experienced and new teacher perspectives on the extent to which existing practices met the targeted outcomes. Additionally, teachers offered numerous suggestions for additional practices that would better support teachers' preparedness for taking on their teaching positions. These findings were reported back to the intended users, and a variety of immediate steps were subsequently implemented in order to resolve the problem. Both teachers and administrators reported a sense of awareness raising and strategic improvement as a result of the evaluation efforts. This example not only points to the characteristics of effective teacher induction programs (see also Fenton-Smith & Torpey, 2013) but also demonstrates how teacher-led internal evaluations can result in immediately visible impacts on program design and delivery.

External Evaluation to Judge Value and Effectiveness

In a high-stakes evaluation in a U.S. public school district, a team of evaluators aimed to estimate the impact and effectiveness of a computer-based supplementary reading program for English language learners (ELLs) at the elementary-school level.[7] The project can be regarded as a more conventional instance of "summative" evaluation in that the district had provided substantial funding to implement the program (in over 2,000 schools) and wanted to know if it was effective, if it warranted continuation, and, by implication, whether the expenditure of state tax dollars was justified. The evaluation used a quasiexperimental design, assessed student reading ability as a key indicator of program effectiveness, and collected information from a number of additional sources to better understand whether supplementary reading instruction was improving the reading abilities of ELLs.

Notable about the evaluation context were the many stakeholders with a vested interest in program success who hoped for (and expected) a finding that the program had increased student reading ability. Given the keen (and politicized) interest in results, the evaluators took special precautions to ensure that the findings would be as persuasive as possible to key intended evaluation users, stakeholder groups, and audiences. Initially, assessment results suggested no improvements in student reading after participation in the program. Crucially, this potentially explosive finding was addressed in an intentional and strategic way to avoid the very real possibility of nonuseful evaluation in this case—namely, a backlash and rejection of the report and its recommendations. To do so, the assessment results were further explored through additional, contextualized (and more qualitative) analyses, which found a number of alternative explanations for the ostensible lack of impact on student learning (e.g., inconsistent administration). Furthermore, these additional findings were carefully emphasized via intentional evaluation reporting strategies (e.g., using research literature to buttress conclusions) that rendered findings in such a way as to be maximally cogent to deeply skeptical audiences.

The approach to evaluation in this instance is instructive in that the focus on usefulness and users was used strategically and tactically to avoid a potential weakness in externally mandated, summative-type evaluations: outsider evaluators producing findings that fail to meet the needs or respond to the concerns of local program stakeholders. Moreover, this evaluation illustrates the challenge posed by language assessment—as an indicator of instructional effectiveness or intervention impact—for program evaluation purposes. Often there is a need for multiple data sources to contextualize assessment results and shed light on what student performance actually means in the context of program processes, which in turn helps enhance the usefulness of this specific (and privileged) type of evaluation information (see Elder, 2005).

Evaluation as an Integral Part of Innovation

In a final example, this evaluation took place in conjunction with the introduction of a new course and associated materials and instruction in an academic English program at a university in Thailand.[8] Learner needs and interests served as the starting point for designing a new task-based syllabus, which was then implemented by a group of local teachers in a one-year experimental course that emphasized language performance abilities and learner strategies, primarily through the use of extended task work and focus-on-form pedagogy, and culminating in assessments that reflected academic target tasks. Formative evaluation was designed into the new course from the outset to illuminate how learners and teachers reacted to the design of the course and the pedagogic tasks themselves and to inform immediate instructional improvements or other adjustments needed in delivery of the course. Evaluation methods included learner reactions to tasks, daily learning notebooks, end-of-course surveys, classroom observations, teacher and student interviews, and evaluator field notes. After the initial semester of new course delivery, findings suggested that learners had developed not only their ability to deploy integrated language skills but also their independence in taking responsibility for their own learning and in terms of strategies for language learning. Findings also indicated a decrease in learners' previously reported "obsession" with grammatical rules and an appreciation of the real-world relevance of the new course design and tasks. However, it was also found that both teachers and learners found the syllabus to be overly ambitious, with too much to cover in the amount of time available; that learners desired considerably more guidance from teachers throughout the various stages of extended task work; and that both teachers and learners required time to come to understand and appreciate the new, task-based approach to teaching and learning. Evaluation findings were then used formatively to make immediate adjustments, including the addition of an introductory unit on the approach to language learning adopted in the course; the development of an introductory workshop and teacher's guide to instruction; a reduction in the number of tasks; the addition of specific guidance in working through the tasks; the identification of key opportunities for provision of learning-oriented feedback within each of the tasks; and the consolidation and organization of the teaching and learning materials.

Important in this example is the way in which evaluation provided insights into both positive impacts of the task-based innovation and concerns with its implementation. Thus, the actual process of program delivery was illuminated as it played out, from the lived perspectives of the primary stakeholders—learners and teachers. This focus on revealing what actually happened during implementation then enabled reflection on its effectiveness and especially the identification of adjustments needed for better program delivery. The evaluators were also able to observe an important reality in relation to many language teaching innovations: both teachers and learners required some time to come to terms with and appreciate the task-based teaching and learning process, and this realization suggests considerations that might be built into teacher and learner development more explicitly (see chapters 10 and 11).

Summary and Recommendations

As exemplified in the aforementioned cases, evaluation may play a critical role in initial design and delivery of innovative language education, providing an evidentiary basis for understanding what works as intended and suggesting areas in need of immediate improvement. Evaluation can also make an important contribution in existing programs, in which teachers or other stakeholders perceive the need for change, in which participatory monitoring of diverse program components is called for, or in a number of other circumstances. Indeed, any ethical educational endeavor should probably incorporate ongoing inquiry into the array of educational processes and affordances designed to bring about student learning. To use evaluation effectively, however, it will need to be implemented in ways that are systematic and trustworthy and that satisfactorily meet the needs of stakeholders who stand to gain (or lose) the most from the program and its evaluation. This chapter has described the key dimensions of how evaluation might best be approached to achieve these important aims. Most importantly, to ensure the effective use of any evaluative methods or tools, there must be a clear understanding of the job to be done before the right "tool," approach, or procedure can be selected to accomplish it. Thus, thoughtful, deliberate evaluation planning, as well as attention to high-quality implementation, is needed so that stakeholders can make sound educational decisions toward greater educational effectiveness. The following recommendations highlight important dimensions of adequate evaluation practice along these lines.

12.1.   Specify intended uses of evaluation.

    a.   Evaluation is a fundamentally pragmatic and practical endeavor that seeks to make tangible, concrete impacts on language education. As such, research is unequivocal that a clear specification of evaluation use (at the beginning of project planning) is a key methodological component helping ensure the ultimate usefulness of evaluation-based program inquiry.

    b.   Educators and other stakeholders will be able to identify a potentially endless list of uses they want to pursue. Educators should thus engage in a process of prioritization to ensure that evaluation is feasibly achievable given constraints of time and resources.

12.2.   Identify intended users of evaluation.

    a.   Evaluation serves to realize the interests and information needs of specific identifiable people, not vague, passive audiences (Patton, 2008). As such, those who are most likely to use evaluation must be clearly identified and engaged in specifying their intended evaluation uses.

    b.   Users of evaluation should be chosen in such a way as to increase the likelihood of meaningfully productive use. Prioritization of users may be necessary. Optimal candidates are those who have decision-making power and care the most about program success. Note also that usefulness is enhanced when intended user groups include representatives from diverse program constituencies (e.g., students, parents, employers). In this way, evaluation becomes more of a democratic endeavor that responds to the needs of interested and impacted parties.

12.3.   Specify the focus of evaluation.

    a.   Useful evaluation requires a clear articulation of the object(s) of investigative focus. In evaluation projects, an "evaluation question" should be conceived that articulates the specific program elements users wish to investigate ("What we want to know about the program is . . . ").

    b.   Different kinds of information may be relevant in answering evaluation questions about particular program elements; fitting indicators should be considered carefully such that they are illuminated by data-collection methods. Student and teacher opinions, learner performance abilities, resource demands, and so on are examples of types of indicators, for which diverse methods of collecting data would be required (e.g., student and teacher opinions might be operationalized via questionnaires, interviews, or focus groups, whereas learner performance abilities might best be observed through task-based assessments).

12.4. *Select or create evaluation data-collection instruments in systematic ways.*

    a. Choose evaluation methods that will (i) yield specified, needed evidence; (ii) tap into relevant sources of information (indicators); and (iii) enable use by actual intended users. These features should be established prior to and separate from the ultimate selection of specific data-collection tools.

    b. Wherever possible, use multiple evaluation methods (and "mixed-method" data-collection designs) as a means of triangulating interpretations (i.e., shedding light on the evaluation focus from multiple perspectives).

    c. Ensure that primary intended users and other key stakeholders (i) agree on methods choices, (ii) are aware of the types of information they are likely to receive, and (iii) regard both as sufficiently accurate and trustworthy for their evaluation decision or action purposes.

    d. Decisions about evaluation validity and reliability should be made on the basis of (i) in-situ, contextualized standards of trustworthiness or accuracy and (ii) the ability of a particular data-collection method to enable sufficiently adequate and appropriate evaluation use by intended users.

12.5. *Take steps to ensure use of evaluation (and monitor for unintended and harmful uses).*

    a. At the conclusion of evaluation projects, strategies should be taken to help enhance the likelihood of use. For example, reporting should be conducted in intentional ways (e.g., targeting particular user audiences; delivering information in maximally effective formats). Findings should be kept in front of evaluation users, particularly when new use opportunities arise.

    b. Misuse of findings should be anticipated and strategically neutralized. Resistance from critical audiences should be carefully considered and countered as necessary on the basis of evidence that has accrued through data collection.

12.6. *Provide for inclusive, democratic participation.*

The usefulness and productiveness of evaluation is increased when it proceeds democratically, with everyone "on board" and reflecting the desires and goals of a program majority (ideally). Inclusion of relevant stakeholders in all aspects of evaluation (e.g., planning, implementation, reporting, use) increases interest, investment, ownership, and the likelihood of evaluation responding to the needs of interested parties.

12.7.   Encourage ongoing, cyclical practice.

    a.   Evaluation typically fails to be useful when it is undertaken sporadi-
cally and reactively (e.g., solely in response to accountability mandates
and other external forces). For program inquiry to be consistently
meaningful and useful, evaluation should be an ongoing, iterative
practice that generates new findings and contingent cycles of inquiry
and educational development.

    b.   Ultimately, evaluation is impactful when understood (and imple-
mented) as an integral component of educational delivery (see chapter 8). Quality language education involves symbiotic relationships
between three programmatic elements (in equal proportions): (i)
engaging, coherent curricular structures and sequences of learning;
(ii) motivating best instructional practices that respond well to student needs; and (iii) useful evaluation and assessment procedures that
help educators and other stakeholders understand and improve teaching and learning.

Notes

1 For a detailed overview of a use-focused approach to evaluation of language educational programs, see Norris and Watanabe (2007). Other useful resources on conducting language program evaluation are Brown (1995) and Lynch (1996, 2003).

2 Brown (1995), Lynch (1996, 2003), and Sinicrope and Watanabe (2008) list the range
of evaluation tools that can be used in language program evaluation.

3 See Greene (2007) for mixed-method approaches to social inquiry and evaluation; see
also the National Science Foundation's (Frechtling & Sharp, 1997) *User-Friendly Handbook for Mixed Methods Evaluations*.

4 See Mackay, Wellesley, and Bazergan (1995); and Mackay, Wellesley, Tasman, and Bazergan (1998)

5 See Williams (2007).

6 See Yang (2009).

7 See Llosa and Slayton (2009).

8 See McDonough and Chaikitmongkol (2007).

13

IMPLICATIONS FOR TECHNOLOGY-MEDIATED LANGUAGE LEARNING AND INSTRUCTION

In this final chapter we consider implications of various topics, challenges, and recommendations raised in the preceding 12 chapters as they relate to the use of technology in language education—or, otherwise conceived, as language learning is inevitably integrated into technology-mediated educational environments and practices. Digital technologies are a relatively recent frontier for education generally, and one that is already transforming how human beings teach and learn in an increasingly connected world where computer-mediated communication (CMC) is becoming the norm for a variety of conventionally face-to-face activities. Likewise for language education, digital technologies have created unique possibilities for language learning and language use, and they will continue to do so as platforms, software, applications, and devices continue to evolve. Accordingly, a robust and active research agenda has emerged, alongside technological developments, to better understand how various technological affordances and environments might foster language acquisition, as well as how technology-mediated communication is changing both the practices of L2 learning and the norms of language use.

In the following sections we explore *some* of the most important technology-related dimensions of language learning and language pedagogy for instructors, students, and course designers. Of course, a single chapter cannot do justice to this vast and ever-expanding topic, but we hope that the ideas considered here will promote careful consideration of some of the major implications. Overall, we advance the general idea that the deployment of technology in language instruction—or the situating of language learning within technology-mediated educational environments—must be motivated by a clear rationale that both draws upon what is known about effective approaches to instructed language learning and makes the most of the technological possibilities at hand, within the limitations of the given educational context. Although this may seem self-evident (and goes to the purpose of this volume), technology-mediated language learning (TMLL) has historically proceeded on the basis of little consideration or understanding of specifically how a digital tool, practice, or environment might actually enhance or otherwise moderate language acquisition processes and outcomes. To redress this state of affairs, we discuss some of what seem to be the most salient and current research- and practice-based issues with respect to planning, implementing, and monitoring the quality of TMLL.

Second Language Acquisition and TMLL

Due to the quick rise, development, and widespread use of new technologies, we are currently witnessing what Worth has called an "evolution in education"—a paradigm shift in how people acquire knowledge and at least attempt to learn languages (as cited in Davies, 2011). Given that real-life communication is itself increasingly technology mediated, computer-based technologies (i.e., desktop, laptop, smartphone, tablet, interactive whiteboard, etc.) have by now also permeated almost all areas of language education, giving rise to a burgeoning subfield of SLA: TMLL.[1]

Sketching Out the TMLL Landscape

Building upon early interests in computer-assisted language learning (CALL), TMLL has become a widely branched field related to a broad range of resources that provide language learning opportunities, including software programs, Web-based environments, online applications, games, and distance or hybrid learning approaches to education (see Chapelle & Voss, 2016; Davies, 2011; Godwin-Jones, 2013; Hubbard, 2015; Thomas, Reinders, & Warschauer, 2014). Although CALL traditionally focused on the use of computer programs that sought to "teach" language in the form of stimulus-response patterns, the advent of the Internet and, in particular Web 2.0, resulted in more interactive, immersive forms of learning software. Along these lines, some commercial computer programs and packages have sought to provide a comprehensive learning approach that mimics the second language (L2) immersion experience (though to varying degrees of success). In the wake of burgeoning online applications, these software programs have begun to either incorporate Web-based features into their systems or they have issued Web-based supplementary materials, thus offering more blended and diversified language learning solutions. In addition to this more traditional software-package approach, completely online applications have begun to provide mobile language learning solutions that are accessible—either free of charge or subscription based—on various computer and mobile devices (Cunningham, 2015; Wagner & Kunnan, 2015).

Besides software and applications that are intended directly for language learning, instructors and researchers have adapted and made use of a range of Web-based communication and information technologies, as well as games, in order to facilitate language learning. For example, freely available interactive speaking capabilities such as Microsoft Skype, Cisco WebEx, and Google Hangouts have been adopted for educational purposes, especially in distance or hybrid learning courses (Hampel & Hauck, 2004; Strambi & Bouvet, 2003). Although these and other videoconferencing technologies naturally help bridge geographical distance, they also facilitate increased "live" L2 communication opportunities. Accordingly, social apps are increasingly popular among language learners, allowing them to connect with speakers from the target language and culture.

Innovative teachers have also endeavored to adapt live, online, multiparticipant computer games for language teaching. Rather than (or in addition to) fighting or competing against other players, users may be tasked with creating and living in the virtual world around them, including interacting and cooperating with other players in an online world and in whatever language is being used there. For example, educators have harnessed various collaborative tasks included in the open gaming environment in order to teach English in several contexts (see Smolčec, 2014, for an overview). Although some instructors have used it as a means to foster students' writing skills (O'Donnell, 2012), others have built entire EFL curricula around the game space (Hausrath, 2012). Given the popular demand for educational purposes, the developers of some commercial games have even launched collections of curricular building blocks, modules, activities, and teaching tasks for encouraging language learning.

A core acquisition-related feature across game-based applications is that they facilitate social interaction. Other Web-based environments, such as the video-sharing platform YouTube or wikis, are examples of similar, highly cooperative environments that allow for collaborative modification, restructuring, or deletion of content. When working in these computer- or Web-based settings, Davies (2011) notes, learners themselves "become active members of an online program" (p. 13), having the power and freedom to view, build, change, and restructure content (Churches, 2009; McLoughlin & Lee, 2007). Thus, as these information and communication technologies rapidly expand, they are building "online communities where people can come together to learn and build knowledge cooperatively" (Davies, 2011, p. 13). The notions of interaction, cooperation, and creation seem to have become the pillars of a new type of social learning that has emerged from the increasing use of technology. Overall, Davies (2011) summarized this new form of learning as follows:

> The current generation in Canada and the United States, for example, are increasingly tech savvy and are accessing and learning information in a manner contrary to traditional top-down teaching methods. Today's

learners, who have access to the Web and who use social software, often construct meaning through bottom-up, self-directed learning approaches. This is the new mode of learning.

(p. 14)

Hence, social learning can be considered a new paradigm that has increasingly gained momentum in today's information age, in which new technologies constitute "pedagogical tools that stem from their affordances of sharing, communication and information discovery" (McLoughlin & Lee, 2007, p. 666).

TMLL and SLA

Computers and the Internet, then, have taken up increasing and more varied roles in the instructed L2 learning process, including those of teacher, materials provider, input resource, assessor, and classroom context or setting, among others. The exploration of such possibilities has in turn raised some key theoretical questions about the relationship of technology with SLA (see the discussion of the SLA theory and technology relationship in Chapelle, 2009): What does this potentially new type of social or computer-mediated learning mean for language learning and teaching? Are language learning processes and outcomes somehow different when we use CALL technology? If so, how is TMLL different from face-to-face learning, and what are the advantages and disadvantages?

It is important to point out that evidence accumulated from several decades of research into computer-mediated language instruction—from 1970 to 2006—does indicate that, generally speaking, learning occurs in these environments at least as well as in comparable, non-computer-mediated classrooms (Grgurović, Chapelle, & Shelley, 2013). Although more evidence-based practice and research is needed to understand the full impact of TMLL on adult learners' L2 acquisition processes, as well as how L2 development can be effectively promoted, computer technology provides a number of potential advantages for language learning, especially with rapid advances in available technologies. First, the traditional distinctions between foreign and second language learning are increasingly blurred as the Internet provides for a third space where anyone, regardless of geography, has access to essentially unlimited input and interaction with foreign languages. This also begs the question of what the target of SLA might be for any given language, and all the more so for English (the language of the Internet, by and large), where new varieties of communication (e.g., text chat) are emerging in conjunction with these new spaces. Second, social communication for language learning can also be facilitated through the advent of technology, providing a much greater possibility for accessing speakers of the target language in a wide variety of environments and modalities of communication. Third, technology may offer certain advantages not otherwise easily accessible for learners to work in a "safe" or sheltered environment on their language learning. For example, online chat provides for a relatively spontaneous type of communication that is nevertheless less immediate than face-to-face speaking. It is also subject to longer pauses and the possibility for visual reflection on the text-based messages, which may allow for more focus on form that is still embedded within an obviously communicative setting. Similarly, learners may be more willing to engage in interactions with target language interlocutors in a potentially less threatening face-to-face speaking environment (e.g., working with avatars might enable the lowering of affective filters). Finally, technology in general, and the Web in particular, provides students with "an enormous amount of information literally at their fingertips" (Davies, 2011, p. 15). Generally, technology might be a way of providing much greater, carefully selected or graded input, such that some restrictions of traditional classroom-based learning (e.g., a static textbook, or L2 input provided only during class) can be lifted. If SLA is dependent on learners working with large amounts of language data input, this goal can certainly be facilitated by technology.

However, the degree to which TMLL is effective ultimately depends on how instructors, learners, and researchers use computer technologies (Chapelle, 2012a). Although various applications certainly can facilitate L2 interaction and learning, technology—if used without care—can just as easily be ineffectual or even detrimental to learning. Some scholars have observed that technology can be a distraction if L2 learners are not familiar with a given medium and, thus, have to spend more time figuring out technical aspects than focusing on the language learning task at hand. Warschauer (2006), for instance, observed a beginner-level French class in which learners were required to use multimedia. Yet, although the teacher touted an innovative use of technology to promote learner engagement, students spent most of their time talking in English about how to create a PowerPoint presentation instead of practicing their French. Hence, using technology for its own sake should be avoided, and pedagogical and theoretical considerations should always drive the deployment of technological tools.

An implication we want to stress here, then, is that care should be taken to use technology in intentional ways that clearly support language instruction and facilitate L2 acquisition, and not because of technology's fashionable educational appeal. Stanley (2013) points out that in adopting TMLL, "there is a real danger of teachers developing *Everest syndrome*" (p. 3; italics in the original)—that is, teachers may feel the urge to use and implement a form of technology simply because it is new and innovative (i.e., "because it is there"). However, the goal of L2 instruction should be the development of proficiency in the target language, not the use of new and exciting technology. It is easy for teachers and course designers to lose sight of this seemingly self-evident point.

Accordingly, when implementing TMLL, it would be beneficial for L2 instructors and materials designers to consider the following critical questions (adapted from Chapelle, 2001):

1. Does a certain activity or learning affordance offer language *learning* potential or only the potential for language use?

2.   Is the activity or affordance appropriate (or inappropriate) for a particular learner (or learner group)?
3.   Does the use of technology have students focus on meaning, as well as form?
4.   Does the activity or affordance have a positive, potentially motivating impact on learners?
5.   Is the activity or affordance practical?

With these considerations (among others) in mind, good TMLL practice will involve being explicit about how a particular use of technology specifically supports the accomplishment of language learning objectives. Developers and designers of learning materials should be able to justify how technology-based products or supplements help promote SLA, based on instructed SLA theory, as well as the growing empirical knowledge base of technology-mediated SLA. Furthermore, once technology-supported learning materials are employed in actual L2 instruction, ongoing and systematic evaluation and assessment should be implemented in order to support claims about how (and whether) TMLL instruction results in targeted language acquisition processes and outcomes (see the sections on assessment and evaluation that follow).

TMLL and Learner Individual Differences

Unsurprisingly, many of the well-known cognitive, social, psychological, and cultural factors or dispositions that learners bring with them to the language learning experience—proficiency, aptitude, working memory, personality, and so on—impact language learning in technology-mediated environments as well. Moreover, some variables—such as readiness for computer-mediated learning, technology experience and training, and attitudes toward CALL, among others—are unique to TMLL environments and entail especially important influences on learning effectiveness. Accordingly, research on TMLL and individual differences (IDs) is motivated by the promise and goal of using information on learner motivation, attitudes, aptitude, and so on to maximize the potential of technology-mediated instruction. However, despite the importance of learner variability in TMLL, the diversity of contexts and digital tools makes it difficult (at this stage) to make wide-ranging generalizations about the impacts of ID variables beyond a specific technology-mediated learning environment addressed in any given study (see Sauro, 2012). Nevertheless, certain patterns and general recommendations have emerged that can helpfully inform, in a general way, instructional design and delivery.

First, there is evidence that the established variables of ID in SLA (see chapters 2 and 3) appear to impact learning in technology-mediated environments as well, and sometimes in ways that have unique implications for language learning. For example, *gender* appears to be a factor in predicting computer literacy, as in the finding by Oza, Demirezen, and Pourfeiz (2015), in which female college students (in Turkey) tend to have less technological literacy and experience, though this observation is yet to be validated in other contexts. *Age* can affect computer literacy as well (older learners typically having less, at least in the current era), and also the effectiveness of interaction during telecollaboration, particularly when large age differences exist between speaking partners (King, 2010; Lee, 2004). *Proficiency* also impacts TMLL, affecting whether learners use and benefit from digital tools in ways intended by course designers or instructors (Fischer, 2012). Lower proficiency learners, in particular, are prone to use software in idiosyncratic ways, taking less advantage of feedback and annotation options, and engaging in fewer problem-solving strategies compared to higher level students (Belz, 2001; Desmarais et al., 1998; Grgurović, Chapelle, & Shelley, 2013). Low proficiency may also be a barrier to understanding instructions delivered in computer software applications, thereby rendering intended learning processes inaccessible (e.g., Llosa & Slayton, 2009). By contrast, higher proficiency students have advantages especially well suited to TMLL in that they are more autonomous and self-directed, able to access more affordances delivered in the target language, and more able to use learning strategies such as metacognition (all important variables for success in digital environments; Hubbard & Romeo, 2012). Finally, *aptitude* and *working memory* have interesting implications for TMLL. For example, low-memory learners—typically disadvantaged in their ability to learn from input and interaction—seem to benefit from synchronous chat room communication in that they have the opportunity to recycle typed responses from their interlocutors and use it in their own L2 output (Gruba & Clark, 2010; Payne & Ross, 2005; Payne & Whitney, 2002). Certainly in this last example, technology seems to offer certain advantages not otherwise easily accessible to learners for working in "safe" or sheltered environments on their language learning; chat, in this instance, provides a relatively spontaneous type of communication that is nevertheless subject to pauses and reflection that may allow for more focus on form.

An important and broad area of TMLL research—focusing on the ostensibly affective-oriented aspects of learner diversity—investigates relationships between the more dynamic ID variables and TMLL. Main findings in this area suggest that specific modalities (e.g., gaming) or particular design features (providing training in using the specific technology per se) can influence learner motivation, attitudes, preferences, anxiety, identities, and so on. For example, a common finding across research on online gaming and social networking sites is that the relative anonymity offered by technology-mediated communication can mitigate the *anxiety* learners experience in face-to-face interactions and thereby increase learners' *willingness to communicate* (WTC; deHaan, 2005, Peterson, 2010, 2011; Reinders & Wattana, 2014).[2] In addition—and adding to the diversity and complexity of TMLL research—certain ID variables are understood to interact with one another. For example, proficiency can impact anxiety such that less proficient students participating in synchronous CMC are prone to more anxiety, particularly when talking with native-speaker interlocutors.[3]

The diversity of TMLL and ID issues aside, we argue that there are three practical implications for instructors and course designers arising out of TMLL research to date (these are framed and discussed in the next section in terms of the TESOL Technology Standards Framework [Healy et al., 2008] for CALL):

1. Given the importance of *digital literacy* in successful TMLL, learners must be trained in the "foundational knowledge and skills in technology for a multi-lingual world" (Healey et al., 2008, p. 21).
2. Given the importance of *autonomous, self-directed* learning in TMLL, instructional design must enable learners to effectively "use technology-based tools as aids in the development of their language learning competence as part of formal instruction and for further learning" (Healey et al., 2008, p. 25).
3. Given the importance of learner *culture* and cultural differences arising in learning environments, instructional design should enable participants to use "technology in socially and culturally appropriate, legal, and ethical ways" (Healey et al., 2008, p. 23).

Each of these dimensions is explored in further detail in this chapter, by way of providing concrete suggestions for the design of language learning experiences in TMLL environments.

Digital Literacy

A consistent finding in TMLL research is that technological literacy and readiness to engage in TMLL are crucially important for technology to enhance learning. Considerable differences in technological familiarity are likely to be found among distinct learner populations (e.g., low-literate, low-education immigrants), though even university students—often regarded as technologically savvy and proficient with the latest devices—also need training in the use of technology specific to particular language educational platforms. A number of studies have found, for example, that college-age students at North American universities—involved in blended and hybrid learning—lack the *specific* skills needed to benefit from TMLL and "specialized CALL tasks" (Winke & Goertler, 2008, p. 496; see also Barrette, 2001; Goertler, Bollen, & Gaff, 2012; Winke, Goertler, & Azumie, 2010).

Given these findings, a key area of concern has been how best to support and train learners in their use of digital technology. Chun, Lai, and Morrison (2013), for example, suggest three major areas to address: (a) affective and attitudinal support, (b) technical support, and (c) learning support. Three similar categories are identified by Hubbard and Romeo (2012):

- *Technical training:* addressing (a) general use of applications (audio-video recording, speed controls in media players, advanced searching in Google); (b) use of language-specific applications (keyboarding skills in a foreign character sets); and (c) options and controls in dedicated applications.

- *Pedagogical training:* making students aware of language learning processes, such as the difference between top-down and bottom-up processing, output, or interaction. Because learners have more choices in online or hybrid learning and more individual control over their learning processes, it becomes important for learners to make the right pedagogical choices on the basis of knowledge about how language learning proceeds.
- *Strategic training:* addressing enhancement of learner strategies, such as metacognition, or the effective use of particular technological affordances, such as clicking on hypertext links (Chun & Plass, 1996) or responding to computer-generated feedback (Heift, 2002).

Starting with technical training, the TESOL Technology Standards Framework (2008) identifies various technical skills needed for minimum-level, rudimentary uses of educational technology. For example, learners should be able to "demonstrate basic operational skills in using various technology tools and internet browsers" (Healey et al., 2008, p. 21), including powering devices on and off, saving and editing files and folders, editing in documents, and performing basic Internet browser functions, such as using e-mail. In addition, learners should be able "to use available input and output devices (e.g., keyboard, mouse, printer, headset, microphone, media player, electronic whiteboard)" and understand L2 orthography on keyboards (Healey et al., 2008, p. 23). Learners should also have knowledge of technology security, the use of security software, and how to secure personal information. Finally, learners should be able to troubleshoot technological problems by accessing help menus, seeking out technical help from relevant sites or individuals, and, in the case of children, avoiding inappropriate or adult content.

Autonomy

An important aspect of TMLL is how learners must often engage in the educational experience on their own and, consequently, must manage independent learning in productive ways. Some learners will be better able to do this than others, which again raises the issue of learner training and the importance of making learners aware of *how* to learn in technology-mediated environments effectively.

Such skills will partly involve what Fischer (2012) calls "general exploitation strategies" insofar as students will need to know how to get the most out of digital tools specifically for language learning purposes. We know that SLA is dependent on learners working with large amounts of data and input, which can certainly be facilitated by technology; however, learners will need training in how to take advantage of this potentiality. Exploitation strategies will include an ability to use technology-based "productivity tools" (Healey et al., 2008, p. 25), which refers to the use of technology for enhancing language production (e.g., word processing, presentation software, Web design) and comprehension (translators, electronic dictionaries). Exploitation strategies also include the use of digital tools for technology-mediated communication and collaboration, which will require using comments functions, wikis, interactive whiteboards, and CMC, as well as platforms for communication such as blogs, podcasts, and movie-making tools.

Effective TMLL also calls for training learners in relevant SLA principles (i.e., pedagogical training, noted previously), as well as specific learning strategies (e.g., metacognition) known to enhance language acquisition (i.e., aforementioned strategic training). This means that language learners will need to have skills in using "technology to support autonomy, lifelong learning, creativity, metacognition, collaboration, personal pursuits, and productivity" (as stipulated in the TESOL standards; Healey et al., 2008, p. 28). Recommendations in this area issue out of various research findings, though primary among these is the importance of *motivation*. Motivation has been a central focus in CALL and TMLL research, given the ostensible and inherently appealing aspects of gaming, social networking, CMC, and so on and their potential for motivation-related language learning benefits (e.g., reducing anxiety, increasing learner control, choice, WTC). Motivation is primarily important in TMLL because of its relationship with *autonomy* (i.e., taking control of learning, reflecting, making decisions). Autonomy is a key variable in TMLL because technology-mediated environments place increased demands on learners for self-regulation, metacognition, independent action and decision making. Learners, then, need "skills and strategies inherent in an autonomous approach, such as the ability to organize and reflect on learning, monitor progress, identify gaps, and solve problems" (Murphy & Hurd, 2011, p. 45).

A clear implication of the aforementioned findings and recommendations, then, is the importance for technology-mediated instructional design to proceed on the basis of student needs and, to the extent practicable, some idea of a learner's ID profile (or the most salient IDs in the targeted learner group): "the teacher's recognition of diversity [is] paramount and needs to be supported by seeking as much information as is reasonably necessary" (Adams & Nicolson, 2011, p. 33). Feedback via assessment and evaluation thus becomes crucial for instructional design. In addition, because the technology-mediated environment will itself exert motivational influence on learners, in multiple possible directions, it will be worthwhile keeping track of that relationship in general, especially where the technology is new to the learners. Various innovations might aid in this aim, such as some kind of periodic motivational tracking over the course of lessons (face-to-face or virtual) to see how learners are responding to instruction and how motivation varies. One also wonders whether it is comparatively easy or useful to automate the collection of information about students' motivational profiles (e.g., via an online version of the Strategy Inventory of Language Learning, or SILL, or the Beliefs About Language Learning Inventory, or BALLI), incorporate these into a kind of needs analysis at the class level, and then turn results into a set of pedagogical suggestions. Whatever the future holds for these sorts of innovations, it will be important to have insights into the diversity of TMLL learner profiles and to use this information for tailored instruction.

Culture

It is well known that differences in culture—and educational culture—can impact learning in negative or positive ways (see chapter 11). The same applies in TMLL, particularly where there are mismatches between the culture of the learner and some aspect of the technology-mediated environment, be it materials, activities, the instructor, or other learners. Synchronous text chat or spoken interaction, mediated and increasingly common via various Web 2.0 applications, has a unique capability to bring learners and instructors from different cultures into close communicative contact, not only with clear potential benefits, but also with the possibility of "clash" when cultures, morals, and expectations about learning differ (Ware, 2005; Ware & Kramsch, 2005). Moreover, educational ideologies and values latent within instructional design can conflict with the L1 or background culture of learners. For example, learners may come from cultures that do not value student autonomy, which seems to be one of the most important assumptions underlying success in blended or fully online learning environments, especially those that involve large degrees of self-access (Peters & Shi, 2011). The importance of learner L1 culture has led to a number of recommendations for students that help mitigate issues arising from cultural differences (particularly as they relate to CMC). For example, in general, learners should be made aware that "communication conventions differ across cultures, communities, and contexts" and accordingly be able to accommodate different communication styles online (Healey et al., 2008, p. 23). This suggests that learners should be trained to identify similarities and differences in local and global communication, which involves being aware of appropriate communication styles in particular contexts (e.g., not using all caps with English-speaking interlocutors) and the ways in which CMC can be interpreted or misinterpreted (with respect to register, expected content of messages, turn taking, etc.). In addition, learners need to know appropriate and ethical "use[s] of private and public information" given how these considerations vary between different cultures (Healey et al., 2008, p. 25). For example, learners should be aware that public information, such as photographs of oneself or others, in one community may be considered private in another. On the topic of culture, it is important to stress the possible advantages of TMLL for developing intercultural competence, a priority learning objective in recent language education research and practice (Belz & Thorne, 2006). CMC, in particular, offers valuable opportunities for interaction with speakers from other cultures and the development of intercultural sensibilities. Moreover, such interactions involve various methods of presenting personal information and building relationships, and blogs and personal websites can be used to communicate a learner's "Web biography" for these purposes (Belz & Thorne, 2006). Using technology in this way, however, involves presenting (and creating) personal identities, and instructional designers and teachers need to consider this potential in TMLL given the sociopolitical and identity dimensions of language instruction noted in chapter 4. TMLL offers certain affordances for the expression and creation—and constraint—of the L2 self, which can be an empowering experience on the one hand, but also repressive and marginalizing on the other. On the positive side, Lee and Hoadley (2006) point out that massively multiplayer online role-playing games (MMORPGs), among other virtual spaces available on the Internet, "allow [. . .] players to construct identity [which] is an important lever that may help align identity formation with learning activities" (p. 3). In this way, MMORPGs and other virtual digital spaces can be realistic playgrounds for tentative and exploratory identity formation. In addition, the close relationship between identity representation (and formation) and social media (e.g., Facebook, Twitter, blogging) can be exploited as a language learning space that is imbued intentionally with an identity focus.

In sum, learner diversity is a key determiner of L2 learning engagement and attainment, a variable that becomes even more complex when technology mediation is added to language learning and teaching. The hoped-for pedagogical solution in TMLL—as in classroom-based instructed SLA—is to use information on learner needs and acquisitional profiles to tailor instruction in optimal ways for particular students. We would argue, though, that research is not quite at the stage where findings have established general principles that can concretely guide instructional design based on learner IDs. However, perhaps the main affordance provided by technology—in the area of learner diversity—is that it creates an unprecedented flexibility for learners to (a) engage in a wide variety of technology-mediated tasks; (b) select from a multitude of Internet-available texts; and (c) interact with a variety of real and virtual interlocutors (within a variety of real and simulated environments) in ways that can accommodate differences in personal needs, learning styles, motivations, and identities.

Key Pedagogical Concepts for TMLL

The importance of considering learner diversity notwithstanding, we turn now to general pedagogical considerations for TMLL given current best practices in language pedagogy. The key ideas raised in chapter 5—many related to a task-based approach to language teaching—encapsulate some of the most important teaching and language learning principles from pedagogical research to date. Returning to these ideas (and drawing on similar arguments in González-Lloret & Ortega, 2014b), we suggest that if technology mediation is to help foster development of an additional language, it must work in the service of pedagogical principles that generally call for (a) engagement in language learning tasks that learners are likely to encounter in future L2 use, (b) a "learning-by-doing" instructional approach, (c) instructional focus on learner needs, (d) primacy of social interaction during instruction with a variety of partners and peer groups, and (e) sundry aids and affordances that scaffold learners in effective ways (especially through provision of feedback) and aid language development. TMLL, then, will need to be guided by what we know works best, in general terms, to promote language acquisition in instructional settings.

First, we have argued that *task* is the optimal unit by which to organize instructional language learning (see also Doughty & Long, 2003b, on using tasks to design distance education), noting, however, that TBLT is much more than the mere deployment of task-like activities. Thus, commonly identified features of tasks provide a useful reference for designing effective TMLL experiences and for which a number of examples can be found in TMLL research. For example, the requirement that tasks and activities be fundamentally *goal oriented* is evidenced by various online affordances such as Internet webquests (directed, collaborative lessons involving the collection of information via Web research) or multiplayer online games where learners must collaboratively negotiate a simulated social space and solve a series of problems or challenges toward some ultimate goal (González-Lloret, 2003; Sykes, 2014). Moreover, wikis, gaming, webquests, and other goal-directed online activities—if designed well—will often entail *problem-based learning*, which is central to an experiential, "learning-by-doing" approach to language instruction, by providing learners with real challenges that stimulate their cognitive, conative, and especially linguistic engagement. In addition, CMC platforms in general (e.g., chat rooms, telecollaboration, interactive learning communities), with their potential for real-time communication, offer opportunities for working with language *holistically*, asking learners to surmount challenges and accomplish linguistic goals using complex language in real time with a primary focus on communicative meaning. TMLL is also appealing for its potential to provide *authentic* texts, interactions, scenarios, environments, and so on that bear a similarity to—or replicate directly—the types of communicative encounters learners will want and need to experience in the real world. Along these lines, the unit of "task" further recommends itself for TMLL when we consider that many potential real-world activities interesting to students are themselves technology mediated, most notably various types of online L2 communication, such as writing e-mails, sending texts, posting on message boards, navigating social networks (Twitter, Facebook, etc.), or participating in audiographic conferencing and other online educational environments (e.g., massive open online courses, or MOOCs; González-Lloret & Ortega, 2014a).

Of course, the aforementioned suggestions relate to various recommended aspects of *task design* (particularly manipulations of task complexity) that will need to be considered carefully—vis-à-vis specific learning objectives—so as to effectively promote the known benefits of task-based communication (e.g., more frequent interaction, negotiation of meaning, focus on form, increased accuracy, fluency, complexity; Robinson, 2011; Van den Branden, Bygate, & Norris, 2009). Task design will also need to ensure that learning can be sequenced in rational ways, steadily increasing task difficulty (via subordinate pedagogical tasks) toward a level of complexity approximating real-world performance. As a TMLL example, asynchronous or semisynchronous text chat would seem to offer options for controlling and simplifying task complexity (e.g., more time for planning and editing) in ways that offer opportunities for language practice and analysis before proceeding on to more difficult performances in synchronous written or spoken digitally mediated communication (Adams & Alwi, 2014). We suggest, then, that if TMLL is generally guided in its design by the aforementioned ideas, technology seems especially well placed to enhance language learning via the known sine qua non principles of language instruction and task design.

In addition to task considerations, instruction for TMLL must issue out of a fundamentally learner-centered orientation to language pedagogy, which starts in the first instance with the identification of instructional objectives, tasks, and other related educational supports that respond to the learning goals of students. Hence, *needs analysis* will be crucial for any TMLL instructional sequence or module. Moreover, although the recommended methodologies for classroom-based needs analyses will be relevant for TMLL also (most notably J. D. Brown, 2009, and Long, 2005a), González-Lloret (2014) points out (as discussed previously) that digital course designers and instructors must also ascertain levels of student digital literacy, available resources, technology accessibility, and support (see the section in this chapter on evaluation). Moreover, forces of globalization enacted via the Internet have created new reasons for learning language (e.g., contributing to Internet-based fandoms), as well as new L2 targets (e.g., forms of international, lingua franca English used on the Internet and via technology in general), which further call for careful identification of specifically technology-related learner aims and desires.

We have also emphasized the importance of exposure to language *input* in instructed SLA and the widely held view that effective selection, manipulation, and presentation of L2 input is crucial to successful language learning. It has been suggested specifically that instruction must provide learners with frequent, rich, and authentic language input (see also Doughty & Long, 2003b). To this end, the virtually unlimited access to *authentic texts* via the Internet is a critically important contribution of technology, one that has greatly expanded the possibilities of incorporating real-life input into language instruction in all modalities (oral, aural, written, and visual). Moreover, because language instruction requires *interesting, relevant content*, the abundance of authentic online texts, recorded realia, live interlocutors, virtual environments, and other forms of Web-based media provide potentially highly compelling, motivating materials and experiences. Indeed, the potential for authenticity from Internet-based texts and environments allows for the exploration of socially situated language use as particular forms are used to convey meaning and accomplish various communicative functions, all within particular registers and genres that define specific discourse communities. All of these dimensions are combined together during Internet-supported communication, making the Web a kind of repository of "real" language use that can be studied, analyzed, learned from, and participated in. On a related note, we point out that the potential for using authentic online texts fundamentally changes the nature of language learning materials, away from, say, the static orientation of physical textbooks, toward more interactive, Internet-based materials—or even collaboratively constructed materials—in which Web 2.0 affordances, such as blogs, wikis, video sharing, and mash-ups, can be used by learners and instructors to create their own locally relevant language learning texts.

TMLL will also call for strategies and techniques that *enhance the salience of input* in ways that support L2 acquisition. Technology would seem to enable many possibilities for strategic input modification and the focusing of learner attention on less salient form-meaning pairings. Affordances such as hyperlinks to explanatory text or online dictionaries—or glossing features such as mouse-overs or pop-ups—can provide synonyms, antonyms, paraphrases, definitions, or even translations that help learners notice or process key features of L2 input (Lee & Lee, 2013). Moreover, Web 2.0 features such as tagging pictures or text in social media or other interactive platforms might offer collaborative options for input enhancement (and lexical or grammatical learning) in ways that meet local communicative needs and goals in real time (Godwin-Jones, 2006).

A key source of meaningful input will come from *opportunities for interaction* with peers and other expert interlocutors (Long, 1981, 1996), a clear area of advantage for technology-mediated instruction. Interaction is a cornerstone principle in SLA and a primary driver of language acquisition because it allows not only the processing of input but also the production and monitoring of output (Chapelle, 1998), especially when expert partners help scaffold learner development via interactional moves known to benefit SLA during communication (primarily feedback of various kinds). The most obvious and eagerly leveraged technological affordance in this category is the use of synchronous CMC, and the preeminent example of CMC is, arguably, the use of telecollaboration. Telecollaboration makes a significant contribution to TMLL because it brings L2 speakers together to engage in real-time, authentic, primarily oral-aural communication (Guth & Helm, 2010). Accordingly, one of the key drivers of learning arising out of interaction is the *negotiation of meaning*, which occurs when tasks are fundamentally communicative and require partners to work collaboratively to accomplish a linguistic goal (Chapelle, 1998). Negotiation within telecollaboration has received sustained attention in TMLL research given its importance for developing intercultural competence, among other competencies (Belz & Thorne, 2006). Interaction during CMC is known to create misunderstandings, miscommunications, unexpectedness, or surprises when speakers compare and contrast their cultural beliefs and opinions with those of their partners (from a different L1 culture). These exchanges, when paired with intensive reflection and post hoc follow-up discussions, are understood to result in deepened awareness about the target culture, the learners' own culture, and cultural difference generally (Canto, de Graaff, & Jauregi, 2014).

We also note that using digital technology to enhance interaction should go beyond traditional, classroom-based conceptualizations of communication and negotiation. That is, CMC should be implemented to take advantage of the multimodality that is possible online given the different types of communication that can happen simultaneously. Videoconferencing and audiographic conferencing, for example, involve groups of learners integrating audio, video, photo images, text chat, file sharing, and other screen graphics (e.g., PowerPoint slides, screen sharing) into their collaborative activities, all of which create novel and complex ways of interacting and negotiating meaning during L2 communication (Canto, de Graaff, & Jauregi, 2014).[4]

Another notable feature of interaction is its ability to promote *cooperative and collaborative learning* (Doughty & Long, 2003b). Technology-mediated environments offer many possibilities for collaboration in that they allow students to chat, read, comment on, edit, and amend one another's texts, videos, blogs, websites, and so on. Furthermore, one of the main advantages of collaborative learning is to encourage learners to do analytic work that *facilitates focus on form*. Interestingly, evidence suggests that specific collaborative digital tools will provide different learning advantages related to particular L2 linguistic features. To take an example, Oskoz and Elola (2014) found that collaborative writing tasks provided different benefits when learners used wikis versus chat rooms to jointly write L2 texts. Wikis—primarily involving reading and editing of typed text—encouraged learners to focus more on linguistic form in that students in the study concentrated more on microtextual elements, such as correcting one another's grammatical errors. By contrast, the use of chat rooms by the students—involving largely spoken discourse between learners—seem to generate more discussion about macrotextual elements, such as rhetorical structure and organization.

Finally, many of the aforementioned examples and recommendations of TMLL support our general recommendation that instruction try to utilize *various scaffolding devices* to fill gaps in learner knowledge. Along these lines, Chapelle (1998) recommends that technology-mediated language instruction should help learners "in comprehending semantic and syntactic aspects of linguistic input," as well as in "notic[ing] errors in their own output, and [. . .] correct[ing] these errors" (p. 23). To these ends, scaffolding from *implicit feedback* such as recasts, clarification requests, and other implicit interactional phenomena during synchronous and asynchronous CMC interaction will focus learners on troublesome aspects of their L2 use. Likewise, scaffolding from *explicit feedback* on learner output—both by peers and instructors—via blogs, text chat, message boards, wikis, and so on, will help draw attention to formal aspects of linguistic form, particularly where there are persistent interlanguage errors (Chapelle, 1998; Solares, 2014).

Students can also focus on linguistic form by engaging in intentional *analysis of language*, an activity supported by various online or software-based concordancing platforms (e.g., MicroConcord, Wordsmith, AntConc, MonoConc, and ParaConc). Concordancers enable learners to perform analyses of L2 corpora (e.g., analyzing keywords in context, word frequency, frequency of collocations or colligations), which promotes *inductive language learning* (Doughty & Long, 2003b) and awareness about key linguistic patterns unique to specific L2 registers and genres (Lixun, 2004).

An additional purpose for linguistic analysis is to emphasize *reflective learning* and have learners engage in important metalevel reflections that consolidate language knowledge and skills (Dewey, 1938). To this end, assessment-driven feedback, for which technology is known to play a useful auxiliary role, is crucial for language learning (Winke, 2014; see the section later in this chapter on assessment). We note here the close similarity between learning-oriented or scenario-based assessment frameworks—which are increasingly computer mediated—and the typical task cycles in TBLT, where formative assessment plays an important role throughout the process. One might envision, then, technology-supported innovations where task-based lessons are programmed and delivered via a "smart" technology that also involves a variety of opportunities for automated feedback along the way (which, indeed, is increasingly what a lot of the computer-based formatively oriented assessments look like).

In sum, we suggest that the aforementioned general principles of language pedagogy will productively guide TMLL toward effective learning experiences. Indeed, the various professional standards of technology-mediated language instruction noted previously[5] have sought to codify many of these ideas into benchmarks of practice so as to ensure high-quality use of digital tools for language teaching and learning. Finally, we note an encouraging trend in CALL and technology-mediated language instruction specifically toward the combined and creative use of Web 2.0 affordances (i.e., Internet sites that enable user-generated content, usability, and interoperability). Web 2.0 tools—used in combination with one another—seem to allow for a certain instructional creativity and flexibility, which is in keeping with a postmethod, hybrid approach to contemporary language teaching, and contrasts (positively, in our view) with the prepackaged CALL software approaches of days past that seem to have diminished along with the notion of "methods-based" language teaching.

Teaching Language Skills in TMLL

Technology mediation also presents a number of particular benefits, as well as some challenges, for extending these general pedagogic principles to the teaching and learning of specific language skills. In this section we summarize how technology is used in L2 skills instruction, providing examples and discussing advantages and caveats (see Levy & Stockwell, 2013; Thomas, Reinders, & Warschauer, 2014, for comprehensive overviews). Although we distinguish between various language modalities as relevant, it will become clear that the use of digital tools and media increasingly blurs the traditional four-skills distinction and draws more typically upon the combined use of L2 skills and an integrated-skills approach to L2 instruction. It is even possible that technology and CMC are seeing new language skills emerge (e.g., an ability somewhere between literacy and oracy arising out of text chat and messaging applications), suggesting that the notion of communicative skills might need to be fundamentally reconceptualized in the increasingly technology-mediated future. Notwithstanding this increasing breakdown of clear-cut boundaries between the traditional skills, we discuss recent developments in research and practice in terms of their primary focus on L2 reading, listening, speaking, and writing.

Reading

L2 teachers have taken advantage of a number of digital tools to support reading instruction, including quick and extensive access to authentic target language texts, the ability to add hyperlinks, and various enhancements of the reading experience via the use of supportive visual input. We focus here on three main components of the computer-supported L2 reading process: (a) word recognition, (b) language comprehension, and (c) text interpretation (see also Park et al., 2014).

Although TMLL opportunities for helping adult L2 learners focus on reading still seem to be rare, technology has been found to provide some advantages with respect to fostering L2 word recognition and decoding processes, including individualization, topical variety, and high learner motivation (see Chun, 2006, or Macaruso & Rodman, 2011, for more detailed discussions). For example, if the target language operates under a completely different writing system, learners may want to practice L2 word recognition, including phonological decoding and phoneme awareness. Although there is an abundance of technology-mediated opportunities to practice word recognition for younger L1 and L2 learners, possibilities for L2 adult learners are more limited. More typically the case, however, it has been argued that many (though certainly not all) adult L2 learners tend to be fully literate in their L1. Therefore, they may be less interested in word recognition than in automatizing their word recognition processes (Park et al., 2014). For example, Fukkink, Hulstijn, and Simis (2005) found that technology-supported automaticity training in the L2 promotes faster lexical access, allowing learners to systematically practice accuracy and fluency (see also Li, 2010). Thus, text-to-speech apps or natural readers[6] could be used by learners in individualized ways as they allow learners to vary the dialect and pace of either single words, whole sentences, or even entire paragraphs. Hence, technology-enhanced L2 reading instruction has the potential to provide individualized training, allowing learners to work independently and practice new vocabulary, or review previously taught words, which promotes automaticity of word recognition.

With regard to L2 text comprehension, several studies have investigated how technology can be used to facilitate comprehension in two core areas: vocabulary and syntax. In terms of vocabulary instruction, research has focused on the use of technological tools ranging from electronic dictionaries (Koyama & Takeuchi,

2007) to Web-based activities, as well as word lists (Makoto, 2006), translation tools (Abraham, 2008; Poole, 2012), and multimedia glossing (e.g., Tabatabaei & Shams, 2011; Yanguas, 2009). For instance, research finds that the deployment of multimedia glosses is positively related to vocabulary acquisition (e.g., Proctor et al., 2011). In the case of multimedia glosses, online reading texts can be manip-ulated so learners have the opportunity to open a pop-up window that then pro-vides either a visual of the word or concept, a textual definition, or a combination of both in order to aid comprehension. The input provided in the gloss can be adapted, depending on the learner type (i.e., visual, aural, textual). As shown in Figure 13.1, for example, learners can click on a phrase like "the mammoth and the mastodon" and be provided with a picture of the two extinct animals.

With regard to hand-held electronic dictionaries, Koyama and Takeuchi (2007) found that learners who used electronic dictionaries looked up more words in less time than learners who used print dictionaries (though, interestingly, the larger number of lookups did not lead to increased L2 reading comprehension).

Digital technology may also be useful for facilitating L2 learners' syntactic processing. Warschauer and Park (2012), for example, observed that traditional block formatting of text may not be the most efficient way to promote read-ing proficiency. In light of research that has found that readers can take in 9–15 characters at a time before moving their eyes (Demb, Boynton, & Heeger, 1997), visual-syntactic text formatting (VSTF) has become a promising form of computer-assisted syntactic structuring, or "digital scaffolding" (Park et al., 2014,

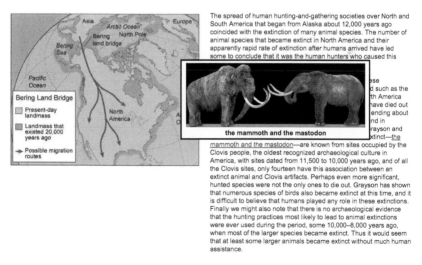

FIGURE 13.1   Multimedia gloss implemented in a computer-based reading text. Adapted from Schedl and O'Reilly (2014). Copyright © 2014 Educa-tional Testing Service. Modified by permission of Educational Testing Service, the copyright owner.

p. 271). To promote syntactic processing, VSTF "breaks sentences up at salient clause and phrase boundaries, and presents visual clusters across multiple rows to denote syntactic hierarchies" (Park et al., 2014, p. 271). Additionally, various electronic display elements, such as font size and style, text and background color, line and page length, and page layout, can be employed to transform the text into salient patterns, thus facilitating more efficient eye movement and syntactic processing, which aids retention and integration of multiphrase sentences. Eye-tracking studies have found VSTF to improve reading speed, comprehension, content retention, and awareness of linguistic patterns (Park et al., 2014; Walker et al., 2005, 2007; Warschauer, Park, & Walker, 2011).

Finally, text interpretation can be aided via technology by means of blogs and CMC. Blogging environments provide textual feedback and annotations, which encourage readers to negotiate textual meaning through CMC-based interaction and thereby develop deeper (cultural, content, and linguistic) understandings (Park et al., 2014). Moreover, computer-mediated interaction between learners and teachers may also be beneficial to L2 reading comprehension and text interpretation, as online discussions can help learners clarify L2 texts and develop interpretation skills by facilitating reflection and metacognitive skills (Carico & Logan, 2004; Downes, 2004; Grisham & Wolsey, 2006).

These kinds of relatively obvious technology-mediated reading affordances aside, a considerable current challenge has to do with the degree to which TMLL research investigates the different kinds of reading that are uniquely called upon for the Internet, where massive amounts of information distributed across different sources requires enhanced skimming and scanning skills, efficient processing, ability to judge relevance, and so on. It would seem that, depending on the learning objectives of a course or curriculum, reading instruction may be needed that enhances specific reading skills for technology-mediated environments (the Internet in particular).

Listening

In the case of listening instruction, there appear to be clear benefits from TMLL, with research showing that digital technology in general and the Internet in particular can foster L2 listening skills and strategies more efficiently and effectively than traditional approaches (Chen & Zhang, 2011; see also Romeo & Hubbard, 2008).

Two TMLL approaches have been increasingly used in L2 listening instruction over the past years: the implementation of help options in multimedia L2 listening (Grgurović & Hegelheimer, 2007; Robin, 2007) and the use of computer-mediated audio- and videoconferencing technologies (Yanguas, 2009). Computer-mediated audio- and videoconferencing technologies such as Skype or WebEx provide unique opportunities for more integrated, communicative types of listening tasks (Hampel & Hauck, 2004; Wang, 2004). Rising in popularity with increased global access to high-speed Internet connections, videoconferencing technology has been employed in distance-learning programs (Hampel & Hauck, 2004; Strambi & Bouvet, 2003) and blended-learning contexts, allowing learners to practice L2 listening skills while interacting with target language speakers. Despite the increased use of audio- and videoconferencing, however, the clarity and reliability of streaming sound and video remain problematic (e.g., Hampel & Hauck, 2004; Levy et al., 2010; Wang, 2004), especially across the global scope of technological differences, thereby often interfering with otherwise sound educational goals. However, when the technology functions properly, communication through videoconferencing has been found to be fairly comparable to face-to-face interaction (Cotos, 2011; Levy & Stockwell, 2013). Furthermore, emerging devices may offer new affordances, such as mobile technology for "live," on-the-spot listening (e.g., using a mobile phone to follow directions, or listen to audio guides at the zoo or museum), which would appear to be a relatively stable platform (i.e., compared to streaming sound and video), allowing learners to integrate listening practice while moving through physical environments (e.g., museums, train stations, city streets).

Help options are supportive features that enhance aural input and include L1 translations, accompanying transcripts or subtitles (Grgurović & Hegelheimer, 2007; Pujolà, 2002), images (Zhou & Yang, 2004), and videos (Smidt & Hegelheimer, 2004), as well as dictionaries and the option to slow down or repeat the audio text (Hsu, 1994). Hsu (1994), for instance, investigated how adult ESL learners used relatively simple practices such as audio repetition, written transcripts, and dictionaries while listening to a story streamed on a computer. She found transcripts to be the most frequently used scaffolding option, though this finding might also reflect the timing of the study in the early days of Internet familiarity. In a similar study, Pujolà (2002) investigated the use of subtitles by 22 beginner EFL students when watching videos for the purpose of training L2 listening skills. Learners varied considerably in how they used help options. Although accompanying texts were frequently viewed by learners at all proficiency levels, more proficient learners used the text only as a backup option. By contrast, lower proficiency learners relied heavily on the transcripts, to the extent that at times "they were doing a reading task instead of listening" (Pujolà, 2002, p. 253). Grgurović and Hegelheimer (2007) expanded this line of research, examining 18 adult ESL learners' use of subtitles and transcripts for listening comprehension tasks. In contrast to Hsu's study, however, learners preferred subtitles over transcripts. Grgurović and Hegelheimer thus argued for giving users more control over help options and allowing learners to skip help altogether "to accommodate different learning styles and preferences" (p. 61).

One overarching implication from these findings, then, is that multimedia TMLL affordances should provide a variety of help options, which learners can selectively deploy to customize L2 activities according to their individual needs. Thus, when promoting learners' L2 listening abilities, a variety of needed support options would include, for example, subtitles, transcripts, and multimedia glosses, as well as the ability to moderate input speed and replay audio segments. Research seems to suggest that there is no single support option that is effective across learner types and that L2 learners use different help or auxiliary options in highly individualized ways. However, help options should be provided only to the extent that they support the skill that is practiced. That is, they should not allow learners to completely rely on the given option to avoid practicing the actual target skill—indeed, at some point learners will probably need to learn how to deal with unmanipulated listening input, so they should be exposed to the same and work with it on a regular basis.

Speaking

Research on fostering speaking ability via TMLL is still relatively limited, though some attention has focused on the teaching of specific aspects, or microskills, of speaking. A major area of investigation thus far has focused on phonological microskills, including pronunciation (Chun, 2013; Kawai & Hirose, 2000; Molholt & Hwu, 2008; Neumeyer et al., 2000; Tanner & Landon, 2009), intonation (Levis & Pickering, 2004), and vowel qualities (Wang & Munro, 2004). Wang and Munro (2004), for example, investigated computer-assisted vowel contrast training for Chinese ELLs and found improved and lasting oral production in learners who worked with TMLL compared to learners who did not. They asked six English speakers to record 71 word pairs containing three vowel contrasts /i/-/I/, /u/-/ʊ/, and /e/-/æ/, and they then created synthetic variants of each stimulus that differed in pitch and acoustic distinctness. In an identification task in which the listeners heard single words through headphones (e.g., "hid," "heed") learners had to identify the correct word by clicking labeled buttons ("heed," "hid") on a computer screen. A salient aspect highlighted in their study, and arguably the main implication for TMLL (Chun, 2013; Olsen, 2014), is the ability of digital tools such as these to provide individualized learning-oriented feedback.

Providing feedback on pronunciation can be challenging, especially for instructors who may themselves be L2 learners of the language they teach. Therefore, Chun (2013) suggests that computers can be used to provide real-time feedback to learners "in the form of visual displays of articulatory activity and its acoustic consequences in actual speech output" (p. 2). Visual acoustic (i.e., waveform or spectrographic analyses) and articulatory displays (i.e., visualizations of how sounds, words, and sentences are articulated or produced by speech organs) are implemented in a number of learning software platforms. Programs such as Audacity, Enhance, Praat, RTSPECT, Speech Analyzer, and Wave Surfer can be used to operationalize computer-supported pronunciation practice (see Godwin-Jones, 2009). We concur, however, with the observation by Neri, Cucchiarini, Strik, and Boves (2002) that ideal computer-assisted pronunciation training software would need to provide opportunities additionally for input, output, and feedback—in other words, an expanded understanding of pronunciation instruction (and not just high-tech visual displays of acoustic phenomena).

In addition to activities that focus directly on the development of L2 speaking microskills, research has shown that TMLL tasks that are not directly targeted at speaking can still have an impact on oral production skills. In an early technology study, Borrás and Lafayette (1994), for example, investigated the use of video subtitles and their effect on speaking ability. They found higher oral performance results in terms of effectiveness, accuracy, organization, and fluency for learner groups that watched videos with subtitles compared to those who watched videos without subtitles. More recently, Payne and Whitney (2002), investigating whether L2 spoken proficiency can be indirectly developed through synchronous CMC in chat rooms, found that written chat communication in an online course increased participants' *oral* production skills. Although it is still unclear, as the authors maintain, how the differing characteristics of written CMC and face-to-face teaching relate to L2 oral proficiency development, they speculate that chat rooms can foster oral production skills in two ways: (a) output enhancement and (b) use of language without the benefit of gesture. L2 learners in the study had greater opportunity to produce output in the L2 as a result of the fact that multiple participants were able to write at the same time in the chat program. They recognize that "[t]his situation would be disastrous in a classroom, but it works online" (Payne & Whitney, 2002, p. 24). In addition, whereas face-to-face classroom interaction allows learners to draw upon gestures and body language, in text-based chat rooms learners are restricted to written language only, to communicate without recourse to nonverbal channels of communication. That being the case, writing or typing their contributions requires an even closer monitoring of output—because there are no nonverbal strategies available—thus drawing even greater attention to the production process. There is also the possibility that the semispontaneous nature of written chat enables a degree of reflective focus-on-form attention that is not possible during face-to-face spoken interaction, allowing learners to notice more about the use of language (also with visual support of the written words they and others produce) as it occurs in a somewhat slower pattern of interaction.

Finally, more and more activities aimed at promoting L2 speaking feature tasks that require the computer to recognize and respond to learner output (Levy & Stockwell, 2013). As part of the TOEFL *Practice Online Speaking Series*, for example, learners can receive automatically scored feedback on their speaking as they try out sample assessment tasks from the TOEFL exam; feedback is provided in the areas of pronunciation, fluency, vocabulary, and grammar. Beyond automated scoring, automatic speech recognition and spoken dialogue systems allow for scripted, as well as increasingly open-response, dialogues (e.g., Ramanarayanan et al., 2015), offering what will be considerable potential for future pedagogic application as these technologies continue to become more accurate and robust to variations in learners and contexts of communication. In particular, the area of natural language processing research and its use for constructing interactive avatars within virtual environments is receiving increased attention in L2 learning applications (Sykes, 2008, 2014; Vincenti & Braman, 2011). Given the understanding that immersion in a given L2 is among the preferred ways to acquire certain aspects of the target language, L2 instructors are aiming to increase students' speaking time by engaging them in communication in synthetic immersive environments that may be otherwise unavailable.

Along similar lines, Second Life and SimCity are prominent, cost-free examples of virtual reality immersion that have been growing over the past decade. In early 2007, Cooke-Plagwitz estimated that over 200 universities were involved in Second Life at the time, creating virtual replications of their physical grounds for educational purposes.[7] In addition to academic institutions, language institutes such as the British Council and the Goethe-Institut have either obtained islands in already existing virtual realities or have started to create their own virtual spaces, featuring locations that allow learners to interact in either transactional or interactional ways with others or with computer avatars while engaging in everyday tasks such as service encounters or doctor visits. Thus, learners can practice speaking, listening, and other interactional skills while they also acquire incidental or intentionally seeded cultural knowledge.

However, we note that uncontrolled or poorly planned incursions into virtual environments can have disadvantages. For instance, the software and graphic requirements for applications such as Second Life may exceed the capabilities of many personal computers. Moreover, it is a characteristic of online virtual worlds such as Second Life that users have a great deal of freedom and autonomy. Thus, instructors cannot always control where learners may wander in Second Life and students may encounter inappropriate material. In addition to these issues, it takes considerable time, expertise, and money to prepare and create a virtual world, especially one that is geared toward effective language learning.

Writing

Writing is an essential skill for many multilingual individuals with educational and professional aspirations and also for those seeking to merely "get by" in a target culture. In addition to writing longer texts such as reports and essays, texting, blogging, e-mailing, and chatting have become daily occurrences in most workplace contexts (Timpe Laughlin, Wain, & Schmidgall, 2015). Adopting these real-life tasks for L2 writing instruction has inspired a body of research that investigates the effects of technology on writing. The affordances that have been investigated include blogging (Arnold, Ducate, & Kost, 2009; Kol & Schcolnik, 2008), automated writing evaluation (Chapelle, Cotos, & Lee, 2015; Chen & Cheng, 2008), use of laptop computers in L2 classrooms (Zheng, Warschauer, & Karkas, 2013), and interactive learning environments as contexts for fostering L2 writing abilities beyond morphosyntactic accuracy (Xing, Wing, & Spencer, 2008).

Two technologies have been particularly prevalent in computer-assisted L2 writing instruction (see also Hegelheimer & Lee, 2014): (a) collaborative writing environments (CWE) and (b) automated writing evaluation (AWE). The Internet provides new collaborative writing opportunities using CMC tools such as blogs, wikis, Blackboard, Moodle, and Google Docs (Elola & Oskoz, 2010; Kessler, 2009; Kost, 2011). Blogs are among the most widely used and researched TMLL approaches in L2 writing instruction. Research has revealed different collaboration patterns among learners using blogs, ranging from individual writing with no collaboration, to shared writing processes, such as brainstorming and outlining (Kost, 2011) and peer editing (Bradley, Lindstrom, & Rystedt, 2010). Although collaborative efforts tend to result in higher quality texts, especially with regard to organization and content development, true collaboration in the text production process has generally been found to be rare (Elola & Oskoz, 2010; Hegelheimer & Lee, 2014; Kessler, 2009; Lee, 2010).

Moreover, computer-based CWEs introduce new issues for L2 writing assignments. Although some learners report that they feel less pressured when producing a writing assignment with peers—and receiving feedback from peers—than with a teacher (e.g., Hegelheimer & Lee, 2014; Mulligan & Garofalo, 2011), others regard collaboration and feedback from peers as potentially embarrassing (Dippold, 2009; Hyland & Hyland, 2006; Storch, 2005), a finding that seems particularly prevalent in the context of Asian cultures (Hegelheimer & Lee, 2014).

In addition to CWEs, AWE is increasingly used to facilitate L2 writing. AWE systems provide automated feedback on a written text by analyzing the usage of linguistic features. Several AWE tools have been used operationally in L2 writing instruction (e.g., Criterion®, Intelligent Academic Discourse Evaluator, IntelliMetric, MY Access!®, WriteToLearn). Criterion, for example, developed by Educational Testing Service, is an online AWE program designed as an instructional tool for high school and college classrooms. In addition to providing a holistic score that ranges from one to six, it also offers sentence-level diagnostic feedback on various aspects of writing, including grammar, mechanics, usage, style, organization, and development (see Chapelle, Cotos, & Lee, 2015, for a detailed description).

AWE software has been found beneficial for a number of reasons. First, AWE software can function as a teaching assistant, reducing the teacher's role in the time-consuming task of providing (instant) feedback on multiple iterations of student writing. As Warschauer (2009) observed, "a major advantage of automated writing evaluation was that it engaged students in autonomous activity while freeing up teacher time" (p. 109). Secondly, AWE software has been found to aid and encourage self-correction and revision by learners (Cotos, 2011; Grimes & Warschauer, 2006; Warschauer, 2009). Moreover, Criterion, in particular, has been found to significantly reduce article and preposition errors in students' writing (Chodorow, Gamon, & Tetreault, 2010).

Although students seem to perceive the use of AWE software positively overall (Warschauer, 2009), the technology to date has some limitations. Although fairly reliable with regard to detecting mechanical and grammatical errors (Dikli, 2006), AWE solutions tend to fall short on providing feedback about content and discourse features (Attali & Burnstein, 2006; Hegelheimer & Lee, 2014). Moreover, research into the functionality of AWE software needs to investigate the use and functionality of AWE in different cross-cultural and cross-linguistic contexts in order to provide feedback to learners on different L1-based writing errors. Thus, although AWE frees up teacher time, the L2 instructor remains a crucial player in the TMLL writing process to facilitate, guide, and provide particular kinds of feedback on learners' L2 writing development that AWE cannot currently supply, such as coherence, cohesion, and the quality and development of argument structures. Moreover, AWEs have been found to be unreliable at times, requiring instructors to step in and provide feedback for L2 learners.

To summarize, the notion of discrete skills has become increasingly blurred in technological environments, and it may even be possible that there are new language skills emerging, somewhere in between literacy and oracy (e.g., text chat, messaging). Although TMLL may draw upon multiple skills in increasingly integrated ways, L2 teachers have the means to determine the main focus—that is, which skills to focus on primarily in a given instructional intervention. In doing so, digital tools provide specific support for particular aspects of the language skill(s) whose development they intend to foster in their students. That is to say, TMLL practice should enhance, in a systematic way, the practice of the targeted skill or subskill. For examples, in L2 reading instruction, multimedia glosses or visual support may scaffold and aid the decoding process, whereas VSTF has been found to facilitate automaticity in the decoding of target language texts. In listening, a key advantage of technology mediation is the ability to manipulate the input—slow down, speed up, repeat, pause—and thus support the development of L2 comprehension skills. For speaking, pronunciation training, based on visual acoustic and articulatory displays that analyze the learner's voice and compare it with L1 speaker norms, providing feedback, exercises, and so on, has been found to help learners develop a more target-like pronunciation. Finally, AWE can be employed to aid L2 learners in becoming more proficient writers, providing corrections and feedback. Moreover, video-mediated communication allows for a focus on more integrated listening and speaking abilities, as well as exposure to potentially different L2 dialects when involving diverse participants distributed around the world (e.g., telecollaboration). At the same time, it bears repeating that language skills in and of themselves do not constitute language proficiency or communicative competence—no amount of pronunciation practice with visual acoustic feedback will result in learners being able to engage in interactive tasks with other speakers. Available skills-based tools should be incorporated judiciously, then, into a pedagogic design that treats language use holistically and comprehensively as the target of learning.

Assessing Student Learning in TMLL

As indicated in the previous section, technology mediation offers numerous possibilities for assessing student learning in potentially efficient and effective ways. However, engaging in useful, ethical, and valid assessment within TMLL classrooms and other settings also raises several important challenges that should be considered. There has been, of course, an explosion of interest in technology-mediated assessment in general over the past 30 years, and the literature on computer-based (CBT), computer-adaptive (CAT), and Internet-based (IBT) testing is considerable (see, e.g., Mills, Potenza, & Fremer, 2005; Parshall et al., 2002; Williamson, Mislevy, & Bejar, 2006; in language testing, see Brown, 2012c; Chapelle, 2001, 2014; Chapelle & Douglas, 2006). By and large, this work has focused on the development of large-scale assessments (e.g., the TOEFL CBT and iBT) and associated concerns with robust and secure delivery platforms, effective examinee-computer interfaces, new item types and accurate construct interpretations, automated scoring, and efficient score reporting. One upshot of this type of work is that language tests, particularly English language tests, have become more widely accessible in diverse regions of the world, and there is some evidence to suggest that large-scale technology-mediated assessments have exerted a substantial washback effect on (English) language education, as teachers and learners focus on developing the abilities assessed in these new forms of assessment (e.g., Wall & Horák, 2008). Similarly, it is likely that learners have come increasingly to expect that they will be assessed via technology, not only because that is how powerful and large-scale assessments do it, but also because communication itself is increasingly technology mediated, as is education.

Turning to the TMLL classroom environment, several implications for assessment derive from recent technological developments. One major and attractive dimension of TMLL is the plethora of assessment applications, authoring tools, Web-based tests, and other affordances that are readily available either cost free or commercially via the Internet.[8] Freeware tools enable teachers to create a variety of simple test task types—including multiple-choice, short-answer, jumbled-sentence, crossword, matching and ordering, and gap-fill exercises—which are then hosted on an Internet site, scored automatically, and provided as feedback to learners about the correctness of their responses. Other freeware options allow teachers to produce Web-based action mazes that confront learners with complex situations that consist of multiple steps, each of which has a number of possible answers, thereby enabling the assessment of learners' higher order abilities (e.g., reasoning, evaluation, decision making). Where more diverse assessment formats are called for, from opinion surveys, to behavioral observations, to constructed-response and selected-response tests, commercial vendors provide comprehensive test development, delivery (e.g., online hosting), scoring, and analysis services. Even more robust assessment possibilities are available from most learning or course management software (LMS or CMS are both commonly used acronyms) providers, with the advantage that assessment is incorporated directly into the design and delivery of technology-mediated courses, all of which occur within an online classroom environment. Thus, for example, Blackboard® makes available a host of assessment development tools, including everything from automated selected-response quizzes, to essays that can be automatically scored for a variety of language features (e.g., spelling, grammar, mechanics, usage, and style, using e-rater®) and checked for plagiarism, to voice recording and analysis software—all integrated into a single course management space where students and teachers interact with each other and course materials and otherwise progress through the class syllabus.[9] Finally, ready-made Web-based assessments of language proficiency or development also exist, both in the form of low-cost and free tools that provide holistic assessments according to commonly known proficiency frameworks.

Given multiple sources of support for Web-based language assessment (see also Brown, 2012c; Chapelle & Douglas, 2006; Davidson & Coombe, 2012; Golonka et al., 2014; González-Lloret, 2013; Roever, 2001; Shin, 2012), the possibilities for TMLL educators to engage in various types of assessment in the technology-mediated environment seem virtually endless, and the support provided is sophisticated to the extent that only minimal technological know-how is required for taking advantage of these resources. One major challenge, of course, is cost. Assessment services by LMS providers, for example, only come with an institution's subscription to that provider, and the freeware applications that are available tend to emphasize only traditional types of selected-response item formats. Perhaps the most important concern with these tools and resources, though, is that they cannot replace the need for assessment literacy among the test developers and users (as outlined in chapter 7); in other words, Web-based and other computerized assessment tools are only useful to the extent that their intended uses have been carefully defined, appropriate methods articulated to such uses, validity of interpretations about learners aligned with what actually gets assessed, and consequences actually shown to support teaching and learning (Chapelle, 2001).

A key potential advantage of many of the web- and software-based assessment tools is the possibility of automated scoring of test performances. Thus, where scoring can be accomplished by the computer, it is likely that the consistency and reliability of test scores will be increased, and the work of teachers can be redirected to making use of the information provided by test scores (i.e., as opposed to spending considerable amounts of time generating the scores in the first place). Perhaps the key contribution of automated scoring to notions of assessment for learning, though, is the possibility of providing learners with immediate feedback on their achievements, diagnosing areas of learning need, and otherwise increasing the efficiency of the formative assessment cycle. The image of language learners interacting autonomously with only a "smart" computer device of some kind is certainly an attractive and potentially highly lucrative one. However, care should be taken in the design of TMLL education, such that the realities of what is possible, and what might be advisable pedagogically, are separated from profit-driven hopes of the marketplace. Clearly, automated scoring of selected-response items (e.g., multiple choice, true-false), as well as highly constrained and brief constructed-response items (e.g., gap fill), is commonplace now, and it provides easy access to formative feedback on assessments that target language and other types of *knowledge* (e.g., vocabulary items, grammar rules). Similarly, as indicated in the previous section on skills instruction, automated pronunciation feedback is available in the form of highly sophisticated acoustic analysis software that compares a learner's production to that of (a variety of) native-speaker norms. Indeed, there are hundreds of pronunciation training apps, websites, and software packages available via the Internet (and there is some, though mixed, evidence of their effectiveness at helping learners develop pronunciation, intonation, and speech rhythm skills; see Golonka et al., 2014). Commercial providers of TMLL have taken full advantage of these relatively limited types of automated assessment to create feedback systems that ostensibly identify areas of learning need and push learners to develop them. Of course, the development of discrete and explicit language knowledge of the sort tested on these assessments is a far cry from the communicative language proficiency that is targeted in contemporary notions of language education (see chapters 2, 5, and 6 in this volume). It is also apparent that learners and teachers have to learn how to utilize feedback that is provided by such automated assessments—for example, a visual acoustic display is not immediately interpretable to most viewers, nor does it automatically indicate how learners should adjust their speech.

Much more challenging, and more interesting for language assessment, is the automated scoring of communicative, constructed-response item types and the provision of meaningful and accurate feedback. Here, the focus is on extended language use in writing and speaking for actual communicative purposes of a variety of kinds that are authentic to learners' needs for learning the language. Led chiefly by research at ETS that takes advantage of natural language processing capabilities, impressive strides have been made in the automated scoring of language production (see, e.g., Shermis & Burstein, 2013; Williamson, Mislevy, & Bejar, 2006; Xi, 2010; Xi et al., 2008; Xi et al., 2012; Zechner et al., 2015). In terms of writing, for example, ETS's e-rater engine has proven to be quite reliable in automated scoring based on a variety of language features underlying expository essay writing, focusing primarily on

- errors in grammar (e.g., subject-verb agreement);
- usage (e.g., preposition selection);
- mechanics (e.g., capitalization);
- style (e.g., repetitious word use);
- discourse structure (e.g., presence of a thesis statement, main points); and
- vocabulary usage (e.g., relative sophistication of vocabulary).

To some extent, as well, it incorporates features of discourse organization and content development in producing scores for a variety of large-scale standardized assessments, including the TOEFL iBT. This approach has been developed further into the Criterion tool, designed specifically as a way of providing formative feedback on essay writing for the features listed previously.[10] In terms of essay writing and automated scoring or feedback, then, the state of the art is such that a considerable array of language features can be accurately identified and scored, and tools are available for easy incorporation of English-language essay assessment into TMLL settings. Of course, the identification of language use patterns and the creation of scores may or may not translate into valid interpretations regarding a given learner's abilities or needs—that depends entirely on the intended uses of the assessment scores and the types of interpretations users want to make. For example, what is challenging, and also subject to ongoing research and development, is the automated scoring of different writing genres and tasks (i.e., not just essays), as well as distinct attributes of writing performance, such as content responsibility, creativity, argumentative effectiveness, and so on.

Automated scoring of speaking has also made considerable advances in recent years, though it lags behind writing assessment due to the major challenge that speech input cannot be controlled to the same extent as written input (i.e., voices vary, whereas what is typed into a keyboard does not). Still, combinations of speech recognition technology and natural language processing (NLP) algorithms have led to sophisticated automatic assessment possibilities. SpeechRater™, for example, combines a variety of technologies in order to interpret L2 speech and produce a "profile" of the speaker's proficiency based on a number of linguistic dimensions, including fluency, pronunciation, vocabulary usage, and prosody. Although this tool is capable of providing formative feedback in these dimensions of spoken performance—as it is used currently in the TOEFL Practice Online program—it does so on only a restricted range of task types (i.e., spontaneous, relatively brief responses to a prompt question). Research at ETS is underway to extend these capabilities to a variety of other task types and with a focus on a broader array of spoken features.[11] For automated assessment of both writing and speaking, then, although numerous possibilities exist for eliciting and scoring individual performances on relatively fixed task types, these should be incorporated into language teaching with some degree of caution. Xi's (2010) concerns still hold today:

> However, it is also important to realize that the accuracy of feedback given by computers, although acceptable in low-stakes practice environments with instructor support, leaves considerable room for improvement to emulate the judgment of trained linguists. Further, no current research has addressed the stability of automated feedback across performance samples. Finally, the effects of automated feedback on learning, especially over an extended period of time, are under-explored and deserve special research efforts.
>
> (p. 298)

To date, the majority of advances in automated scoring and feedback for language assessment have been related to individual, monologic speech and writing. However, as introduced previously, L2 learning targets typically incorporate interactive communication as a high-priority goal of instruction. There is, accordingly, considerable current interest in developing dialogic and multiparticipant computerized assessment that would enable such abilities to be elicited in extended performances across a variety of task types. One possibility here is for the use of "smart" technology that involves the examinee in interactions with an automated interlocutor that is trained (i.e., programmed) to ask questions, elicit clarifications, probe deeper, provide feedback (critically), and otherwise behave in ways that help elicit the abilities of the examinee to engage in relatively authentic interactions. For example, research at ETS under the title of "Trialogues" has explored the possibility of simulating various language-use scenarios in a virtual environment where a learner or learners interact with one or more computerized avatars that guide the conversation (e.g., in a library, in a school classroom) through multiple turns (e.g., So et al., 2015). This type of assessment will no doubt continue to develop in the immediate future, and consideration should be given to the possibilities for incorporating smart, multiparticipant automated interactions into TMLL settings, though not in the immediate future. A major current challenge here, of course, is the considerable resource demand underlying such computerized assessments, involving very sophisticated technological skills, high-end computer delivery platforms, graphic design expectations, and so on. Additionally, there is as yet little evidence of the validity of automatically generated scores for informing the variety of interpretations about productive ability that teachers, learners, and others might want or need to make.

Moving beyond automated assessments—that is, when the expectation for computerized scoring and feedback is not at stake—numerous possibilities exist for tapping into interactive, situated, task-based, and other authentic assessments within technology-mediated settings. In terms of speaking and listening, Skype and related audio- and videoconferencing technologies have made possible the facilitation of live, face-to-face conversations and other interactions involving two or (many) more participants, and it would be a relatively easy matter to incorporate a variety of Web-based, interactive assessments (e.g., with remote native speakers, between learners in a class) into a TMLL environment (see, e.g., Ockey, 2013). For example, the Ohio State University ESL program uses Skype for placement and proficiency assessment of incoming students.[12] Another key feature of technology mediation is the capacity to elicit, record, and archive large amounts of language data in a variety of forms. Thus, for example, online synchronous (e.g., chat) or asynchronous (e.g., discussion board) texts may be used as classroom-based assessment data for analyzing learner language use, pragmatics and turn-taking skills, engagement and participation, content orientation, and so on, and all of that may be given a longitudinal dimension if such activities are repeated over the course of, say, a semester (e.g., Kol & Schcolnik, 2008). Teachers can take advantage of the capacity of technology environments to capture much more easily the ways in which learners are using and developing language, and formative feedback can be easily directed to individual learners or classes on the basis of the actual, recorded texts.

Similarly, assessments may be devised intentionally to capture the ways in which learners are utilizing technology for language learning and other communication purposes (see González-Lloret, 2013; Shin, 2012). Thus, webquests, participation in virtual communities and online exchanges, and gaming all offer opportunities to record, examine, and provide feedback on not only language use but also technology use, as learners engage in the various affordances of the corresponding environments. For example, Sykes (2014) describes the use of formative assessment within a virtual Spanish language environment, where learners had to adhere to certain pragmalinguistic and sociopragmatic expectations in communication in order to advance through various situations in a game; where learners did not produce the expected pragmatic turns, they were forced to "restart" at an earlier point in the game, thereby offering immediate formative feedback on their communicative success. In another formative assessment example, Hwang and Chang (2011) developed a formative assessment system for mobile-adaptive learning, where learners were prompted (on their smartphones) periodically to answer questions about cultural learning targets as they engaged in site-based (i.e., in-person) examination of cultural artifacts; where learners answered test questions incorrectly, they were directed to additional information and other learning resources until they were able to respond correctly. In a more summative assessment example, Aoki and Molnár (2013) collected extensive evidence from a semester-long telecollaboration exchange between English learners in Japan and Hungary, focusing their assessment on participation patterns in the weekly exchanges, the quality of products that resulted from the projects that were in focus for the exchanges, and depth of learner self-reflection as indicated in learners' essays about the exchange projects.

As these and other examples suggest, there are numerous possibilities for integrating assessment into TMLL environments. An increasing array of technological tools makes the elicitation, recording, and scoring of language knowledge and performance abilities relatively accessible, and a variety of uses for technology-mediated assessment have been explored, ranging from large-scale proficiency assessment to automated formative assessments to summative assessment based on rich data collection (and even extending beyond to new notions such as "stealth" assessment, where processes invisible to the learner are used to direct them toward individually meaningful experiences and learning targets; see Shute & Kim, 2014). Although numerous possible advantages have been suggested for these developments, such as increased autonomy and individualization of assessment according to learner needs, automated provision of feedback, and improved learning outcomes, research-based evidence supporting these uses is as yet incomplete, so any commitment to technology-mediated assessment should also be made with a reasonable degree of caution. Moving beyond technological fascination with what might be possible, it is critically important to bear in mind major challenges associated with the different possibilities, such as cost and resource demands, the overwhelming amount of assessment data that can be generated and requires scoring and analysis, and the potential alienation of learners who are not familiar with technological expectations. Although it is important for developers and innovators working with TMLL to be aware of the variety of possibilities outlined here, it is equally if not more important that the basic expectations for any assessment (as indicated in chapter 7), and particularly formative assessment, be built into educational design from the outset. Winke (2014), for example, discusses the careful consideration of roles to be played by assessment in an online-delivered language course, the selection of specific assessment methods that reflected the pedagogic orientation and emphases of the course, the deliberate implementation of assessment by course instructors such that learners understood and participated in the process, and the considered reflection of information about language development that was offered by assessments. It is this kind of situated, intentional use of assessment that we would encourage within TMLL environments.

Curriculum Development and Design in TMLL

Online courses, blended learning environments, self-access learning, and flipped classroom contexts are rapidly increasing in popularity, placing broadly differing demands on the design of language learning experiences. For example, some distance-learning courses are conceived entirely from scratch and originally conceptualized from a TMLL perspective (e.g., Strambi & Bouvet, 2003; Trinder, 2003). In other cases, existing courses are converted to an online-delivered format, whereas in other contexts, an online component may simply be added to an existing face-to-face course for a so-called hybridized model of instruction (see Levy & Stockwell, 2013). Still other courses, modules, and programs are designed for fully autonomous, learner-centered instruction, primarily through interaction with a "smart" computer software program or through applications that take advantage of crowd-sourced materials on the Internet. Although the development of curricula for online learning courses, modules, and components should also follow established procedures for the design of face-to-face learning sequences (i.e., needs analysis, goals and objectives, a syllabus), a main question in TMLL curriculum and course development concerns the systematic incorporation of technology components into the design process, a complex endeavor that "requires the careful integration of a number of elements, both pedagogical and technical, in a principled way" (Levy & Stockwell, 2013, p. 19).

A major tenor in designing technology-mediated curricula and online learning environments is the idea that the focus should not be placed on the tools and technologies but on how to "account for the new processes and actions associated with Web 2.0 technologies, infowhelm (the exponential growth in information), increasing ubiquitous personal technologies or cloud computing" (Churches,

2009, par. 1). Along these lines, and reinterpreting Bloom's (1956) taxonomy (see chapter 9) for technology-mediated learning, Churches (2009b) adds the layer of communication to the original six levels of cognitive complexity for ordering typical learning activities (see Figure 13.2).

As an essential skill in the 21st century, Churches argues that although collaboration is not "an integral part of the learning process for the individual, you don't have to collaborate to learn, but often your learning is enhance [*sic*] by doing so" (p. 8). Thus, L2 instruction needs to also account for collaboration in technology-mediated learning environments, drawing upon the collaborative and communicative nature of many Web technologies (e.g., wikis, blogs, Google Docs, social networks, and LMSs). For example, Bloom's higher order thinking skill of evaluating could be supported by asking learners to identify and bookmark target language websites that, for instance, provide useful information to solve a given problem. At a later stage—corresponding to synthesis—learners could be tasked with collaboratively designing and writing their own blog surrounding the topic or problem at hand.

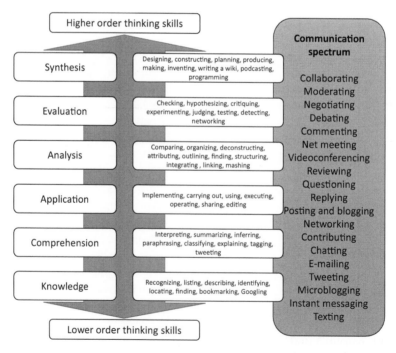

FIGURE 13.2 Churches' (2009) interpretation of Bloom's digital taxonomy and the communication spectrum. Adapted from Churches (2009). Licensed under the Creative Commons Attribution-ShareAlike 4.0 International License.

Although Churches' (2009b) interpretation of Bloom's taxonomy is aimed at technological learning, some aspects need to be taken into account particularly for TMLL. For example, as Churches (2009a) argued, bookmarking as "a resource is of no value if the resource is inappropriate, invalid, out of date or inaccurate" (par. 1). However, given that this seemingly simple activity of bookmarking a website is embedded in a Web 2.0 context, demands and thus targeted learning outcomes for L2 learners may be slightly different. For instance, when asking learners to identify and bookmark target language websites that deal with a specific problem, they may be challenged by a different kind of reading experience, where massive amounts of information distributed across different sources calls for enhanced skimming or scanning skills, efficient processing, ability to judge relevance, and so on. Thus, (sub)processes, as well as the final product, may need to be accounted for when conceptualizing learning objectives in the process of designing a TMLL curriculum, module, or lesson.

Although the aforementioned points constitute initial ideas, much more research into affordances and constraints of TMLL curricula is needed. Nielson (2014), for instance, has observed that "there is very little empirical research on how to establish effective online classes for the delivery of foreign language instruction" (p. 296). Nevertheless, researchers have recently begun to investigate implementations of technology-mediated curricula and courses to better understand how Web-based environments particularly mediate instruction. In particular, research has investigated distance learning via TBLT, exploring how this approach to curriculum and course design reacts to the integration of digital educational tools (e.g., González-Lloret & Ortega, 2014b; Hampel, 2006; Hampel & Hauck, 2004; Lai, Zhao, & Wang, 2011; Nielson, 2014; Solé & Mardomingo, 2004). TBLT has been proposed as an ideal approach for online curriculum design because the TBLT conceptual framework can accommodate the characteristically student-centered, self-paced, and individualized dimension of TMLL well: "many target tasks can be accomplished over the internet or through simulations and [. . .] students can easily work at their own pace at a distance" (Nielson, 2014, p. 296). Indeed, one might imagine a particular TMLL affordance whereby numerous independent learning modules could be produced, graded by complexity, and then accessed according to the needs or interests of learners or the design of an educational program (which would all be accomplished efficiently in a technology-mediated environment). Potentially, TBLT would be able to support just such an innovation given the rationales provided by TBLT researchers for task and instructional sequencing (see chapter 9).

Whether TBLT provides an optimal curricular organizational structure for TMLL remains an empirical question to be explored, of course. To this end, a recent study from Nielson (2014) has tried to "confirm that the [TBLT] principles for course design that work so well in other contexts are, in fact, a good fit for distance language learning" (p. 296). She outlines a case study on how to structure and evaluate an online task-based Chinese course. Adopting the TBLT framework, her course development began with a needs analysis, surveying learners of Chinese about their goals and motivations for learning Chinese. The resulting course content was composed primarily of video and audio input, whereas a textbook was avoided as it "would not have matched the real-world needs of the Chinese students" (p. 299). The course was designed around five target scenarios and supplemented with 30-minute synchronous CMC sessions, available for each individual learner. The CMC sessions, in which learners could speak with a Chinese speaker, were implemented as a form of practice and preparation for the final performance-based oral assessment. Nielson's findings suggest that the TBLT approach to course design was a success with positive impacts on student learning. However, she also points out that technology impacted the content of the curriculum (a target task was changed to a phone conversation to accommodate the online format), and there was some doubt as to whether skills learned via technology would transfer to face-to-face contexts. In this example, then, technology had a type of washback effect on the program, transforming the nature of the curriculum and, arguably, the nature of learning. These unintended consequences suggest the need for vigilant monitoring to ensure that technology-mediated affordances are enabling instruction to consistently target intended learning outcomes (see the section on evaluation later in this chapter).

One lesson to take away from the aforementioned TBLT development approaches is that it is important to determine in a systematic way whether a type of technology is helping mobilize (or, by contrast, undermining) a favored pedagogical approach in a particular L2 context. Chapelle (2014) proposes that "[i]mplementing and evaluating successful technology-mediated TBLT becomes possible with carefully defined task characteristics" that take into account how technology also mediates L2 learning (p. 328). To this end, Chapelle (2014) juxtaposes task qualities proposed by González-Lloret and Ortega (2014a) with the CALL task framework proposed in Chapelle (2001), synthesizing both into a framework of task design that can guide materials and curriculum designers, L2 instructors, researchers, and evaluators (see Table 13.1).

Table 13.1 is meant to provide a framework by which course and curriculum designers can start to systematically structure, organize, and evaluate technology-mediated curricula in terms of established task features and theoretical TBLT principles. To this end, Chapelle (2014) suggests that the task characteristics proposed in Table 13.1 should be investigated empirically in different contexts to further inform the design, development, and implementation of technology-mediated L2 instruction. Doing so, however, calls for the implementation of continuous evaluation to monitor the influence of technology-related aspects on L2 instruction. Chapelle (2014) cautions that course designers should "be cognizant of the non-neutrality of technology" (p. 329). That is to say, technology and its integration into the design of learning tasks influences—either directly or indirectly—L2 learning experiences (as the study from Nielson shows). When evaluating a given learning experience, then, it is critical to take into account whether and how a

TABLE 13.1 Computer-Assisted Task-Based Language Learning and Teaching Framework (Adapted From Chapelle, 2014)

Authenticity	Learning tasks should mirror tasks learners will encounter in the real world outside of the L2 learning environment.
Primary Focus on Meaning	Tasks should contain an incidental focus on meaning, drawing learners' attention to meaning even though tasks may also include a focus on form.
Learner Fit and Learner Centeredness	Closely interconnected with the needs analysis and goal determination in curriculum design and course planning, tasks should provide adequate opportunities for engagement while accounting for learners' needs and goals, as well as learners' individual characteristics.
Language Learning Potential and Reflective Learning	Stemming from Dewey's theory of reflective learning, task design needs to provide opportunities for students to reflect on their educational engagement and learning process (see also Winke, 2014).
Positive Impact and Reflective Learning	Comparable to washback, the use of technology may provide an additional learning experience that students may transfer to other learning opportunities outside of the immediate learning environment, thus applying the same technology (skills) for future L2 learning (see also Solares, 2014).
Practicality	Tasks should be practical and feasible in their implementation.
Goal Orientation	Tasks should have a communicative goal rather than provide the mere platform for exercising language forms. Depending on the task, these communicative purposes can range from writing a wiki entry to scanning an online newspaper article for information to negotiating in synchronous CMC.

technological affordance is operationalizing the desired learning outcomes of the curriculum. The aforementioned framework of task features may ultimately help confirm whether the principles for curriculum and course design are an adequate fit for a technology-enhanced learning context.

To our thinking, then, the most viable approach to TMLL curriculum and course design is the use of a TBLT syllabus and a set of systematically constructed and selected tasks that are well suited to a particular group of students within a particular TMLL context. Technology is conspicuously pervasive in contemporary L2 instruction such that is has become central to many L2 teaching approaches, TBLT especially (Chapelle, 2014; González-Lloret & Ortega, 2014b). Accordingly, González-Lloret and Ortega (2014a) situate TBLT in the midst of technology and CALL, arguing that TBLT can provide a suitable framework to organize technology-enhanced designs for L2 instruction. Conversely, TBLT curricula can benefit from the application of technology given that synchronous and asynchronous forms of CMC have become widely used in real-life contexts. Moreover, technology allows for a larger amount of modularity in curriculum design, where numerous independent task-based learning modules could be produced and graded by complexity and then accessed according to needs or interests of the learners or program. Thus, both perspectives—technology and TBLT—are complementary to the extent that they form a "theoretical symbiosis" with practical synergies for the purpose of designing technology-mediated TBLT syllabi (González-Lloret & Ortega, 2014a, p. 4).

Supporting Teachers in TMLL Instruction

It should go without saying that instructors play a key role in the success of language education, and—like conventional classroom teaching—certain types of TMLL are reliant on high-quality teacher performance.[13] Accordingly, teachers need specific types of skills, resources, and supports in order to deliver technology-mediated instruction effectively, especially given the unique dimensions of TMLL for learners and institutions. Although much of what is recommended in the teacher-training research literature applies to preparing instructors for TMLL as well, it should be clear from the previous discussion that certain learner needs, tools, and learning processes are unique to technology-mediated environments and require dedicated instructional support. This places demands on teachers to develop specific pedagogical knowledge, skills, and dispositions that maximize the learning potential of the various types of affordances available in TMLL.

At the most basic level, just as learners need to have a certain amount of technological literacy, so too do instructors need to have "foundational knowledge and skills" in technology for professional purposes (Healey et al., 2008, p. 29). This includes knowledge of basic technological concepts and operational competence in a wide variety of platforms, as well as awareness of the many technology supports available for language instruction and how to use them in a particular setting. Basic technical competence also requires knowing how to use technology in "socially and culturally appropriate, legal, and ethical ways" (Healey et al., 2008). Doing so will require ongoing professional development, which might involve (among other things) participating in workshops and webinars, attending local or national conferences on TMLL topics, or joining one of many online communities dedicated to supporting teachers in using technology for language instruction. It should be noted, though, that teachers are not always receptive to use of technology for language instruction. Teachers can hold certain prejudices against TMLL (Constantinides, 2013), and, on a related note, evidence suggests that the use of technology in teaching practice is related to teacher interest in technology (Egbert, Paulus, & Nakamichi, 2002). It may be, then, that aspects of teacher training and professional development will need to include development of particular dispositions (e.g., valuing, demystifying, and reducing anxiety with TMLL) conducive to use of digital tools in language teaching.

The basics of digital literacy aside, language teachers must be able to integrate "pedagogical knowledge and skills with technology to enhance language teaching and learning" (Healey et al., 2008). This point may be self-evident at this stage in that well-trained teachers would ideally be familiar with the various issues raised in this chapter and the TMLL research literature generally. That is, instructors should be able to shrewdly identify and evaluate digital resources suitable for the teaching context (Healey et al., 2008), these decisions informed by empirically based SLA research and careful professional reflection. Teachers must also be able to "coherently integrate technology into their pedagogical approaches" such that there are explicit and cogent rationales for why a particular use of technology enhances language acquisition (Healey et al., 2008, p. 32). A key orientation in this teaching approach will be to have teachers focus their instructional efforts more on the individual learner and the use of technology to facilitate self-directed learning rather than on predetermined and group-driven learning processes (Reinders & Darasawang, 2012). This aim raises again the importance of fostering key learner attributes such as motivation, autonomy, and student reflection on learning. Skilled TMLL instructors will provide students with specific strategies to enhance self-directed learning, such as techniques for monitoring and increasing motivation. To this end, Hurd (2006) suggests that instructors have learners set goals and engage in positive self-talk or self-encouragement. Teachers should also encourage learners to be active agents in their learning, as well as encourage independent decision making and support learners in their decisions and choices as individuals. Instructors might also help learners cope with the frustration, isolation, or anxiety that are prone to occur when students engage in language learning remotely (Murphy & Hurd, 2011). Supportive feedback also helps keep motivation high, as does creating a sense of community where student decisions can be discussed and shared with classmates and teachers alike (Murphy & Hurd, 2011). Teachers may also need to be advocates for self-directed learning given that there "may be considerable resistance to autonomy among learners who are more comfortable with an approach that puts the teacher firmly in control" (p. 45).

Effective implementation of TMLL will also involve being practical about curricular design given the known institutional constraints that impinge on TMLL, particularly in contexts where resources and expertise are limited. Belz and Müller-Hartmann (2003) found that a university-level telecollaboration program was hindered by "misalignment of academic calendars, local patterns of socialization into the teaching profession, institution-specific classroom scripts, systems of learning assessment, student workloads, and the physical layouts of local institutions and social forms of classroom collaboration" (p. 71). Negotiating these sorts of hazards will require administrative savvy, organizational skills, and an awareness of what TMLL planning requires, such as sufficient time for preparation and piloting, all of which will require broad consultation with the various institutional support entities (especially in schools and colleges) that will need to be coordinated in order to bring off TMLL successfully (Reinders & Darasawang, 2012).

A key area of knowledge and skill will be the use of technology for feedback and assessment (Healey et al., 2008, p. 36), assessment literacy being a known challenge for language instructors. We refer the reader to the relevant sections in this chapter and emphasize that instructors and course designers will need to have training, expertise, and support systems—these also reliant on digital tools—to collect and use information on student learning for the enhancement of teaching and learning. Moreover, given the importance of autonomy, motivation, learning strategies, conducive dispositions (e.g., intercultural competence), and so on, TMLL instructors will need to be knowledgeable about the principles and practices of formative assessment and its implementation in digital environments (e.g., being proficient in the design and implementation of online surveys, electronic portfolios, online test construction applications). Beyond the assessment of language skills and learning dispositions, teachers also need to be competent in evaluating educational, administrative, and technological elements of the program, including "the effectiveness of specific student uses of technology" (Healey et al., 2008, p. 38).

The final recommendation from the TESOL technology standards calls for "language teachers to use technology to improve communication, collaboration, and efficiency" (Healey et al., 2008, p. 38). On the one hand, teachers must be proficient in using technology for administrative purposes, such as communicating and collaborating with peers, students, administrative staff, and other program stakeholders. Instructors will also need to use technology to facilitate effective communication between students for pedagogical purposes, such as maintaining various types of electronic fora (e.g., blog, chat, message board, use of social media, document sharing) for online learning communities. Again, given the observation that full realization of learner autonomy and self-directed learning are unlikely to occur without instructor intervention, communication with students becomes a crucial part of what Murphy (2008) calls a "pedagogic dialogue" such that learners take on the role of "active agents [. . .] constructing and assuming control of a personally meaningful and effective interface between themselves, their attributes and needs, and the features of the learning context" (C. White, 2008, p. 7, cited in Murphy & Hurd, 2011).

Engaging learners in such a way will call for teachers to use technology effectively for localizing and individualizing instruction and meeting the particular needs of diverse and potentially dispersed groups of learners. Conducting needs analyses, as noted prior, will go a long way toward tailoring TMLL in useful ways for targeted learners, including specific uses of technology given specific learning goals. However, needs analyses and curriculum development efforts may well encounter certain challenges in TMLL given the diversity of globally remote participants, particularly in fully distance-based programs. Given the realities of learner diversity, technology would seem to offer unique potentialities for automated or computer-guided learning, particularly the use of Web 3.0 capabilities, to individualize input and instruction based on individual learner activities and interests. One might imagine, for example, GPS tracking of learners via mobile devices and the automated supply of vocabulary or other relevant input depending on the environment the learner happens to be visiting (a train station, a supermarket, a hospital, etc.). Organizing these sorts of affordances, however, will likely place high demands on whatever system or technology infrastructure is supporting the learner in this endeavor, particularly in terms of alignment with individual needs and curricular goals, the ongoing assessment of development, and the provision of meaningful and useful feedback.

For the time being, then, instructors will be primarily responsible for organizing locally relevant, learner-tailored instructional experiences. To this end, the Internet would seem to offer a wealth of options for selecting relevant texts, video, audio, and other input that will be of interest to global student audiences. That said, teachers or course designers who select texts and organize interactive learning experiences will need to be mindful of how learners use language in ways that are both global and local. For example, localizing instruction in technology-mediated environments will require that teachers be aware of how language learning and teaching happen in virtual, transnational spaces where global varieties of a L2, particularly lingua franca forms of English, are commonly needed for online business or educational uses. An implication of this point relates to how TMLL research and practice emanates from predominantly western nations and academic centers. Thus, the adoption of technology-mediated education has been relatively limited in nonwestern societies (for reasons similar to lack of innovation in terms of more communicative orientations to language teaching), and because the use of educational technology is "nonneutral" and mediates learning in potentially biased ways (Preuss & Morway, 2012), teachers and instructors will need to take care that the use of the Internet—and other technology-mediated tools that circulate cultural ideologies (many of these increasingly commercial)—does not repeat the colonizing tendencies of globalized English instruction from days past. Teachers and course designers, then, will need to be vigilant to ensure that TMLL—now global in scope and reach—is a force for liberation and empowerment, rather than political oppression, hegemony, or economic exploitation (Preuss & Morway, 2012).

Finally, providing teachers with ongoing training and development (all the more important for TMLL as techniques and technologies develop and evolve at rapid pace) can be well supported by many of the same technology-mediated affordances that enhance language education for students. For example, we have noted in chapter 11 the various support resources offered to teachers via the Internet, such as webinars and instructional video, blogs, supplementary input, activities, and tasks, assessment tools, research publications related to materials and teaching, and so on, all of which offer unprecedented opportunities for access and sharing of professional knowledge and experiences.

Additional potentialities for teacher training and technology support come from research on language teacher education by distance (LTED), which has been quick to identify the helpfulness of CMC for creating virtual learning communities that are crucial to successful teacher-training programs (Hall & Knox, 2009). Some such communities are publicly available (in the form of Yahoo Groups) and exist in support of learning sites. The sites typically include membership-based online communities of teachers who work collaboratively by sharing materials and answering one another's questions. Professional online communities are also created for dedicated teacher-training programs—again via LTED programs— and likewise offer a variety of CMC affordances that enable sharing of materials, syllabi, and video teaching demonstrations, as well as opportunities to exchange ideas with peers and teacher trainers (Hall & Knox, 2009).

One example of using CMC for teacher-training purposes—also relevant to the issues of culture and localization noted previously—comes from a study by Müller-Hartmann (2006) in which language teacher trainees in Germany (teaching English) and the U.S. (teaching a variety of languages) engaged in inter-cultural competence training by participating in the very same telecollaboration course they were to facilitate later for language students. The training program combined experiential learning, model teaching, and intensive reflection using synchronous CMC, e-mail, and text chat. U.S. and German teachers discussed movies, books, and other cultural artifacts via CMC and were challenged to question one another on cultural stereotypes and other issues from the various texts. Subsequent to the CMC discussions, student teachers were asked to reflect on their interactions in a variety of ways, including a group discussion with the home teacher-trainee group, creating cultural "dos and don'ts" lists, and writing a reflective essay (integrating academic literature) analyzing the telecollaboration experience. The conflicts, misunderstandings, and "emotional turmoil" that arose out of the discussions—along with intensive reflection—deepened the student teachers' cultural knowledge, sharpened their skills for relating to the L2 culture, and developed critical cultural awareness of the target culture, all of which developed their intercultural interactional abilities. Moreover, the experience of becoming intercultural speakers and sharing in technology-mediated instruction with their partner teacher-trainees also provided valuable firsthand experience in the "analysis of international telecollaborative encounters" (Müller-Hartmann, 2006, p. 81).

In sum, such online collaborative communities of practice may be seen as crucial for successful online teacher training, and we conclude this section listing a number of additional factors identified by Reinders (2009) as best programmatic practices for training teachers to deliver technology-mediated language instruction (see Table 13.2).

Evaluating TMLL

As technology is incorporated into the design and delivery of innovative language education experiences, program evaluation can and should play a crucial role in facilitating evidence-based decision making in relation to all phases of language instruction. Perhaps the prototypical purpose for evaluating TMLL has been

TABLE 13.2 Factors in High-Quality Teacher-Training Programs for TMLL (Adapted From Reinders, 2009)

1. Access to computers and relevant devices with ongoing technology support
2. Time for learners to implement and learn about TMLL concepts and affordances (both during and after a training course)
3. Recognition for successful implementation of technology-mediated instruction
4. Modeling and constructing of authentic tasks and relating theory to practice through practical examples and applications (shifting teacher-trainee thinking to an understanding of specifically how technology is implemented in a language teaching situation)
5. Experiencing technology from the learner's perspective and learning about technology by using technology
6. Ongoing pedagogical support (mentoring, online communities of practice)
7. Opportunities and encouragement to reflect on the implications of technology at a broader level

to compare the effectiveness of courses and programs that feature technological innovations with "traditional" face-to-face instruction. For example, Sanders (2005) compared traditional university Spanish classes with a hybrid model that replaced class meetings with online automated exercises and synchronous discussions as a way of accommodating high enrollment demands. After three quarters of instruction, outcomes assessments—including vocabulary, grammar, and reading tests; an American Council on the Teaching of Foreign Languages (ACTFL) Oral Proficiency Interview; and an ACTFL Writing Proficiency Test—suggested equivalent achievements by the TMLL learners except in the area of writing proficiency. Although test-based outcomes or effectiveness evaluations of this sort can be useful in pointing to the overall impact of course or program delivery, and thereby perhaps inform decisions about whether the innovation should be sustained or not, an exclusive focus on outcomes may not offer much guidance in situations where the purpose of evaluation is to understand how and why TMLL is or is not functioning or what might be done to improve it (see, e.g., Llosa & Slayton, 2009). Comparing outcomes between technology-based and face-to-face instruction may also be misleading, in that the TMLL instructional option may be increasingly the only viable or preferred approach for a given teaching and learning context. Following recommendations in chapter 12, then, our basic suggestion here is that the intended uses and users of TMLL evaluation must be determined first and foremost, and that specific, focused uses related to the situated (i.e., context-specific) challenges of a given technology-mediated lesson, class, course, module, or program should drive the evaluation.

One likely and high-priority use for evaluation in relation to TMLL has to do with the determination of learner and teacher needs in relation to language learning and teaching targets and technological demands or expectations of the instructional design. Needs analysis has been mentioned throughout this volume as a crucial starting point in program design, providing essential information about the purposes for learning, as well as the contextual constraints and affordances that shape what is possible in terms of pedagogy. In particular, for TMLL, needs analysis (NA) should uncover the roles played by technology in mediating both the types of communication abilities learners are developing and the ways in which pedagogy is delivered. Along these lines, in a useful overview, González-Lloret (2014) identified the following dimensions of TMLL that NA should seek to elucidate: (a) target language use tasks and the contexts, especially digital, within which they occur (e.g., getting directions from a person vs. getting directions from a smartphone); (b) digital tools required for language task accomplishment and their demands on learners and users (e.g., using the phone vs. using a website for making hotel reservations); (c) digital literacy experience and abilities of the learners and teachers (including how to operate hardware and software, how to gather and evaluate information, how to manipulate media, and how to communicate in digital environments); and (d) access to technology (including regional differences, capacity and energy requirements, Internet reliability, and availability of support). Gathering information about these features from diverse sources (e.g., teachers and learners themselves, local technology experts, employers) through multiple methods (e.g., surveys and interviews, observations, document analyses) provides an empirical basis for the overall design of feasible TMLL instruction and, potentially, for raising awareness among educational decision makers, teachers, and learners alike about the realities of technology-mediated communication and pedagogy.

A second likely focus for evaluation in TMLL education is the determination of how learners and teachers respond to technological innovations in terms of both the behaviors and the processes they engage in during instruction, as well as their affective reactions to working with technology (for general recommendations, see Phillips, McNaught, & Kennedy, 2012; Ruhe & Zumbo, 2009). Here, the purpose of evaluation is largely formative, with information gathered in order to understand how well specific aspects of the educational design are functioning and what might need to be changed in order for teaching and learning to happen as intended. At the broadest level, evaluation might monitor whether, how, and to what extent technological affordances are actually utilized as intended in instruction, including, for example, (a) access, interface, and navigation (e.g., automated tracking of which parts of a website or software program are accessed by learners and teachers and which are not); (b) time spent on technology-mediated learning tasks and how time is used (e.g., total amount of time a learner spends within a virtual community and proportion of time spent on distinct activities there); and (c) technical problems that occur (e.g., number and type of "help" requests made within a telecollaboration platform). Most LMSs (e.g., Blackboard®) automatically log and report detailed information regarding such factors, and overall patterns in usage data can provide valuable feedback on the extent to which technology is being utilized and functioning as intended.

Turning to the specific domain of TMLL, a number of features have been identified as particularly salient for educational design and therefore in need of evaluative attention. These include the roles that teachers take in guiding learning and the skills they possess for working with technology, the design of pedagogic language tasks within technological settings, and in particular the learners themselves—how they interact with learning content, how they participate in learning communities, how they focus their metacognitive strategies, and how they respond to TMLL designs and, especially, learning supports provided (Hampel & de los Arcos, 2013). Interestingly, it may be that *language* learning presents an especially challenging case for technology mediation in terms of the requirements (at least in contemporary notions of effective language learning, such as those outlined in this volume) for critical features that are perhaps not as prevalent in other learning domains, like (a) persistent interaction in multiple modalities among learners, teachers, and potentially others; (b) the need to continually monitor and provide focused feedback on learner language development; (c) the challenge of tracking and demonstrating language learning achievements; and (d) the possibility of diverse learner backgrounds, expectations, aptitudes, and other IDs that will affect their responses to both language learning and technology mediation (see, e.g., Oliver, Kellogg, & Patel, 2012). By far the most common methodology for collecting data on any of these factors is the use of questionnaires that ask learners and teachers to indicate their behaviors, as well as their affective perceptions, in relation to various features of the technology-mediated learning setting. For example, survey questionnaires have been used to

- determine the amount of teacher implementation of TMLL in language classrooms, as well the as reasons for greater or lesser use (e.g., in EFL classrooms in Li & Walsh, 2011);
- determine motivating features (e.g., access to resources, interaction with a wide array of target language speakers, novelty and "real-world" relevance of language learning online) and demotivating features (e.g., challenge of organizing asynchronous and remote-participation class sessions, technical glitches, lack of time, and increased workload or hours spent on work outside of class) of TMLL (e.g., Cai & Zhu, 2012); and
- determine the level of enjoyment, satisfaction, usefulness, learning gains, and other learner reactions to TMLL pedagogy (e.g., Pardo-Ballester, 2012; Solares, 2014).

Another source of data that may be particularly salient for examining learning-related behavior in TMLL settings has to do with the automatic archiving of actual language performance data. Thus, when synchronous chat sessions, telecollaborative exchanges, discussion boards, blogs, wikis, or role-playing games form a part of the pedagogic design, the interactive discussions and corresponding language produced may be analyzed in various ways to determine what learners are doing, what they are focusing on and responding to in the input and their own production, how they are dealing with communication challenges, and so on (e.g., Adams & Nik, 2014; Canto, de Graff, & Jauregi, 2014; Oskoz & Elola, 2014; Sauro, 2014).

Another approach to evaluation in TMLL has to do with the analysis of language learning as the holistic interaction of a variety of factors and processes that bring about specific language learning products. Thus, on the one hand, specific pedagogic tasks might be analyzed to determine not only what language features seemed to be acquired upon task completion but also whether learners and teachers engaged with the tasks as designed and whether there was a relationship between the type of engagement and the learning outcome. For example, Ma (2008) evaluated a computer-based vocabulary learning program to determine whether the amount of time spent on vocabulary learning tasks, dictionary word look-up behavior, and production of new words in computer exercises were predictive of receptive or productive vocabulary learning over the course of a 100-minute pedagogic task session (findings indicated predictability for receptive, but not productive, learning). Similarly, Kennedy and Miceli (2013) evaluated the addition of a collaborative online wiki project outside of regular beginning Italian classes, and they found that even though learners successfully produced the types of wiki pages that were envisioned, they perceived the technical problems and collaborative demands to be overly challenging, to the extent that they expressed disinterest in further learning via online group-based projects. Although these task-specific evaluations can illuminate what works with specific pedagogic interventions, larger scale evaluations might incorporate evidence on numerous aspects of the TMLL setting, as a given pedagogic design is delivered over longer instructional sequences. For example, Lai, Zhao, and Wang (2011) evaluated a fully task-based syllabus and materials that involved both synchronous and asynchronous tasks delivered in a virtual online high school program. Over the course of a semester, they collected data through surveys of teachers and learners, weekly blog entries by learners, weekly debriefing of teachers, observations and data capture from synchronous class sessions, end-of-semester course evaluations by learners, learner performance assessments administered on the final exam, and end-of-semester teacher interviews. They also collected performance data and background survey information from a comparison class that also met online but did not adopt the task-based syllabus and materials. These rich data sources allowed the evaluators to identify numerous advantages to the task-based online course (e.g., learner individualization, increased participation, enhanced monitoring of language development, facilitation of focus on form through extensive use of online annotation tools), as well as challenges specific to the influence of technology on task design (e.g., instability of platforms for synchronous spoken communication, anonymity or ambiguity of online communication, the need for schematization and contextualization of language used in tasks online), all pointing clearly to the need for learner and teacher strategy training in the design of the online TBLT course in addition to other specific improvements.

In sum, although evaluations that ask "Does it work?" or "Is it better than X?" will persist as a commonly presumed primary goal, the ever-evolving reality of TMLL suggests that the pursuit of answers to other questions might prove more useful in supporting innovation. Indeed, establishing parameters for determining whether a particular software package, learning community, online task, or other TMLL intervention is effective or not has itself proven to be an ambiguous goal, and effectiveness evaluations often seem to lead to conflicting findings (see, e.g., evaluations of Rosetta Stone by Rockman et al., 2009, vs. Nielson & Doughty, 2008). Perhaps a preferred evaluation strategy would be to utilize evaluation intentionally throughout TMLL innovation, from design, to delivery, to impact analysis, in an ongoing cycle of understanding, improving, and ensuring the quality of language education. Where evaluation has been incorporated as an integral part of TMLL interventions (e.g., Hill & Tschudi, 2008; Nielson, 2014; Rogan & San-Miguel, 2013), with distinct questions asked and answered empirically at different stages of program development and delivery, the result seems to be the production of syllabi, materials, and instructional strategies that (a) respond to learners' actual needs, (b) are tried out and improved simultaneously with teaching and learning, and (c) lead to the achievement of targeted language learning outcomes.

Summary

It is clear that technology mediation will continue to exert a substantial and exponentially increasing influence on all aspects of language instruction, from expectations for L2 acquisition, to materials development, to assessment and evaluation. The fact that technological media, tools, and other affordances will continue to rapidly evolve also suggests that we may not yet know very well what best practices entail. As such, we would like to conclude this chapter by reiterating the basic recommendation that careful thought about useful language pedagogy—which is informed by what we know from the various considerations raised and sources cited throughout this volume—should drive the design of any and all language educational experiences, including those that occur in technology-mediated environments.

Notes

1 Note that the terms CALL (computer-assisted language learning) and TMLL (technology-mediated language learning) are used somewhat interchangeably in the literature, with CALL being the historically preceding term, but TMLL emerging more recently, reflective of the fact that technology interactions with learning are potentially much broader than just "computer assistance." Here, we adopt TMLL unless referring to specific prior uses of the term CALL.

2 Research on the established ID variables of *personality* and *learning strategy* (with the exception of enhancing metacognition)—at the present time—show equivocal results, with no clear patterns indicating that personality, learning strategy, or learning style impact learning via technology-mediated instruction (Beauvois & Eledge, 2013; Desmarais et al., 1998; Hubbard & Romeo, 2012).

3 In such instances, Satar and Özdener (2008) recommend having low-proficiency learners engage in text chat with familiar, non-native-speaking partners.

4 It is worth noting in passing that text-based chat, although possessing many of the key features of interactive communication, does not seem to foster negotiation of meaning to the extent expected from an ostensibly interactive, technology-mediated modality (Ortega, 2009a).

5 The TESOL Technology Standards Framework, and see also the International Society for Technology's National Educational Technology Standards for Teachers (Cennamo, Ross, & Ertmer, 2010)

6 Natural Reader, http://www.naturalreaders.com/

7 See Monash Chinese Island at http://www.virtualhanyu.com/ as an example of a virtual themed island for Chinese learners.

8 See overview of Web-based testing tools at http://elearningindustry.com/free-testing-tools-for-online-education

9 Blackboard, http://www.blackboard.com/

10 Automated Scoring of Writing Quality, https://www.ets.org/research/topics/as_nlp/writing_quality/

11 Automated Scoring of Speech, https://www.ets.org/research/topics/as_nlp/speech/

12 Oral Proficiency Assessment, http://esl.ehe.osu.edu/home/testing/spoken-english/

13 Of course, fully autonomous self-access models of TMLL, which only involve the interaction of a learner and a computer, rule out most intervention by a teacher, though it is questionable to what extent such models are appropriate for the majority of language learners and learning settings worldwide.

REFERENCES AND SUGGESTED READINGS

Abraham, L. B. (2008). Computer-mediated glosses in second language reading comprehension and vocabulary learning: A meta-analysis. *Computer Assisted Language Learning*, *21*(3), 199–226.

Abrahamsson, N., & Hyltenstam, K. (2009). Age of onset and nativelikeness in a second language: Listener perception versus linguistic scrutiny. *Language Learning*, *59*(2), 249–306.

Achiba, M. (2003). *Learning to request in a second language: A study of child interlanguage pragmatics*. Clevedon, UK: Multilingual Matters.

Adair-Hauck, B., Glisan, E. W., Koda, K., Swender, E. B., & Sandrock, P. (2006). The Integrated Performance Assessment (IPA): Connecting assessment to instruction and learning. *Foreign Language Annals*, *39*(3), 359–382.

Adams, R., & Alwi, N. A. N. M. (2014). Prior knowledge and second language task production in text chat. In M. González-Lloret & L. Ortega (Eds.), *Technology-mediated TBLT: Researching technology and tasks* (pp. 51–78). Amsterdam, The Netherlands: John Benjamins.

Adams, H., & Nicolson, M. (2011). Learner diversity. In M. Nicolson, L. Murphy, & M. Southgate (Eds.), *Language teaching in blended contexts* (pp. 29–42). Edinburgh, UK: Dunedin Academic Press.

Adams, R. J., & Newton, J. (2009). TBLT in Asia: Constraints and opportunities. *Asian Journal of English Language Teaching*, *19*(1), 1–17.

Adams, R. J., & Nik, N. (2014). Prior knowledge and second language task production in text chat. In M. González-Lloret & L. Ortega (Eds.), *Technology-mediated TBLT: Researching technology and tasks* (pp. 51–78). Amsterdam, The Netherlands: John Benjamins.

Adamson, B., & Davison, C. (2003). Innovation in English language teaching in Hong Kong: One step forward, two steps sideways? *Prospect*, *18*, 27–41.

Alcón Soler, E., & García Mayo, M. P. (2008). Focus on form and learning outcomes in the foreign language classroom. In J. Philp, R. Oliver, & A. Mackey (Eds.), *Child's play? Second language acquisition and the younger learner* (pp. 173–192). Amsterdam, The Netherlands: John Benjamins.

Alderson, J. C. (2005). *Diagnosing foreign language proficiency: The interface between learning and assessment.* New York, NY: Continuum.

Alderson, J. C. (Ed.). (2009). *The politics of language education: Individuals and institutions.* Bristol, UK: Multilingual Matters.

Alderson, J. C., & Beretta, A. (Eds.). (1992). *Evaluating second language education.* Cambridge, UK: Cambridge University Press.

Aljaafreh, A., & Lantolf, J. P. (1994). Negative feedback as regulation and second language learning in the zone of proximal development. *Modern Language Journal, 78,* 465–483.

American Association for Higher Education (AAHE). (1994). *Nine principles of good practice for assessing student learning.* Retrieved from http://www.academicprograms.calpoly.edu/pdfs/assess/nine_principles_good_practice.pdf

Andersen, R. W., & Shirai, Y. (1994). Discourse motivations for some cognitive acquisition principles. *Studies in Second Language Acquisition, 16,* 133–156.

Anderson, L. W., & Krathwohl, D. R. (2001). *A taxonomy for learning, teaching, and assessing: A revision of Bloom's taxonomy of educational objectives.* New York, NY: Longman.

Anderson, N. J. (2012). Student involvement in assessment: Healthy self-assessment and effective peer assessment. In C. A. Coombe, P. Davidson, B O'Sullivan, & S. Stoynoff (Eds.), *Cambridge guide to second language assessment* (pp. 187–197). Cambridge, UK: Cambridge University Press.

Aoki, K., & Molnár, P. (2013). Issues of student assessment in international telecollaborative project-based learning. *ICT in Education.*

Arnold, N., Ducate, L., & Kost, C. (2009). Collaborative writing in wikis. In L. Lomicka & G. Lord (Eds.), *The next generation: Social networking and online collaboration in foreign language learning* (Vol. 8, pp. 115–144). San Marcos, TX: CALICO Monograph Series.

Assessment Reform Group. (2002). *Assessment for Learning: 10 principles research-based principles to guide classroom practice.* London, UK: Assessment Reform Group.

Attali, Y., & Burnstein, J. (2006). Automated essay scoring with e-rater® V.2. *The Journal of Technology, Learning, and Assessment, 4*(3). Retrieved from http://www.jtla.org

Ausubel, D. P. (1963). *The psychology of meaningful verbal learning.* New York, NY: Grune and Stratton.

Bachman, L. (1990). *Fundamental considerations in language testing.* Oxford, UK: Oxford University Press.

Bachman, L. F., & Palmer, A. S. (1996). *Language testing in practice: Designing and developing useful language tests.* Oxford, UK: Oxford University Press.

Bachman, L. F., & Palmer, A. S. (2010). *Language assessment in practice.* Oxford, UK: Oxford University Press.

Bailey, N., Madden, C., & Krashen, S. D. (1974). Is there a "natural sequence" in adult second language learning? *Language Learning, 24,* 235–243.

Baker, S. C., & MacIntyre, P. D. (2000). The role of gender and immersion in communication and second language orientations. *Language Learning, 50,* 311–341.

Baralt, M., Gilabert, R., & Robinson, P. (Eds.). (2014). *Task sequencing and instructed second language learning.* London, UK: Bloomsbury.

Bardovi-Harlig, K. (2000). *Tense and aspect in second language acquisition: Form, meaning, and use.* Oxford, UK: Wiley-Blackwell.

Bardovi-Harlig, K. (2013). Developing L2 pragmatics. *Language Learning, 63*(1), 68–86.

Barrette, C. M. (2001). Students' preparedness and training for CALL. *CALICO Journal, 19*(1), 5–35.

Bartholome, L. (1994). Beyond the methods fetish: Toward a humanizing pedagogy. *Harvard Educational Review, 64*(2), 173–194.

Basturkmen, H. (2012). Review of research into the correspondence between language teachers' stated beliefs and practices. *System, 40*, 282–295.

Beauvois, M. H., & Eledge, J. (2013). Personality types and megabytes: Student attitudes toward computer mediated communication (CMC) in the language classroom. *CALICO Journal, 13*(2 & 3), 27–45.

Becker, K. (2007, November). Instructional ethology: Reverse engineering for serious design of educational games. *Proceedings of the 2007 Conference on Future Play* (pp. 121–128). Association for Computing Machinery.

Bell, D. (2007). Do teachers think that methods are dead? *ELT Journal, 61*(2), 135–143.

Bell, J. (2012). Teaching mixed-level classes. In A. Burns & J. C. Richards (Eds.), *The Cambridge guide to pedagogy and practice in second language teaching* (pp. 86–94). Cambridge, UK: Cambridge University Press.

Bell, J., & Gower, R. (2011). Writing course materials for the world: A great compromise. In B. Tomlinson (Ed.), *Materials development in language teaching* (pp. 135–150). Cambridge, UK: Cambridge University Press.

Belz, J. A. (2001). Institutional and individual dimensions of transatlantic group work in network-based language teaching. *ReCALL, 13*(2), 213–231.

Belz, J. A. (2003). Linguistic perspective on the development of intercultural communicative competence in telecollaboration. *Language Learning & Technology, 7*(2), 68–117.

Belz, J. A., & Müller-Hartmann, A. (2003). Teachers as intercultural learners: Negotiating German-American telecollaboration along the institutional fault line. *Modern Language Journal, 87*(1), 71–89.

Belz, J. A., & Thorne, S. L. (2006). Introduction: Internet-mediated intercultural foreign language education and the intercultural speaker. In J. A. Belz & S. L. Thorne (Eds.), *Internet-mediated intercultural foreign language education* (pp. viii–xxv). Boston, MA: Heinle & Heinle.

Benevides, M., & Valvona, C. (2008). *Widgets*. New York, NY: Pearson.

Benson, P. (2011). *Teaching and researching autonomy* (2nd ed.). London, UK: Pearson.

Bernhardt, E. B. (2011). *Understanding advanced second language reading*. New York, NY: Routledge.

Biber, D., Nekrasova, T., & Horn, B. (2011). The effectiveness of feedback for L1-English and L2 writing development: A meta-analysis. *TOEFL iBT Research Report No. TOEFLiBT-14*. Princeton, NJ: Educational Testing Service.

Bigelow, M., & Watson, J. (2012). The role of educational level, literacy, and orality in L2 learning. In S. M. Gass & A. Mackey (Eds.), *The Routledge handbook of second language acquisition* (pp. 461–475). New York, NY: Routledge.

Birch, B. (2007). *English L2 reading: Getting to the bottom*. Mahwah, NJ: Lawrence Erlbaum.

Birdsong, D. P. (1992). Ultimate attainment in second language acquisition. *Language, 68*, 705–755.

Birdsong, D. P. (1999). Introduction: Whys and why nots of the critical period hypothesis for second language acquisition. In D. P. Birdsong (Ed.), *Second language acquisition and the critical period hypothesis* (pp. 1–22). Mahwah, NJ: Lawrence Erlbaum.

Bitchener, J. (2012). A reflection on 'the language learning potential' of written CF. *Journal of Second Language Writing, 21*(4), 348–363.

Bitchener, J., & Ferris, D. R. (2012). *Written corrective feedback in second language acquisition and writing*. New York, NY: Routledge.

Black, P., & Wiliam, D. (1998). Assessment and classroom learning. *Assessment in Education: Principles, Policy and Practice, 5*(1), 7–74.

Black, P., & Wiliam, D. (2012). Assessment for learning in the classroom. In J. Gardner (Ed.), *Assessment and learning* (pp. 11–32). London, UK: Sage.

Blake, R. J. (2000). Computer mediated communication: A window on L2 Spanish inter-language. *Language Learning & Technology, 4*(1), 120–136.

Bloom, B. S. (Ed.). (1956). *Taxonomy of educational objectives. 1. Cognitive domain.* New York, NY: David McKay.

Bolitho, R. (2003). Materials for language awareness. In B. Tomlinson (Ed.), *Developing materials for language learning* (pp. 422–425). London, UK: Continuum.

Borg, S. (2003). Teacher cognition in language teaching: A review of research on what language teachers think, know, believe, and do. *Language Teaching, 36*, 81–109.

Borg, S. (2006). Conditions for teacher research. *English Teaching Forum, 44*, 22–27.

Borg, S., & Al-Busaidi, S. (2012). Teachers' beliefs and practices regarding learner autonomy. *ELT Journal, 66*, 283–292.

Borrás, I., & Lafayette, R. C. (1994). Effects of multimedia courseware subtitling on the speaking performance of college students of French. *The Modern Language Journal, 78*(i), 61–75.

Boxer, D. (2013). Speaking. In P. Robinson (Ed.), *The Routledge encyclopedia of second language acquisition* (pp. 599–604). London, UK: Routledge.

Bradley, L., Lindstrom, B., & Rystedt, H. (2010). Rationalities of collaboration for language learning in a wiki. *ReCALL, 22*(2), 247–264.

Braine, G. (Ed.). (2013). *Non-native educators in English language teaching.* New York, NY: Routledge.

Breen, M. (1984). Process syllabus for the language classroom. In C. J. Brumfit (Ed.), *General English syllabus design ELT document* (pp. 47–60). Oxford, UK: Pergamon Press.

Brett, D., & González-Lloret, M. (2009). Technology-enhanced materials. In M. H. Long & C. J. Doughty (Eds.), *The handbook of language teaching* (pp. 351–369). Malden, MA: Wiley-Blackwell.

Brett, P. (1997). A comparative study of the effects of the use of multimedia on listening comprehension. *System, 25*(1), 39–53.

Brindley, G. (1994). Task-centred assessment in language learning: The promise and the challenge. In N. Bird, P. Falvey, A. Tsui, D. Allison, & A. McNeill (Eds.), *Language and learning: Papers presented at the annual international language in education conference (Hong Kong, 1993)* (pp. 73–94). Hong Kong: Hong Kong Education Department.

Brinton, D. M., Snow, M. A., & Wesche, M. B. (2003). *Content-based second language instruction.* Ann Arbor, MI: University of Michigan Press.

British Council. (2011). *EAQUALS core inventory for general English.* London, UK: Author.

Brooks, P. J., Kempe, V., & Sionov, A. (2006). The role of learner and input variables in learning inflectional morphology. *Applied Psycholinguistics, 27*(2), 185–209.

Brown, H. D. (2000). *Teaching by principles: An interactive approach to language pedagogy.* White Plains, NY: Longman.

Brown, H. D. (2004). *Language assessment: Principles and classroom practices.* White Plains, NY: Pearson.

Brown, H. D. (2007). *Principles of language learning and teaching.* White Plains, NY: Pearson.

Brown, J. D. (1995). *The elements of language curriculum: A systematic approach to program development.* Boston, MA: Heinle & Heinle.

Brown, J. D. (2009). Foreign and second language needs analysis. In M. Long & C. J. Doughty (Eds.), *The handbook of language teaching* (pp. 269–293). Malden, MA: Wiley-Blackwell Publishing.

Brown, J. D. (2012a). Developing rubrics for language assessment. In J. D. Brown (Ed.), *Developing, using, and analyzing rubrics in language assessment with case studies in Asian and Pacific languages* (pp. 13–32). Honolulu, HI: National Foreign Languages Resource Center Publications.

Brown, J. D. (2012b). EIL curriculum development. In L. Alsagoff, S. L. McKay, G. Hu, & W. A. Renandya (Eds.), *Principles and practices for teaching English as an international language* (pp. 147–167). New York, NY: Routledge.

Brown, J. D. (2012c). Research on computers in language testing: Past, present, and future. In M. Thomas, H. Reinders, & M. Warschauer (Eds.), *Contemporary computer-assisted language learning* (pp. 73–94). New York, NY: Bloomsbury.

Brown, J. D. (2014). *Testing in language programs: A comprehensive guide to English language assessment.* Honolulu, HI: JD Brown Publishing.

Brown, J. D., & Hudson, T. (1998). Alternatives in language assessment. *TESOL Quarterly, 32*(4), 653–675.

Brown, J. D., & Hudson, T. (2002). *Criterion-referenced language testing.* Cambridge, UK: Cambridge University Press.

Brown, J. D., Hudson, T., Norris, J. M., & Bonk, W. (2002a). *An investigation of second language task-based performance assessments.* Honolulu, HI: University of Hawai'i Press.

Brown, J. D., Hudson, T. D., Norris, J. M., & Bonk, W. (2002b). *Investigating task-based second language performance assessment.* Honolulu, HI: University of Hawai'i Press.

Brown, M. W. (2009). The teacher-tool relationship: Theorizing the design and use of curriculum materials. In J. T. Remillard, B. A. Herbel-Eisenmann, & G. M. Lloyd (Eds.), *Mathematics teachers at work: Connecting curriculum materials and classroom instruction* (pp. 17–36). New York, NY: Routledge.

Brown, S., & Larson-Hall, J. (2012). *Second language acquisition myths: Applying second language research to classroom teaching.* Ann Arbor, MI: University of Michigan Press.

Bruner, J. S. (1966). *Toward a theory of instruction.* Cambridge, MA: Harvard University Press.

Bruner, J. S. (1973). *The relevance of education.* New York, NY: Norton.

Bruner, J. S. (1975). From communication to language: A psychological perspective. *Cognition, 3,* 255–287.

Burns, A. (2006). Teaching speaking: A text-based syllabus approach. In E. Usó-Juan & A. Martínez-Flor (Eds.), *Current trends in the development and teaching of the four language skills* (pp. 235–258). Berlin, Germany: Mouton de Gruyter.

Butler, R. (1988). Enhancing and undermining intrinsic motivation: The effects of task-involving and ego-involving evaluation on interest and performance. *British Journal of Educational Psychology, 58*(1), 1–14.

Butler, Y. G. (2011). The implementation of communicative and task-based language teaching in the Asia-Pacific region. *Annual Review of Applied Linguistics, 31,* 36–57.

Bygate, M. (2006). Areas of research that influence L2 speaking instruction. In E. Usó-Juan & A. Martínez-Flor (Eds.), *Current trends in the development and teaching of the four language skills* (pp. 159–186). Berlin, Germany: Mouton de Gruyter.

Bygate, M., Norris, J. M., & Van den Branden, K. (2015). Task-based language teaching. In C. Chapelle (Ed.), *Blackwell encyclopedia of applied linguistics.* Cambridge, UK: Wiley-Blackwell. doi:10.1002/9781405198431.wbeal1467

Byrd, P. (2001). Textbooks: Evaluation for selection and analysis for implementation. In M. Celce-Murcia (Ed.), *Teaching English as a second or foreign language* (3rd ed., pp. 415–427). Boston, MA: Heinle & Heinle.

Byrnes, H. (2002). The role of task and task-based assessment in a content-oriented collegiate foreign language curriculum. *Language Testing, 19*(4), 425–443.

Byrnes, H., & Manchón, R. M. (Eds.). (2014). *Task-based language learning: Insights from and for writing.* Philadelphia, PA: John Benjamins.

Byrnes, H., Maxim, H., & Norris, J. (2010). Realizing advanced L2 writing development in a collegiate curriculum: Curricular design, pedagogy, assessment [Monograph]. *Modern Language Journal, 94.*

Cai, S., & Zhu, W. (2012). The impact of an online learning community project on university Chinese as a foreign language students' motivation. *Foreign Language Annals, 45,* 307–329.

Call, M. L. S. (1985). Auditory short-term memory, listening comprehension, and the input hypothesis. *TESOL Quarterly, 19,* 765–781.

Canadian Language Benchmarks. (2012). *For English as a second language.* Retrieved from http://www.cic.gc.ca/english/pdf/pub/language-benchmarks.pdf

Canagarajah, A. S. (1999). *Resisting linguistic imperialism in English teaching.* Oxford, UK: Oxford University Press.

Canagarajah, A. S. (2005). *Reclaiming the local in language policy and practice.* Mahwah, NJ: Lawrence Erlbaum.

Canagarajah, A. S. (2007). Lingua franca English, multilingual communities, and language acquisition. *Modern Language Journal, 91*(Suppl.), 923–939.

Canagarajah, A. S., & Ben Said, S. (2010). English language teaching in the outer and expanding circles. In J. Maybin & J. Swann (Eds.), *The Routledge companion to English language studies* (pp. 157–170). Oxford, UK: Routledge.

Canale, M. (1983a). From communicative competence to communicative language pedagogy. In J. C. Richards & R. W. Schmidt (Eds.), *Language and communication* (pp. 2–27). London, UK: Longman.

Canale, M. (1983b). On some dimensions of language proficiency. In J. Oller (Ed.), *Issues in language testing research* (pp. 333–342). Rowley, MA: Newbury House.

Canale, M., & Swain, M. (1980). Theoretical bases of communicative approaches to second language teaching and testing. *Applied Linguistics, 1*(1), 1–47.

Candlin, C. N. (1984). Syllabus design as a critical process. *ELT Documents,* (118), 29–46.

Canto, S., de Graaff, R., & Jauregi, K. (2014). Collaborative tasks for negotiation of intercultural meaning in virtual worlds and video-web communication. In M. González-Lloret & L. Ortega (Eds.), *Technology-mediated TBLT: Researching technology and tasks* (pp. 183–214). Amsterdam, The Netherlands: John Benjamins.

Carico, K. M., & Logan, D. (2004). A generation in cyberspace: Engaging readers through online discussions. *Language Arts, 81*(4), 293–302.

Carless, D. (2007). Learning-oriented assessment: Conceptual bases and practical implications. *Innovations in Education and Teaching International, 44*(1), 57–66.

Carless, D. (2009). Learning-oriented assessment: Principles, practice, and a project. In L. Meyer, S. Davidson, H. Anderson, R. Fletcher, P. Johnston, & M. Rees (Eds.), *Tertiary assessment and higher education student outcomes: Policy, practice, and research* (pp. 79–90). Wellington, NZ: Ako Aotearoa.

Carless, D. (2011). *From testing to productive student learning: Implementing formative assessment in Confucian-heritage settings.* New York, NY: Routledge.

Carless, D. (2013). Innovation in language teaching and learning. In C. Chapelle (Ed.), *The Encyclopedia of Applied Linguistics*. Cambridge, UK: Wiley-Blackwell. doi:10.1002/9781405198431.wbeal0540

Carroll, J. B. (1965). The prediction of success in intensive foreign language training. In R. Glaser (Ed.), *Training, research, and education* (pp. 87–136). Pittsburgh, PA: University of Pittsburgh Press.

Carroll, J. B., & Sapon, S. (1959). *The modern languages aptitude test*. San Antonio, TX: Psychological Corporation.

Celce-Murcia, M., Dörnyei, Z., & Thurrell, S. (1995). Communicative competence: A pedagogically motivated model with content specifications. *Issues in Applied Linguistics, 6*(2), 5–35.

Cennamo, K. S., Ross, J. D., & Ertmer, P. A. (2010). *Technology integration for meaningful classroom use: A standards-based approach*. Belmont, CA: Wadsworth, Cengage Learning.

Chafe, W. (1985). Linguistic differences produced by differences between speech and writing. In D. R. Olsen, N. Torrance, & A. Hilyard (Eds.), *Literacy and language learning: The nature and consequences of reading and writing* (pp. 105–123). Cambridge, UK: Cambridge University Press.

Chambless, K. S. (2012). Teachers' oral proficiency in the target language: Research on its role in language teaching and learning. *Foreign Language Annals, 45*, 141–162.

Chamot, A. U., Barnhardt, S., El-Dinary, P. B., & Robbins, J. (1999). *The learning strategies handbook*. White Plains, NY: Addison Wesley Longman.

Chang, Y.-F. (2009). 'I no say you say is boring': The development of pragmatic competence in L2 apology. *Language Sciences, 32*, 408–424.

Chapelle, C. A. (1998). Multimedia CALL: Lessons to be learned from research on instructed SLA. *Language Learning & Technology, 2*(1), 21–39.

Chapelle, C. A. (2001). *Computer applications in second language acquisition: Foundations for teaching, testing and research*. Cambridge, UK: Cambridge University Press.

Chapelle, C. A. (2009). The relationship between second language acquisition theory and computer-assisted language learning. *The Modern Language Journal, 93*, 741–753.

Chapelle, C. A. (2012a). Computer-assisted language learning effectiveness research. In C. Chapelle (Ed.), *The encyclopedia of applied linguistics*. Cambridge, UK: Wiley-Blackwell. doi:10.1002/9781405198431.wbeal0176

Chapelle, C. A. (2012b). Conceptions of validity. In G. Fulcher & F. Davidson (Eds.), *The Routledge handbook of language testing* (pp. 21–33). New York, NY: Routledge.

Chapelle, C. A. (2014). Afterword: Technology-mediated TBLT and the evolving role of the innovator. In M. González-Lloret & L. Ortega (Eds.), *Technology-mediated TBLT: Researching technology and tasks* (pp. 323–334). Amsterdam, The Netherlands: John Benjamins.

Chapelle, C. A., Chung, Y-R., & Xu, J. (Eds.). (2008). *Towards adaptive CALL: Natural language processing for diagnostic language assessment*. Ames, IA: Iowa State University.

Chapelle, C. A., Cotos, E., & Lee, J. (2015). Validity arguments for diagnostic assessment using automated writing evaluation. *Language Testing, 32*(3), 385–405.

Chapelle, C., & Douglas, D. (2006). *Assessing language through computer technology*. Cambridge, UK: Cambridge University Press.

Chapelle, C., & Voss, E. (2016). 20 years of technology and language assessment in language learning and technology. *Language Learning & Technology, 20*(2), 116–128.

Chaudron, C., Doughty, C. J., Kim, Y., Kong, D. K., Lee, J., Lee, Y. G., & Urano, K. (2005). A task-based needs analysis of a tertiary Korean as a foreign language program. In M.

Long (Ed.), *Second language needs analysis* (pp. 225–261). Cambridge, UK: Cambridge University Press.

Chen, C-F. E., & Cheng, W. E. (2008). Beyond the design of automated writing evaluation: Pedagogical practices and perceived learning effectiveness in EFL writing classes. *Language Learning & Technology, 12*(2), 94–112.

Chen, L., & Zhang, R. (2011). Web-based CALL to listening comprehension. *Current Issues in Education, 13*(4). Retrieved from http://cie.asu.edu/

Cheng, H. F., & Dörnyei, Z. (2007). The use of motivational strategies in language instruction: The case of EFL teaching in Taiwan. *International Journal of Innovation in Language Learning and Teaching, 1*(1), 153–174.

Chodorow, M., Gamon, M., & Tetreault, J. (2010). The utility of article and preposition error correction systems for English language learners: Feedback and assessment. *Language Testing, 27*(3), 419–436.

Chun, D. M. (2002). *Discourse intonation in L2: From theory and research to practice.* Amsterdam, The Netherlands: John Benjamins.

Chun, D. M. (2006). CALL technologies for L2 reading. In L. Ducate & N. Arnold (Eds.), *Calling on CALL: From theory and research to new directions in foreign language teaching* (Vol. 5, pp. 131–170). San Marcos, TX: CALICO.

Chun, D. M. (2013). Computer-assisted pronunciation teaching. In C. A. Chapelle (Ed.), *The encyclopedia of applied linguistics.* Cambridge, UK: Wiley-Blackwell. doi:10.1002/9781405198431.wbeal0172

Chun, D. M., & Plass, J. (1996). Effects of multimedia annotations on vocabulary acquisition. *Modern Language Journal, 80*(2), 183–198.

Churches, A. (2009). *Bloom's digital taxonomy.* Retrieved March 6, 2015, from http://edorigami.wikispaces.com/Bloom%27s+Digital+Taxonomy

Clahsen, H., Meisel, H., & Pienemann, M. (1983). *Deutsch als Zweitsprache: der Spracherwerb ausländischer Arbeiter.* Tübingen, Germany: Gunter Narr.

Coffin, C. (2006). Learning the language of school history: The role of linguistics in mapping the writing demands of the secondary school curriculum. *Journal of Curriculum Studies, 38*(4), 413–429.

Cohen, A. D. (2008). Teaching and assessing L2 pragmatics: What can we expect from learners? *Language Teaching, 41*(2), 213–235.

Cohen, A. D., Oxford, R. L., & Chi, J. C. (2001). *Learning style survey: Assessing your own learning styles.* Minneapolis, MN: Center for Advanced Research on Language Acquisition, University of Minnesota.

Constantinides, M. (2013). Integrating technology on initial training courses: A survey amongst CELTA tutors. In B. Zhou (Ed.), *Explorations of language teaching and learning with computational assistance* (pp. 230–245). Hershey, PA: Information Science Reference.

Cook, G. (2000). *Language play, language learning.* Oxford, UK: Oxford University Press.

Cook, V. (1994). Universal grammar and the learning and teaching of second languages. In T. Odlin (Ed.), *Perspectives on pedagogical grammar* (pp. 25–48). Cambridge, UK: Cambridge University Press.

Cook, V. (2001). *Second language learning and language teaching.* Oxford, UK: Oxford University Press.

Cooke-Plagwitz, J. (2008). New directions in CALL: An objective introduction to second life. *CALICO Journal, 25*(3), 547–557.

Coppieters, R. (1987). Competence differences between native and near native speakers. *Language, 63*, 544–573.

Costa, P. T., & McCrae, R. R. (1992). *NEO-PI-R: Professional manual.* Odessa, FL: Psychological Assessment Resources.

Cotos, E. (2011). Review of Wimba voice 6.0 collaboration suite. *Language Learning & Technology, 15*(1), 29–35.

Council of Chief State School Officers (CCSSO). (2012). *Framework for English language proficiency development standards corresponding to the common core state standards and the next generation science standards.* Washington, DC: Author.

Council of Europe. (2001). *Common European framework of reference for languages: Learning, teaching, assessment.* Cambridge, UK: Cambridge University Press.

Crandall, E., & Basturkmen, H. (2004). Evaluating pragmatics-focused materials. *ELT Journal, 58*(1), 38–49.

Cronbach, L., & Snow, R. (1977). *Aptitudes and instructional methods: A handbook for research on interactions.* New York, NY: Irvington.

Crookes, G. (2009a). Radical language teaching. In M. H. Long & C. Doughty (Eds.), *The handbook of language teaching* (pp. 595–609). Malden, MA: Wiley-Blackwell.

Crookes, G. (2009b). *Values, philosophies, and beliefs in TESOL: Making a statement.* Cambridge, UK: Cambridge University Press.

Crookes, G. (2013). Critical language pedagogy. In C. Chapelle (Ed.), *Blackwell encyclopedia of applied linguistics.* Cambridge, UK: Wiley-Blackwell. doi:10.1002/9781405198431. wbeal0284

Cross, J. (2009). Effects of listening strategy instruction on news videotext comprehension. *Language Teaching Research, 13*, 151–176.

Cumming, A. (1989). Writing expertise and second language proficiency. *Language Learning, 39*, 81–141.

Cunningham, K. J. (2015). Duolingo. *TESL-EJ, 19*(1). Retrieved from http://www.tesl-ej. org/wordpress/issues/volume19/ej73/ej73m1/

Curry, N. (2014). Using CBT with anxious language learners: The potential role of the learning advisor. *Studies in Self-Access Learning Journal, 5*(1), 29–41.

Curry, N., & Mynard, J. (2014). Editorial: Directions in self-access learning. *Studies in Self-Access Learning Journal, 5*(1), 1–7.

Dalton-Puffer, C. (2011). Content and language integrated learning: From practice to principles? *Annual Review of Applied Linguistics, 31*, 182–204.

Darling-Hammond, L., & Falk, B. (2013). *Teacher learning through assessment: How student-performance assessments can support teacher learning.* Washington, DC: Center for American Progress.

Darling-Hammond, L., Wei, R. C., Andree, A., Richardson, N., & Orphanos, S. (2009). *Professional learning in the learning profession.* Washington, DC: National Staff Development Council.

Davidson, F., & Lynch, B. (2002). *Testcraft: A teacher's guide to writing and using language test specifications.* New Haven, CT: Yale University Press.

Davidson, P., & Coombe, C. (2012). Computerized language assessment. In C. Coombe, P. Davidson, B. O'Sullivan, & S. Stoynoff, S. (Eds.), *The Cambridge guide to second language assessment* (pp. 267–273). Cambridge, UK: Cambridge University Press.

Davies, G., Otto, S. E. K., & Rüschoff, B. (2014). Historical perspectives on CALL. In M. Thomas, H. Reinders, & M. Warschauer (Eds.), *Contemporary computer-assisted language learning* (pp. 19–38). London, UK: Bloomsbury.

Davies, J. R. (2011). Second-language acquisition and the information age: How social software has created a new mode of learning. *TESL Canada Journal, 28*(2), 11–19. Retrieved from http://dx.doi.org/10.18806/tesl.v28i2.1069

Davis, E. A., & Krajcik, J. S. (2005). Designing educative curriculum materials to promote teacher learning. *Educational Researcher, 34,* 3–14.

Davis, J. McE. (2011). *Using surveys for understanding and improving foreign language programs.* (NetWork #61) [PDF document]. Honolulu, HI: University of Hawai'i, National Foreign Language Resource Center. Retrieved from http://hdl.handle.net/10125/14549

Davis, J. McE. (2014, July 23). *Using classroom assessment to enhance teaching and learning.* Invited workshop delivered at US Foreign Service Institute.

Davis, L. E. (2013). Language assessment in program evaluation. In C. A. Chapelle (Ed.), *Blackwell encyclopedia of applied linguistics.* New York, NY: Wiley-Blackwell. doi:10.1002/9781405198431.wbeal0604

Davis, L. E., & Kondo-Brown, K. (2012). Assessing student performance: Types and uses of rubrics. In J. D. Brown (Ed.), *Developing, using, and analyzing rubrics in language assessment with case studies in Asian and Pacific Languages* (pp. 33–56). Honolulu, HI: National Foreign Languages Resource Center Publications.

de Bot, K. (1992). A bilingual processing model: Levelt's 'Speaking' model adapted. *Applied Linguistics, 13*(1), 1–24.

de Bot, K. (1996). The psycholinguistics of the output hypothesis. *Language Learning, 46,* 529–555.

de Jong, N. H. (2005). Can second language grammar be learned through listening? An experimental study. *Studies in Second Language Acquisition, 27*(2), 205–234.

de Jong, N. H., & Perfetti, C. A. (2011). Fluency training in the ESL classroom: An experimental study of fluency development and proceduralization. *Language Learning, 61*(2), 533–568.

de la Fuente, M. (2002). Negotiation and oral acquisition of L2 vocabulary: The roles of input and output in the receptive and productive acquisition of words. *Studies in Second Language Acquisition, 24,* 81–112.

De Ridder, I. (2002). Visible or invisible links: Does the highlighting if hyperlinks affect incidental vocabulary learning, text comprehension, and the reading process? *Language Teaching & Technology, 6*(1), 123–146.

DeGraaf, R. (1997). The eXperanto experiment: Effects of explicit instruction on second language acquisition. *Studies in Second Language Acquisition, 19,* 249–275.

deHaan, J. (2005). Learning language through video games: A theoretical framework, an evaluation of game genres and questions for future research. In S. P. Schaffer & M. L. Price (Eds.), *Interactive convergence: Critical issues in multimedia* (pp. 229–239). Oxford, UK: Inter-Disciplinary Press.

DeKeyser, R. (1997). Beyond explicit rule learning: Automatising second language morphosyntax. *Studies in Second Language Acquisition, 22,* 499–533.

DeKeyser, R. (2007). Skill acquisition theory. In B. VanPatten & J. Williams (Eds.), *Theories in second language acquisition* (pp. 97–113). Mahwah, NJ: Lawrence Erlbaum.

Dekeyser, R. (2012). Age effects in second language learning. In S. M. Gass & A. Mackey (Eds.), *The Routledge handbook of second language acquisition* (pp. 442–460). New York, NY: Routledge.

Della Chiesa, B., Scott, J., & Hinton, C. (Eds.). (2012). *Languages in a global world—Learning for better cultural understanding.* Paris, France: OECD Publishing.

Demb, J. B., Boynton, G. B., & Heeger, D. J. (1997). Brain activity in the visual cortex predicts individual differences in reading performance. *Proceedings of the National Academy of Science, 94,* 13363–13366.

Desmarais, L., Duquette, L., Renié, D., & Laurier, M. (1998). Evaluating learning and inter-actions in a multimedia environment. *Computers and the Humanities, 31*(3), 327–349.

Dewaele, J.-M. (2007). Predicting language learners' grades in the L1, L2, L3 and L4: The effect of some psychological and sociocognitive variables. *International Journal of Multi-lingualism, 4*(3), 169–197.

Dewaele, J.-M. (2013). The link between foreign language classroom anxiety and psychoti-cism, extraversion, and neuroticism among adult bi- and multilinguals. *Modern Language Journal, 97*(3), 670–684.

Dewaele, J.-M., & Furnham, A. (1999). Extraversion: The unloved variable in applied lin-guistics research. *Language Learning, 49*, 509–544.

Dewey, J. (1938). *Experience and education.* Toronto, Canada: Collier-MacMillan Canada Ltd.

Dikli, S. (2006). An overview of automated scoring of essays. *The Journal of Technology, Learn-ing, and Assessment, 5*(1), 3–35.

Dippold, D. (2009). Peer feedback through blogs: Student and teacher perceptions in an advanced German class. *ReCALL, 21*(1), 18–36.

Dörnyei, Z. (2001). New themes and approaches in L2 motivation research. *Annual Review of Applied Linguistics, 21*, 43–59.

Dörnyei, Z. (2005). *The psychology of the language learner: Individual differences in second lan-guage acquisition.* Mahwah, NJ: Lawrence Erlbaum.

Dörnyei, Z. (2007). Creating a motivating classroom environment. In J. Cummins & C. Davison (Eds.), *International handbook of English language teaching* (Vol. 2, pp. 719–731). New York: Springer.

Dörnyei, Z. (2009). *The psychology of second language acquisition.* Oxford, UK: Oxford Uni-versity Press.

Dörnyei, Z., & Csizér, K. (1998). Ten commandments for motivating language learners: Results of an empirical study. *Language Teaching Research, 2*, 203–229.

Dörnyei, Z., & Ottó, I. (1998). Motivation in action: A process model of L2 motivation. *Working Papers in Applied Linguistics (Thames Valley University, London), 4*, 43–69.

Dörnyei, Z., & Skehan, P. (2003). Individual differences in L2 learning. In C. Doughty & M. Long (Eds.), *The handbook of second language acquisition* (pp. 589–630). Malden, MA: Wiley-Blackwell.

Doughty, C. J. (2003). Instructed SLA: Constraints, compensation, and enhancement. In C. Doughty & M. Long (Eds.), *The handbook of second language acquisition* (pp. 256–310). Malden, MA: Wiley-Blackwell.

Doughty, C. J. (2013). Assessing aptitude. In A. Kunnan (Ed.), *The companion to language assessment* (pp. 23–46). New York, NY: Wiley-Blackwell.

Doughty, C., & Long, M. H. (Eds.). (2003a). *The handbook of second language acquisition.* London, UK: Wiley-Blackwell.

Doughty, C., & Long, M. H. (2003b). Optimal psycholinguistic environments for distance foreign language learning. *Language Learning and Technology, 7*(3), 50–80.

Downes, S. (2004). Educational blogging. *EDUCAUSE Review, 39*(5), 14–26.

Duff, P. A. (2012). Identity, agency, and second acquisition. In S. M. Gass & A. Mackey, *The Routledge handbook of second language acquisition* (pp. 410–426). New York, NY: Routledge.

Dulay, H. C., & Burt, M. K. (1973). Should we teach children syntax? *Language Learning, 23*, 245–258.

Dulay, H. C., & Burt, M. K. (1974). Natural sequences in child second language acquisition. *Language Learning, 24*, 37–53.

East, M. (2012). *Task-based language teaching from the teachers' perspective: Insights from New Zealand* (Vol. 3). Amsterdam, The Netherlands: John Benjamins.

East, M. (2015). Coming to terms with innovative high-stakes assessment practice: Teachers' viewpoints on assessment reform. *Language Testing, 32*, 101–120.

Egbert, J., & Hanson-Smith, E. (Eds.). (2007). *CALL environments: Research, practice, and critical issues.* Alexandria, VA: TESOL.

Egbert, J., Paulus, T., & Nakamichi, Y. (2002). The impact of CALL instruction on language classroom technology use: A foundation for rethinking CALL teacher education? *Language Learning & Technology, 6*(3), 108–126.

Ehrman, M. E. (1996). *Understanding second language learning difficulties.* Thousand Oaks, CA: Sage.

Ehrman, M. E., & Leaver, B. L. (2003). Cognitive styles in the service of language learning. *System, 31*, 393–415.

Elder, C. (2005). Evaluating the effectiveness of heritage language education: What role for testing? *International Journal of Bilingual Education and Bilingualism, 8*(2–3), 196–212.

Ellis, N. C. (1996). Sequencing in SLA: Phonological memory, chunking and points of order. *Studies in Second Language Acquisition, 18*, 91–126.

Ellis, N. C. (2006). Cognitive perspectives on SLA: The associative cognitive CREED. *AILA Review, 19*, 100–121.

Ellis, N. C. (2007). The associative-cognitive CREED. In B. VanPatten & J. Williams (Eds.), *Theories in second language acquisition* (pp. 77–95). Mahwah, NJ: Lawrence Erlbaum Associates.

Ellis, N. C., & Sinclair, S. (1996). Working memory in the acquisition of vocabulary and syntax: Putting language in good order. *Quarterly Journal of Experimental Psychology, 49A*, 234–250.

Ellis, R. (1989). Are classroom and naturalistic acquisition the same? A study of the classroom acquisition of German word order rules. *Studies in Second Language Acquisition, 11*, 305–328.

Ellis, R. (1992). Learning to communicate in the classroom. *Studies in Second Language Acquisition, 14*(1), 1–23.

Ellis, R. (1993). The structural syllabus and second language acquisition. *TESOL Quarterly, 27*(1), 91–113.

Ellis, R. (1997a). SLA and language pedagogy. *Studies in Second Language Acquisition, 19*(1), 69–92.

Ellis, R. (1997b). *SLA research and language teaching.* Oxford, UK: Oxford University Press.

Ellis, R. (2003). *Task-based language learning and teaching.* Oxford, UK: Oxford University Press.

Ellis, R. (2007). The differential effects of corrective feedback on two grammatical structures. In A. Mackey (Ed.), *Conversational interaction in second language acquisition* (pp. 339–360). Oxford, UK: Oxford University Press.

Ellis, R. (2008). *The study of second language acquisition* (2nd ed.). Oxford, UK: Oxford University Press.

Ellis, R. (2011). Macro- and micro-evaluations of task-based teaching. In B. Tomlinson (Ed.), *Materials development in language teaching* (pp. 21–35). Cambridge, UK: Cambridge University Press.

Ellis, R. (2015). Researching acquisition sequences: Idealization and de-idealization in SLA. *Language Learning, 65*, 181–209.

Ellis, R., & Shintani, N. (2014). *Exploring language pedagogy through second language acquisition research.* London, UK: Routledge.

Elola, I., & Oskoz, A. (2010). Collaborative writing: Fostering foreign language and writing conventions development. *Language Learning & Technology, 14*(3), 51–71.

Erlam, R. (2005). Language aptitude and its relationship to instructional effectiveness in second language acquisition. *Language Teaching Research, 9,* 147–171.

Eskey, D. E. (1988). Holding in the bottom: An interactive approach to the language problems of second language readers. In P. Carrell, J. Devine, & D. E. Eskey (Eds.), *Interactive approaches to second language reading* (pp. 93–100). Cambridge, UK: Cambridge University Press.

Eskey, D. E. (2005). Reading in a second language. In E. Hinkel (Ed.), *Handbook of research in second language teaching and learning* (pp. 563–579). Mahwah, NJ: Lawrence Erlbaum.

Eskildsen, S. W. (2015). What counts as a developmental sequence? Exemplar-based L2 learning of English questions. *Language Learning, 65,* 33–62.

Eslami, Z. R., & Fatahi, A. (2008). Teachers' sense of self-efficacy, English proficiency, and instructional strategies: A study of nonnative EFL teachers in Iran. *TESL EJ, 11,* 1–19.

Farrell, T. S. C., & Ives, J. (2015). Exploring teacher beliefs and classroom practices through reflective practice: A case study. *Language Teaching Research, 19,* 594–610.

Farrell, T. S. C., & Mallard, C. (2006). The use of reception strategies by learners of French as a foreign language. *The Modern Language Journal, 90*(3), 338–352.

Fenton-Smith, B., & Torpey, M. J. (2013). Orienting EFL teachers: Principles arising from an evaluation of an induction program in a Japanese university. *Language Teaching Research, 17*(2), 228–250.

Ferris, D. R. (2003). *Response to student writing: Research implications for second language students.* Mahwah, NJ: Lawrence Erlbaum.

Ferris, D. R. (2011). *Treatment of error in second language student writing.* Ann Arbor, MI: University of Michigan Press.

Ferris, D. R., & Hedgcock, J. S. (2014). *Teaching L2 composition: Purpose, process, and practice.* New York, NY: Routledge.

Feryok, A. (2010). Language teacher cognitions: Complex dynamic systems? *System, 38,* 272–279.

Fischer, R. (2012). Diversity in learner usage patterns. In G. Stockwell (Ed.), *Computer-assisted language learning: Diversity in research and practice* (pp. 14–32). Cambridge, UK. Cambridge University Press.

Fleisher, D. (2007). *Evaluation use: A survey of the U.S. American Evaluation Association members.* Unpublished Master's thesis, Claremont Graduate University.

Flowerdew, J. (2009). Corpora in language teaching. In M. H. Long & C. J. Doughty (Eds.), *The handbook of language teaching* (pp. 327–350). Malden, MA: Wiley-Blackwell.

Frechtling, J., & Sharp, L. (1997). *User-friendly handbook for mixed methods evaluations.* Retrieved from http://www.nsf.gov/pubs/1997/nsf97153/start.htm

French, L. M., & O'Brien, I. (2008). Phonological memory and children's second language grammar learning. *Applied Psycholinguistics, 29*(3), 463–487.

Fukkink, R. G., Hulstijn, J. H., & Simis, A. (2005). Does training in second-language word recognition skills affect reading comprehension? An experimental study. *The Modern Language Journal, 89,* 54–75.

Fulcher, G. (2010). *Practical language testing.* London, UK: Hodder Education.

Fulcher, G. (2012). Assessment literacy for the language classroom. *Language Assessment Quarterly, 9,* 113–132.

Gagné, R. M. (1968). Presidential address of division 15 learning hierarchies. *Educational Psychologist, 6*(1), 1–9.

Gagné, R. M., & Briggs, I. J. (1979). *Principles of instructional design*. New York, NY: Holt Reinhart.

Gagné, R. M., Wager, W. W., Golas, K. C., & Keller, J. M. (2005). *Principles of instructional design*. Belmont, CA: Wadsworth/Thomson Learning.

Gardner, R. C. (1985). *Social psychology and second language learning: The role of attitudes and motivation*. London, UK: Edward Arnold.

Gardner, R. C., & Lambert, W. E. (1972). *Attitudes and motivation in second language learning*. Rowley, MA: Newbury House.

Garet, M. S., Porter, A. C., Desimone, L., Birman, B. F., & Yoon, K. S. (2001). What makes professional development effective? Results from a national sample of teachers. *American Educational Research Journal, 38*(4), 915–945.

Garnier, M., & Schmitt, N. (2016). Picking up polysemous phrasal verbs: How many do learners know and what facilitates this knowledge? *System, 59*, 29–44.

Garton, S., & Graves, K. (2014). Materials in ELT: Looking ahead. In S. Garton & K. Graves (Eds.), *International perspectives on materials in ELT* (pp. 270–279). New York, NY: Palgrave Macmillan.

Gascoigne, C. (2006). Toward an understanding of incidental input enhancement in computerized L2 environments. *CALICO Journal, 24*(1), 147–162.

Gass, S. M., & Mackey, A. (2007). Input, interaction, and output in second language acquisition. In B. VanPatten & J. Williams (Eds.), *Theories in second language acquisition: An introduction* (pp. 175–200). Mahwah, NJ: Lawrence Erlbaum.

Gatbonton, E. (2008). Looking beyond teachers' classroom behaviour: Novice and experienced ESL teachers' pedagogical knowledge. *Language Teaching Research, 12*, 161–182.

Genesee, F., & Upshur, J. A. (1996). *Classroom-based evaluation in second language education*. Cambridge, UK: Cambridge University Press.

Gilabert, R. (2004). *Task complexity and L2 narrative oral production*. Unpublished Ph.D. dissertation, University of Barcelona, Spain.

Godwin-Jones, R. (2006). Emerging technologies, tag clouds in the blogosphere: Electronic literacy and social networking. *Language Learning & Technology, 10*(2), 8–15.

Godwin-Jones, R. (2009). Personal learning environments. *Language Learning & Technology, 13*(2), 3–9.

Godwin-Jones, R. (2013). Emerging technologies for language learning. In C. A. Chapelle (Ed.), *The encyclopedia of applied linguistics* (pp. 1882–1886). Cambridge, UK: Wiley-Blackwell.

Goertler, S., Bollen, M., & Gaff, J. (2012). Students' readiness for and attitudes toward hybrid FL instruction. *CALICO Journal, 29*(2), 297–320.

Goh, C. (2000). A cognitive perspective on language learners' listening comprehension problems. *System, 28*, 55–75.

Goh, C. (2002). Exploring listening comprehension tactics and their interaction patterns. *System, 30*, 185–206.

Goldberg, L. R. (1992). The development of markers for the Big-Five factor structure. *Psychological Assessment, 4*(1), 26–42.

Goldberg, L. R. (1993). The structure of phenotypic personality traits. *American Psychologist, 48*, 26–34.

Goldschneider, J. M., & DeKeyser, R. M. (2001). Explaining the "natural order of L2 morpheme acquisition" in English: A meta-analysis of multiple determinants. *Language Learning, 51*, 1–50.

Golonka, E. M., Bowles, A. R., Frank, V. M., Richardson, D. L., & Freynik, S. (2014). Technologies for foreign language learning: A review of technology types and their effectiveness. *Computer Assisted Language Learning, 27*(1), 70–105.

González-Lloret, M. (2003). Designing task-based CALL to promote interaction: En busca de esmeraldas. *Language Learning & Technology, 7*(1), 86–104.

González-Lloret, M. (2013). Technologies for performance-based assessment. In M. L. Pérez-Cañado (Ed.), *Competency-based language teaching in higher education* (pp. 169–180). Dordrecht, ND: Springer.

González-Lloret, M. (2014). The need for needs analysis in technology-mediated TBLT. In M. González-Lloret & L. Ortega (Eds.), *Technology-mediated TBLT: Researching technology and tasks* (pp. 23–50). Amsterdam, The Netherlands: John Benjamins.

González-Lloret, M., & Ortega, L. (2014a). Toward technology-mediated TBLT: An introduction. In M. González-Lloret & L. Ortega (Eds.), *Technology-mediated TBLT: Researching technology and tasks* (pp. 1–22). Amsterdam, The Netherlands: John Benjamins.

González-Lloret, M., & Ortega, L. (Eds.). (2014b). *Technology-mediated TBLT: Researching technology and tasks.* Amsterdam, The Netherlands: John Benjamins.

Goo, J. (2012). Corrective feedback and working memory capacity in interaction-driven L2 learning. *Studies in Second Language Acquisition, 34*(3), 445–474.

Goodman, K. S. (1967). Reading: A psycholinguistic guessing game. *Journal of the Reading Specialist, 6*(4), 126–135.

Goto Butler, Y. (2011). The implementation of communicative and task-based language teaching in the Asia-Pacific region. *Annual Review of Applied Linguistics, 31*, 36–57.

Grabe, W. (2001). Reading-writing relations: Theoretical perspectives and instructional practices. In D. Belcher & A. Hirvela (Eds.), *Linking literacies: Perspectives on L2 reading-writing connections* (pp. 15–47). Ann Arbor, MI: University of Michigan Press.

Grabe, W. (2003). Reading and writing relations: Theoretical perspectives and instructional practices. In B. Kroll (Ed.), *Exploring the dynamics of second language writing* (pp. 242–262). Cambridge, UK: Cambridge University Press.

Grabe, W. (2009). *Reading in a second language: Moving from theory to practice.* Cambridge, UK: Cambridge University Press.

Grabe, W., & Stoller, F. (2011). *Teaching and researching reading.* Harlow, UK: Pearson.

Graham, S., & Macaro, E. (2008). Strategy instruction in listening for lower-intermediate learners of French. *Language Learning, 58*, 747–783.

Grau Sempere, A., Mohn, M. C., & Pieroni, R. (2009). Improving educational effectiveness and promoting internal and external information-sharing through student learning outcomes assessment. In J. M. Norris, J. McE. Davis, C. Sinicrope, & Y. Watanabe (Eds.), *Toward useful program evaluation in college foreign language education* (pp. 139–162). Honolulu, HI: University of Hawai'i, National Foreign Language Resource Center.

Graves, K. (2000). *Designing language courses: A guide for teachers.* Boston, MA: Heinle & Heinle.

Gray, J. (Ed.). (2013). *Critical perspectives on language teaching materials.* New York, NY: Palgrave Macmillan.

Greene, J. C. (2007). *Mixed methods in social inquiry.* San Francisco, CA: Wiley-Blackwell.

Gregg, K. (2003). SLA theory: Construction and assessment. In C. J. Doughty & M. H. Long (Eds.), *The handbook of second language acquisition* (pp. 831–865). Oxford, UK: Wiley-Blackwell.

Grgurović, M., Chapelle, C. A., & Shelley, M. C. (2013). A meta-analysis of effectiveness studies on computer technology-supported language learning. *ReCALL, 25*(2), 165–198.

Grgurović, M., & Hegelheimer, V. (2007). Help options and multimedia listening: Students' use of subtitles and the transcript. *Language Learning & Technology, 11*(1), 45–66.

Gries, S. T. (2008). Corpus analysis and second language acquisition data. In P. Robinson & N. C. Ellis (Eds.), *Handbook of cognitive linguistics and second language acquisition* (pp. 406–431). London, UK: Routledge.

Grimes, D., & Warschauer, M. (2006). *Automated essay scoring in the classroom*. Paper presented at the American Educational Research Association San Francisco, CA.

Grisham, D. L., & Wosley, T. D. (2006). Recentering the middle school classroom as a vibrant learning community: Students, literacy, and technology intersect. *Journal of Adolescent & Adult Literacy, 49*, 648–660.

Gruba, P., & Clark, C. (2010). The use of social networking sites for foreign language learning: An autoethnographic study of Livemocha. *Proceedings of Ascilite Sydney 2010*, 164–173.

Guilloteaux, M. J., & Dörnyei, Z. (2008). Motivating language learners: A classroom-oriented investigation of the effects of motivational strategies on student motivation. *TESOL Quarterly, 42*(1), 55–77.

Guth, S., & Helm, F. (Eds.). (2010). *Telecollaboration 2.0: Language, literacies and intercultural learning in the 21st century*. Berlin, Germany: Peter Lang.

Hadfield, J., & Dörnyei, Z. (2013). *Motivating learning*. Harlow, UK: Longman.

Hall, D. R., & Knox, J. S. (2009). Language teacher education by distance. In A. Burns & J. C. Richards (Eds.), *The Cambridge guide to second language teacher education* (pp. 218–229). Cambridge, UK: Cambridge University Press.

Halliday, M. A. (1993). Towards a language-based theory of learning. *Linguistics and Education, 5*(2), 93–116.

Hamada, M., & Koda, K. (2008). Influence of first language orthographic experience on second language decoding and word learning. *Language Learning, 58*(1), 1–31.

Hampel, R. (2006). Rethinking task design for the digital age: A framework for language teaching and learning in a synchronous online environment. *ReCALL, 18*, 105–121.

Hampel, R., & de los Arcoz, l. A. (2013). Interacting at a distance: A critical review of the role of ICT in developing the learner-context interface in a university language programme. *Innovation in Language Learning and Teaching, 7*(2), 158–178.

Hampel, R., & Hauck, M. (2004). Towards an effective use of audioconferencing in distance learning courses. *Language Learning & Technology, 8*(1), 66–82.

Hamp-Lyons, L., & Tavares, N. (2011). Interactive assessment: A dialogic and collaborative approach to assessing learners' oral language. In D. Tsagari & Ildikó Csépes (Eds.), *Classroom-based language assessment* (pp. 29–46). Frankfurt, Germany: Peter Lang.

Hanaoka, O., & Izumi, S. (2012). Noticing and uptake: Addressing pre-articulated covert problems in L2 writing. *Journal of Second Language Writing, 21*(4), 332–347.

Harklau, L. A. (2002). The role of writing in classroom second language acquisition. *Journal of Second Language Writing, 11*, 329–350.

Harrington, M., & Sawyer, M. (1992). L2 Working memory capacity and L2 reading skill. *Studies in Second Language Acquisition, 14*(1), 25–38.

Hauptman, P. C. (1971). A structural approach versus a situational approach to foreign-language teaching. *Language Learning, 21*, 235–244.

Hausrath, Z. (2012). First curriculum: Teaching English as a second language with Minecraft. Retrieved from http://tesolbuilders.blogspot.com/search?updated-min=2012–01–01T00:00:00–05:00&updated-max=2013–01–01T00:00:00–05:00&max-results=5

Healey, D., Hegelheimer, V., Hubbard, P., Ioannou-Georgiou, S., Kessler, G., & Ware, P. (2008). *TESOL technology standards framework*. Alexandria, VA: Teachers of English to Speakers of Other Languages, Inc. (TESOL).

Hedgcock, J. S. (2005). Taking stock of research and pedagogy in L2 writing. In E. Hinkel (Ed.), *Handbook of research in second language teaching and learning* (pp. 597–613). Mahwah, NJ: Lawrence Erlbaum.

Hedgcock, J. S. (2012). Second language writing processes among adolescent and adult learners. In E. L. Grigorenko, E. Mambrino, & D. D. Preiss (Eds.), *Handbook of writing: A mosaic of perspectives and views* (pp. 219–237). New York, NY: Psychology Press.

Hedgcock, J. S., & Lefkowitz, N. (1996). Some input on input: Two analyses of student response to expert feedback on L2 writing. *Modern Language Journal, 80,* 287–308.

Hegelheimer, V., & Lee, J. (2014). The role of technology in teaching and researching writing. In M. Thomas, H. Reinders, & M. Warschauer (Eds.), *Contemporary computer-assisted language learning* (pp. 287–302). London, UK: Bloomsbury.

Heift, T. (2002). Learner control and error correction in ICALL: Browsers, peekers, and adamants. *CALICO Journal, 19*(2), 295–313.

Hess, N. (2001). *Teaching large multilevel classes.* Cambridge, UK: Cambridge University Press.

Hill, Y. Z., & Tschudi, S. (2008). A utilization-focused approach to the evaluation of a web-based hybrid conversational Mandarin program in a North American university. *Teaching English in China: CELEA Journal, 31*(5), 37–54.

Hinkel, E. (2002). *Second language writers' text.* Mahwah, NJ: Lawrence Erlbaum.

Hinkel, E. (2006). Current perspectives on teaching the four skills. *TESOL Quarterly, 40*(1), 109–131.

Hinkel, E. (2010). Integrating the four skills: Current and historical perspectives. In R. B. Kaplan (Ed.), *Oxford handbook in applied linguistics* (pp. 110–126). Oxford, UK: Oxford University Press.

Hiver, P. (2013). The interplay of possible language teacher selves in professional development choices. *Language Teaching Research, 17*(2), 210–227.

Honeyfield, J. (1977). Simplification. *TESOL Quarterly, 11*(4), 431–440.

Horwitz, E. K. (1985). Using student beliefs about language learning and teaching in the foreign language methods course. *Foreign Language Annals, 18,* 333–340.

Horwitz, E. K. (1988). The beliefs about language learning of beginning university foreign language students. *Modern Language Journal, 72*(3), 283–294.

Horwitz, E. K. (2001). Language anxiety and achievement. *Annual Review of Applied Linguistics, 21,* 112–126.

Horwitz, E. K., Horwitz, M. B., & Cope, J. (1986). Foreign language classroom anxiety. *Modern Language Journal, 70,* 125–132.

Horwitz, E. K., Tallon, M., & Luo, H. (2009). Foreign language anxiety. In J. C. Cassady (Ed.), *Anxiety in schools: The causes, consequences, and solutions for academic anxieties* (pp. 95–115). New York, NY: Peter Lang.

Housen, A., & Pierrard, M. (Eds.). (2008). *Investigations in instructed second language acquisition.* Berlin, Germany: Mouton de Gruyter.

Hsu, J. (1994). *Computer assisted language learning (CALL): The effect of ESL students' use of interactional modifications on listening comprehension.* Ames, IA: Iowa State University, Department of Curriculum and Instruction, College of Education.

Hu, G. (2002). Potential cultural resistance to pedagogical imports: The case of communicative language teaching in China. *Language Culture and Curriculum, 15*(2), 93–105.

Hu, G. (2005). Contextual influences on instructional practices: A Chinese case for an ecological approach to ELT. *TESOL Quarterly, 39*(4), 635–660.

Hu, M., & Nation, I. S. P. (2000). Unknown vocabulary density and reading comprehension. *Reading in a Foreign Language, 13*(1), 403–430.

Hu, Z., & McGrath, I. (2011). Innovation in higher education in China: Are teachers ready to integrate ICT in English language teaching? *Technology, Pedagogy and Education, 20*(1), 41–59.

Hubbard, P. (2008). Twenty-five years of theory in the CALICO journal. *CALICO Journal, 25*(3), 387–399.

Hubbard, P. (2015). *An invitation to CALL: Foundations of computer-assisted language learning.* Retrieved from http://web.stanford.edu/~efs/callcourse/

Hubbard, P., & Romeo, K. (2012). Diversity in learner training. In G. Stockwell (Ed.), *Computer-assisted language learning: Diversity in research and practice* (pp. 33–48). Cambridge, UK: Cambridge University Press.

Hudson, T. (2007). *Teaching second language reading.* Cambridge, UK: Cambridge University Press.

Huhta, M., Vogt, K., Johnson, E., & Tulkki, H. (2013). *Needs analysis for language course design: A holistic approach to ESP.* Cambridge, UK: Cambridge University Press.

Hurd, S. (2006). Towards a better understanding of the dynamic role of the distance language learner: Learner perceptions of personality, motivation, roles and approaches. *Distance Education, 27*(3), 299–325.

Hutchinson, T., & Waters, A. (1987). *English for specific purposes.* Cambridge, UK: Cambridge University Press.

Hwang, G. J., & Chang, H. F. (2011). A formative assessment-based mobile learning approach to improving the learning attitudes and achievements of students. *Computers & Education, 56*(4), 1023–1031.

Hyland, K. (2004). *Genre and second language writing.* Ann Arbor, MI: University of Michigan Press.

Hyland, K. (2007). Genre pedagogy: Language, literacy and L2 writing instruction. *Journal of Second Language Writing, 16,* 148–164.

Hyland, K. (2009). *Academic discourses.* London, UK: Continuum.

Hyland, K., & Hyland, F. (2006). *Feedback in second language writing: Contexts and issues.* Cambridge, UK: Cambridge University Press.

Hyland, K., & Wong, L. C. (Eds.). (2013). *Innovation and change in English language education.* London, UK: Routledge.

Hymes, D. H. (1966). Two types of linguistic relativity. In W. Bright (Ed.), *Sociolinguistics* (pp. 114–158). The Hague, Belgium: Mouton de Gruyter.

Interagency Language Roundtable (ILR). (2012). *ILR language proficiency skill level descriptions.* Retrieved April 2, 2013, from http://www.govtilr.org/skills/ilrscle1.htm

Ioup, G., Boustagoui, E., Tigi, M., & Moselle, M. (1994). Reexamining the critical period hypothesis: A case of successful adult SLA in a naturalistic environment. *Studies in Second Language Acquisition, 16,* 73–98.

Ishihara, N., & Cohen, A. D. (2010). *Teaching and learning pragmatics: Where language and culture meet.* Harlow, UK: Pearson.

Izumi, S. (2003). Comprehension and production processes in second language learning: In search of the psycholinguistic rationale of the output hypothesis. *Applied Linguistics, 24*(2), 168–196.

Jacobs, G. M., & Farrell, T. S. C. (2001). Paradigm shift: Understanding and implementing change in second language education. *TESL-EJ, 5.* Retrieved from http://www.kyoto-su.ac.jp/information/tesl-ej/ej17/toc.html

Janzen, J., & Stoller, F. (1998). Integrating strategic reading in L2 instruction. *Reading in a Foreign Language, 12*(1), 251–269.

Jenkins, J. (2000). *The phonology of English as an international language: New models, new norms, new goals.* Oxford, UK: Oxford University Press.

Jenkins, J. (2003). *World Englishes: A resource book for students:* London, UK: Routledge.

Jenkins, J. (2012). English as a Lingua Franca from the classroom to the classroom. *ELT Journal, 66*(4), 486–494.

Jeon, E. H., & Kaya, T. (2006). Effects of L2 instruction on interlanguage pragmatic development: A meta-analysis. In J. M. Norris & L. Ortega (Eds.), *Synthesizing research on language learning and teaching* (pp. 165–211). Amsterdam, The Netherlands: John Benjamins.

Jia, G., & Fuse, A. (2007). Acquisition of English grammatical morphology by native Mandarin-speaking children and adolescents: Age-related differences. *Journal of Speech, Language and Hearing Research, 50,* 1280–1299.

Jin, K.-A. (2002). The effect of teaching listening strategies in the EFL classroom. *Language Research, 38*(3), 987–999.

Johns, A. M. (Ed.). (2002). *Genre in the classroom: Multiple perspectives.* Mahwah, NJ: Lawrence Erlbaum.

Johnson, E. R. (2012). *Academic language and academic vocabulary: RTI strategies for content learning.* Sacramento, CA: Achievement For All Publishers.

Johnson, K. E. (2006). The sociocultural turn and its challenges for second language teacher education. *TESOL Quarterly, 40*(1), 235–257.

Johnson, K. E. (2009). *Second language teacher education: A sociocultural perspective.* New York, NY: Routledge.

Jolly, D., & Bolitho, R. (2011). A framework for materials writing. In B. Tomlinson (Ed.), *Materials development in language teaching* (pp. 107–150). Cambridge, UK: Cambridge University Press.

Jordan, G. (2004). *Theory construction in second language acquisition.* Amsterdam, The Netherlands: John Benjamins.

Jordan, R. R. (1997). *English for academic purposes.* Cambridge, UK: Cambridge University Press.

Kachru, B. B. (1986). *The alchemy of English: The spread, functions and models of nonnative Englishes.* Oxford, UK: Pergamon.

Kane, M. (2012). Articulating a validity argument. In G. Fulcher & F. Davidson (Eds.), *The Routledge handbook of language testing* (pp. 34–47). New York, NY: Routledge.

Kartchava, E., & Ammar, A. (2013). Learners' beliefs as mediators of what is noticed and learned in the language classroom. *TESOL Quarterly, 48*(1), 86–109.

Kasper, G., & Roever, C. (2005). Pragmatics in second language learning. In E. Hinkel (Ed.), *Handbook of research in second language teaching and learning* (pp. 317–334). Mahwah, NJ: Lawrence Erlbaum.

Kasper, G., & Rose, K. R. (2002). *Pragmatic development in a second language.* Mahwah, NJ: Wiley-Blackwell.

Kato, S. (2012). Bridging theory and practice: Developing lower-level skills in L2 reading. *The Language Learning Journal, 40*(2), 193–206.

Kauffman, D. (2005). Curriculum prescription and curriculum constraint: Second-year teachers' perceptions. In N. W. Paper (Ed.), NGT Working Paper (Project on the Next Generation of Teachers. Cambridge, MA). Retrieved from http://www.gse.harvard.edu/~ngt/Prescription%20&%20 Constraint.pdf

Kawai, G., & Hirose, K. (2000). Teaching the pronunciation of Japanese double-mora phonemes using speech recognition technology. *Speech Communication, 30*(2–3), 131–143.

Keck, C., Iberri-Shea, G., Tracy-Ventura, N., & Wa-Mbaleka, S. (2006). Investigating the empirical link between task-based interaction and acquisition: A quantitative meta-analysis. In J. M. Norris & L. Ortega (Eds.), *Synthesizing research on language learning and teaching* (pp. 91–131). Amsterdam, The Netherlands: John Benjamins.

Keenan, E., & Comrie, B. (1977). Noun phrase accessibility and universal grammar. *Linguistic Inquiry, 8*, 63–99.

Kennedy, C., & Miceli, T. (2013). In piazza online: Exploring the use of wikis with beginner foreign language learners. *Computer Assisted Language Learning, 26*(5), 389–411.

Kern, R. G. (2014). Technology as *Pharmakon*: The promise and perils of the Internet for foreign language education. *Modern Language Journal, 98*, 330–347.

Kessler, G. (2009). Student-initiated attention to form in wiki-based collaborative writing. *Language Learning & Technology, 13*(1), 79–95.

Kiddle, T. (2013). Developing digital language learning materials. In B. Tomlinson (Ed.), *Developing materials for language teaching* (2nd ed., pp. 189–206). London, UK: Bloomsbury.

Kiely, R., & Rea-Dickins, P. (2005). *Program evaluation in language education*. London, UK: Palgrave Macmillan.

King, T. (2010). The CrossCall Project: Cross-sector computer-assisted language learning. In F. Helm & S. Guth (Eds.), *Telecollaboration 2.0 for language and intercultural learning* (pp. 437–452). Berlin, Germany: Peter Lang.

Knight, S. (1994). Dictionary use while reading: The effects on comprehension and vocabulary acquisition for students of different verbal abilities. *The Modern Language Journal, 78*, 285–299.

Koda, K. (2005). *Insights into second language reading*. New York, NY: Cambridge University Press.

Kol, S., & Schcolnik, M. (2008). Asynchronous forums in EAP: Assessment issues. *Language Learning & Technology, 12*(2), 49–70.

Kolb, D. A. (1984). *Experiential learning: Experience as the source of learning and development* (Vol. 1). Englewood Cliffs, NJ: Prentice-Hall.

Konoeda, K., & Watanabe, Y. (2008). Task-based critical pedagogy in Japanese EFL classrooms. *Readings in Language Studies, 1*, 45–61.

Kormos, J. (1999). The effect of speaker variables on the self-correction behavior of L2 learners. *System, 27*, 207–221.

Kormos, J. (2012). The role of individual differences in L2 writing. *Journal of Second Language Writing, 21*, 390–403.

Kormos, J., & Sáfár, A. (2008). Phonological short term-memory, working memory and foreign language performance in intensive language learning. *Bilingualism: Language and Cognition, 11*(2), 261–271.

Kost, C. (2011). Investigating writing strategies and revision behavior in collaborative wiki projects. *CALICO Journal, 28*(3), 606–620.

Koyama, T., & Takeuchi, O. (2007). Does look-up frequency help reading comprehension of EFL learners? Two empirical studies of electronic dictionaries. *CALICO Journal, 25*(1), 110–125.

Kramsch, C. (2014). Teaching foreign languages in an era of globalization: Introduction. *Modern Language Journal, 98*, 296–311.

Krashen, S. D. (1982). *Principles and practice in second language acquisition*. Oxford, UK: Pergamon.

Krashen, S. D., & Terrell, T. D. (1983). *The natural approach: Language acquisition in the classroom*. Hayward, CA: Alemany Press.

Kubanyiova, M. (2007). Developing a motivational teaching practice in EFL teachers in Slovakia: Challenges of promoting teacher change in EFL contexts. *TESL-EJ, Special Issue: Language Education Research in International Contexts, 10*, 1–17.

Kubanyiova, M. (2009). Possible selves in language teacher development. In Z. Dörnyei & E. Ushioda (Eds.), *Motivation, language identity and the L2 Self* (pp. 314–332). Bristol, UK: Multilingual Matters.

Kubanyiova, M. (2015). Knowledge base of language teachers. In C. A. Chapelle (Ed.), *Encyclopedia of applied linguistics*. Cambridge, UK: Wiley-Blackwell. doi:10.1002/9781405198431.wbeal1415

Kumaravadivelu, B. (1994). Intake factors and intake processes in adult language learning. *Applied Language Learning, 5*, 33–71.

Kumaravadivelu, B. (2008). *Cultural globalization and language education*. New Haven, CT: Yale University Press.

Kumaravadivelu, B. (2012). *Language teacher education for a global society: A modular model for knowing, analyzing, recognizing, doing, and seeing*. New York, NY: Routledge

Kurvers, J. (2007). Development of word recognition skills of adult L2 beginning readers. In N. Faux (Ed.), *Low educated second language and literacy acquisition: Research, policy and practice* (pp. 23–44). Richmond, VA: Virginia Commonwealth University.

Kurvers, J., & van de Craats, I. (2007). *What makes the illiterate language learning genius?* Paper presented at the conference on Low Educated Second Language and Literacy Acquisition: Research Policy and Practice, Newcastle upon Tyne.

Kurvers, J., Van Hout, R., & Vallen, T. (2006). Discovering language: Metalinguistic awareness of adult illiterates. In I. Van, J. de Craats, M. Kurvers, & Young-Scholten (Eds.), *Low educated adult second language and literacy acquisition: Proceedings of the inaugural symposium* (pp. 69–88). Utrecht, The Netherlands: LOT.

Lai, C., & Morrison, B. (2013). Towards an agenda for learner preparation in technology-enhanced language learning environments. *CALICO Journal, 30*(2), 154–162.

Lai, C., Zhao, Y., & Wang, J. (2011). Task-based language teaching in online ab initio foreign language classrooms. *Modern Language Journal, 95*(s1), 81–103.

Lamie, J. M. (2005). *Evaluating change in English language teaching*. Basingstoke, UK: Palgrave Macmillan.

Lamy, M.-N., & Hampel, R. (2007). *Online communication in language learning and teaching*. New York, NY: Palgrave Macmillan.

Lantolf, J. P. (Ed.). (2000). *Sociocultural theory and second language learning*. Oxford, UK: Oxford University Press.

Lantolf, J. P. (2009). Dynamic assessment: The dialectical integration of instruction and assessment. *Language Teaching, 42*, 355–368.

Lantolf, J. P. (2011). The sociocultural approach to second language acquisition. In D. Atkinson (Ed.), *Alternative approaches to second language acquisition* (pp. 57–72). Abingdon, UK: Routledge.

Lantolf, J. P., & Poehner, M. E. (2004). Dynamic assessment of L2 development: Bringing the past into the future. *Journal of Applied Linguistics, 1*(1), 49–72.

Lantolf, J. P., & Poehner, M. E. (Eds.). (2008). *Sociocultural theory and the teaching of second languages*. London, UK: Equinox.

Lantolf, J. P., & Poehner, M. E. (2011a). Dynamic assessment in the classroom: Vygostkian praxis for second language development. *Language Teaching Research, 15*(1), 11–33.

Lantolf, J. P., & Poehner, M. E. (2011b). *Dynamic assessment in the foreign language classroom: A teacher's guide* (2nd ed.). State College, PA: The Pennsylvania State University, Center for Advanced Language Proficiency Education and Research.

Lantolf, J. P., & Thorne, S. L. (2006). *Sociocultural theory and the genesis of second language development*. Oxford, UK: Oxford University Press.

Lantolf, J. P., & Thorne, S. L. (2007). Sociocultural theory and second language learning. In B. VanPatten & J. Williams (Eds.), *Theories in second language acquisition: An introduction* (pp. 201–224). Mahwah, NJ: Lawrence Erlbaum.

Larsen-Freeman, D., & Anderson, M. (2011). *Techniques and principles in language teaching*. Oxford, UK: Oxford University Press.

Larson-Hall, J. (2008). Weighing the benefits of studying a foreign language at a younger starting age in a minimal input situation. *Language Research, 24*(1), 35–63.

Lave, J., & Wenger, E. (1991). *Situated learning: Legitimate peripheral participation.* Cambridge, UK: Cambridge University Press.

Leaver, B. L., & Willis, J. R. (2004). *Task-based instruction in foreign language education: Practices and programs.* Washington, DC: Georgetown University Press

Lee, D. J. (1981). Interpretation of morpheme rank ordering in L2 research. In P. Dale & D. Ingram (Eds.), *Child language: An international perspective* (pp. 261–272). Baltimore, MD: University Park Press.

Lee, H. W., & Lee, J. H. (2013). Implementing glossing in mobile-assisted language learning environments: Directions and outlook. *Language Learning & Technology, 17*(3), 6–22.

Lee, H. W., Lim, K. Y., & Grabowski, B. L. (2008). Generative learning: Principles and implications for making meaning. In J. M. Spector, M. D. Merrill, J. van Merriënboer, & M. P. Driscoll (Eds.), *Handbook of research on educational communications and technology* (pp. 111–124). Mahwah, NJ: Lawrence Erlbaum.

Lee, J. J., & Hoadley, C. M. (2006). Online identity as a leverage point for learning in massively multiplayer online role playing games (MMORPGs). *Proceedings of the Sixth International Conference on Advanced Learning Technologies (ICALT'06)* (pp. 761–763).

Lee, J. J., & VanPatten, B. (2003). *Making communicative language teaching happen.* New York, NY: McGraw-Hill.

Lee, L. (2004). Learners' perspectives on networked collaborative interaction with native speakers of Spanish in the US. *Language Learning & Technology, 8*(1), 83–100.

Lee, L. (2010). Exploring wiki-mediated collaborative writing: A case study in an elementary Spanish course. *CALICO Journal, 27*(2), 260–276.

Leki, I., Cumming, A., & Silva, T. (2008). *A synthesis of research on second language writing in English.* New York, NY: Routledge.

Lenzing, A. (2015). Exploring regularities and dynamic systems in L2 development. *Language Learning, 65*, 89–122.

Levelt, W. J. M. (1989). *Speaking: From intention to articulation.* Cambridge, MA: MIT Press.

Levelt, W. J. M. (1992). Accessing words in speech production: Stages, processes and representations. *Cognition, 42*, 1–22.

Levis, J., & Pickering, L. (2004). Teaching intonation in discourse using speech visualization technology. *System, 32*(4), 505–524.

Levy, M., Blin, F., Siskin, C., & Takeuchi, O. (Eds.). (2010). *WorldCALL: International perspectives on computer assisted language learning.* New York, NY: Routledge.

Levy, M., & Stockwell, G. (2013). *CALL dimensions: Options and issues in computer-assisted language learning.* New York, NY: Routledge.

Lew, A. W. M. (2011). Aligning CALL with the theory and practice of instructed SLA. *Teachers College, Columbia University Working Papers in TESOL & Applied Linguistics, 11*(2), 20–22.

Li, J. (2010). Learning vocabulary via computer-assisted scaffolding for text processing. *Computer Assisted Language Learning, 23*(3), 253–275.

Li, L., & Walsh, S. (2011). "Seeing is believing": Looking at EFL teachers' beliefs through classroom interaction. *Classroom discourse, 2*(1), 39–57.

Li, L., & Walsh, S. (2011). Technology uptake in Chinese EFL classes. *Language Teaching Research, 15*, 99–125.

Li, S. (2013). The interactions between the effects of implicit and explicit feedback and individual differences in language analytic ability and working memory. *Modern Language Journal, 97*(3), 634–654.

Liddicoat, A. J., & Scarino, A. (2013). *Intercultural language teaching and learning*. New York, NY: Wiley-Blackwell.

Lightbown, P. M., & Spada, N. (1990). Focus-on-form and corrective feedback in communicative language teaching: Effects on second language learning. *Studies in Second Language Acquisition, 12*(4), 429–448.

Lightbown, P. M., & Spada, N. (2013). *How languages are learned*. Oxford, UK: Oxford University Press.

Linck, J. A., Osthus, P., Koeth, J. T., & Bunting, M. F. (2014). Working memory and second language comprehension and production: A meta-analysis. *Psychonomic Bulletin & Review, 21*(4), 861–883.

Littlewood, W. (2004). The task-based approach: Some questions and suggestions. *ELT Journal, 58*(4), 319–326.

Littlewood, W. (2007). Communicative and task-based language teaching in East Asian classrooms. *Language Teaching, 40*(3), 243–249.

Livingston, S. A., & Zieky, M. (1982). *Passing scores: A manual for setting standards of performance on educational and occupational tests*. Princeton, NJ: Educational Testing Service.

Lixun, W. (2004). Exploring parallel concordancing in English and Chinese. *Language Learning & Technology, 5*(3), 174–184.

Llosa, L., & Slayton, J. (2009). Using program evaluation to inform and improve the education of young English language learners in US schools. *Language Teaching Research, 13*(1), 35–54.

Lo Bianco, J. (2014). Domesticating the Foreign: Globalization's effects on the place/s of languages. *Modern Language Journal, 98*, 312–325.

LoCastro, V. (2001). Large classes and student learning. *TESOL Quarterly, 35*(3), 493–496.

Loewen, S. (2011). Focus on form. In E. Hinkel (Ed.), *Handbook of research in second language teaching and learning* (pp. 576–592). New York, NY: Routledge.

Loewen, S. (2015). *Introduction to instructed second language acquisition*. New York, NY: Routledge.

Long, M. H. (1981). Input, interaction and second language acquisition. In H. Winitz (Ed.), *Native language and foreign language acquisition* (Vol. 379, pp. 259–278). New York, NY: Annals of the New York Academy of Sciences.

Long, M. H. (1983). Does second language instruction make a difference? A review of the research. *TESOL Quarterly, 17*, 359–382.

Long, M. H. (1996). The role of linguistic environment in second language acquisition. In W. Ritchie & T. Bhatia (Eds.), *Handbook of second language acquisition* (pp. 413–468). New York, NY: Dunedin Academic Press.

Long, M. H. (2000). Focus on form in task-based language teaching. In R. Lambert & E. Shohamy (Eds.), *Language policy and pedagogy: Essays in honor of A. Ronald Walton* (pp. 179–192). Amsterdam, The Netherlands: John Benjamins.

Long, M. H. (2005a). Methodological issues in learner needs analysis. In M. H. Long (Ed.), *Second language needs analysis* (pp. 19–76). Cambridge, UK: Cambridge University Press.

Long, M. H. (2005b). *Second language needs analysis*. Cambridge, UK: Cambridge University Press.

Long, M. H. (2009). Methodological principles for language teaching. In M. H. Long & C. J. Doughty (Eds.), *The handbook of language teaching* (pp. 373–394). Malden, MA: Wiley-Blackwell.

Long, M. H. (2015). *Second language acquisition and task-based language teaching*. Malden, MA: Wiley-Blackwell.

Long, M. H., & Crookes, G. (1992). Three approaches to task-based syllabus design. *TESOL Quarterly*, *26*(1), 27–56.

Long, M. H., & Norris, J. M. (2000). Task-based language teaching and assessment. In M. Byram (Ed.), *Encyclopedia of language teaching* (pp. 597–603). London, UK: Routledge.

Loo, A. (2010). Large language classes. *Tapestries*, *4*, 47–66.

López-Barrios, M., & de Debat, E.V. (2014). Global vs. local: Does it matter? In S. Garton & K. Graves (Eds.), *International perspectives on materials in ELT* (pp. 37–52). New York, NY: Palgrave Macmillan.

Low, E. L. (2014). *Pronunciation for English as an international language: From research to practice.* Hoboken, NJ: Routledge.

Lowie, W., & Verspoor, M. (2015). Variability and variation in second language acquisition orders: A dynamic reevaluation. *Language Learning*, *65*, 63–88.

Lu, Z., & Liu, M. (2011). Foreign language anxiety and strategy use: A study with Chinese undergraduate EFL learners. *Journal of Language Teaching and Research*, *2*, 1298–1305.

Luoma, S. (2004). *Assessing speaking.* Cambridge, UK: Cambridge University Press.

Lynch, B. K. (1996). *Language program evaluation: Theory and practice.* New York, NY: Cambridge University Press.

Lynch, B. K. (2003). *Language assessment and programme evaluation.* Edinburgh, UK: Edinburgh University Press.

Lyster, R., & Saito, K. (2010). Oral feedback in classroom SLA: A meta-analysis. *Studies in Second Language Acquisition*, *32*, 265–302.

Ma, Q. (2008). Empirical CALL evaluation: The relationship between learning process and learning outcome. *CALICO Journal*, *26*(1), 108–122.

Macaruso, P., & Rodman, A. (2011). Efficacy of computer-assisted instruction for the development of early literacy skills in young children. *Reading Psychology*, *32*, 172–196.

MacIntyre, P. D. (1999). Language anxiety: A review of the research for language teachers. In D. J. Young (Ed.), *Affect in foreign language and second language learning* (pp. 24–45). Boston, MA: McGraw-Hill.

MacIntyre, P. D., Burns, C., & Jessome, A. (2011). Ambivalence about communicating in a second language: A qualitative study of French immersion students' willingness to communicate. *Modern Language Journal*, *95*(1), 81–96.

MacIntyre, P. D., Clement, R., Dornyei, Z., & Noels, K. A. (1998). Conceptualizing willingness to communicate in a L2: A situational model of l2 confidence and affiliation. *Modern Language Journal*, *82*(4), 545–562.

MacIntyre, P. D., & Gardner, R. C. (1991). Language anxiety: Its relation to other anxieties and to processing in native and second languages. *Language Learning*, *41*, 513–534.

Mackay, R., Wellesley, S., & Bazergan, E. (1995). Participatory evaluation. *ELT Journal*, *49*(4), 308–317.

Mackay, R., Wellesley, S., Tasman, D., & Bazergan, E. (1998). Using institutional self-evaluation to promote the quality of language and communication training programmes. In P. Rea-Dickens & K. P. Germaine (Eds.), *Managing evaluation and innovation in language teaching: Building bridges* (pp. 111–131). London, UK: Longman.

Mackey, A., Abbuhl, R., & Gass, S. M. (2012). Interactionist approach. In S. M. Gass & A. Mackey (Eds.), *The Routledge handbook of second language acquisition* (pp. 7–23). Abingdon, UK: Routledge.

Mackey, A., & Goo, J. (2007). Interaction research in SLA: A meta-analysis and research synthesis. In A. Mackey (Ed.), *Conversational interaction in second language acquisition: A collection of empirical studies* (pp. 407–451). Oxford, UK: Oxford University Press.

Mackey, A., Philp, J., Egi, T., Fujii, A., & Tatsumi, T. (2002). Individual differences in working memory, noticing of interactional feedback and L2 development. In P. Robinson (Ed.), *Individual differences and instructed language learning* (pp. 181–209). Amsterdam, The Netherlands: John Benjamins.

Mackey, A., & Sachs, R. (2012). Older learners in SLA research: A first look at working memory, feedback, and L2 development. *Language Learning, 62*(3), 704–740.

Makino, T. (1980). *Acquisition order of English morphemes by Japanese adolescents.* Tokyo, JP: Shinozaki Shorin Press.

Makoto, Y. (2006). L1 and L2 glosses: Their effects on incidental vocabulary learning. *Language Learning & Technology, 10*(3), 14–21.

Malone, M. E. (2013). The essentials of assessment literacy: Contrasts between testers and users. *Language Testing, 30*(3), 329–344.

Mama, M., & Hennessy, S. (2013). Developing a typology of teacher beliefs and practices concerning classroom use of ICT. *Computers & Education, 68*, 380–387.

Manchón, R. M. (Ed.). (2011). *Learning-to-write and writing-to-learn in an additional language.* Amsterdam, The Netherlands: John Benjamins.

Manning, C. (2014). Considering peer support for self-access learning. *Studies in Self-Access Learning Journal, 5*(1), 50–57.

Markee, N. (1997). *Managing curricular innovation.* Cambridge, UK: Cambridge University Press.

Marsh, C. J. (2009). *Key concepts for understanding curriculum.* New York, NY: Routledge.

Martinez, R., & Schmitt, N. (2012). A phrasal expressions list. *Applied Linguistics, 33*(3), 299–320.

Martínez-Flor, A., Usó-Juan, E., & Alcón Soler, E. (2006). Toward acquiring communicative competence through speaking. In E. Usó-Juan & A. Martínez-Flor (Eds.), *Current trends in the development and teaching of the four language skills* (pp. 139–157). Berlin, Germany: Mouton de Gruyter.

Masgoret, A. M., & Gardner, R. C. (2003). Attitudes, motivation, and second language learning: A meta-analysis of studies conducted by Gardner and associates. *Language Learning, 53*, 123–163.

Masoura, E. V., & Gathercole, S. E. (2005). Phonological short-term memory skills and new word learning in young Greek children. *Memory, 13*, 422–429.

Masuhara, H., Haan, M., Yi, Y., & Tomlinson, B. (2008). Adult EFL courses. *ELT Journal, 62*, 294–312.

Masuhara, H., & Tomlinson, B. (2008). General English materials. In B. Tomlinson (Ed.), *English language teaching materials* (pp. 17–37). London, UK: Continuum.

Matsuda, P. K. (2003). Second language writing in the twentieth century: A situated historical perspective. In B. Kroll (Ed.), *Exploring the dynamics of second language writing* (pp. 15–34). Cambridge, UK: Cambridge University Press.

Matsuda, P. K., Cox, M., Jordan, J., & Ortmeier-Hooper, C. (2010). *Second-language writing in the composition classroom: A critical sourcebook.* New York, NY: Bedford.

McCrae, R. R., & Costa, P. T. (2003). *Personality in adulthood: A five-factor theory perspective* (2nd ed.). New York, NY: Guilford Press.

McDonough, J., Shaw, C., & Masuhara, H. (2013). *Materials and methods in ELT: A teacher's guide.* Malden, MA: Wiley-Blackwell.

McDonough, K. (2007). Interactional feedback and the emergence of simple past activity verbs in L2 English. In A. Mackey (Ed.), *Conversational interaction in second language acquisition: A collection of empirical studies* (pp. 323–338). Oxford, UK: Oxford University Press.

McDonough, K., & Chaikitmongkol, W. (2007). Teachers' and learners' reactions to a task-based EFL course in Thailand. *TESOL Quarterly, 41*, 107–132.

McDonough, K., & Mackey, A. (2006). Responses to recasts: Repetitions, primed production and linguistic development. *Language Learning, 56*(4), 693–720.

McGrath, I. (2002). *Materials evaluation and design for language teaching.* Edinburgh, UK: Edinburgh University Press.

McGrath, I. (2007). Textbooks, technology and teachers. In O. Alexander (Ed.), *New approaches to materials development for language learning* (pp. 343–358). Berlin, Germany: Peter Lang.

McGrath, I. (2013). *Teaching materials and the roles of EFL/ESL teachers: Practice and theory.* London, UK: Bloomsbury.

McKay, S. L. (1993). *Agendas for second language literacy.* Cambridge, UK: Cambridge University Press.

McKay, S. L. (2002). *Teaching English as an international language: Rethinking goals and approaches.* Oxford, UK: Oxford University Press.

McLoughlin, C., & Lee, M. (2007). Social software and participatory learning: Pedagogical choices with technology affordances in the Web 2.0 era. *Proceedings Ascilite Singapore.* Retrieved from http://www.ascilite.org.au/conferences/singapore07/procs/mcloughlin.pdf

Meisel, J., Clahsen, H., & Pienemann, M. (1981). On determining developmental stages in natural second language acquisition. *Studies in Second Language Acquisition, 3*, 109–135.

Merrill, P. F. (1978). Hierarchical and information processing task analysis: A comparison. *Journal of Instructional Development, 1*(2), 35–40.

Meunier, F. (2012). Formulaic language and language teaching. *Annual Review of Applied Linguistics, 32*, 111–129.

Milleret, M., & Silveira, A. S. (2009). The role of evaluation in curriculum development and growth of the UNM Portuguese program. In J. M. Norris, J. McE. Davis, C. Sinicrope, & Y. Watanabe (Eds.), *Toward useful program evaluation in college foreign language education* (pp. 57–82). Honolulu, HI: University of Hawaii, National Foreign Language Resource Center.

Millrood, R. (2002). Teaching heterogeneous classes. *ELTJ, 56*(2), 128–136.

Mills, C. Potenza, M., Fremer, J., & Ward, W. (2002). *Computer-based testing: Building the foundation for future assessments.* Mahwah, NJ: Lawrence Erlbaum.

Mills, C. N., Potenza, M. T., Fremer, J. J., & Ward, W. C. (Eds.). (2005). *Computer-based testing: Building the foundation for future assessments.* New York, NY: Routledge.

Mills, N. A. (2013). Action research: Bridging theory and practice. *Academic Exchange Quarterly, 17*(1), 95–100.

Mishan, F. (2005). *Designing authenticity into language learning materials.* Bristol, UK: Intellect.

Mishan, F. (2013). Demystifying blended learning. In B. Tomlinson (Ed.), *Developing materials for language teaching* (2nd ed., pp. 207–224). London, UK: Bloomsbury.

Mitchell, R., Myles, F., & Marsden, E. (2013). *Second language learning theories.* London: Routledge.

Modiano, M. (2009). EIL, native-speakerism, and the failure of European ELT. In F. Sharifian (Ed.), *English as an international language* (pp. 55–80). Bristol, UK: Multilingual Matters.

Mody, R. (2013). *Needs analysis report: Maharashtra English Language Initiative for Secondary Schools (ELISS).* Mumbai, UK: British Council.

Mok, M. (Ed.). (2013). *Self-directed learning oriented assessment in the Asia-Pacific.* New York, UK: Springer.

Molholt, G., & Hwu, F. (2008). Visualization of speech patterns for language learning. In V. M. Holland & F. P. Fisher (Eds.), *The path of speech technologies in computer assisted language learning: From research toward practice* (pp. 91–122). New York, NY: Routledge.

Montgomery, J. L., & Baker, W. (2007). Teacher-written feedback: Student perceptions, teacher self-assessment, and actual teacher performance. *Journal of Second Language Writing, 16*, 82–99.

Moore, A. (2015). *Understanding the school curriculum: Theory, politics and principles.* New York, UK: Routledge.

Mori, Y. (1999). Epistemological beliefs and language learning beliefs: What do language learners believe about their learning? *Language Learning, 49*(3), 377–415.

Moskovsky, C., Alrabai, F., Paolini, S., & Ratcheva, S. (2013). The effects of teachers' motivational strategies on learners' motivation: A controlled investigation of second language acquisition. *Language Learning, 63*(1), 34–62.

Moyer, A. (2013). *Foreign accent: The phenomenon of non-native speech.* Cambridge, UK: Cambridge University Press.

Mukundan, J., & Ahour, T. (2010). A review of textbook evaluation checklists across four decades (1970–2008). In B. Tomlinson & H. Masuhara (Eds.), *Research for materials development in language learning: Evidence for best practice* (pp. 336–352). London, UK: Continuum.

Müller-Hartmann, A. (2006). How to teach intercultural communicative competence via telecollaboration. In J. A. Belz & S. L. Thorne (Eds.), *Internet-mediated intercultural foreign language education* (pp. 63–84). Boston, MA: Heinle & Heinle.

Mulligan, C., & Garofalo, R. (2011). A collaborative writing approach: Methodology and student assessment. *The Language Teacher, 35*(3), 5–10.

Munby, J. (1978). *Communicative syllabus design: A sociolinguistic model for defining the content of purpose-specific language programmes.* Cambridge, UK: Cambridge University Press.

Muñoz, C. (2008). Age-related differences in foreign language learning. Revisiting the empirical evidence. *International Review of Applied Linguistics (IRAL), 46*(3), 197–220.

Murphy, L. (2008). Supporting learner autonomy: Developing practice through the production of courses for distance learners of French, German, and Spanish. *Language Teaching Research, 12*(1), 83–102.

Murphy, L., & Hurd, S. (2011). Fostering learner autonomy and motivation in blended teaching. In M. Nicolson, L. Murphy, & M. Southgate (Eds.), *Language teaching in blended contexts* (pp. 43–56). Edinburgh, UK: Dunedin Academic Press.

Mushayikwa, E., & Lubben, F. (2009). Self-directed professional development: Hope for teachers working in deprived environments? *Teaching and Teacher Education, 25*, 375–382.

Musumeci, D. (2009). History of language teaching. In M. Long & C. Doughty (Eds.), *Handbook of language teaching* (pp. 42–62). Cambridge, UK: Wiley-Blackwell.

Myers, I. B., & McCaulley, M. H. (1985). *Manual: A guide to the development and use of the Myers-Briggs type indicator.* Palo Alto, CA: Consulting Psychologists Press.

Nassaji, H., & Geva, E. (1999). The contribution of phonological and orthographic processing skills to adult ESL reading: Evidence from native speakers of Farsi. *Applied Psycholinguistics, 20*, 241–267.

Nassaji, H., & Swain, M. (2000). A Vygotskian perspective on corrective feedback in L2: The effect of random versus negotiated help in the learning of English articles. *Language Awareness, 8*, 34–51.

Nation, I. S. P. (2005). Teaching and learning vocabulary. In E. Hinkel (Ed.), *Handbook of research in second language teaching and learning* (pp. 581–595). Mahwah, NJ: Lawrence Erlbaum.

Nation, I. S. P. (2001). *Learning vocabulary in another language.* Cambridge, UK: Cambridge University Press.

Nation, I. S. P. (2009). *Teaching ESL/EFL reading and writing.* New York, NY: Routledge.

Nation, I. S. P. (2013). *Learning vocabulary in another language* (2nd ed.). Cambridge, UK: Cambridge University Press.

Nation, I. S. P., & Beglar, D. (2007). A vocabulary size test. *The Language Teacher, 31*(7), 9–13.

Nation, I. S. P., & Macalister, J. (2010). *Language curriculum design.* New York, NY: Routledge.

Nation, I. S. P., & Macalister, J. (Eds.). (2013). *Case studies in language curriculum design: Concepts and approaches in action around the world.* New York, NY: Routledge.

Nel, N., & Müller, H. (2010). The impact of teachers' limited English proficiency on English second language learners in South African schools. *South African Journal of Education, 30,* 635–650.

Neri, A., Cucchiarini, C., Strik, H., & Boves, L. (2002). The pedagogy-technology interface in computer-assisted pronunciation training. *Computer Assisted Language Learning, 15*(5), 441–468.

Neumeyer, L., Franco, H., Digalakis, V., & Weintraub, M. (2000). Automatic scoring of pronunciation quality. *Speech Communication, 30*(2–3), 83–93.

Nielson, K. B. (2014). Evaluation of an online, task-based Chinese course. In M. González-Lloret & L. Ortega (Eds.), *Technology-mediated TBLT: Researching technology and tasks* (pp. 295–321). Amsterdam, The Netherlands: John Benjamins.

Nielson, K. B., & Doughty, C. (2008). *Rosetta Stone™ evaluation.* College Park, MD: Center for Advanced Study of Languages.

Norris, J. M. (2000). Purposeful language assessment. *English Teaching Forum, 38*(1), 18–23.

Norris, J. M. (2005). Using developmental sequences to estimate ability with English grammar: Preliminary design and investigation of a web-based test. *Second Language Studies, 24*(1), 24–128.

Norris, J. M. (2006). The why (and how) of assessing student learning outcomes in college foreign language programs. *Modern Language Journal, 90*(4), 590–597.

Norris, J. M. (2008). *Validity evaluation in language assessment.* New York: Peter Lang.

Norris, J. M. (2009). Task-based teaching and testing. In C. Doughty & M. Long (Eds.), *The handbook of language teaching* (pp. 578–594). Malden, MA: Wiley-Blackwell.

Norris, J. M. (2015). Thinking and acting programmatically in task-based language teaching: Essential roles for program evaluation. In M. Bygate (Ed.), *Domains and directions in the development of TBLT: A decade of plenaries from the international conference* (pp. 27–57). Amsterdam, The Netherlands: John Benjamins.

Norris, J. M. (2016). Current uses for task-based language assessment. *Annual Review of Applied Linguistics, 36,* 230–244.

Norris, J. M., & Davis, J. (Eds.). (2015). *Student learning outcomes assessment in college foreign language programs.* Honolulu, HI: National Foreign Language Resource Center.

Norris, J. M., Davis, J., Sinicrope, C., & Watanabe, Y. (Eds.). (2009). *Toward useful program evaluation in college foreign language education.* Honolulu, HI: University of Hawaii, National Foreign Language Resource Center.

Norris, J. M., & Ortega, L. (2000). Effectiveness of L2 instruction: A research synthesis and quantitative meta-analysis. *Language Learning, 50,* 417–528.

Norris, J. M., & Ortega, L. (Eds.). (2006). *Synthesizing research on language learning and teaching.* Amsterdam, The Netherlands: John Benjamins.

Norris, J. M., & Ortega, L. (2010). Timeline: Research synthesis. *Language Teaching, 43,* 61–79.

Norris, J. M., & Pfeiffer, P. C. (2003). Exploring the use and usefulness of ACTFL oral proficiency ratings and standards in college foreign language departments. *Foreign Language Annals, 36,* 572–581.

Norris, J. M., & Watanabe, Y. (2007). *Roles and responsibilities for evaluation in foreign language programs.* Honolulu, HI: University of Hawaii, National Foreign Language Resource Center.

Norris, J. M., & Watanabe, Y. (2013). Program evaluation. In C. Chapelle (Ed.), *The encyclopedia of applied linguistics.* Cambridge, UK: Wiley-Blackwell. doi:10.1002/9781405198431. wbeal0963

North, B. (2014). *The CEFR in practice.* Cambridge, UK: Cambridge University Press.

Norton, B. (2000). *Identity and language learning.* Harlow, UK: Pearson.

Ntelioglou, B. Y., Fannin, J., Montanera, M., & Cummins, J. (2014). A multilingual and multimodal approach to literacy teaching and learning in urban education: A collaborative inquiry project in an inner city elementary school. *Frontiers in Psychology, 5,* 533.

Nunan, D. (1988). *Syllabus design.* Oxford, UK: Oxford University Press.

Nunan, D. (1991). Communicative tasks and the language curriculum. *TESOL Quarterly, 25,* 279–295.

Nunan, D. (2004). *Task-based language teaching.* Cambridge, UK: Cambridge University Press.

Nunan, D. (2005). Important tasks of English education: Asia-wide and beyond. Asian EFL Journal. *Asian EFL Journal, 7*(3), 5–8.

O'Brien, I., Segalowitz, N., Collentine, J., & Freed, B. (2006). Phonological memory and lexical, narrative, and grammatical skills in second-language oral production by adult learners. *Applied Psycholinguistics, 27,* 377–402.

Ockey, G. (2013). Assessment of listening. In C. Chapelle (Ed.), *The encyclopedia of applied linguistics.* Cambridge, UK: Wiley-Blackwell. doi:10.1002/9781405198431.wbeal0048

O'Donnell, L. (2012). *Teacher's guide: Five ways Minecraft (and other video games) can boost student writing skills.* Retrieved from http://liamodonnell.com/feedingchange/2012/04/16/ teachers-guide-five-ways-minecraft-and-other-video-games-can-boost-student-writing-skills/

O'Grady, W. (2005). *Syntactic carpentry: And emergentist approach to syntax.* Mahwah, NJ: Lawrence Erlbaum.

O'Grady, W. (2008). The emergentist program. *Lingua, 118,* 447–464.

O'Grady, W. (2010). An emergentist approach to syntax. In H. Narrog & B. Heine (Eds.), *The Oxford handbook of linguistic analysis* (pp. 257–283). Oxford, UK: Oxford University Press.

O'Grady, W. (2015). Processing determinism. *Language Learning, 65*(1), 6–32.

Ohta, A. S. (2000). Rethinking interaction in SLA: Developmentally appropriate assistance in the zone of proximal development and the acquisition of L2 grammar. In J. P. Lantolf (Ed.), *Sociocultural theory and second language learning* (pp. 51–78). Oxford, UK: Oxford University Press.

O'Keeffe, A., Clancy, B., & Adolphs, S. (2011). *Introducing pragmatics in use.* New York, NY: Routledge.

Oliver, K., Kellogg, S., & Patel, R. (2012). An investigation into reported differences between online foreign language instruction and other subject areas in a virtual school. *CALICO Journal, 29,* 269–296.

Olson, C. B., & Land, R. (2007). A cognitive strategies approach to reading and writing instruction for English language learners in secondary school. *Research in the Teaching of English, 41,* 269–303.

Olson, D. J. (2014). Benefits of visual feedback on segmental production in the L2 classroom. *Language Learning & Technology, 18*(3), 173–192.

Omaggio-Hadley, A. (2000). *Teaching language in context, 3rd ed.* Boston, MA: Heinle & Heinle.

O'Malley, J. M., & Chamot, A. U. (1990). *Learning strategies in second language acquisition.* Cambridge, UK: Cambridge University Press.

Ortega, L. (2007). Second language learning explained? SLA across nine contemporary theories. In B. VanPatten & J. Williams (Eds.), *Theories in second language acquisition: An introduction* (pp. 225–250). Mahwah, NJ: Lawrence Erlbaum.

Ortega, L. (2009a). Interaction and attention form in L2 text-based computer-mediated communication. In A. Mackey & C. Polio (Eds.), *Multiple perspectives in interaction in second language acquisition: Second language research in honor of Susan M. Gass* (pp. 226–253). New York, NY: Taylor and Francis.

Ortega, L. (2009b). Sequences and processes in language learning. In C. Doughty & M. Long (Eds.), *The handbook of language teaching* (pp. 81–105). Malden, MA: Wiley-Blackwell.

Ortega, L. (2009c). *Understanding second language acquisition.* London, UK: Hodder Education.

Ortega, L. (2012). Epilogue: Exploring L2 writing—SLA interfaces. *Journal of Second Language Writing, 21*, 404–415.

Ortega, L. (2013). SLA for the 21st century: Disciplinary progress, transdisciplinary relevance, and the bi/multilingual turn. *Language Learning, 63*(Suppl. 1), 1–24.

Oskoz, A., & Elola, I. (2014). Promoting foreign language collaborative writing through the use of Web 2.0 tools and tasks. In M. González-Lloret & L. Ortega (Eds.), *Technology-mediated TBLT: Researching technology and tasks* (pp. 115–148). Amsterdam, The Netherlands: John Benjamins.

Oxford, R. L. (2011). *Teaching and researching language learning strategies.* Harlow, UK: Pearson.

Oxford, R. L., & Anderson, N., 1995: State of the art: A crosscultural view of language learning styles. *Language Teaching, 28*, 201–215.

Oza, H., Demirezen, M., & Pourfeiz, J. (2015). Digital device ownership, computer literacy, and attitudes toward foreign and computer-assisted language learning—5th World Conference on Learning, Teaching and Educational Leadership, WCLTA 2014. *Procedia—Social and Behavioral Sciences, 186*, 359–366.

Pae, T. (2013). Skills-based L2 anxieties revisited: Their intra-relations and their inter-relations with general foreign language anxiety. *Applied Linguistics, 34*(2), 232–252.

Paltridge, B. (2001). Genre, text type and the English for academic purposes (EAP) classroom. In A. M. Johns (Ed.), *Genre in the classroom: Multiple perspectives* (pp. 69–88). Mahwah, NJ: Lawrence Erlbaum.

Pan, L., & Block, D. (2011). English as a "global language" in China: An investigation into learners' and teachers' language beliefs. *System, 39*, 391–402.

Pardo-Ballester, C. (2012). CALL evaluation: Students' perception and use of LoMasTv. *CALICO Journal, 29*, 532–547.

Park, Y., Zheng, B., Lawrence, J., & Warschauer, M. (2014). Technology-enhanced reading environments. In M. Thomas, H. Reinders, & M. Warschauer (Eds.), *Contemporary computer-assisted language learning* (pp. 267–285). London, UK: Bloomsbury.

Parshall, C., Spray, J., Kalohn, J., and Davey, T. (2002). *Practical considerations in computer-based testing.* New York, NY: Springer.

Patton, M. Q. (2008). *Utilization-focused evaluation* (4th ed.). Thousand Oaks, CA: Sage.

Patton, M. Q. (2012). *Essentials of utilization-focused evaluation.* Thousand Oaks, CA: Sage.

Payne, J. S., & Ross, B. M. (2005). Synchronous CMC, working memory, and L2 oral proficiency development. *Language Learning & Technology, 9*(3), 35–54.

Payne, J. S., & Whitney, P. J. (2002). Developing L2 oral proficiency through synchronous CMC: Output, working memory, and interlanguage development. *CALICO Journal, 20*(1), 7–32.

Pawlak, M., Mystkowska-Wiertelak, A., & Bielak, J. (2015). *Autonomy in second language learning: Managing the resources.* New York, NY: Springer.

Peacock, M. (2001). Match or mismatch? Learning styles and teaching styles in EFL. *International Journal of Applied Linguistics, 11*(1), 20.

Pellettieri, J. (2000). Negotiation in cyberspace: The role of chatting in the development of grammatical competence. In M. Warschauer & R. Kern (Eds.), *Network-based language teaching: Concepts and practice* (pp. 59–86). Cambridge, UK: Cambridge University Press.

Pennycook, A. (2001). *Critical applied linguistics: A critical introduction.* Mahwah, NJ: Lawrence Erlbaum.

Perrachione, T. K., Lee, J., Ha, L. Y. Y., & Wong, P. C. M. (2011). Learning a novel phonological contrast depends on interactions between individual differences and training paradigm design. *Journal of the Acoustical Society of America, 130,* 461–472.

Pervin, L. A., & John, O. P. (2001). *Personality: Theory and research* (8th ed.). New York, NY: Wiley-Blackwell.

Peters, H., & Shi, L. (2011). Teaching community languages in blended contexts. In M. Nicolson, L. Murphy, & M. Southgate (Eds.), *Language teaching in blended contexts* (pp. 187–202). Edinburgh, UK: Dunedin Academic Press.

Petersen, K., & Mackey, A. (2009). *Interaction, modality and learning: Comparing the effectiveness of computer-generated and face to face recasts.* Paper presented at the SLRF, Michigan State University.

Peterson, C., & Al-Haik, A. (1976). The development of the defense language aptitude battery. *Educational and Psychological Measurement, 36,* 369–380.

Peterson, M. (2010). Computerized games and simulations in computer-assisted language learning: A meta-analysis of research. *Simulation & Gaming, 41*(1), 72–93.

Peterson, M. (2011). Digital gaming and second language development: Japanese learners' interactions in a MMORPG. *Digital Culture & Education, 3*(1), 56–73.

Phillips, R., McNaught, C., & Kennedy, G. (2012). *Evaluating e-learning: Guiding research and practice.* New York, NY: Routledge.

Phillipson, R. (1992). *Linguistic imperialism.* Oxford, UK: Oxford University Press.

Piaget, J. (1967). *Six psychological studies.* New York, NY: Random House.

Pica, T. (1983). Adult acquisition of English as a second language under different conditions of exposure. *Language Learning, 33*(4), 465–497.

Pica, T. (1992). The textual outcomes of native speaker/non-native speaker negotiation: What do they reveal about second language learning? In C. Kramsch & S. McConnell-Ginet (Eds.), *Text in context: Crossdisciplinary perspectives on language study* (pp. 198–237). Lexington, MA: D.C. Heath.

Pica, T., Kanagy, R., & Falodun, J. (1993). Choosing and using communicative tasks for second language instruction. In G. Crookes & S. M. Gass (Eds.), *Tasks in a pedagogical context* (pp. 9–34). Cleveland, UK: Multilingual Matters.

Pienemann, M. (1984). Psychological constraints on the teachability of languages. *Studies in Second Language Acquisition, 6,* 186–214.

Pienemann, M. (1998). *Language processing and second language acquisition: Processability theory.* Amsterdam, The Netherlands: John Benjamins.

Pienemann, M. (2005). *Cross-linguistic aspects of processability theory.* Amsterdam, The Netherlands: John Benjamins.

Pienemann, M. (2007). Processability theory. In B. VanPatten & J. Williams (Eds.), *Theories in second language acquisition*. Mahwah, NJ: Lawrence Erlbaum.

Pienemann, M. (2015). An outline of processability theory and its relationship to other approaches to SLA. *Language Learning, 65*, 123–151.

Pienemann, M., Johnston, M., & Brindley, G. (1988). Constructing an acquisition based procedure for second language assessment. *Studies in Second Language Acquisition, 10*, 217–243.

Pienemann, M., & Keßler, J. (Eds.). (2011). *Studying processability theory*. Amsterdam, The Netherlands: John Benjamins.

Pimsleur, P. (1966). *The Pimsleur language aptitude battery*. New York, NY: Harcourt, Brace, Jovanovic.

Pintrich, P. R. (2000). The role of goal orientation in self-regulated learning. In M. Boekaerts, P. R. Pintrich, & M. Zeidner (Eds.), *Handbook of self-regulation* (pp. 451–502). San Diego, CA: Dunedin Academic Press.

Plonsky, L. (2011). The effectiveness of second language strategy instruction: A meta-analysis. *Language Learning, 61*, 993–1038.

Plonsky, L., & Oswald, F. L. (2014). How big is 'big'? Interpreting effect sizes in L2 research. *Language Learning, 64*, 878–912.

Poehner, M. (2008). Both sides of the conversation: The interplay between mediation and learner reciprocity in dynamic assessment. In J. P. Lantolf & M. Poehner (Eds.), *Sociocultural theory and the teaching of second languages* (pp. 33–56). London, UK: Equinox.

Polio, C. (2012). The relevance of second language acquisition theory to the written error correction debate. *Journal of Second Language Writing, 21*, 375–389.

Poole, R. (2012). Concordance-based glosses for academic vocabulary acquisition. *CALICO Journal, 29*(4), 679–693.

Poulisse, N. (1997). Language production in bilinguals. In J. Kroll & A. M. B. de Groot (Eds.), *Tutorials in bilingualism: Psycholinguistic perspectives* (pp. 201–224). Mahwah, NJ: Lawrence Erlbaum.

Poulisse, N., & Bongaerts, T. (1994). First language use in second language production. *Applied Linguistics, 15*, 36–57.

Prabhu, N. S. (1990). There is no best method—Why? *TESOL Quarterly, 24*(2), 161–176.

Preuss, C., & Morway, C. (2012). Caught in the web: Overcoming and reproducing hegemony in Azerbaijan. *Language Learning & Technology, 16*(2), 87–102.

Prichard, C. (2008). Evaluating L2 readers' vocabulary strategies and dictionary use. *Reading in a Foreign Language, 20*(2), 216–231.

Proctor, C., Dalton, B., Uccelli, P., Biancarosa, G., Mo, E., Snow, C., & Neugebauer, S. (2011). Improving comprehension online: Effects of deep vocabulary instruction with bilingual and monolingual fifth graders. *Reading and Writing, 24*(5), 517–544.

Pujolà, J-T. (2002). CALLing for help: Researching language learning strategies using help facilities in a web-based multimedia program. *ReCALL, 14*(2), 235–262.

Purpura, J. E. (2004). *Assessing grammar*. Cambridge, UK: Cambridge University Press.

Purpura, J. E. (2009). The impact of large-scale and classroom-based language assessments on the individual. In C. Weir & L. Taylor (Eds.), *Language testing matters: Investigating the wider social and educational impact of assessment—Proceedings of the ALTE Cambridge conference, April 2008* (pp. 301–325). Cambridge, UK: Cambridge University Press.

Purpura, J. E., & Turner, C. E. (2014). *Learning-oriented assessment in language classrooms: Using assessment to gauge and promote language learning*. New York, NY: Routledge.

Qi, C. H. (2013). Special issue on curriculum studies. In U. University of New Mexico (Ed.), *Scientific Research Open Access*. Retrieved from http://www.scirp.org/Index.aspx

Qualifications and Curriculum Authority. (2001). *Planning for learning in the foundation stage.* London, UK: Author.

Ramanarayanan, V., Suendermann-Oeft, D., Ivanovy, A. V., & Evanini, K. (2015). A distributed cloud-based dialog system for conversational application development. *Proceedings of the 16th Annual SIGdial Meeting on Discourse and Dialogue (SIGDIAL 2015),* September 2–4, Prague, Czech Republic.

Ramanathan, V. (2005). *The English-vernacular divide: Postcolonial language politics and practice.* Clevedon, UK: Multilingual Matters.

Rea-Dickins, P. (2006). Currents and eddies in the discourse of assessment: A learning-focused interpretation. *International Journal of Applied Linguistics, 16*(2), 163–188.

Rea-Dickins, P. (2007). Classroom based assessment: Possibilities and pitfalls. In E. Hinkel (Ed.), *Handbook of research in second language teaching and learning* (pp. 506–520). London, UK: Lawrence Erlbaum.

Reid, J. (1995). *Learning styles in the ESL/EFL classroom.* Boston, MA: Heinle & Heinle.

Reigeluth, C. M. (Ed.). (1999). *Instructional-design theories and models: A new paradigm of instructional theory.* Mahwah, NJ: Lawrence Erlbaum.

Reinders, H. (2009). Technology and second language teacher education. In A. Burns & J. C. Richards (Eds.), *The Cambridge guide to second language teacher education* (pp. 230–237). Cambridge, UK: Cambridge University Press.

Reinders, H., & Darasawang, P. (2012). Diversity in language support. In G. Stockwell (Ed.), *Computer-assisted language learning: Diversity in research and practice* (pp. 49–70). Cambridge, UK: Cambridge University Press.

Reinders, H., & Wattana, S. (2014). Can I say something? The effects of digital game play on willingness to communicate. *Language Learning & Technology, 18*(2), 101–123.

Reves, T. (1982). *What makes a good language learner?* Unpublished Ph.D. dissertation, Hebrew University.

Révész, A. (2011). Task complexity, focus on L2 constructions, and individual differences: A classroom-based study. *Modern Language Journal, 95*(Suppl.), 162–181.

Richards, J. C. (1985). *The context of language teaching.* Cambridge, UK: Cambridge University Press.

Richards, J. C. (1990). *The language teaching matrix.* Cambridge, UK: Cambridge University Press.

Richards, J. C. (2001). *Curriculum development in language teaching.* Cambridge, UK: Cambridge University Press.

Richards, J. C., & Rodgers, T. (2001). *Approaches and methods in language teaching* (2nd ed.). Cambridge, UK: Cambridge University Press.

Richey, R. C. (2000). The future role of Robert M. Gagné in instructional design. In R. C. Richey (Ed.), *The legacy of Robert M. Gagné* (pp. 255–281). New York, NY: Syracuse University.

Robin, R. (2007). Commentary: Learner-based listening and technological authenticity. *Language Learning & Technology, 11*(1), 109–115.

Robinson, P. (1995). Attention, memory, and the 'Noticing Hypothesis.' *Language Learning, 45,* 283–331.

Robinson, P. (1997). Generalizability and automaticity of second language learning under implicit, incidental, enhanced, and instructed conditions. *Studies in Second Language Acquisition, 19,* 233–247.

Robinson, P. (Ed.). (2001a). *Cognition and second language instruction.* Cambridge, UK: Cambridge University Press.

Robinson, P. (2001b). Task complexity, cognitive resources and syllabus design: A triadic framework for examining task influences on SLA. In Peter Robinson (Ed.), *Cognition and second language instruction* (pp. 285–317). Cambridge, UK: Cambridge University Press.

Robinson, P. (2001c). Task complexity, task difficulty and task production: Exploring interactions in a componential framework. *Applied Linguistics, 22*(1), 27–57.

Robinson, P. (2003). The cognition hypothesis, task design and adult task-based language learning. *Second Language Studies, 21*(2), 45–107.

Robinson, P. (2007a). Aptitudes, abilities, contexts and practice. In R. DeKeyser (Ed.), *Practice in a second language: Perspectives from cognitive psychology and applied linguistics* (pp. 256–286). New York, NY: Cambridge University Press.

Robinson, P. (2007b). Criteria for classifying and sequencing pedagogic tasks. In Maria del Pilar Garcia-Mayo (Ed.), *Investigating tasks in formal language learning* (pp. 7–27). Clevedon, Avon, UK: Multilingual Matters.

Robinson, P. (2009). Syllabus design. In M. H. Long & C. J. Doughty (Eds.), *The handbook of language teaching* (pp. 294–310). Malden, MA: Wiley-Blackwell.

Robinson, P. (2011). *Second language task complexity: Researching the cognition hypothesis of language learning and performance.* Amsterdam, The Netherlands: John Benjamins.

Rockman et al. (2009). *Rosetta stone evaluation report.* Retrieved from http://resources. rosettastone.com/CDN/us/pdfs/Rockman-Evaluation-Report.pdf

Roehr, K. (2007). Metalinguistic knowledge and language ability in university-level L2 learners. *Applied Linguistics, 29*, 67–106.

Roehr, K. (2008). Linguistic and metalinguistic categories in second language learning. *Cognitive Linguistics, 19*, 67–106.

Roever, C. (2001). Web-based language testing. *Language Learning & Technology, 5*(2), 84–94.

Rogan, F., & San Miguel, C. (2013). Improving clinical communication of students with English as a second language using online technology: A small scale evaluation study. *Nurse Education in Practice, 13*(5), 400–406.

Romeo, K., & Hubbard, P. (2008). Pervasive CALL learner training for improving listening proficiency. *Proceedings of the WorldCALL Conference,* Fukuoka, Japan, August, 2008. Retrieved from http://www.j-let.org/~wcf/proceedings/d-009.pdf

Rose, H. (2015). Researching language learning strategies. In B. Paltridge & A. Phakiti (Eds.), *Research methods in applied linguistics* (pp. 421–438). New York, NY: Bloomsbury.

Rossiter, M. J., Abbott, M. L., & Kushnir, A. (2016). L2 vocabulary research and instructional practices: Where are the gaps? *TESL-EJ, 20*(1). Retrieved from http://www. tesl-ej.org/wordpress/issues/volume20/ej77/ej77a6/

Rost, M. (2005). L2 listening. In E. Hinkel (Ed.), *Handbook of research in second language teaching and learning* (pp. 503–527). Mahwah, NJ: Lawrence Erlbaum.

Rost, M., & Ross, S. (1991). Learner use of strategies in interaction: Typology and teachability. *Language Learning, 41*, 235–268.

Ruhe, V., & Zumbo, B. (2009). *Evaluation in distance education and e-learning: The unfolding model.* New York, NY: Guilford Press.

Russell, J., & Spada, N. (2006). The effectiveness of corrective feedback for the acquisition of L2 grammar: A meta-analysis of the research. In J. M. Norris & L. Ortega (Eds.), *Synthesizing research on language learning and teaching* (pp. 133–164). Amsterdam, The Netherlands: John Benjamins.

Saito, Y., Horwitz, E. K., & Garza, T. J. (1999). Foreign language reading anxiety. *Modern Language Journal, 83*, 202–218.

Samuda, V. (2005). Expertise in pedagogic task design. In K. Johnson (Ed.), *Expertise in second language learning and teaching* (pp. 150–164). New York, NY: Palgrave Macmillan.

Samuda, V., & Bygate, M. (2008). *Tasks in second language learning.* New York, NY: Palgrave Macmillan.

Sanders, R. F. (2005). Redesigning introductory Spanish: Increased enrollment, online management, cost reduction, and effects on student learning. *Foreign Language Annals, 38*(4), 523–532.

Santos, M., Darling-Hammond, L., & Cheuk, T. (2012). *Teacher development to support English language learners in the context of common core state standards.* Retrieved December 28, 2014, from http://ell.stanford.edu/sites/default/files/pdf/academic-papers/10-Santos%20LDH% 20Teacher% 20Development% 20FINAL.pdf

Saraceni, C. (2013). Adapting courses—A personal view. In B. Tomlinson (Ed.), *Developing materials for language teaching* (pp. 49–62). London, UK: Bloomsbury.

Sarwar, Z. (2001). Innovations in large classes in Pakistan. *TESOL Quarterly, 35*(3), 497–500.

Satar, H. M., & Özdener, N. (2008). The effects of synchronous CMC on speaking proficiency and anxiety: Text versus voice chat. *Modern Language Journal, 92*(4), 595–613.

Sato, M. (2013). Beliefs about peer interaction and peer corrective feedback: Efficacy of classroom intervention. *Modern Language Journal, 97*(3), 611–633.

Sauro, S. (2012). L2 performance in text-chat and spoken discourse. *System, 40,* 335–348.

Sauro, S. (2014). Lessons from the fandom: Technology-mediated tasks for language learning. In M. González-Lloret & L. Ortega (Eds.), *Technology-mediated TBLT: Researching technology and tasks* (pp. 239–262). Amsterdam, The Netherlands: John Benjamins.

Savignon, S. J. (1983). *Communicative competence: Theory and classroom practice; texts and contexts in second language learning.* Reading, MA: Addison-Wesley.

Schedl, M., & O'Reilly, T. (2014). *Development and evaluation of prototype tasks for an enhanced iBT TOEFL reading test.* Paper presented at the 2014 TOEFL research colloquium, Princeton, NJ.

Schmidt, R. (1990). The role of consciousness in second language learning. *Applied Linguistics, 11,* 129–158.

Schmidt, R., & Frota, S. (1986). Developing basic conversational ability in a second language: A case study of an adult learner of Portuguese. In R. R. Day (Ed.), *Talking to learn: Conversation in second language acquisition* (pp. 237–326). Rowley, MA: Newbury House.

Schmitt, N. (Ed.). (2004). *Formulaic sequences: Acquisition, processing and use.* Amsterdam, The Netherlands: John Benjamins.

Schmitt, N. (2008). Instructed second language vocabulary learning. *Language Teaching Research, 12*(3), 329–363.

Schumann, J. (1979). The acquisition of English negation by speakers of Spanish: A review of the literature. In R. E. Anderson (Ed.), *The acquisition and use of Spanish and English as first and second languages* (pp. 3–32). Washington, DC: TESOL.

Schumann, J. (1987). The expression of temporality in basilang speech. *Studies in Second Language Acquisition, 9,* 21–41.

Schutz, N. W., & Derwing, B. L. (1981). The problem of needs assessment in English for specific purposes: Some theoretical and practical considerations. In R. Mackay & J. D. Palmer (Eds.), *Languages for specific purposes: Program design and evaluation* (pp. 29–45). Rowley, MA: Newbury House.

Segalowitz, N. (2003). Automaticity and second languages. In C. J. Doughty & M. H. Long (Eds.), *The handbook of second language acquisition* (pp. 382–408). Malden, MA: Wiley-Blackwell.

Segalowitz, N. (2010). *Cognitive bases of second language fluency*. London, UK: Routledge.

Seidlhofer, B. (2004). Research perspectives on teaching English as a lingua franca. *Annual Review of Applied Linguistics, 24*, 209–239.

Seidlhofer, B. (2011). *Understanding English as a lingua franca*. Oxford, UK: Oxford University Press.

Selinker, L. (1972). Interlanguage. *IRAL, 10*(3), 209–231.

Service, E., & Kohonen, V. (1995). Is the relation between phonological memory and foreign language learning accounted for by vocabulary acquisition? *Applied Psycholinguistics, 16*, 155–172.

Shamim, F. (2012). Teaching large classes. In A. Burns & J. C. Richards (Eds.), *The Cambridge guide to pedagogy and practice in second language teaching* (pp. 95–102). Cambridge, UK: Cambridge University Press.

Shamim, F. (2013). Towards an understanding of teachers' resistance to innovation. In A. Ahmed, M. Hanzala, F. Saleem, & G. Cane (Eds.), *ELT in a changing world: Innovative approaches to new challenges* (pp. 87–106). Newcastle, UK: Cambridge Scholars Press.

Sheen, Y. (2007). The effect of corrective feedback, language aptitude and learner attitudes on the acquisition of English articles. In A. Mackey (Ed.), *Conversational interaction in second language acquisition* (pp. 301–322). Oxford, UK: Oxford University Press.

Sheen, Y. (2008). Recasts, language anxiety, modified output and L2 learning. *Language Learning, 58*(4), 835–874.

Shehadeh, A., & Coombe, C. A. (2012). *Task-based language teaching in foreign language contexts: Research and implementation*. Amsterdam, The Netherlands: John Benjamins.

Shermis, M. D., & Burstein, J. (2013). *Handbook of automated essay evaluation: Current applications and new directions*. New York, NY: Routledge.

Shin, S. (2012). Web-based language testing. In C. Coombe, P. Davidson, B. O'Sullivan, & S. Stoynoff (Eds.), *The Cambridge guide to second language assessment* (pp. 274–279). Cambridge, UK: Cambridge University Press.

Shintani, N. (2011). A comparative study of the effects of input-based and production-based instruction on vocabulary acquisition by young EFL learners. *Language Teaching Research, 15*(2), 137–158.

Shintani, N. (2012). Input-based tasks and the acquisition of vocabulary and grammar: A process-product study. *Language Teaching Research, 16*(2), 253–279.

Shintani, N., & Wallace, M. P. (2014). The effectiveness of listening support on L2 learners' listening comprehension ability: A meta-analysis. *English Teaching and Learning, 38*(3), 71–101.

Shute, V. J. (2007). *Focus on formative feedback*. Princeton, NJ: Educational Testing Service.

Shute, V. J., & Kim, Y. (2014). Formative and stealth assessment. In J. M. Spector, M. D. Merrill, J. Elen, & M. J. Bishop (Eds.), *Handbook of research on educational communications and technology* (pp. 311–321). New York, NY: Springer.

Siegal, M. (1996). The role of learner subjectivity in second language sociolinguistic competency: Western women learning Japanese. *Applied Linguistics, 17*, 356–382.

Silva, T. (1993). Toward an understanding of the distinct nature of L2 writing: The ESL research and its implications. *TESOL Quarterly, 27*, 657–677.

Simpson-Vlach, R., & Ellis, N. (2010). An academic formulas list: New methods in phraseology research. *Applied Linguistics, 31*(4), 487–512.

Sinicrope, C., & Watanabe, Y. (2008). *Overview of common evaluation methods*. Retrieved from http://www.nflrc.hawaii.edu/evaluation/files/Watanabe&Sinicrope_Eval%20Methods_resources.pdf

Skehan, P. (1986). Cluster analysis and the identification of learner types. In V. Cook (Ed.), *Experimental approaches to second language acquisition* (pp. 81–94). Oxford, UK: Pergamon.

Skehan, P. (1996). A framework for the implementation of task-based instruction. *Applied Linguistics*, *17*, 38–62.

Skehan, P. (1998). *A cognitive approach to language learning*. Oxford, UK: Oxford University Press.

Skehan, P. (2001). Tasks and language performance assessment. In M. Bygate, P. Skehan, & M. Swain, (Eds.), *Researching pedagogic tasks: Second language learning, teaching, and testing* (pp. 167–185). London, UK: Longman.

Skehan, P. (2002). Theorising and updating aptitude. In P. Robinson (Ed.), *Individual differences and instructed language learning* (pp. 69–93). Amsterdam, The Netherlands: John Benjamins.

Skehan, P. (2003). Task-based instruction. *Language Teaching*, *36*, 1–34.

Skehan, P. (2012). Language aptitude. In S. M. Gass & A. Mackey, *The Routledge handbook of second language acquisition* (pp. 381–395). New York, NY: Routledge.

Skehan, P. (Ed.). (2014). *Processing perspectives on task performance*. Amsterdam, The Netherlands: John Benjamins.

Skehan, P., & Foster, P. (2001). Cognition and tasks. In P. Robinson (Ed.), *Cognition and second language instruction* (pp. 183–205). Cambridge, UK: Cambridge University Press.

Smidt, E., & Hegelheimer, V. (2004). Effects of online academic lectures on ESL listening comprehension, incidental vocabulary acquisition, and strategy use. *Computer Assisted Language Learning*, *17*(5), 517–556.

Smith, B. (2003). The use of communication strategies in computer-mediated communication. *System*, *31*, 29–53.

Smolčec, M. (2014). Using Minecraft for learning English. *TESL-EJ*, *18*(2). Retrieved from http://www.tesl-ej.org/wordpress/issues/volume18/ej70/ej70int/

Snow, M. (2005). A model of academic literacy for integrated language and content instruction. In E. Hinkel (Ed.), *Handbook of research in second language teaching and learning* (pp. 693–712). Mahwah, NJ: Lawrence Erlbaum.

Snow, R. (1989). Aptitude-treatment interaction as a framework for research on individual differences in learning. In P. Ackerman, R. J. Sternberg, & R. Glaser (Eds.), *Learning and individual differences: Advances in theory and research* (pp. 13–59). New York, NY: W.H. Freeman.

Snow, R., Federico, P., & Montague, W. (1980). *Aptitude, learning, and instruction* (Vols 1 & 2). Hillsdale, NJ: Lawrence Erlbaum.

So, Y., Zapata-Rivera, D., Cho, Y., Luce, C., & Battistini, L. (2015). Using trialogues to measure English language skills. *Journal of Educational Technology & Society*, *18*(2), 21–32.

Solares, M. E. (2014). Textbooks, tasks, and technology: An action research study in a textbook bound EFL context. In M. González-Lloret & L. Ortega (Eds.), *Technology-mediated TBLT: Researching technology and tasks* (pp. 79–114). Amsterdam, The Netherlands: John Benjamins.

Solé, C. R. i., & Mardomingo, R. (2004). Trayectorias: A new model for online task-based learning. *ReCALL*, *16*(1), 145–157.

Song, S., & Kellogg, D. (2011). Word meaning as a palimpsest: A defense of sociocultural theory. *Modern Language Journal*, *95*, 589–604.

Spada, N., & Tomita, Y. (2010). Interactions between type of instruction and type of language feature: A meta-analysis. *Language Learning*, *60*, 263–308.

Spencer-Oatey, H., & Franklin, P. (2009). *Intercultural interaction: A multidisciplinary approach to intercultural communication.* Hampshire, UK: Palgrave Macmillan.

Stanley, G. (2013). *Language learning with technology: Ideas for integrating technology in the classroom.* Cambridge, UK: Cambridge University Press.

Stauble, A. E. (1978). The process of creolization: A model for second language development. *Language Learning, 28,* 29–54.

Stern, H. H. (1993). Fundamental concepts of language teaching. *Studies in Second Language Acquisition, 7,* 251–253.

Storch, N. (2005). Collaborative writing: Product, process and students' reflections. *Journal of Second Language Writing, 14,* 153–173.

Strambi, A., & Bouvet, E. (2003). Flexibility and interaction at a distance: A mixed-mode environment for language learning. *Language Learning & Technology, 7*(3), 81–102.

Sullivan, K., & Collett, P. (2014). Editorial. *Studies in Self-Access Learning Journal, 5*(4), 315–319.

Suskie, L. A. (2009). *Assessing student learning: A common sense guide.* San Francisco, CA: Jossey-Bass.

Swaffar, J. K., & Urlaub, P. (Eds.). (2014). *Transforming postsecondary foreign language teaching in the United States.* New York, NY: Springer.

Swain, M. (1985). Communicative competence: Some roles of comprehensible input and comprehensible output in its development. In S. M. Gass & C. G. Madden (Eds.), *Input in second language acquisition* (pp. 235–253). Rowley, MA: Newbury House.

Swain, M. (1995). Three functions of output in second language learning. In G. Cook & B. Seidlhofer (Eds.), *Principle and practice in applied linguistics: Studies in honour of H. G. Widdowson* (pp. 125–144). Oxford, UK: Oxford University Press.

Swain, M. (2000). The output hypothesis and beyond: Mediating acquisition through collaborative dialogue. In J. P. Lantolf (Ed.), *Sociocultural theory and second language learning* (pp. 97–114). Oxford, UK: Oxford University Press.

Swain, M. (2005). The output hypothesis: Theory and research. In E. Hinkel (Eds.), *Handbook of research in second language teaching and learning* (pp. 471–483). Mahwah, NJ: Lawrence Erlbaum.

Swain, M., Kinnear, P., & Steinman, L. (2011). *Sociocultural theory in second language education: An introduction through narratives.* Bristol, UK: Multilingual Matters.

Swain, M., & Lapkin, S. (1982). *Evaluating bilingual education.* Clevedon, Avon, UK: Multilingual Matters.

Swales, J. (1990). *Genre analysis: English in academic and research settings.* Cambridge, UK: Cambridge University Press.

Swales, J. (1991). ESP development worldwide. In C. Luzares (Ed.), *Proceedings of the ESP state-of-the-art conference* (pp. 11–19). Manila, Philippines: De La Salle University.

Swales, J., & Feak, C. (2012). *Academic writing for graduate students* (3rd ed.). Ann Arbor, MI: University of Michigan Press.

Swan, M., & Walter, C. (1990). *The new Cambridge English course 2: Teacher's book.* Cambridge, UK: Cambridge University Press.

Swender, E., Conrad, D., & Vicars, R. (2012). *ACTFL proficiency guidelines 2012.* Alexandria, VA: American Council for the Teaching of Foreign Languages.

Sykes, J. M. (2008). *A dynamic approach to social interaction: Synthetic immersive environments and Spanish pragmatics.* Unpublished PhD Dissertation, University of Minnesota, Minneapolis, MN.

Sykes, J. M. (2014). TBLT and synthetic immersive environments. In M. González-Lloret & L. Ortega (Eds.), *Technology-mediated TBLT: Researching technology and tasks* (pp. 150–182). Amsterdam, The Netherlands: John Benjamins.

Tabatabaei, O., & Shams, N. (2011). The effect of multimedia glosses on online computer-ized L2 text comprehension and vocabulary learning of Iranian EFL learners. *Journal of Language Teaching and Research, 2*(3), 714–725.

Taguchi, N. (2008). Cognition, language contact, and the development of pragmatic com-prehension in a study-abroad context. *Language Learning, 58*(1), 33–71.

Taguchi, N. (2014). English-medium education in the global society: Introduction to the special issue. *IRAL, 52*(2), 89–98.

Takimoto, M. (2009). The effects of input-based tasks on the development of learners' pragmatic proficiency. *Applied Linguistics, 30*(1), 1–25.

Tanner, M. W., & Landon, M. M. (2009). The effects of computer-assisted pronunciation readings on ESL learners' use of pausing, stress, intonation, and overall comprehensibil-ity. *Language Learning & Technology, 13*(3), 51–65.

Tarone, E. (2000). Getting serious about language play: Language play, interlanguage vari-ation, and second language acquisition. In B. Swierzbin, F. Morris, M. Anderson, C. Klee, & E. Tarone (Eds.), *Social and cognitive factors in SLA: Proceedings of the 1999 second language research forum* (pp. 31–54). Somerville, MA: Cascadilla Press.

Tarone, E. (2005). Speaking in a second language. In E. Hinkel (Ed.), *Handbook of research in second language teaching and learning* (pp. 485–502). Mahwah, NJ: Lawrence Erlbaum.

Tarone, E., Bigelow, M., & Hansen, K. (2009). *Literacy and second language oracy*. Oxford, UK: Oxford University Press.

TESOL. (2006). TESOL pre-k-12 proficiency standards framework. Alexandria, VA: TESOL.

Thomas, J. (1983). Cross-cultural pragmatic failure. *Applied Linguistics, 4*(2), 91–112.

Thomas, M., & Reinders, H. (Eds.). (2010). *Task-based language teaching and technology*. New York, NY: Continuum.

Thomas, M., Reinders, H., & Warschauer, M. (Eds.). (2014). *Contemporary computer-assisted language learning*. London, UK: Bloomsbury.

Timpe, V. (2013). *Assessing intercultural language learning: The dependence of receptive socioprag-matic competence and discourse competence on learning opportunities and input*. Frankfurt a.M., Germany: Peter Lang.

Timpe-Laughlin, V., Wain, J., & Schmidgall, J. (2015). *Defining and operationalizing the con-struct of pragmatic competence: Review and recommendations*. (Research Report No. RR-15-06). Princeton, NJ: Educational Testing Service.

Tomlinson, B. (Ed.). (2003). *Developing materials for language teaching*. London, UK: Continuum.

Tomlinson, B. (Ed.). (2008). *English language teaching materials: A critical review*. London, UK: Continuum.

Tomlinson, B. (Ed.). (2011). *Materials development in language teaching* (2nd ed.). Cambridge, UK: Cambridge University Press.

Tomlinson, B. (2012). Materials development for language learning and teaching. *Language Teaching: Surveys and Studies, 45*(2), 143–179.

Tomlinson, B. (Ed.). (2013). *Applied linguistics and materials development*. London, UK: Bloomsbury.

Tomlinson, B., & Masuhara, H. (2004). *Developing language course materials*. Singapore: RELC Portfolio Series.

Tomlinson, C. A. (2014). *The differentiated classroom: Responding to the needs of all learners* (2nd ed.). London, UK: Pearson.

Towell, R., & Tomlinson, P. (1999). Language curriculum development research at univer-sity level. *Language Teaching Research, 3*(1), 1–32.

Trim, J. L. M., Richterich, R., van Ek, J. A., & Wilkins, D. A. (1973). *Systems development in adult language learning*. Strasbourg, France: Council of Europe.

Trinder, R. (2003). Conceptualization and development of multimedia courseware in the tertiary educational context: Juxtaposing approach, content and technology considerations. *ReCALL, 15*(1), 79–93.

Tseng, W. T., Dörnyei, Z., & Schmitt, N. (2006). A new approach to assessing strategic learning: The case of self-regulation in vocabulary acquisition. *Applied Linguistics, 27*(1), 78–102.

Tsui, A. B. M. (2003). *Understanding expertise in teaching*. Cambridge, UK: Cambridge University Press.

Turner, C. E. (2012). Classroom assessment. In G. Fulcher & F. Davison (Eds.), *The Routledge handbook of language testing* (pp. 61–74). New York, NY: Routledge.

Turner, C. E., & Purpura, J. E. (2016). Learning-oriented assessment in second and foreign language classrooms. In D. Tsagari & J. Banerjee (Eds.), *Handbook of second language assessment* (pp. 255–272). Boston, MA/Berlin, Germany: De Gruyter.

Tyler, R. W. (1948, September). How can we improve high-school teaching? *The School Review, LVI*, 387–399.

Underwood, P. R. (2012). Teacher beliefs and intentions regarding the instruction of English grammar under national curriculum reforms: A theory of planned behavior perspective. *Teaching and Teacher Education, 28*, 911–925.

Ur, P. (2005). *A course in language teaching*. Cambridge, UK: Cambridge University Press.

Ushioda, E., & Dörnyei, Z. (2012). Motivation. In S. M. Gass & A. Mackey (Eds.), *The Routledge handbook of second language acquisition* (pp. 396–409). New York, NY: Routledge.

Usó-Juan, E., & Martínez-Flor, A. (2006). Approaches to language learning and teaching: Towards acquiring communicative competence through the four skills. In E. Usó-Juan & A. Martínez-Flor (Eds.), *Current trends in the development and teaching of the four language skills* (pp. 3–25). Berlin, Germany: Mouton de Gruyter.

Van den Branden, K. (2006a). Training teachers: Task-based as well? In K. Van den Branden (Ed.), *Task-based language education: From theory to practice* (pp. 217–248). Cambridge, UK: Cambridge University Press.

Van den Branden, K. (Ed.). (2006b). *Task-based language education: From theory to practice*. Cambridge, UK: Cambridge University Press.

Van den Branden, K. (2009). Diffusion and implementation of innovations. In M. Long & C. Doughty (Eds.), *The handbook of language teaching* (pp. 659–672). Oxford, UK: Wiley-Blackwell.

Van den Branden, K., Bygate, M., & Norris, J. M. (Eds.). (2009). *Task-based language teaching: A reader*. Amsterdam, The Netherlands: John Benjamins.

Vandergrift, L. (1999). Facilitating second language listening comprehension: Acquiring successful strategies. *ELT Journal, 53*(3), 168–176.

Vandergrift, L. (2003). Orchestrating strategy use: Toward a model of the skilled second language listener. *Language Learning, 53*(3), 463–493.

Vandergrift, L. (2004). Listening to learn or learning to listen? *Annual Review of Applied Linguistics, 24*, 3–25.

Vandergrift, L. (2015). *Listening: Theory and practice in modern foreign language competence*. Retrieved from https://www.llas.ac.uk/resources/gpg/67

Vandergrift, L., & Goh, C. (2012). *Teaching and learning second language listening: Metacognition in action*. New York, NY: Routledge.

Vandergrift, L., & Tafaghodtari, H. M. (2010). Teaching L2 students how to listen does make a difference: An empirical study. *Language Learning, 60*, 470–497.

VanPatten, B. (2002). Processing instruction: An update. *Language Learning*, *52*(4), 755–803.

VanPatten, B. (2004). Input processing in SLA. In B. VanPatten (Ed.), *Processing instruction: Theory, research, and commentary* (pp. 5–32). Mahwah, NJ: Lawrence Erlbaum.

VanPatten, B. (2007). Input processing in second language acquisition. In B. VanPatten & J. Williams (Eds.), *Theories in second language acquisition* (pp. 115–136). Mahwah, NJ: Lawrence Erlbaum.

VanPatten, B. (2012). Input processing. In S. M. Gass & A. Mackey (Eds.), *The Routledge handbook of second language acquisition* (pp. 268–281). Abingdon, UK: Routledge.

VanPatten, B. (2013). Mental representation and skill in instructed SLA. In J. W. Schwieter (Ed.), *Innovative research and practices in second language acquisition and bilingualism* (pp. 3–22). Amsterdam, The Netherlands: John Benjamins.

VanPatten, B., & Benati, A. (2010). *Key terms in second language acquisition*. London, NY: Continuum.

Vatz, K., Tare, M., & Jackson, S. R., & Doughty, C. J. (2013). Aptitude-treatment interaction studies in second language acquisition: Findings and methodology. In G. Granena & Mike Long (Eds.), *Sensitive periods, language aptitude, and ultimate L2 attainment* (pp. 273–292). Amsterdam, The Netherlands: John Benjamins.

Vellenga, H. (2004). Learning pragmatics from ESL & EFL textbooks: How likely? *TESL-EJ*, *8*(2). Retrieved from http://tesl-ej.org/ej30/a3.html

Vincenti, G., & Braman, J. (Eds.). (2011). *Multi-user virtual environments for the classroom: Practical approaches to teaching in virtual worlds*. Hershey, PA: IGI Publishing.

Vygotsky, L. S. (1978). *Mind in society: The development of higher psychological processes*. Cambridge, MA: Harvard University Press.

Wagner, E., & Kunnan, A. J. (2015). The Duolingo English test. *Language Assessment Quarterly*, *12*(3), 320–331.

Walker, R., Gordon, A. S., Schloss, P., Fletcher, C. R., Vogel, C. A., & Walker, S. (2007). *Visual-syntactic text formatting: Theoretical basis and empirical evidence for impact on human reading*. Paper presented at the IEEE Professional Communication Conference, Seattle, WA.

Walker, S., Schloss, P., Fletcher, C. R., Vogel, C. A., & Walker, R. (2005). Visual-syntactic text formatting: A new method to enhance online reading. *Reading Online*, *8*(6).

Wall, D., & Horák, T. (2008). The impact of changes in the TOEFL examination on teaching and learning in Central and Eastern Europe: Phase 2, coping with change. *ETS Research Report Series*, *2008*(2), i–105.

Wallace, C. (2001). Reading. In R. T. Carter & D. Nunan (Eds.), *The Cambridge guide to teaching English to speakers of other languages* (pp. 21–28). Cambridge, UK: Cambridge University Press.

Wang, X., & Munro, M. (2004). Computer-based training for learning English vowel contrasts. *System*, *32*, 539–552.

Wang, Y. (2004). Supporting synchronous distance language learning with desktop videoconferencing. *Language Learning & Technology*, *8*(3), 90–121.

Ware, P. (2005). Missed communication in online communication: Tensions in a German American telecollaboration. *Language, Learning & Technology*, *9*(2), 64–89.

Ware, P., & Kramsch, C. (2005). Toward an intercultural stance: Teaching German and English through telecollaboration. *Modern Language Journal*, *89*(2), 190–205.

Warschauer, M. (2006). *Laptops and literacy: Learning in the wireless classroom*. New York, NY: Teachers College Press.

Warschauer, M. (2009). Learning to write in the laptop classroom. *Writing & Pedagogy*, *1*(1), 101–112.

Warschauer, M., & Park, Y. (2012). Re-envisioning reading in English as a foreign language. *JACET-KANTO Journal, 8*, 5–13.

Warschauer, M., Park, Y., & Walker, R. (2011). Transforming digital reading with visual-syntactic text formatting. *The JALT CALL Journal, 7*(3), 255–270.

Watanabe, Y., Davis, J. McE., & Norris, J. M. (2012). *A utilization-focused approach to developing, mapping, and assessing student learning outcomes in college foreign language programs.* Honolulu, HI: Foreign Language Program Evaluation Project National Foreign Language Resource Center, University of Hawaii at Manoa.

Waters, A. (2009a). Advances in materials design. In M. H. Long & C. J. Doughty (Eds.), *The handbook of language teaching* (pp. 311–326). Malden, MA: Wiley-Blackwell.

Waters, A. (2009b). Managing innovation in English language education. *Language Teaching, 42*(4), 421–458.

Watkins, S., Curry, N., & Mynard, J. (2014). Piloting and evaluating a redesigned self-directed learning curriculum. *Studies in Self-Access Learning Journal, 5*, 58–78.

Watson Todd, R. (2013). Large-sized language classes. In C. Chapelle (Ed.), *The encyclopedia of applied linguistics.* Cambridge, UK: Wiley-Blackwell. doi:10.1002/9781405198431.wbeal0666

Wedell, M. (2009). *Planning for educational change: Putting people and their contexts first.* London, UK: Continuum.

Weidemann, A. (2002). Overcoming resistance to innovation: Suggestions for encouraging change in language teaching. *Per Linguam, 18*(1). doi:http://dx.doi.org/10.5785/18–1–7. Retrieved May 6, 2015, from http://perlinguam.journals.ac.za/pub/article/view/7.

Weir, C. J. (2001). The formative and summative uses of language test data: Present concerns and future directions. In C. Elder & A. Davies (Eds.), *Experimenting with uncertainty: Essays in honour of Alan Davies* (pp. 117–125). Cambridge, UK: Cambridge University Press.

Wenden, A. (1999). An introduction to metacognitive knowledge and beliefs in language learning. *System, 27*, 435–441.

Wertsch, J. V. (1997). *Vygotsky and the formation of the mind.* Cambridge, MA: Harvard University Press.

Wesche, M. (1981). Language aptitude measures in streaming, matching students with methods, and diagnosis of learning problems. In K. C. Diller (Ed.), *Individual differences and universals in language learning aptitude* (pp. 119–154). Rowley, MA: Newbury House.

White, C. (2008). Language learning strategies in independent learning: An overview. In S. Hurd & T. Lewis (Eds.), *Language learning strategies in independent settings* (pp. 3–24). Clevedon, Avon, UK: Multilingual Matters.

White, J. (2008). Speeding up acquisition of his and her: Explicit L1/L2 contrasts help. In J. Philp, R. Oliver, & A. Mackey (Eds.), *Child's play? Second language acquisition and the younger learner* (pp. 193–228). Amsterdam, The Netherlands: John Benjamins.

White, L. (2007). Linguistic theory, universal grammar, and second language acquisition. In B. VanPatten & J. Williams (Eds.), *Theories in second language acquisition: An introduction* (pp. 37–55). Mahwah, NJ: Lawrence Erlbaum.

White, L. (2012). Universal grammar, crosslinguistic variation and second language acquisition. *Language Teaching, 45*(3), 309–328.

White, L., & Genesse, F. (1996). How native is near-native? The issue of ultimate attainment in adult second language acquisition. *Second Language Research, 12*, 233–265.

White, R. V. (1988). *The ELT curriculum: Design, innovation and management.* Oxford: Basil Blackwell.

WIDA. (2012). *2012 amplification of the English language development standards, Kindergarten-Grade 12.* Madison, WI: University of Wisconsin.

Widdowson, H. G. (1978). Notional-functional syllabuses: 1978, part IV. In C. H. Blatchford and J. Schachter (Eds.), *On TESOL '78* (pp. 33–35). Washington, DC: TESOL.

Widdowson, H. G. (1990). *Aspects of language teaching.* Oxford, UK: Oxford University Press.

Widdowson, H. G. (2000). On the limitations of linguistics applied. *Applied Linguistics, 21*(1), 3–25.

Wiggins, G. P. (1998). *Educative assessment: Designing assessments to inform and improve student performance.* San Francisco, CA: Jossey-Bass.

Wiggins, G. P., & McTighe, J. (2005). *Understanding by design.* Alexandria, VA: ASCD.

Wiggins, G. P., & McTighe, J. (2007). *Schooling by design: Mission, action, and achievement.* Alexandria, VA: ASCD.

Wiggins, G. P., & McTighe, J. (2011). *The understanding by design guide to creating high-quality units.* Alexandria, VA: ASCD.

Wiliam, D. (2010). The role of formative assessment in effective learning environments. In H. D. Dumont, D. Istance, & F. Benavides (Eds.), *The nature of learning: Using research to inspire practice* (pp. 135–159). Paris, France: Organisation for Economic Co-operation and Development.

Wiliam, D. (2011). *Embedded formative assessment.* Bloomington, IN: Solution Tree Press.

Wilkins, D. A. (1974). Notional syllabuses and the concept of a minimum adequate grammar. In S. P. Corder & E. Roulet (Eds.), *Linguistic insights in applied linguistics* (pp. 119–128). Paris: Didier.

Wilkins, D. A. (1976). *Notional syllabuses.* Oxford, UK: Oxford University Press.

Williams, E. (2007). Extensive reading in Malawi: Inadequate implementation or inappropriate innovation? *Journal of Research in Reading, 30*(1), 59–79.

Williams, J. D. (2003). *Preparing to teach writing: Research, theory, and practice.* Mahwah, NJ: Lawrence Erlbaum.

Williams, J. N. (2005). Learning without awareness. *Studies in Second Language Acquisition, 27*(2), 269–304.

Williams, J. N. (2012). Working memory and SLA. In S. M. Gass & A. Mackey (Eds.), *The Routledge handbook of second language acquisition* (pp. 427–441). New York, NY: Routledge.

Williams, J. N., & Lovatt, P. J. (2003). Phonological memory and rule learning. *Language Learning, 53*(1), 67–121.

Williams, J. N., & Lovatt, P. J. (2005). Phonological memory and rule learning. *Language Learning, 55*(1), 177–233.

Williams, M. (2014). Is technology a silver bullet for language teaching and learning? *The Guardian.* Retrieved from http://www.theguardian.com/teacher-network/teacher-blog/2014/may/12/technology-language-teaching-learning-pedagogy

Williamson, D. M., Mislevy, R. J., & Bejar, I. I. (Eds.). (2006). *Automated scoring of complex tasks in computer-based testing.* Mahwah, NJ: Lawrence Erlbaum.

Willis, D. (1990). *The lexical syllabus.* London, UK: Collins.

Willis, D., & Willis, J. (2007). *Doing task-based teaching.* Oxford, UK: Oxford University Press

Willis, J. (1996). *A framework for task-based learning.* Harlow, UK: Longman.

Willis, J., & Willis, D. (1989). *Collins COBUILD English course.* London, UK: Collins.

Winke, P. (2011). Evaluating the validity of a high-stakes ESL test: Why teachers' perceptions matter. *TESOL Quarterly, 45*(4), 628–660.

Winke, P. (2014). Formative, task-based oral assessments in an advanced Chinese-language class. In M. González-Lloret & L. Ortega (Eds.), *Technology-mediated TBLT: Researching technology and tasks* (pp. 263–294). Amsterdam, The Netherlands: John Benjamins.

Winke, P., & Goertler, S. (2008). Did we forget someone? Students' computer access and literacy for CALL. *CALICO Journal, 25*(3), 482–509.

Winke, P., Goertler, S., & Amuzie, G. L. (2010). Commonly-taught and less-commonly-taught language learners: Are they equally prepared for CALL and online language learning? *Computer Assisted Language Learning, 23*(3), 53–70.

Wittrock, M. C. (1974). Learning as a generative process. *Educational Psychology, 19*(2), 87–95.

Wittrock, M. C. (1985). Teaching learners generative strategies for enhancing reading comprehension. *Theory Into Practice, 24*(2), 123–126.

Wylie, E. C., Gullickson, A., Cummings, K., Egelson, P., Noakes, L., Norman, K., & Veeder, S. (2012). *Improving formative assessment practice to empower student learning.* Thousand Oaks, CA: Corwin.

Xi, X. (2010). Automated scoring and feedback systems: Where are we and where are we heading? *Language Testing, 27*(3), 291–300.

Xi, X., Higgins, D., Zechner, K., & Williamson, D. M. (2008). Automated scoring of spontaneous speech using SpeechRaterSM v1. 0. *ETS Research Report Series, 2008*(2), i–102.

Xi, X., Higgins, D., Zechner, K., & Williamson, D. M. (2012). A comparison of two scoring methods for an automated speech scoring system. *Language Testing, 29,* 371–394.

Xing, M., Wang, J., & Spencer, K. (2008). Raising students' awareness of cross-cultural contrastive rhetoric in English writing via an e-learning course. *Language Learning & Technology, 12*(2), 71–93.

Xu, S., & Connelly, F. M. (2009). Narrative inquiry for teacher education and development: Focus on English as a foreign language in China. *Teaching and Teacher Education, 25,* 219–227.

Yang, W. (2009). Evaluation of teacher induction practices in a US university English language program: Towards useful evaluation. *Language Teaching Research, 13*(1), 77–98.

Yanguas, I. (2009). Multimedia glosses and their effect on L2 text comprehension and vocabulary learning. *Language Learning & Technology, 13*(2), 48–67.

Yasuda, S. (2011). Genre-based tasks in foreign language writing: Developing writers' genre awareness, linguistic knowledge, and writing competence. *Journal of Second Language Writing, 20*(2), 111–133.

Yates, G. C. R. (2000). Applying learning style research in the classroom: Some cautions and the way ahead. In R. J. Riding & S. G. Rayner (Eds.), *Interpersonal perspectives on individual differences* (pp. 347–364). Stamford, CI: Ablex.

Zannirato, A., & Sánchez-Serrano, L. (2009). Using evaluation to design foreign language teacher training in a literature program. In J. M. Norris, J. McE. Davis, C. Sinicrope, & Y. Watanabe (Eds.), *Toward useful program evaluation in college foreign language education* (pp. 98–118). Honolulu, HI: University of Hawai'i Press.

Zechner, K., Chen, L., Davis, L., Evanini, K., Lee, C. M., Leong, C. W. Wang, X., & Yoon, S-Y. (2015). *Automated scoring of speaking tasks in the test of English-for-teaching (TEFT™).* Princeton, NJ: ETS Research Report Series.

Zhan, S. (2008). Changes to a Chinese pre-service language teacher education program: Analysis, results and implications. *Asia-Pacific Journal of Teacher Education, 36,* 53–70.

Zhang, X., & Lantolf, J. P. (2015). Natural or artificial: Is the route of L2 development teachable? *Language Learning, 65,* 152–180.

Zheng, B., Warschauer, M., & Farkas, G. (2013). Digital writing and diversity: The effects of school laptop programs on literacy processes and outcomes. *Journal of Educational Computing Research, 48*(3), 267–299.

Zheng, X., & Davison, C. (2008). *Changing pedagogy: Analyzing ELT teachers in China.* New York, NY: Continuum.

Zheng, Y., & Cheng, L. (2008). Test review: College English Test (CET) in China. *Language Testing, 25*(3), 408–417.

Zhou, G., & Yang, S. (2004). The effects of visual aid on EFL listening comprehension. *Journal of PLA University of Foreign Languages, 27*(3), 58–62.

Zwiers, J. (2008). *Building academic language: Essential practices for content classrooms.* San Francisco, CA: Wiley-Blackwell.

INDEX